REPUBLIC OF DEBTORS

Detail from *The Forlorn Hope*, newspaper masthead, ca. 1800, negative
number 49720. Collection of the New-York Historical Society.

REPUBLIC
OF DEBTORS

*Bankruptcy in the Age of
American Independence*

BRUCE H. MANN

HARVARD UNIVERSITY PRESS

Cambridge, Massachusetts
London, England

2002

Library of Congress Cataloging-in-Publication Data
Mann, Bruce H.
Republic of debtors : bankruptcy in the age of American independence / Bruce H. Mann.
p. cm.
Includes bibliographical references and index.
ISBN 0-674-00902-9
1. Debt—United States. 2. Consumer credit—United States. 3. Bankruptcy—United
States. I. Title.

HG3766 .M29 2002
332.7'5'0973—dc21
2002068619

CONTENTS

For Elizabeth

ACKNOWLEDGMENTS

For their unfailing helpfulness and good cheer as I passed countless happy hours in their collections, I am grateful to the librarians, archivists, and staffs of the Historical Society of Pennsylvania, the Library Company of Philadelphia, the Pennsylvania Historical and Museum Commission, the Philadelphia City Archives, the New-York Historical Society, the New York Public Library, the New York City Municipal Archives, the Manuscripts Division of the Library of Congress, the National Archives—Northeast Region (Boston), the American Antiquarian Society, the Massachusetts Historical Society, the Boston Public Library, the Baker Library of the Harvard University Graduate School of Business Administration, the Harvard Law School Library, the Virginia Historical Society, the Library of Virginia, the Connecticut Historical Society, the Connecticut State Library, the Maryland Historical Society, the Historical Society of Delaware, the Firestone Library of Princeton University, the Missouri Historical Society, the Huntington Library, and the Historic New Orleans Collection. In a more material vein, I am indebted to the National Endowment for the Humanities, the University of Pennsylvania Research Foundation, and the University of Pennsylvania Law School for their generous support of my research.

The project first took shape as a book at the Rockefeller Foundation Study Center in Bellagio, surely the most perfect place to write one can imagine. Unsuspecting colleagues at the Columbia University Seminar in Early American History and the laws schools of Washington University in St. Louis and Harvard, Syracuse, and Yale universities invited me to try out various ideas at their seminars and workshops. I am particularly grateful to my friends and colleagues at the remarkable McNeil Center for Early American Studies, upon whom former director and founding father, Richard S. Dunn, inflicted me not once, but twice—both times to my great benefit, if not to theirs. An earlier version of Chapter 5 appeared in the *William and Mary Quarterly*, where then-editor Michael McGiffert shepherded it with his customary enthusiasm and attention to detail. Serendipitously, the manuscript arrived at Harvard University Press just as Kathleen McDermott did, to my good fortune. Richard Audet was an admirably meticulous copyeditor.

Christine Leigh Heyrman and Christopher L. Tomlins have been good friends as well as kind readers. That I finished the book at all owes much to their encouragement. Once I did, Cornelia Hughes Dayton read the manuscript closely and made numerous valuable suggestions. Elizabeth Warren doubtless rues the day she asked the question that lengthened this project—an innocent inquiry about why Congress took so long to enact a bankruptcy law—but she deserves the dedication anyway. Those who know her know some of the reasons why. Those who know us know others. She, I hope, knows the rest.

INTRODUCTION

W hen news reached the New Gaol in New York late in March 1800 that Congress had passed a bankruptcy bill, the debtors imprisoned there gathered "to celebrate the auspicious event." They enjoyed "a rich repast of social conversation, on the prospect of returning to the world, and the bosom of our relatives and friends," then drank a series of seventeen formal and volunteer toasts: "The Bankrupt Law, this Godlike act." "God forgive those of our creditors, who have reviled us and persecuted us, and spoke all manner of evil against us, for the sake of money." "May imprisonment for debt, with its corrupt and destructive consequences, no longer deface God's image." "May the pride of every debtor be to pay his just debts, if ever in his power; and shun offers of credit in future as destructive to his life, liberty, and property." "May wisdom and justice draw the line between the honest and fraudulent debtor."[1]

"This Godlike act" was the controversial, short-lived Bankruptcy Act of 1800—the high-water mark of debtor relief in the eighteenth century. "Controversial" because it enabled debtors to escape debts they could not repay and, moreover, granted that boon only to commercial debtors whose success had allowed them to amass debts that were beyond the means of less prosperous debtors. "Short-lived" because it was too ideologically charged to survive the Jeffersonian revolution. The tide of reform quickly receded, but the Act nonetheless marked a transformation in the moral and political economy of eighteenth-century America. Virtually every toast offered in its honor by the debtors imprisoned in New York turned deeply rooted attitudes toward insolvency and bankruptcy on their head. Earlier in the century, bankruptcy relief was not so much controversial as unthinkable. By 1800 debtors and creditors alike desired it.

Whether a society forgives its debtors and how it bestows or withholds forgiveness are matters of economic and legal consequence. They also go to the heart of what a society values. Consider, for example, Samuel Moody, minister at York, Maine, who in 1715 related to his congregation the scriptural lesson of the widow who approached the prophet Elisha, distressed that "the Creditor is come to take unto him my two Sons to be bond men." When Elisha learned that she had no property left save one pot of oil, he instructed her to gather all the empty vessels she could and fill them from that one pot, which she did. When she returned to Elisha with news of the miracle, he told her, "Go, sell the oyl, and pay the debt, and live thou and thy children of the rest." From this text Moody drew seven doctrines, three of which run throughout the eighteenth century and, therefore, throughout this book: "That it is a sad and lamentable thing to be deeply in Debt." "Debts must be paid, tho' all go for it." And "Such as are Distressed by reason of Debt, are Objects of Pity and Charity; and Good People will Compassionate their Condition, and Consider what may be done for them."[2]

Moody assumed the existence of a moral economy of debt. Although that moral economy weakened as the eighteenth century unfolded and never held sway unchallenged even when it was strongest, it nonetheless established the ideal against which debtors and creditors measured themselves and each other and to which they gave legal expression. It was an ideal that presupposed the dependence of debtors and the omnipotence and inherent justness of creditors. Within that framework inability to pay was a moral failure, not a business risk. Like other moral failures, such as fornication or drunkenness, it called forth sanctions that to modern eyes were disturbingly punitive.

Moody's words fell on the ears of people who were unavoidably in debt. The homiletic injunction "neither a borrower nor a lender be" expresses an ideal that has never described reality in commercial societies. More to the point, it never could. Unless commerce consists of simultaneous exchanges of goods or services and the payment for them—that is, unless buyers immediately pay sellers in cash or in kind—people must conduct business on promises. In America in the eighteenth century the promises could be oral promises to pay, entries in account books, promissory notes jotted on scraps of paper, formal bonds on printed forms, or bills of public credit, to name the most common kinds. Whatever their form, the promises created debts and transformed the people who made and received them into debtors and creditors.

Debt was an inescapable fact of life in early America. One measure of how thoroughly this was so is the pervasiveness of debts owed and owing in probate inventories.[3] Another is the predominance of debt actions in civil litigation, not to mention the vast number of account books that have survived that never found their way into litigation.[4] Still another is that promises to pay were themselves a medium of exchange, circulating as money through factoring of open accounts and assignment of notes and bonds. Debt cut across regional, class, and occupational lines. Whether one was an Atlantic merchant or a rural shopkeeper, a tidewater planter or a backwoods farmer, debt was an integral part of daily life.

Ubiquity, however, is not uniformity. Debt meant different things to different people. To some, it represented entrepreneurial opportunity. To others, a burdensome necessity. To still others, it signified destitution. Debt could also be different things to the same people at different times, as individual debtors slipped from prosperity. Common to all was the uncertainty that faced both debtors and creditors when indebtedness became

{3}

insolvency. What should become of debtors and their property when what they owned was not enough to pay what they owed? Did creditors' claims to repayment of what they had lent extend to the bodies of the debtors to whom they had lent it? Could creditors imprison their debtors or bind them to service? Could insolvent debtors ever hope for release from their debts, short of repayment in full? Samuel Moody answered these questions one way, the festive debtors in the New Gaol another. Between them lay a culture of debt that changed in the eighteenth century, and with it the responses to insolvency.

The book I have written is about those changes. Put briefly, the rapid spread of written credit instruments in the increasingly commercialized economies before the Revolution marked the intrusion of impersonal market relations into lives that until then had been governed more communally. The assignability of notes and bonds severed the connection between debts and their underlying social relations, thereby making possible a transformation in the relations between debtors and creditors. At the same time, paper money permitted more people to participate more freely in the economy, while the sudden emergence of a consumer marketplace created both wants and the promise of satisfying them. These trends, which began before the Revolution, accelerated after it. Large-scale speculation in land and government securities transformed the interdependency between creditor and debtor and had far-reaching social, economic, political, and legal consequences. The rise of speculation as the investment of choice helped redefine insolvency from a moral delict to an economic one for which imprisonment seemed an inappropriately criminal punishment. In part, this was because when speculative schemes failed, as they did in droves in the financial collapse of the 1790s, numerous prominent men found themselves imprisoned for their debts or fugitives from their creditors. Their presence in the pool of insolvent debtors confounded the normal expectations of social and economic status and altered the political dimensions of debtor relief. When Congress, in response, considered bankruptcy legislation that would relieve only large commercial debtors, the resulting debate went to the heart of what the character of the new nation should be.

The fundamental dilemma was that debt and insolvency were the antithesis of republican independence, yet they pervaded all reaches of American society. Everyone stood somewhere on the continuum of indebtedness that ran from prosperity to insolvency, whether in their own right or by their dependence on a husband, a father, a master, or an owner. That had always been the case in early America. But whereas the problem of insolvency had once been limited to relatively simple issues of enforcing debtors' obligations, at century's end it encompassed more complicated questions of commerce and agriculture, vice and virtue, nationalism and federalism, dependence and independence, even slavery and freedom—all of which have particular resonance in the Revolutionary era.

As we shall see, the redefinition of insolvency from sin to risk, from moral failure to economic failure, was not complete by the end of the eighteenth century. Nor is it yet. Although weakened, Moody's moral economy of debt still shaped attitudes toward insolvency in the Revolutionary era, whether as an ideal to be guided by or as a hindrance to be rejected. Its continued influence assured that insolvency could never be simply an economic issue but rather one with religious, moral, social, political, legal, and ideological dimensions as well. In the chapters that follow we will observe debtors, creditors, lawyers, judges, legislators, ministers, writers, and others struggling with how the law should address the inability of men and women to repay their debts, whether through insolvency, bankruptcy, or imprisonment. At bottom, they were struggling with the place of failure in the new republic.

❦ I ❧

DEBTORS AND CREDITORS

The most trifling Actions that affect a Man's Credit, are to be regarded
. . . Creditors are a kind of People, that have the sharpest Eyes and Ears,
as well as the best Memories of any in the World.

George Fisher, *The American Instructor* (1753)

D r. John Morgan of Philadelphia understood the essence of credit. His advertisement in the *Aurora* in 1797 informed the public that he "continues practice as usual in the Venereal Disease." To assure discretion, "[a]n Alley adjoins the house"—particularly useful, since the house stood across Chestnut Street from the Bank of the United States—"and Secrecy with Honor will be duly observed." He required only that his patients pay in cash at the time of treatment, "as delicacy in the subject precludes all enquiry."[1] The good doctor knew that he could not conduct his business on credit. After all, one does not extend credit to strangers without first inquiring into their reputation for creditworthiness, which Morgan obviously could not do without creating new, presumably less flattering, reputations for his clients. So cash it was.

Most businesses did not operate under Morgan's peculiar constraints.

Nonetheless, as his advertisement illustrates, credit and reputation were inseparable. Indeed, "reputation" had been among the nonfinancial definitions of "credit" for two hundred years.[2] Advice manuals linked them explicitly, noting that a reputation for punctual payment, industry, thrift, and moderation made one "Lord of another Man's Purse." Although not the intended audience, swindlers and confidence men were among those who took such advice to heart, fraudulently obtaining credit by falsifying reputations for creditworthiness.[3] Credit could be won or lost even on noneconomic reputational matters. Gerard Beekman, for example, a prominent New York dry-goods merchant before the Revolution, took pains to correct his brother's business letters after hearing others remark on his "bad Spelling" and advised him with no apparent self-awareness that "it will be to your own Credit to improv in that Sience." And when the London textile wholesalers and cargo merchants Perkins, Buchanan & Brown learned that "wicked and designing people" were circulating "a most infamous false Report" that they were Catholics to undermine their business, they hastened to restore their reputations—and their credit—by assuring their correspondents in Virginia and Maryland that they and their families "as far back as we have any knoledge of them" were "firme Protestants" and that they had "not one Roman Catholick Relation in the World." Whether Beekman and the London merchants had in mind money or character is a meaningless question—in their world "credit" implied both.[4]

Merchants and traders constantly inquired into the creditworthiness of potential customers. Before Dun & Bradstreet pioneered centralized credit reporting in the nineteenth century, the decision to extend or withhold credit rested on personal ties or experience, or, absent those, on second- or third-hand information reported by someone whom the creditor knew— in short, on reputation, rumor, opinion, even fact. The letters of merchants and their agents or attorneys fairly brim with queries and responses about the probity and financial circumstances of prospective borrowers. Although not yet reduced to a market commodity itself, as it eventually would be, credit information clearly had value, which traders such as Mark Pringle of Baltimore and lawyers such as Harrison Gray Otis of Boston played upon when they offered it as a way of ingratiating themselves with distant merchants. If, as Pelatiah Webster wrote late in the century, credit "gives hearts ease, it gives wealth, 'tis a nurse of every social virtue," then determining if the person with whom one was dealing was "of credit" carried particular moment.[5]

The symbiosis of credit and reputation meant that neither could stand without the other. William Black of Williamsburg, Virginia, for example, implored James Mercer in 1771 not to distrain him for a debt that was still yielding interest because such a public step "in a County where, as yet, I am a Stranger . . . woud be very hurtfull" to his reputation and thus to his credit. A generation later, when William Priestman announced that he would auction Michael Krafft's note at the coffeehouse in Philadelphia—which readers would know meant that Krafft had failed to pay it—Krafft published a letter to the public explaining the circumstances and charging that Priestman had advertised the sale "merely for the purpose of injuring my character." Similarly, when Noah Webster, a staunch Federalist, sought to impugn the character of Alexander James Dallas, an equally staunch Republican, he did so by publishing a report that Dallas was overdrawn at the Bank of Pennsylvania, which moved Dallas to threaten to sue him for credit libel to redress the injury to his credit and reputation.[6] Even creditors bent on collecting their due could be sensitive to the connection, as was the London creditor who ordered that an attachment be served on a Philadelphia debtor "as privately as" could be managed "so that his character may suffer as little as possible." In the same spirit, creditors sometimes lent their names to help restore fallen debtors to credit, as George Meade's creditors did in a published testimonial that he had treated them honestly and impartially in his efforts to repay them, which they hoped would persuade others to do business with him.[7]

Credit and reputation became one when a creditor lent money on nothing more than the debtor's oral promise to repay, or even on the unstated understanding that the debtor would eventually repay the debt. Debts of that sort, however, were not business debts—they were social ones. For Virginia planters in the mid-eighteenth century, extending credit to neighbors on terms of honor rather than contract was a mark of respect as well as a form of patronage, depending on the recipient. Such loans were relationships, not transactions, and as such were governed by rules of etiquette, not law. Social lending was not just a southern phenomenon, although the elaborate social conventions that guided it were. When John Moore, a merchant in New York before the Revolution and a Loyalist exile after, loaned £500 to Peter Jay, a fellow merchant, "without the least shadow of security, confiding entirely on Mr. Jays honor, and being a member of our club whom I esteemed and respected, I felt as easy, as if I had been well secured."[8] The great weakness of social debts, of course, was that, as creatures of etiquette rather than law, they were harder to collect if requests for repayment were thought gauche.

For all the weight placed on credit and reputation, debtors and creditors alike knew that neither was sufficient to guarantee repayment. In truth, nothing was, but law at least provided different mechanisms to make some measure of repayment more likely. First among these were the legal forms that debt could take. Then there were the procedural rules of debt collection, which came into play when debtors failed to pay debts when they were due. And, lastly, when simple default became insolvency, law governed the disposition of the debtor's person and property. This final stage is what concerns us most, but we must first study the two that preceded it. To understand how the law treated failure, we must first learn how debtors and their creditors sparred within the law when default had not yet worsened into insolvency, which in turn begins with the legal form of the debt itself.

"Legal form" has several measures. It can refer to whether the debtor's promise to repay is express or implied; if express, whether written or oral; and if written, whether embodied in a promissory note, a bill, or a bond. It can also refer to whether the debt is secured or unsecured, that is, whether it is guaranteed or not. The nested classifications of the former meaning are most relevant when creditors attempt to collect from debtors who, although perhaps recalcitrant, are nonetheless solvent. The latter distinction—secured or unsecured—matters more when the debtor is insolvent.

Throughout the eighteenth century the form of debt that virtually everyone—rich and poor, urban and rural, even servants, many women, and some slaves—was familiar with was the account book. Books were running accounts of the dealings between creditors and their debtors. Each entry chronicled a transaction—the purchase of goods, the performance of labor services, occasional payments on account. A book was evidence of the debts it listed, but nowhere did it contain an express promise by the debtor to pay for the goods or services received. Rather, it recorded debts for which the law implied a promise to pay. That the promise to pay was implied rather than express did not compromise either the enforceability or popularity of book accounts, but it did shape their salient features. Books were not conclusive evidence of the debts they recorded, only presumptive—debtors were free to counter their creditors' claims with a wide range of controverting evidence, allowing juries to sort out who owed what to whom. This quality, together with the open-ended nature of book accounts, explains why book debts did not bear interest, no matter how long they ran or how high they grew. Although creditors who sued typically prevailed, book accounts nonetheless contained too much intrinsic uncertainty to permit the calculation of interest. On the other hand, book debts were subject to statutes of limitations that barred creditors from suing to collect them after a certain period of time, limitations that did not apply to written promises to pay.[9]

If book accounts were comparatively informal, credit instruments were the epitome of legal formality. English in origin, they were formal instruments by which debtors, over their own signatures, expressly promised to pay specific sums to creditors, either on demand or by a certain date. Written credit instruments came in several precisely defined forms.[10] Bonds, for example, could be conditioned or simple. Both were contracts under seal—which is to say, they contained a device, which once was a wax impression, in addition to the debtor's signature—by which the obligor bound himself to pay a stipulated sum to the obligee on a stated date. Conditioned bonds, which were the more common and useful of the two, differed from simple bonds in that they predicated payment on the obligor's failure to perform a specified condition before the date set for payment. That condition, known as a condition of defeasance, could be either the performance of some act or the payment of a sum of money. Conditioned bonds had myriad uses, most commonly to guarantee the conveyance of land, the delivery of commercial goods, and the repayment of loans. The guarantee lay in their *in terrorem* effect. Failure to perform the condition made the obligor liable for the full amount of the bond, which was typically twice the sum lent or twice the value of the items to be delivered. The law acknowledged the coercion inherent in conditioned bonds by referring to the difference between the amount promised and the value received as the "penalty."[11]

By way of contrast, bills obligatory and promissory notes, the latter also known as notes of hand, were not under seal (not even the fictitious seal represented by the initials "L.S.," or *locus sigilli*). They were promises signed by the debtor to pay the creditor a specified sum within a stipulated time or on demand. Bills generally acknowledged the debt and recited what we would now regard as consideration for the debtor's promise—that, for example, the obligation was for commodities received—whereas notes were simply unadorned promises to pay the named amount, much like IOUs. Bills obligatory were also signed by witnesses while promissory notes were not.

Bills of exchange were a further variant and, for commercial purposes, a very important one. The precursors to modern checks, bills of exchange facilitated long-distance commercial transactions by serving as vehicles for borrowing money, making third-party payment of debts, and moving money from one place to another without having to do so physically. In its plainest form, a bill of exchange was a written order by one person in- structing a second to pay a third. Or, in legalese, a drawer drew on a drawee in favor of a payee. The drawee—whose position in the transac- tion approximated that of the bank where one has a checking account— became liable for payment to the payee only by agreeing to do so when physically presented with the bill—or, again in legalese, by accepting the draft, upon which blessed event the drawee became an acceptor. The party that presented the bill for payment was, technically, the holder of the bill—it might be the original named payee, or someone to whom the payee had endorsed the bill, or subsequent endorsees from intervening endorsers. Upon acceptance, the drawer became liable to the drawee for the amount of the draft.[12] A drawee's refusal to accept a draft had serious consequences for the drawer, the magnitude of which is best captured by observing that rejected bills were referred to as "dishonored." Drawees sometimes refused drafts because they lacked funds to pay them. More often, however, they did so because they lacked confidence in the drawer's ability to reimburse them—in other words, they doubted the drawer's creditworthiness. A dishonored bill of exchange thus reflected directly upon the honor and reputation of its maker and, by extension, upon all his other bills. As Antony Carroll, a young Irish immigrant working in the New York trading house of Gouverneur & Kemble, understood, even one protested bill "would give a bad character to any I might have occasion to draw" in the future.[13] Honor, reputation, and character aside, when payees returned dishonored bills to their drawers and demanded payment—a process known as protesting a bill for nonpayment—the drawer was liable to the payee for the principal sum of the bill, interest from the date of protest, the costs of protest, and, for foreign bills, a surcharge of up to 20 percent of the principal as damages for nonacceptance.[14]

Unlike book debts and oral promises, written credit instruments carried interest, either by contract or by statute. If by contract—which is to say, by agreement between debtor and creditor forged through negotiation or by fiat—the rate of interest and when it would begin to accrue were stipulated in the instrument. If by statute, it was usually in the form of a maximum legal rate of interest, above which lay the forbidden realm of usury. Also unlike book debts and oral promises, written credit instruments were assignable—that is, the creditor could transfer the instrument by endorsing it to a third party, who would then have the right to collect the amount due on it from the debtor, interest and all.

Assignability plays a crucial role in insolvency. A proper credit system requires that debts be transferable, most importantly because the ability to transfer a debt permits the transferors to pay their own debts. With assignability the debtor's promise to pay becomes a kind of currency that circulates from one assignee to another, coming to rest only when whoever holds the written evidence of the promise asks the debtor to make good on it. For example, assignability enables local traders to satisfy their debts to their suppliers by endorsing over the promissory notes they have received from their local customers in payment for goods purchased—that is, by transferring the promises to pay that their customers have made to them. The one who ultimately demands payment of the note from the debtor whose note it is will then be the more distant supplier, not the local trader with whom the debtor had originally dealt. For this process to work, promises to pay must be severed from the transactions that give rise to them and be treated as essentially fungible. Only then can written credit instruments circulate in the economy. Assignability thus promoted economic efficiency by depersonalizing the relationship between debtor and creditor—part of the social cost of commercialization.[15]

Separating written promises to pay from the original relationship between debtor and creditor and allowing them to circulate in the wider economy had two broad, related implications for insolvency. One must remember that the promises often represented hopes as much as they did commitments. Aspiring entrepreneurs who built their businesses on credit incurred debts that they expected to repay with the fruits of their anticipated success. This was so whether they were small traders purchasing goods on credit for resale to the consumers they believed would flock to them or large speculators buying government scrip or land warrants that they intended to sell at great profit before the notes and bonds they had purchased them with fell due. It is, of course, in the nature of markets, not to mention life, that one's hopes do not always come to pass. Yet when the hopes are represented by promises to pay, the debts remain even after the hopes have been disappointed. And if, like flocks of birds, the promises to pay all come home at once when there is not enough room to accommodate them all, insolvency is the result. Assignability kept debtors' promises circulating in the marketplace, making it difficult for debtors to know when they would return for repayment or from what quarter they would come. All that was certain was that reports of a debtor's distress would bring all of his promises back at once.

Written promises to pay did not circulate at par, although they had to be paid at par with interest. That is, when creditors assigned their debtors' notes and bonds, they did not receive the full face value of the notes or bonds in return, whereas the assignees who ultimately collected from the debtors did, plus interest. What creditors actually received was determined by two discounts. One is mathematically straightforward—the right to receive £10 one year from now is not worth £10 today; rather, the present value of that right is whatever lesser amount would grow to £10 in one year's time with the accumulation of interest. Thus, a note for £10, payable in one year, would sell for that lesser amount, additional discounts aside. Additional discounts, however, were never aside. A debtor's promises to pay were only as good as his ability to pay. Other people's perceptions of that ability constituted the debtor's creditworthiness and determined what they were willing to pay for the debtor's written promises. The notes and bonds of debtors who were not creditworthy traded at steeper discounts—that is to say, they fetched less on the market—than the notes and bonds of debtors who were. The result was the private equivalent of currency depreciation—as reports of a debtor's difficulty spread, the price at which assignees would accept his paper dropped, often precipitously. Hence the frequent preoccupation of debtors with reputation and honor.[16]

Despite their technical distinctions the kinds of debt discussed thus far were simply different ways of memorializing debtors' promises to pay. This is not to say that the use of one form or another was a matter of indifference. Whether a debt was on book, bond, bill, or note affected the ease with which a creditor could collect it. Bonds, bills, and notes, for example, foreclosed certain evidentiary objections and procedural delays that book accounts permitted. Attested instruments such as bonds and bills carried greater evidentiary reliability than unattested notes. None of them, however, offered any assurance that they would be paid before others when a debtor slid into insolvency. That was determined by whether a debt, whatever its form, was secured or unsecured.

Debtors could secure their debts in a number of ways, only some of which created secured debts in the technical sense. When creditors asked their debtors to be "made secure," they were asking for something more than assurances that they would be repaid. They were asking for enforceable guarantees separate from the debts themselves. Debtors could furnish these guarantees by securing their creditors or by securing their debts. Both made creditors "secure," but only the latter did so by creating a security interest that gave a creditor a privileged position of priority ahead of other creditors if the debtor became insolvent. A debt is secured in the latter, more precise, meaning when a creditor holds title to or a lien against a particular item of the debtor's property as a pledge for the debtor's promise to pay the debt. If the debtor repays the debt, the creditor releases the title or lien and walks away satisfied. If the debtor fails to pay, the creditor pays himself out of the property he holds in pledge.[17] The most common example is the mortgage, by which the debtor pledges land to a creditor as security for a debt. People often speak of a mortgage as a debt, but it is not—it is the security interest that guarantees repayment of a debt. The most important legal consequence of the mortgage is that the mortgagee—the creditor who holds it—has dibs on the mortgaged property. That is, if the debtor fails to pay the debt, the mortgagee-creditor has priority over all other creditors in using the property to repay the debt it secures. Other creditors may lay claim only to whatever is left over. If several creditors hold mortgages in the same property, priority among them is determined by seniority—that is, by the order in which they received their mortgages. Mortgages are not perfect security—creditors might misjudge land values, or they might not discover that the property already secures other debts, or the debtor-mortgagor might not be the true or sole owner of the property, or prices might decline so much that land becomes worth less than the debt it secures. Nonetheless, secured creditors were the envy of their unsecured comrades.

Creditors could also be made secure by requiring their debtors to recruit sureties—persons who guaranteed the debt by promising to pay the creditor if the debtor did not. Sureties made their promises in writing, either by co-signing the debtor's bill or bond or by executing a separate surety bond. Either way, they became secondarily liable for the debt, which means that they were, in effect, backup debtors who could be compelled to pay only after the primary debtor failed to. In return, they were entitled to indemnification from the debtors whose debts they repaid.

Every suretyship was thus a potential creditor-debtor relationship, both between the original creditor and the surety, and between the surety and the original debtor. The former explains why some insolvent debtors could attribute their ruin to having stood surety for debtors who later failed. And the latter explains why sureties often sought to be "made secure" themselves by the debtors they vouched for. Not surprisingly, sureties almost invariably were friends or relatives of the debtors whose debts they warranted—suretyship rested on blood, affection, and honor, not profit. Family ties notwithstanding, by securing the express written promises that constituted commercial transactions, sureties were creatures of a commercial economy, not a traditional one.[18]

A similar means of securing creditors was for debtors to deposit with their creditors notes they had received by assignment from others in the course of business—a kind of passive suretyship in that the makers of the notes, whose liability on them preceded the assignment, rarely knew that their paper had been pledged to secure someone else's promise. Creditors whose debtors failed to pay them could then sue the obligors of the notes they held as security. Neither this mode of securing creditors nor suretyship gave creditors any legal priority over others in collecting from debtors. They did not create security interests in the legal sense of the term, as mortgages did—although deposited notes bear a passing resemblance to a later device, the chattel mortgage. Rather, they secured creditors by giving them other people to sue if their debtors failed to repay them. The value of the security thus rested on the creditworthiness of the sureties and of the makers of the notes given in pledge. Little wonder, then, that creditors often rejected securities offered by debtors, holding out instead for more creditworthy—or, as creditors put it, "better"—security.

Whether making creditors secure took the form of securing the debt or securing the creditor, it could occur as part of the original credit transaction or later. "Later" is more interesting because it reveals more about the dynamics of credit. Creditworthiness is not a constant. When creditors demanded security after they had extended credit, it was because they had become nervous. They suspected that the debtor's ability to repay had weakened. As long as the debt was not due, there was nothing creditors could do to augment whatever security they had taken, if indeed they had taken any. Once a debt fell due, however, creditors could demand to be made secure in return for not collecting the debt. Far from being simple, such a demand was part of an intricate pas de deux between debtor and creditor. Debtors and creditors alike understood the economic, social, and tactical constraints that deterred creditors from collecting debts as they fell due. For example, creditors who loaned money for the income it generated were often content to collect interest rather than suffer the loss of time and income involved in retrieving the principal and lending it to another debtor. As long as a creditor felt the debt was "safe," forbearance was economically sensible. "Safety" was a function of creditworthiness and security. Impairments in either, or the creditor's own declining fortunes, changed the calculus, triggering a demand for security or payment. There were social restraints as well. Debtors' frequent invocations of "honor" on the eve of the Revolution were reminders of a recent past in which the invocations would have been unnecessary, when debtors expected to be trusted rather than dunned. Despite the commercialization of credit in the eighteenth century, there remained a traditional framework of "neighborly" debts within which forbearance was the rule and demands to pay or provide security were affronts to the debtor's honor or integrity. Like all things traditional, which rest on common adherence to shared premises, the framework lost its power to restrain creditors when only debtors saw such demands as impugning their character.

Economic and social constraints on collecting debts notwithstanding, the most intricate steps in the dance were tactical. If a debtor was not inclined to pay a debt when it became due, and if the creditor was not content to let the debt lie out at interest on the same terms as before, then the dance began in earnest. What gave the interplay between debtors and creditors such urgency at this juncture was that, when the specter of failure loomed, there was no way to end the duet without leaving one party, and usually both, poorer. Even in flush times, debtors and creditors dealt with one another with a weather eye on what the law permitted—bargaining in the shadow of the law, as it were. When insolvency threatened, the shadow lengthened.

Debtors and creditors alike knew that litigation, although frequent, was a last resort. They knew that, as a last resort, it typically began aggressively, even punitively, with the creditor suing out a writ of attachment for the debtor's arrest and imprisonment if he could not post bond or find sureties to guarantee his appearance at court. They knew that procedural rules could delay final judgment for a year or more while tolling the accumulation of interest. They knew that even a final judgment for the creditor simply marked the transition to the further uncertainties and delays of execution process. They knew that writs of execution, when levied, often yielded little or nothing. They knew that imprisonment for debt, however emotionally satisfying to creditors, did little to make repayment more likely. And they knew that when debtor relief was available, whether as poor debtors' oaths or insolvency laws, it beggared debtors without significantly benefiting creditors. How debtors and creditors applied this knowledge to the intricacies of debt collection is our next concern.

William Samuel Johnson was a prominent man after the Revolution—a delegate to the Constitutional Convention and president of Columbia College. Before the Revolution he was a creditor's lawyer in Connecticut—so much so that when he searched for words of condolence to comfort John Hancock of Boston on the death of his son, the most heartfelt he could summon were "His debtors I hope will discharge their accounts without giving you any trouble about them."[19] Much of Johnson's practice consisted of collecting debts for his commercial clients, many of whom lived in New York or Boston, for which he charged 2.5 percent of the amount collected plus costs. Cash was chronically scarce in the eighteenth century, in part because of inflation but also because of British restrictions on the issuance of paper currency and the insistence of British merchants on being paid in specie. Without cash, people relied on promises—the notes, bills, and bonds discussed above. Merchants naturally became the heaviest investors in these written credit instruments, both because they were more likely to receive them in commercial transactions and because of the private banking functions they performed.

Johnson's clients were, in part, bankers, and Johnson was their broker as well as their lawyer. He placed their loans and collected their debts. He also left for posterity the most extensive letters we have—nearly a thousand in all—that treat legal practice before the Revolution. Through them we can recapture the interplay between debtors and creditors that court records only begin to describe. The particulars varied across colonies and decades, but in general outline that interplay was the same throughout America at midcentury, as letters from creditors, debtors, and other lawyers elsewhere will demonstrate.[20]

Relations between creditors and their debtors were not purely bilateral affairs. Creditors were themselves debtors, and debtors often had many creditors. Each debt was a strand in a web of indebtedness that bound debtors and creditors, creditors and other creditors, debtors and other debtors to one another in complex interrelations. Individual decisions to sue could rest as readily on the actions of third parties as on the debtors and creditors themselves. Creditors pressed to pay their own debts dunned their debtors more insistently, not because they feared the "safety" of the debt but because of their own necessity. Facing demands themselves, creditors called in debts that they had formerly been content to leave out at interest.[21] Creditor-debtors up and down the line tried to balance collections from debtors below them and payments to creditors above them. A pharmacist wrote his Boston creditor in 1756 that it was "a very sickly time" and business was good—"I Got three times as much Due to me . . . as I owe you But it wont do to Call upon People for money as soon as they have got the Medacens; however as fast as the people pay me, so fast I will pay you." John Kidd, a Philadelphia dry-goods merchant, told his London suppliers that although tea and sugar were "ready money articles"—cash purchase items—"I assure you what we sell for ready Money is most Commonly 2 or 3 months before we can get paid." Decades later, Benjamin Parke of Fredericksburg, Virginia, apologized to Thomas Hawthorn of Philadelphia that "[t]he promises of those indebted to me hath lead me at different times to promise you, and their noncomplyance has been the cause of my so often disappointing you." Sometimes, of course, the balancing failed. When another of Hawthorn's debtors wrote him that "if I cant get money due me, I cant discharge my Debts," Hawthorn folded the letter, jotted "Hypocritical. Needs no answer" on the fold, and ordered the man sued.[22]

Johnson was not averse to litigation, but he preferred nonlitigated resolutions, knowing that they often required the threat or actual initiation of a lawsuit to attain. He reminded clients that once they sued, they set in motion a train of events that were not necessarily to their advantage, as when he warned two Boston merchants that if they sued rather than negotiated with a debtor whom Johnson reported as "still in good credit," the debtor could delay final judgment for fourteen months, an involuntary extension of credit for which the suspended interest that would otherwise have been due "will well pay him." Or when, after voicing the same caution to another Boston creditor, he added his fear that the debtor, if pressed unseasonably, would tender payment in depreciated Rhode Island or New York currency, which the General Assembly, after an expensive and time-consuming appeal, would probably force the creditor to accept. Many creditors did not need such advice. Gerard Beekman, for example, who sometimes employed Johnson to collect debts, offered to settle with distant debtors for only half of what he claimed, "which I think is better then to go to Law and Imploy Persons so far off, where I dont know Judge or Jury." Other creditors, however, did. Frederick Rhinelander of New York sent a long list of stale debts to Ephraim Kirby, a prominent young Connecticut attorney who had recently published the first volume of American law reports, urging him to take immediate legal action, but Kirby convinced him that it would "be best in most cases to endeavour to secure the debts by friendly negotiations."[23]

Delay was the specter that most haunted Johnson. He complained to Seth Low, a prominent merchant in New York, that "our people are perfectly skilled in all the arts of delay and the badness of the times are unhappily but too good an excuse for their practice of them." Creditors voiced the same complaint, such as Benjamin Pollard of Norfolk, Virginia, who protested that lawyers "continually find ways and means to stave off judgments" and debtors "know they cannot be compelled to pay their debts without five or six years attendance on a law suit." Part of the delay was

inherent in the calendar. County courts in Connecticut held only two sessions each year at which new actions could be filed—April and November.
Unfinished business carried over to adjourned sessions in June and January, but no new actions could begin there. The schedule differed in other
colonies, but every colony limited the frequency of, and therefore access
to, courts of general jurisdiction, where suits for all but the smallest debts
had to begin. Whether the calendar was friend or foe was, of course, a
matter of perspective and circumstance. It was one thing for Johnson to
advise a creditor that, "[a]s the courts are at a distance, I think it will not be
amiss to give the several debtors notice that they will be sued at the next
court if they do not satisfy you before." It was quite another for him to
contemplate the same length of time and complain that debtors know how
long it is before they can be sued and that the knowledge "makes them the
more remiss."[24] Recognizing the difference, lawyers explicitly tied lenience to the court calendar. When Johnson learned that a debtor whom
he had ordered sued had written the creditor to ask his forbearance while
they negotiated security for the debt, he strongly urged his client not to
withdraw the writ because it would be six months before they could sue
the debtor again. Better to let the writ be served and halt the process later
if the debtor offered adequate security.[25]

Other delays were procedural. Debtors on book accounts and unwit-
nessed promissory notes could have up to three separate trials—the standard number of hearings in all civil actions. Debtors did not have to mount
an active defense to secure the delays. They could lose in the first county
court, review to the next county court six months later, lose again there,
and appeal to the superior court for a third trial four to six months later
still before the creditor's judgment would be truly final and execution
could issue.[26] If the debtor ultimately lost, as debtors almost invariably
did, he had to pay court costs as well as the debt. However, since interest
on promissory notes was tolled from the date the debtor was first sued to
the date of final judgment, the savings in interest justified debtors in
stretching out the proceedings and suffering the attendant costs. In practice, the benefits of procedural delay were unavailable to poorer debtors.
The law required losing litigants to give security to review or appeal

adverse decisions. Debtors of limited means, whose prospects of paying a delayed judgment were no better than paying an immediate one, were not likely to find sureties, who, although perhaps charitable, were rarely philanthropic.

These delays had the imprimatur of law. They were neither more nor less than what debtors were entitled to by statute. That, of course, did not prevent Johnson from railing bitterly against debtors who took advantage of what the law allowed them. He denounced one debtor as "a villain of whom we can expect nothing but per necessity." He referred to the advantage as "an unhappy liberty . . . which bad haymasters often here take to keep their creditors out of even their most just due." He complained about "our dilatory forms of law" and about how "[m]iserable have been the delays." He even seemed to relish the plight of a jailed debtor, whose circumstances Johnson regarded as "the just reward of his falsehood, prevarication, and endless tergiversation" after many delays. On the other hand, if a client complained of the delays or questioned Johnson's handling of the suit, Johnson retreated to the lawyerly high ground and loftily declaimed that "[l]awyers, you are sensible, are not to make laws but only to conduct their clients' causes according to the established methods and rules of procedure." Somewhat less defensively, a lawyer in Tennessee attributed his Baltimore clients' "surprise" at not having a judgment two years after first suing to "your not having made yourselves acquainted with the nature of proceedings in Courts of Justice." Given the uniformity of the complaints throughout the period, one suspects that a common response of creditors to such delay was the resigned exasperation that James Mercer of Virginia expressed to his brother in 1784 when he wrote that a debtor at least "had honesty enough to appear [at court] and set aside the office Judgment which will put me off two or three Courts and then I suppose his usual Justice will then suggest to him the propriety of offering me Lands in the Moon or some Hemp instead of money."[27]

Debtors recognized the nature of the advantage that the law placed in their hands. One debtor was "a notable hand at taking advantage of the delays of law." Another, whom Johnson threatened with arrest, invited Johnson to do so. He had been prepared to make a partial payment on account, but, as Johnson reported to his client, "if we chose the law he would let the law have its course and keep you out as long as he could." A third, whom Johnson criticized for keeping the creditor "out of a just debt," replied that "you [the creditor] sold your goods dear, and it was your business to have known that he had this advantage in his hands, and that he should keep you out as long as the law would allow or 'til he could conveniently pay it."[28]

The debtor's assumption that it was the creditor's "business to have known" what constraints law placed on collecting debts is revealing. The individual creditor in question may not in fact have understood the procedure for litigating debts in Connecticut. Johnson, however, did. Knowledgeable players knew both the rules of the game and how the rules shaped their alternatives and expectations. They knew the statutes and court rules that specified how long before a court session writs could be served, what sheriffs and constables could and could not do to make service, how the bond requirements differed on writs of summons and writs of attachment, what consequences defendants suffered for failing to procure the necessary bonds, what prosecution bonds were required of non-resident plaintiffs, how many continuances an absent defendant was allowed and under what circumstances, which actions were reviewable and which were not, what bonds were necessary to review or appeal adverse judgments, how long writs of execution remained valid before they lapsed, how execution process differed on chattels and real property, and so forth.

Players who knew the rules had an advantage. Hence the dynamics of bluffing. Johnson, for example, slipped one past a debtor whom he threatened to sue on a note. Because the note was not due within the time allowed for service and return, Johnson could not sue the debtor at the next scheduled county court. He threatened to anyway, and the debtor, "not knowing . . . what was not in my power to do, gave me a new note on interest on demand." Others, however, were not as timorous. They were the ones of whom Johnson wrote, "[a]s he was sensible the law would not oblige him, he would not allow one farthing of interest," and "[h]e . . . would not by the fear of a suit . . . be intimidated into any allowance of interest." Some debtors seemed to relish the contest, as did one Delaware debtor whose creditor marveled that, after threatening to sue him, he "triumphs in the Opportunity of keeping me out so many Courts."[29]

Underlying, and indeed legitimizing, resort to procedural delay was the fact that "settling" a debt did not necessarily mean paying it. Debtors and creditors alike regarded "due and payable" as discrete, widely separated events. Creditors and their lawyers often did not seek payment but rather assurances that the debt would be repaid—with interest to be paid in the interim, of course. Assurances could take the form of new security or of an entirely new debt obligation. It was not uncommon for debtors to roll book accounts, which did not bear interest, over into notes or bonds, which did, and which also carried procedural advantages that facilitated recovery. Creditors proposed such rollovers as the price of their forbearance, as a condition of further credit, or even, as Gerard Beekman did, as a way of closing accounts and converting book debts into interest-bearing securities in contemplation of retirement. Debtors proposed them to buy more time. Both parties often accepted a rollover as the best deal attainable.[30] As a practice born of necessity, it lent itself to abuse, which the Connecticut General Assembly took note of in 1734 when it enacted penalties against "ill-minded persons" who compelled their debtors "to give mortgages, bills, bonds or notes under hand, for the payment of great and unlawful sums for forbearance, or to trade further with them, upon unreasonable advance, to the great oppression and undoing of many families."[31]

When it became necessary to sue, the most common way to begin was by a writ of attachment or a writ of *capias ad respondendum*. Which writ was a matter of jurisdictional custom. Connecticut courts, for example, issued attachments, eschewing latinate constructions as befit a colony whose ties to England tended to be mediated through its more cosmopolitan neighbors. Pennsylvania and New York, on the other hand, where lawyers were better trained and more anglicized, used *capias* process. The differences between the two were minor, and for our purposes they can be discussed as one. Unlike a summons, an attachment required the debtor to provide security sufficient to satisfy the debt, using his property, if adequate, or his body, if not.[32] The latter alternative was known as "taking" or "arresting" the debtor. A debtor whose person had been attached faced imprisonment if he could not find a bondsman to stand bail—not imprisonment as punishment, although its punitive aspects are undeniable, but imprisonment as a guarantee that the debtor would appear in court. The most obvious reason for the choice of attachment to begin debt actions was that the decision to sue was itself more of a last resort than a beginning. It generally meant that nonjudicial attempts at collection had failed, leaving coercive process as the only way to get the debtor's attention and, perhaps, the debt. The tactical purpose of attachment was not so much to confine the debtor as to obtain security for the debt, either from the debtor or from sympathetic friends or relatives. As Johnson reported to one client in 1762, he thought that if he could arrest a debtor "it is probable his father will give security for him rather than let him go to gaol." On the other hand, since giving security put one's own property at risk, even close family members might decline to purchase a relative's freedom at the cost of endangering their financial futures, choosing instead to let the debtor be imprisoned.[33] Another aim of attachment was to force a debtor to recruit one or two men of means to stand bail. Bail bondsmen did not secure the debt—they guaranteed that the debtor would appear at court. However, their guarantee carried a steep potential cost—they became liable for the debt if the debtor absconded, although creditors often had to sue them to collect.[34]

Not all debtors feared arrest. One Thompson haughtily told Johnson in 1751 that "he does not value an arrest, as he can procure bondsmen, but does not choose it as it may hurt his credit." Another, Robert Sloan, opined to Johnson that "he should be very willing to be arrested" because it would excuse him from the partial payment he had intended to make.[35] Debtors such as Thompson and Sloan, however, were differently circumstanced from other debtors, whether in terms of greater resources, closer familiarity with the process, or simply steadier nerves. Most debtors did not view arrest with equanimity. Solomon Kidder implored Samuel Abbot of Boston in 1766 not to sue him before they could meet—"I had rather give you Ten Dollars then To Have a writ sarved upon me which I never had." Eighteen years later, John Jones "fear'd" coming to Philadelphia, "apprehending some persons in this city would take the opportunity of suing him." John Pintard, hiding outside Newark from his creditors in New York in 1793, captured the fears and anxieties of many less literary-minded debtors when he described how he "coursed the back lane at twilights grey, with all the horrors of a culprit, least a monster,

> sullen of aspect, by the vulgar call'd
> a catchpole—his ample palm
> should haply on ill fated shoulder lay
> of debtor.[36]

Fear of arrest—or, more specifically, fear of the consequences of arrest—promoted a variety of stratagems to avoid being served with a writ of attachment. Samuel Hazard, a Pennsylvania iron manufacturer, suspected one debtor of bribing the constable. Another "has truly been a bird of passage, fixed nowhere, sometimes residing in one town, sometimes in another, and always cautious to avoid every appearance of an officer, and in several instances has used violence to escape." Some debtors kept to their houses—sometimes for years—where they were safe from service of process. Others absconded, fleeing to another colony where distance and procedural rules made arrest unlikely. The latter two ploys figure particularly in our inquiry because they were "acts of bankruptcy" under the federal Bankruptcy Act of 1800—that is, whether a debtor had "kept close" or absconded "with intent unlawfully to delay or defraud his . . . creditors" helped determine whether a debtor qualified for a commission of bankruptcy.[37]

Debtors who received insolvency or bankruptcy relief were not necessarily impoverished. They were deeply in debt, but they were not poor. Most colonial, state, and federal insolvency and bankruptcy systems had debt thresholds that far exceeded the borrowing capacities of genuinely destitute debtors. As a consequence their benefits extended only to debtors whose success had been such that creditors allowed them to amass large debts. By the same token, "keeping close" for any length of time was an option available only to debtors with the financial resources to sustain it. The strategy stemmed from the fact that the law everywhere prohibited sheriffs and constables from forcibly entering a person's dwelling to serve a writ on the occupant. They could enter through an open or unlocked door, climb through an unsecured window, or trick their way inside, but they could not break down a door or otherwise force their way in. Debtors who successfully kept close prevented officers from serving them with process that would have required them to give security, find bail, or be arrested. As a practical matter, only debtors who did not have to leave their houses each day to labor for their sustenance could afford to keep close. By keeping to their houses, they may only have postponed the inevitable, but they also bought time to negotiate a settlement, pursue ventures that might restore their fortunes, or otherwise hope against hope. While confined, they gradually consumed their resources to support themselves and their families. Samuel Hazard lamented in 1757 that his property had been "greatly Lessend in Value by . . . the Unavoidable Expences of my Family dureing near two years Confinement to my House." Daniel King of Salem warned his creditors in 1763 that if they "still insist on Imposabilitys I must Keep house and Spend the Little I intended for my Creditors for I . . . Have tired all my Frinds and Can Doe no more." Abijah Beach, a Connecticut trader who owed over £2,000 to nearly forty creditors in Connecticut and New York, "shut himself up a Prisoner in his own House," where he led "a Life of Inactivity, unprofitable to himself, the Community and his Creditors, and has been obliged to support himself his Wife and seven small Children upon what he had," by dint of which "he is now become greatly insolvent."[38]

On the other hand, the debtors who avoided service by keeping close were not the debtors who went to court only to delay final judgment through reviews and appeals. The latter had the resources both to buy time and to expect that they could use the time so bought to advantage. The former lacked the ability to give bail for appearance or security for each review and appeal and in general had fewer prospects of salvaging their affairs. Or they were judgment debtors who had lost their cases in court and kept to their houses to avoid writs of execution or *capias ad satisfaciendum* by which they would have been seized and held until they paid. They were the debtors who, as Johnson remarked of one, "if arrested can doubtless do no more than to exchange the confinement of his house for that of a gaol."[39] The most famous such debtor was Robert Morris, superintendent of finance in the Revolution and the wealthiest man in America afterward, who for the seven months before he entered debtors' prison in 1798 withstood process servers from his country house outside Philadelphia, which he dubbed "Castle Defiance."[40]

Most debtors presumably did not have to contend with angry creditors and armed henchmen—"Myrmidons," Morris called them, after Achilles' pitiless followers at Troy—lying in wait outside the door, threatening to break or bribe their way in to seize them and deliver them to sheriffs, who could not take such steps themselves. Morris did. At times he treated it as a game of cat and mouse. But he was not playing when he brandished his own weapons and vowed bloodshed before jail, or when he advised his equally insolvent partner, John Nicholson, that he had a right to use deadly force to defend himself against intruders. Morris conducted business from an upper-story window and admitted only family and trusted friends inside. When he had to let in a glazier to repair his windows, he went out on the widow's walk atop his roof, locking the door behind him in case the man had been deputized to serve writs.[41] Nicholson, who shared Morris's sequestration at Castle Defiance until his lawyers advised him that he had to keep to his own house to be safe from arrest, described their position succinctly when he wrote his brother that he and Morris "are keeping garrison at the hills, we can see the city but there are few in it we would trust to see us or admit within our walls, . . . altho we are not in jail, yet we are in a voluntary confinement."[42]

No one would claim typicality for Morris, but he was subject to the same legal process and constraints as lesser debtors. When he asked Nicholson whether his meeting with Richard Stokes "shall be held through the window or whether he may be safely admitted inside the *sacred* Walls of the Sanctum Sanctorum that contains my person," he was calculating a risk that all debtors keeping close understood.[43] The only relief such debtors could look forward to from their self-imposed imprisonment was on Sundays, when writs could not legally be served. As Pintard wrote in his diary one Saturday evening in 1793, "Tomorrow I shall partake of the common priviledges of human nature. Perhaps a poor haunted debtor, feels the good of the institution of the Sabbath, as sensibly as most people." Morris's Monday letters to Nicholson were often tinged with the afterglow of Sunday outings—"Here I am safe and sound after breathing the fresh air of yesterday in some extensive walks," and "Yesterday I never took a pen in hand but spent the whole day with my Family rambling about."[44]

If these conjure images of debtors' promenades on Sundays, flaunting their temporary immunity from arrest, we should remember that home and church—and by extension of the latter, the Sabbath—were traditionally the only places where individuals could invoke limits on the authority of the state to initiate legal action. Even at that, they offered imperfect sanctuary at best. Debtors knew that, just as their houses might not protect them against creditors acting privately—for example, George Knox's threat against Walter Livingston that "By God I will bring up 20 men from New York with me and I will be damned if I dont take him"—Sunday did not guarantee that they would not be abducted and turned over to a sheriff on Monday. Morris and Nicholson received general cautions that it was not safe for them to venture out on Sundays, as well as the occasional, sometimes anonymous, warning of plots to seize them and hold them until Monday when they could be legally arrested. Each time they adjusted their behavior with an eye toward taking advantage of the diminishing legal protections left to them.[45]

The only place left for debtors in Morris's and Nicholson's position to go was jail, which both men ultimately did and where Nicholson remained until he died. However satisfying for frustrated or vindictive creditors, imprisoning debtors did little or nothing to make repayment more likely. As Johnson remarked of one debtor, "I can put him in gaol any day, but that will not pay the debt."[46] This made execution process the last real opportunity for creditors to collect anything.

Judgments that one person owed another money were not self-executing. That is, debtors who lost in court did not instantly reach into their pockets and pay their creditors. They might, of course, but they also might not, in which case additional legal steps were necessary to collect a judgment. Collectively, those steps constituted execution process—writs of execution, *capias ad satisfaciendum, fieri facias,* and *levari facias,* depending on the jurisdiction and on what was to be seized. As with every other phase of litigation, one should think of the writs as the participants did—not as rules that compelled particular results but rather as guidelines that shaped the continuing interactions of debtors and creditors, without necessarily determining them.

In form, execution process was simple. It directed the sheriff to attach the judgment debtor's person or property, depending on the writ, and compel the former or use the latter to satisfy the judgment. In practice, it was subject to two great imponderables—finding the debtor and finding the debtor's property. Debtors could avoid being served with execution process by the same means they avoided attachment or summons—by keeping close or absconding. Levying execution on the debtor's property was rather more problematic. Only nonexempt property could be taken in execution, which in most colonies and states meant that some, usually small, portion of clothing, bedding, necessary household items, farm implements, and tools of a trade were shielded from seizure. Land, which for many debtors was their most valuable asset, could not be attached at all in the plantation colonies and often only under certain conditions in the northern colonies unless the execution was pursuant to a mortgage foreclosure, in which case it was the debtor who had put the property at risk by pledging it to secure a debt. Even when land could legally be levied upon, the levy might yield little or nothing if, for example, there were prior liens against the property or if land was so plentiful or cash so tight that there was no market for selling it. Benjamin Pollard spoke for many southern creditors when he complained "that it is only throwing away money to sue for the recovery of debts, as Landed property cannot be subjected to the payment of them" and that he had "never yet got paid a single judgment" because he had "always found a debtors property so secured by Mortgages or other encumbrances that it could not be touched." The scarcity of money affected real and personal property alike because property taken in execution was sold at public auction, where payment was in cash, not promissory notes. The problem was a persistent one. In 1763 Johnson reported that the sheriff bartered levied goods for rum and other items that he hoped would be more salable after there had been no buyers at auction for want of cash. Twenty years later, James Mercer complained that goods in Virginia were selling at auction for a quarter of their cost for the same reason.[47]

The scarcity of money that dampened auction prices was, of course, the same scarcity of money that inhibited paying debts in the first place. Creditors like John Vining recognized that "the scarcity of cash makes [debts] hard to be got without greatly distressing the people." Robert Morris, in a lament echoed by other propertied debtors throughout the period, wrote, "Hard, very hard, is our Fate to be starving in the midst of plenty for we have abundant property, money however cannot be obtained for any part of it." Daniel Ramsay captured the essence of the dilemma when he wrote from South Carolina in 1788:

> Our sufferings here as to money matters are greater than in the time of the war or just after its close. Instead of growing better our affairs have been gradually growing worse. There are three houses in Charleston each of whom could sue bonds to a greater amount than all the circulating money in the country would pay. Houses and lands will not sell for a fourth of their former value. He that owes but a little though possessed of much property lives by the courtesy of his creditors for if they were to sue his property must be sacrificed and perhaps the debt be unpaid.

Or, as an unknown New York debtor wrote one of his creditors in 1765, making the same point in more personal terms, "you well know that hardly any trading person in this City could pay all the debt they owe were they Emediately pushed for it. I have Real and personal Estate to amount of above Double the Value I owe, after making a Very Sufficient allouance for bad debts."[48]

The outlines of debt collection, of how debtors and creditors bargained in the shadow of the law, changed little from the beginning of the eighteenth century to its end. The single largest variable is one we will consider later—the presence or absence of insolvency or bankruptcy legislation. Apart from that, the only real difference is that debtors after the Revolution faced the beginnings of routinized, professional debt collection. As early as 1788 Samuel Barrett, a Boston justice of the peace, used printed forms to notify debtors that he would sue them unless they paid, with blanks left for the names of the creditor and debtor, their places of residence, the form and amount of the debt, and the length of the remaining grace period before he filed suit. In 1790 James Cebra of New York circulated a broadside offering "his services . . . in the collection of debts." To assure readers of his character, "[a]s collecting of debts is a business of trust," he appended a testimonial signed by fifty-six prominent merchants and lawyers in the city. By 1799 newspapers were printing impersonal advertisements for debt collectors that dispensed with the character references and even the name of the collector and simply offered the service.[49] The personalized, polite duns of pre-Revolutionary lawyers like William Samuel Johnson had not disappeared, but debt collection was more clearly becoming a business.[50]

One constant was the distaste for lawyers, which was shared by creditors and debtors alike and varied little across the decades. When John Pintard, former imprisoned debtor and bankrupt, wrote in his commonplace book that "A Lawyers trade is Villainy licenced by Law," he echoed Thomas Preston, a merchant-creditor forty-five years earlier, who wrote that lawyers are "a sett of Rascalls that are regardless of their Clients Interest, tho they allways take Care to be well paid." Where Benjamin Pollard complained that "such is . . . the chicane of Law that bringing suit to compel payment is nothing [because] the Lawyers continually find ways and means to stave off judgment," Robert Morris angrily declared "my God how these Lawyers delight to shew their cunning and Management without once thinking of the distress they create."[51]

Throughout our period, of course, creditors could choose the time-honored option of "lumping it," whether out of generosity, frustration, or a straightforward calculation of the likelihood of success and the cost of trying. Robert Troup, a leading lawyer in New York at the close of the century, advised two British creditors "to consider your Debt as lost rather than to embark in Suits which will draw after them certain and heavy expense." He explained that "frauds are now so prevalent and oaths so little regarded with us, that where a decided disposition appears to keep property from the hands of Creditors, it seldom happens that Creditors are successful in their endeavours to obtain it." Creditors "generally spend much money, encounter much trouble, suffer much vexation, and at last are compelled to abandon the pursuit as altogether hopeless. Such is unfortunately the state of things that has grown out of the enormous speculations in this Country and the loose morality which French Philosophy is spreading through the world."[52]

We will have occasion to consider Troup's evil trinity of "enormous speculations," "loose morality," and "French Philosophy" at length in later chapters—they figured prominently in the debate over national bankruptcy legislation in the 1790s. For now, let us simply note the unstated implications of his advice: The debtor-creditor relation was a legal one, defined by the formal rules that governed the creation and collection of debts. It also had social, economic, political, and moral dimensions that were not entirely contained within the formal framework of debtor and creditor law. The law prescribed remedies and procedures, but it could not control when those remedies would be available nor how parties would use the procedures. The debtor-creditor relation retained an underlying indeterminacy even as the formal legal system was elevating uniformity and certainty as values. The growing formalism of the relation merely defined the general framework within which debtors and creditors dealt with one another. Insolvency added urgency, even desperation, to the calculus—for creditors as well as debtors.

♀ 2 ♂

THE LAW OF FAILURE

[O]ur Humanity we may distinguish . . . in the particular Relations of Debtor and Creditor; wherein our Conduct may be so far praise-worthy as to convey the brightest Lustre to our Characters; or so far inhuman as to level us with the brute Creation; so far consonant to God's divine Attribute of Mercy, as to draw down a Blessing upon all our Endeavours; or so far repugnant thereto, as to derive a Curse upon every Thing we take in Hand.

Debtor and Creditor (1762)

The biblical parable of the unmerciful servant that was the text for these lines captured both the reality and the ideal of debtor-creditor relations. It told of the king who ordered his servant sold, together with the man's family and possessions, to repay the debt he owed to the king. But when the servant begged for lenience, beseeching the king to "have patience with me, and I will pay thee all," the creditor-king "was moved with compassion, and loosed him, and forgave him the debt." Later, however, the servant imprisoned his own debtor, even though the poor wretch pleaded with him in the same language he had implored the king. When the king learned of the servant's severity, he chastised him for not showing his debtor the same compassion he had shown him and angrily "delivered him to the tormentors" to extract the payment he had formerly forgiven (Matthew 18:23–35).

When Cotton Mather invoked the debtor's plea of the parable—
"Have patience with me, and I will pay thee all"—in 1716, it was to observe that creditors who treated their honest debtors with "Brotherly
Kindness" brought their debtors "into a further Debt, for so much Kind
Usage of them." Half a century later, when it first became the text for a
published discourse, the plea appeared as part of an argument that whoever "has the Interest of his Country at Heart . . . must endeavour all that
in him lies, to extend, repair, and strengthen the great Road of Commerce,
to clear away the Rubs and Difficulties that may impede the Progress of
his Fellow-Labourers therein." In that new context the debtor's plea represented—and was understood as representing—an offered novation of the
original contract between debtor and creditor. Once a mark of religious
compassion, forbearance acquired more explicit trappings of economic
calculation.[1]

Behind this change lay failure. Economic growth, even prosperity,
touched every part of British North America in the first half of the eighteenth century. From the Atlantic fisheries to the shipyards of New York
and Philadelphia, from the commercial farmers of Pennsylvania to the tobacco planters of the Chesapeake, from the loggers of northern New England to the fur traders who spread through the Appalachian backcountry,
from artisans to mechanics to shopkeepers, as well as the merchants and
coastal and inland traders who bound them all together, production
and trade increased. To be sure, economic expansion was not without
fits and starts nor were its benefits evenly distributed, either within or
across regions—indeed, one might argue that widening inequality was a
mark of economic success—but its direction was as inescapable as the
population growth that accompanied it.[2]

The increasingly commercial economies of the eighteenth century created new opportunities for success. They also multiplied the risk of failure.
Agricultural expansion spurred the growth of market towns and ports, with
concentrated populations and market orientations that promoted artisans,
merchants, and the specialization of business enterprise. The lure of greater
local trade opportunities induced people to enter the lists as small traders,
just as the production of agricultural surpluses and the growing demand for

manufactured goods encouraged merchants to become exporters and importers. With the kind of optimism possible in an atmosphere of prosperity and expansion, ambitious men launched their ventures with large aspirations and little capital. Credit bridged the gap, whether for traders who needed goods to trade or farmers who needed land and livestock to expand. Commercial development rode the crest of a rising tide of indebtedness, a tide that reflected the confidence of prosperity as farmers and planters, artisans and shopkeepers, traders and merchants borrowed against anticipated profits to finance the undertakings that they knew—not hoped, but knew—would create them. Their dreams and ambitions took flight on wings of entrepreneurial indebtedness, more enticingly known as investment. Not surprisingly, some faltered while others soared. Crops fail, prices fall, ships sink, warehouses burn, owners die, partners steal, pirates pillage, wars ravage, and people simply make mistakes. In highly leveraged, largely uninsured economies, even single misfortunes can bring ruin. However great the wreckage, debt always remains. Economic growth enabled more people to fail owing greater sums of money to larger numbers of creditors than had been possible in the smaller, more insular local economies of the seventeenth century. This was the reality—the rising risk of failure—that underlay the legal and intellectual transformation of insolvency. It was also the reality that weakened the moral economy of debt.

Commercial lawyers commonly sort themselves into creditors' lawyers and debtors' lawyers. Samuel Moody was a creditors' minister. In truth, there was little in law or religion at the beginning of the eighteenth century that would have permitted him to be anything else. For a brief moment three generations earlier, John Winthrop, John Cotton, Robert Sanderson, and other Puritan writers had argued that credit should be a means of charity rather than a commodity and that creditors—although not, tellingly enough, secured creditors, those with "a surety or a lawfull pleadge"—should be prepared to forgive their debtors. That moment passed, however, and within a few decades even the most pious creditor, such as the Atlantic merchant John Hull of Boston, could regard debts as "righteous" obligations, which could be expiated only by payment in full. Moody's severity nonetheless surprises.[3]

When Moody observed to his Maine parishioners that it was "a sad and lamentable thing to be deeply in Debt," he was expressing compassion for debtors without suggesting that there was or should be any earthly amelioration of their condition. He took special notice of the fact that God himself frequently referred to sin, "the worst thing in the World," by the name debt. When he recounted the parable of the unmerciful servant, it was to demonstrate the harsh rigor of creditors' remedies, with no mention at all that the king forgave his debtor and later punished him for not forgiving his own debtor in turn. To be sure, Moody's uncompromising rigidity on the subject of debt had venerable roots—it echoed the late medieval, pre-Reformation identification of debt with sin for which absolution, and ultimately salvation, required repayment—but, as we shall see, economic reality was overtaking scriptural injunction even as he wrote.[4]

Moody did concede certain moral distinctions among debtors but for spiritual purposes only. Echoing a long-standing secular discrimination between honest bankrupts and fraudulent ones, he distinguished between debtors who "are Diminished and brought Low by the Holy Providence of God; who are Chargeable, neither with Slothfulness nor Prodigality," and those who "have made themselves Poor by hearkening to Satans Temptations, following after vain Persons, living in Pride and Luxury; running into Debt, to support these and other Chargeable Lusts, without Care or Conscience how they should get out again." The former might be "the most Proper Objects of Charity," but the latter were to be pitied more, for they were "Double Debtors"—in debt both to their temporal creditors and to God—whose souls would be cast into the debtors' prison of hell. Moody recognized a further division within the former group between debtors whose distress was the result of some accident or calamity and those who had been brought low by their own improvidence or imprudence, whether gullibility, misplaced trust, or general lack of business acumen. However, he only drew this finer distinction for purposes of cautioning that we should not attribute all failure to providence or conclude that all who have failed are at fault.[5]

To Moody, these moral gradations made no difference in the obligations debtors owed their creditors. The fundamental rule for all debtors, regardless of how they fell into debt, was that "Debts must be paid, tho' all go for it." Scripture and reason alike required that debtors must, if necessary, dispose of everything they own to repay their debts. They must "Sell all, to the very Clothes on their Back; which no Creditor will be so Barbarous as to strip them of"—a reassurance that debtors doubtless heard with some skepticism. To the objection that such severity would reduce debtors to beggary, Moody replied, "If God, in His Providence, has thus brought you; or if you, by Extravagance or Imprudence have brought your selves to Poverty, Poor you must contentedly be . . . It is no Sin to be Poor; but to lie in Debt, is a Sin."[6]

It is in this last reply that Moody showed himself most clearly a creditor's minister. God may bring his people into debt but will do nothing to lift them from insolvency except insofar as they follow the doctrine that "Debts must be paid, tho' all go for it." In that case, and that case only, God might incline the hearts of creditors to show some forbearance, perhaps even compassion. This is the God whom Moody addressed as the "Great Creditor" who casts insolvent souls into the debtors' prison of hell, where Satan is "Gods Gaoler" and the inmates "eat Fire and Brimstone; and drink the Dreggs of Divine Wrath and Fury without any Gaol Delivery, or so much as the Remotest Hope thereof."[7]

To apostrophize God in this manner implicitly acknowledged the authority of temporal creditors, who enjoyed the same powers over debtors' bodies as the "Great Creditor" did over their souls. Indeed, failure to pay one's earthly creditors created, for Moody, a spiritual debt, thereby backstopping the legal remedies of creditors in this life with the wrath of God in the next. Moody further linked creditors sacred and profane in the precepts he laid down for how debtors should conduct themselves in their distress. He drew his listeners' attention to what the debtor in 2d Kings did not do:

She did not Fret against God. . . ; no, nor does she utter any Railing Speeches against the Creditor, how hard so ever he was in prosecuting her. She denies not the Debt, nor Refuseth to Pay. She makes no flattering Promises to the Person, into whose Books she was gotten so deep, of what she was neither likely, nor careful to Perform: Nor does she take any indirect or unwarrantable course, to Evade or Discharge what was Due.

Instead, "[s]he did as the Man of God Directed her. She was willing to Pay her Debt; and willing to part with all her Living." Debtors should not censure their creditors, who "are Debtors as well as you; and have Creditors as sharp on them." Nor should they "Flatter [their] Creditors with fair Promises, or plausible Pretences of what [they] are either unable, or unwilling, and never likely to make good unto them." Debtors who "owe much, and have nothing to Pay . . . must Pay Submission, for the present, and promise more substantial Payment as soon as ever they shall be Able. In the mean time, they must willingly Fare hard, as well as Work hard; and Pray hard too; that they may be as Good as their Promise."[8]

Moody's strictures did not fall on unprepared ears. He simply made explicit what other ministers had left implicit. A generation earlier, Samuel Willard had preached that keeping one's promises implicates both "the honour of God" and "the credit of Religion." Using the language of secured credit, he reasoned that every Christian's promise carries with it a pledge of his conscience as security for his performance of the promise. The consequence of breaking the promise was forfeiture of the pledge, and a man "who hath Forfeited and lost his Conscience . . . hath not only lost his Religion, but his Morality too."[9]

Moody may have described debtors' obligations in greater detail than other writers, but he was not alone in the severity of his sentiments. Cotton Mather, who yielded to no one in the sternness of his judgments, observed in a lecture delivered a few months after Moody's sermons that "One Point of Morality" in which many people were "defective" was their lack of caution in incurring and remaining in debt. Too many people "bring Debts upon themselves, in such a manner, and in such a measure, that a Folly nothing short of Criminal, is to be charged upon them." And once in debt, their delay in repayment is also a crime, "for which they are to be Indicted, as not having the Fear of God before their Eyes." Like Moody, Mather inveighed against the prideful temptations of luxury. People run into debt because "they cannot bear the Humiliations of a Low and Mean Condition in the World." They borrow "for the Supply of their Carnal Appetites." Also like Moody, Mather took it as irrefragable that "[i]f a Man cannot keep out of a Low and Mean Condition, without a plain wrong to the Estates of other Men, he is then most Evidently called of God into a Low and Mean Condition."[10]

On the other hand, whereas Moody interpreted his scriptural text in the harshest light possible, Mather took a text that was, if anything, more severe and softened its application at every turn, even if only slightly. Every precept carried a qualification. "People must not be in Debt unto one another, any further than what is unavoidable." "'Tis the Duty of Christians, to have as few Creditors as ever they can, and owe as little to their Creditors as ever they can," not to have no creditors and owe nothing. Rather than condemn all debt, Mather understood that some debts were "proper" and that the obligation of Christians was not to avoid such debts but to "[c]ome into [them], with the Pace of a Tortoise, and get out of [them], with the Flight of an Eagle."[11]

Mather had a much subtler grasp of debt than Moody. He recognized the difference between debts not yet due and debts past due, and consequently that being in debt was less blameworthy than being a delinquent debtor. A debt is "but as an Embryo, in its Formation, while the Time is not yet come for the Creditor to make his Demand. But it is more fully formed, and makes a very audible Cry, when a Man witholds from another Man, the Possessions, which ought Now to be delivered." This latter state "is not only Being in Debt, but also Lying in Debt: And it is to be avoided with all the Caution imaginable." Mather also saw that the question of when a debtor who was sliding toward insolvency was obliged to inform his creditors of his plight was fraught with difficulty. Commercial debtors especially wavered between hope and despair as their affairs worsened, making it hard to know when a debtor who still hoped for recovery should nonetheless throw in the towel, stop the deepening spiral of debt, and preserve his remaining assets for his creditors. At what point did a debtor's desire to remain in business and regain solvency injure his creditors instead? When did a debtor's persistence bring himself "into ill Terms with Heaven"? Mather did not attempt to answer these questions, but he clearly recognized a problem that any system of debtor relief had to address.[12]

Mather's refusal to lump all debts together and stigmatize them as sinful reflected his acceptance of the inevitability of debt, which in turn led him to caution debtors rather than condemn them. "A Man that is going into Debt, should keep the Eye of Prudence Open." It is folly "[t]o run in the Dark, when One is going into Debt." "For a Man to run into Debt, when he has no Prospect, and perhaps no Purpose of ever getting out," is dishonest. "Men ought often and nicely to Examine the State of their Business, if they would not find themselves irrecoverably Plunged into Debt, before they are aware." "The Man that is got into Debt, ought to get out of it, as fast as he can, and as if it were for his Life."[13]

To be sure, Mather agreed with Moody on the obligations of debtors whose debts were due. A debtor should be "Solicitous in Complying with Time for every Payment" and "Indefatigable in turning every Stone for the Satisfaction of thy Creditor." Debtors brought to insolvency by their own dereliction "ought with a deep Repentance, to abase [them]selves before God, and the World," as well as their creditors. But where Moody read the scriptural lesson of the widow to mean that insolvent debtors should strip themselves bare to satisfy their creditors, Mather saw instead a debtor who did not resort to fraud or deceit to "withold more than is meet, from the Injured Creditors," thereby at least suggesting, contrary to Moody, that although "Debts must be paid," all need not "go for it."[14]

More significantly, Mather, unlike Moody, conceded that some debt was necessary. In his concession lay the seed of a distinction that bedeviled debtor relief in the latter part of the century. Mather recognized that without debt there could be no trade: "It would strangely Cramp the Trade of a People, if it might be no more than the Cash that is running among them." Since "the World so much resolves to Trade upon Credit," Mather granted that "a Man of Capacity and Integrity" who had nothing else to his name but those qualities, might sometimes find them "a Sufficient Fund ... if his Creditors will please have it so." In the end "[n]o Body is Hurt, if the Debt wherewith Trade is carryed on, be kept under a Suitable Regulation."[15] Although Mather did not pursue the point further, his acknowledgment that trade could not exist without credit, coupled with his injunction that "a Due Caution, to Owe no Man any thing, is what every Man should Labour in," was an admission that commercial debts—and, by implication, commercial debtors—were different from other kinds of debt and debtors. And if they were different, then they might merit different forms of relief when their indebtedness became insolvency.

In this Mather, like Moody, was stating more directly what other ministers had noted indirectly. Willard, for one, recognized the importance of trade and argued that "[t]he Wellfare of Humane Society is very much Concerned in" whether people keep their promises. "Man is a Dependent Creature." Because individuals cannot supply all their own wants and needs, "there is mutual Traffick between men and Transactions among them in the Management of it." As "mutual Traffick" cannot be limited to simultaneous exchange, "men must trust one another; and therefore Covenants and Promises must pass between them for the future doing this or that." What permits these promises "to pass for currant between man and man, is truth in the promiser," without which "the Ligament of Humane society is dissolved and Communities must be disbanded."[16]

Mather may have viewed debt more acceptingly than Moody, but ultimately he, too, believed that debtors were morally bound to pay their debts. Only full payment or a creditor's grace could discharge a debt. Partial payment did not satisfy the whole. Insolvency, although pitiable, warranted no relief other than what creditors might be inclined to grant, their hearts "mollified by their seeing the Brokenness of" their debtors' hearts. Where Moody argued that insolvent debtors must surrender everything and, if that was not enough, "must willingly . . . Work hard" until they repaid the last farthing, Mather enlisted the debtor's conscience toward the same end. To Mather, the Roman law that condemned bankrupt debtors to dismemberment was more lenient than "the Conscience of a Debtor [taking] him in hand, and with angry Strokes [telling] him, You have wronged such and such Neighbours; they feel themselves the worse for you every day that comes over their heads; and what Restitution can you make unto them!" Mather did not invoke Moody's image of hell as a debtors' prison, but, not surprisingly, the imagery he did use encouraged full repayment: "An honest Man should feel [debt] as a Load, and groan under the Load; but not cry for, more Weight! as the Miserables that are Pressing to Death use to do." "The Miseries which Debt is accompanied withal" in this world include "to be Despised of ones Neighbour, and be annihilated with a blasted Reputation," "to be exposed unto the Rage, of Provoked Creditors," "to be Dun'd with repeated Indignities," and "to be Vex'd with legal Prosecutions."[17]

The one concession Mather made, and that only a procedural one, was that creditors, before suing their debtors, should first follow the gospel rule of Matthew 18:15–17. That rule, which formed the basis of Congregational church discipline, facilitated reconciliation but only upon the offender's repentance. As applied by Mather to the law of debtor and creditor, it did not contemplate the creditor's forgiveness of the debt. The debtor "should be civilly Addressed . . . by the Creditor, and then by some of his Friends, and be Admonish'd of the Damage that he will bring upon himself, and especially the Wounds upon his Conscience, if he don't fairly pay what he owes." Creditors whose debtors did not respond with a level of repentance that included repayment could then resort to law, secure in the knowledge that they had fulfilled their Christian duty to their debtors. In truth, few creditors availed themselves of the parleying procedure of Matthew 18, even though they almost always preferred to collect their debts without suing for them. Nonetheless, Mather's invocation of the scriptural rule, which he noted with satisfaction was also prescribed "in a famous *Lexicon Juridicum*," underscores the existence of a moral economy of debt in which failure to repay a debt was a moral offense for which the debtor's conscience would suffer the penalty.[18]

Moody and Mather wrote at a time of contest in the economic culture of New England—not surprising, as moral strictures are often asserted most vigorously and censoriously when acceptance of them weakens. Margaret Newell has perceptively described how New Englanders in the early eighteenth century labored to redefine old categories of religion and political economy to accommodate new complexities of trade and finance, which found expression in internal development, vigorous commercial activity, and new habits of consumption that refused to be cabined by traditional social restrictions. For our purposes the most significant spur to this process was paper money, which, because it was nothing more than a reified promise—a debt—called into question ideas and beliefs that once had been certain, such as the meaning of value.[19]

A scant fifteen years before Moody and Mather held forth, the Cambridge Association of ministers had abandoned its objections to usury—opposition to which had been a cornerstone of Puritan commercial theology since the founding. It did so amid a rising tide of popularity of bills of public credit, issued first by Massachusetts in 1690, followed by other colonies in the ensuing decades. By turning debt into a circulating medium of exchange, paper money redressed chronic shortages of specie and credit, stimulated internal trade, and facilitated consumption. As paper money circulated through the colonial economies, touching people whose previous participation in the economy had been conducted by commodity exchanges, it democratized credit, allowing local traders and entrepreneurial farmers to share the aspirations of Atlantic merchants. What some saw as opportunity, others viewed with concern. Writers such as Edward Wigglesworth, Paul Dudley, and Thomas Paine argued that the credit made freely available by paper money encouraged people to spend beyond their means, to consume rather than invest. Rather than be satisfied with a competency appropriate to their station, they complained, people sought to emulate their betters, in the process incurring indebtedness that threatened both their moral and economic independence. To their minds, credit and everything it entailed—the right to engage in commerce, to borrow, to consume—should not be available to all. Although none of the participants in the currency debate expressly linked debtors' obligations to the vices of paper money, they did not have to. Both sprang from the same moral economy.[20]

Debtors do not fail alone. In failure, as in success, they are inextricably tied to their creditors. When a debtor defaults on a debt, the paramount legal question is how the creditor is to be paid. When a debtor defaults on debts to several creditors, the question is how the creditors are to be paid. Although similar, these two questions are not the same, nor is the latter simply the plural form of the former. On the other hand, neither are they entirely different. As a debtor's defaults multiply, the mechanics of how individual creditors collect their debts give way to the competition among creditors to determine who among them will be paid in full, in part, or not at all. Just as solvency and insolvency are not so much inverses of one another as they are overlapping bands on a continuum, the law and practice of debt collection elide into the law and practice of insolvency.

Observers typically analyze debt-related measures by asking if they serve debtors or creditors. Sometimes the dichotomy is apt. Statutes of limitations, which bar plaintiffs from legal redress if they wait too long to file suit, discipline creditors and protect debtors. Gaol-delivery statutes and poor debtors' oaths, which release truly indigent debtors from imprisonment and shield them from future arrest for the same debts, express measured compassion for "unfortunate" debtors. The use of arrest process against debtors, not to mention imprisonment for debt itself, gives creditors considerable raw power over their debtors. Insolvency and bankruptcy laws, on the other hand, defy simple dichotomization. Indeed, any attempt to do so obscures the reality on which they rest—that debtors and creditors are partners in debt, and never more so than when debtors are insolvent.

Insolvency is an imprecise state. It can mean that one's liabilities exceed one's assets or, more narrowly, that the assets legally available to creditors are insufficient to pay one's debts. Or it can mean simply the inability to repay debts as they become due. Compared to bankruptcy, insolvency is rather democratic. Anyone can become insolvent. There are no occupational restrictions or minimum debt requirements to keep out the riffraff. Nor do debtors need the imprimatur of court action to proclaim themselves insolvent. The sole criterion is failure. Bankruptcy, on the other hand, is a legally defined status, conferrable on the select few only by formal adjudication. Merely being hopelessly mired in debt is not enough. With infrequent exceptions before the twentieth century, insolvent debtors could not be declared bankrupt unless they followed certain commercial occupations, amassed debts in excess of a large minimum, and committed statutorily defined acts of bankruptcy. Thus, although insolvency and bankruptcy shared a common origin in the inability of debtors to repay their debts, and despite ample lay usage that treated the terms as synonyms, there were crucial differences. Whether a debtor was insolvent was, at bottom, a question of fact, not law. Debtors could be insolvent even in the absence of any insolvency law. They could be bankrupt, however, only when there were statutes that prescribed the qualifications for bankruptcy, which was the case only sporadically throughout most of American history. All bankrupts were insolvent, but few insolvents were bankrupt.

English law, on the other hand, recognized the distinction continuously from 1543, when a Henrician statute—regarded by historians as the first bankruptcy law for its procedure, despite its lack of a discharge—authorized the imprisonment of debtors who absconded or shut themselves in their houses, the seizure of their property, and its distribution among their creditors. Later statutes in 1571, 1604, and 1623 expanded the acts of bankruptcy that triggered the process and enlarged the powers of the commissioners to ferret out the bankrupt's property and punish both the bankrupt and those who aided his evasions. Bankrupt debtors were presumptively dishonest and fraudulent. They were criminals whose borrowing amounted to theft and who thus should be punished—by hanging, if necessary—and forced to repay. During the seventeenth century, however, the rise of a commercial economy in England introduced people to the power and caprice of the market, which they struggled to make sense of in an outpouring of pamphlets and other writings. As they searched for economic understanding, writers began to see that there were honest bankrupts as well as dishonest ones, that insolvency could result from economic misfortune rather than idle profligacy, and that creditors could oppress debtors as readily as debtors could defraud creditors. Some even argued that a certain level of business failures was a healthy measure of entrepreneurial expansion. A new bankruptcy statute in 1706 acknowledged these distinctions by offering absolution to honest bankrupts while retaining criminal punishment for dishonest ones, thus joining a new appreciation of the market with the old moral economy of debt. For the first time, honest commercial debtors would be shielded from imprisonment, freed from liability for their debts, and returned to the market to compete again—if, of course, they could secure credit. In practice, the frequent difficulty of distinguishing honest bankrupts from dishonest ones created significant ambiguity well into the nineteenth century, but the principle of a discharge for at least some insolvent debtors was established.[21]

Debt and debtors in America rarely merited legislative attention in the seventeenth century, when debt was more typically local and consequently more neighborly. Apart from the occasional statute binding insolvent debtors to their creditors for a term as servants or granting poor debtors release from imprisonment upon oath that their debts were low and their assets even less, relations between debtors and creditors were governed by common law, local custom, and private negotiation.[22] No colony apportioned losses among creditors. The closest any colony came to compelling creditors to act cooperatively rather than competitively when a debtor failed was in 1639, when Maryland enacted a statute that required insolvent debtors to assign their property to their creditors in proportion to their debts. Despite this promising beginning, which prompted one historian to describe the statute—wrongly—as "the first formulated bankruptcy law on the American continent," the statute did not contemplate that creditors were entitled to anything less than the full measure of what they were owed. Debtors had to work off unpaid balances as indentured servants, bound successively to each creditor in declining order of the amount of their debts until every debt had been paid in full. Four decades later, in 1678, Rhode Island discovered how difficult it was to force creditors to share their debtors' assets with one another when it repealed a statute enacted only six weeks earlier that had directed the proportionate distribution of debtors' estates. A world governed by a moral economy of debt did not require much in the way of statutory regulation.[23]

That world changed in the eighteenth century. In fits and starts, colonies began to regard an insolvent debtor's financial and material remains as rightfully belonging to all of the debtor's creditors rather than to the creditor who was quickest to seize them. In part, this recognition was shaped by the growing geographic complexity of credit. Trading networks and the assignment of debt obligations swept debtors into larger economies. Whether or not debtors themselves traveled, their debts did, so that debtors often owed money to distant creditors as well as near ones. For far-off creditors, long-distance debts represented entrepreneurial profit—they were the threads that comprised the webs of commercial connections. They also represented risk. More than local creditors, distant creditors worked with imperfect information, compounded by the slowness with which it traveled. News of a debtor's decline reached faraway creditors after nearer creditors had already had an opportunity to act on the same information. Since priority among unsecured creditors was determined by the order in which they served process on the debtor, and among secured creditors by the order in which they took security in the same property, time was, indeed, money. Creditors who acted earlier took precedence over creditors who acted later. Once one creditor sued, all creditors had to sue to claim a place in line. And sue they did. As Peter Boss of Rhode Island complained to the anonymous creditor who had triggered a rush by all his creditors, "your seizing me Caused all my Creditors to fall on me." Nonlocal creditors thus always ran the risk of losing out to local creditors in the race to repay themselves from the debtor's property.[24]

Without statutory mechanisms for stopping the race and apportioning losses among creditors, distant creditors and their attorneys were more likely to leap into legal action earlier than they might otherwise be inclined to protect their interests. To give just one example: James McEvers, a merchant in New York, was content not to press a Connecticut debtor, one DeForest, too hard for payment. He instructed his lawyer, William Samuel Johnson, not to arrest DeForest but rather to try to negotiate security for the debt. However, when Johnson learned that another creditor, Naphtali Hart Myers, had given an officer writs of attachment to serve on DeForest, he felt he had no choice but to ignore McEvers's instructions and give his own writs against DeForest to the same officer to serve with the others so that McEvers would "be on the same footing with" Myers rather than suffering "while a less favorable creditor is secured."[25]

As Johnson's decision indicates, priority was critical when a debtor was—or was feared to be—insolvent. Creditors may have believed, with Samuel Moody, that "Debts must be paid, tho' all go for it," but they knew that insolvency made these words hortatory rather than prescriptive. Hence the competition among creditors to get paid before the debtor's assets ran out. When unrestrained by statute or contract, the competition played out along two lines—legal priority and preference. The former, as we have seen, was determined by a security interest or by the order of serving an attachment or execution. The latter was a function of the debtor's willingness to pay some creditors but not others. Distressed debtors made such decisions much the way they do today, by calculating which creditors they can put off, which they must buy off, and which they feel most guilty about. Robert Morris divided his unsecured debts—which were indistinguishable from one another in terms of their relative legal priority—into a four-tiered hierarchy of preferences. Debts "which I owe for Money or names disinterestedly lent are of the first class and are to be paid in preference to any others." Debts "contracted with persons whose bodily labour and services I have had are of the second class." Debts "for which I received value or what at the time was deemed a proper consideration are next." Last in preference were "notes for which I am responsible by having lent my name," that is, notes he had endorsed for other debtors. For their part, creditors might try to argue that older debts should be paid before newer ones, as when Samuel Abbot of Boston tried to convince Henry Daggett of New Haven that "it is customary to discharge such Debts first that are first contracted," but their inability to translate this "custom" into law left them to compete with one another for legal priority or preferential payment.[26]

Except for the occasional experiments with bankruptcy, the only ways to persuade or compel creditors to act cooperatively rather than competitively were insolvency proceedings and private composition—one legislative, the other contractual. The two often worked in tandem, even though one was a statutory haven of last resort for debtors and the other a negotiated settlement among debtors and creditors. In thinking of insolvency proceedings as a haven of last resort, one should emphasize "last resort" rather than "haven." Debtors emerged from insolvency proceedings stripped of their substance but not cleansed of their debts. Deprived of their capital, their future exertions were for the benefit of any of their creditors who continued to pursue them. The only advantage to debtors of an insolvency discharge was that it released them from prison and barred creditors from rearresting them for the same debts. The disadvantage to creditors was that it forced them to share a typically small pie and robbed each creditor of his hope that he might win the race for the debtor's assets. A debtor's threat to invoke insolvency process was thus rather like placing a loaded gun to one's head—a threat neither lightly made nor lightly dismissed.

Insolvency process implicitly marked a divide between insolvent debtors who retained property worth distributing and genuinely indigent debtors.[27] For the latter, there was the poor debtor's oath. Indigent debtors whose debts were small and their assets even less and who had been in jail for thirty days could swear to these facts and be thrown back onto the streets whence they had come. The oath was a form of poor relief for debtors so destitute that they had nothing to pay for their food in jail let alone their debts and whose participation in the credit economy was sufficiently limited that they were objects of pity rather than suspicion. Massachusetts had such a provision as early as 1672 for imprisoned debtors whose creditors failed to pay their jail fees and who swore they were worth less than £5, although laboring debtors without dependents might have to pay for their freedom by being bound in service to their creditors. Once a colony accepted the principle of debtors securing their release by swearing to their penury, it was tempting to expand the practice into something resembling a full-scale insolvency proceeding, with notice to creditors and a hearing on the debtor's application for release. In 1698 Massachusetts made the poor debtor's oath the trigger for convening a hearing at which creditors who suspected the debtor of concealing property could decide to pay to keep him in jail for another three months, at the end of which he would be released if no additional property materialized. The law did not apply to debtors who owed more than £500 to any one creditor, but the correlation between wealth and access to credit made it unlikely that this excluded any debtor whose assets totaled less than five pounds. The oath thus made it possible for most indigent debtors to regain their personal freedom, if not their economic freedom.[28]

The poor debtor's oath, however, was not insolvency process, at least not in any analytically useful sense. Insolvency and bankruptcy process create procedures for determining creditors' claims against a debtor and for distributing the debtor's property among his or her creditors in proportion to their claims. Poor debtor's oaths offered neither, nor could they when they applied only to debtors with too little property to be worth distributing. They thus had nothing to do with making creditors act cooperatively and everything to do with limiting their ability to act punitively. If one judges by the relative infrequency of statutes permitting the oaths—Rhode Island, for example, routinely denounced as a notorious debtors' haven, did not allow the oaths until 1798, and even then only with unusually onerous conditions—creditors suffered few restrictions on their power.[29]

Insolvency relief proper, where it existed, was sporadic and typically short-lived. Maryland in 1708 enacted a variant of its 1639 procedure that imprisoned insolvent debtors could invoke voluntarily without having to be bound in service to their creditors. Neither statute discharged debts. The later statute lasted only three years. Maryland thereafter abjured statutory insolvency process until 1774, except for brief revivals in 1725, 1733, and 1735, all of which restored indentured servitude for debtors without wives or children to support. From 1705 to 1720 Virginia permitted insolvent debtors who had been imprisoned for three months and whose debts did not exceed £10 to win release by giving up their property, but creditors could take out new executions for the same debts against any property that remained or was later acquired—a caveat that sharply limited the already narrow appeal of the procedure. Pennsylvania had no insolvency statute at all until 1730, when it replaced debt servitude with a procedure by which imprisoned insolvent debtors who owed no more than £100 could secure their release by rendering a full account under oath and by assigning their property to their creditors, keeping for themselves clothing, bedding, and a small amount of tools up to five pounds in value.

The legislature quickly amended the statute to permit all petty debtors—those who owed less than forty shillings—and all single debtors under the age of forty who owed less than £20 to repay their creditors by service the amounts not satisfied by assignment of their property. It also limited benefit of the act to debtors imprisoned on or before August 1, 1730—a restriction that turned a general insolvency act into a special one.[30]

New York maintained a similar system through a series of temporary laws, beginning in 1730, that typically divided judgment debtors and debtors imprisoned on *mesne* process for three months or more into two categories. Debtors who owed less than two pounds qualified for immediate release upon assigning their property to their creditors, retaining for themselves clothing, bedding, and tools to a total value of twenty or fifty shillings, depending on their marital status. Larger debtors who owed up to £100 could obtain their release in the same manner, but their creditors had the option of keeping them in prison by paying their jail fees. Subsequent enactments varied the numbers, but the basic outline remained the same. Each such temporary law applied only to debtors in prison on the effective date of the statute and usually expired after one year or sometimes two. Although primarily gaol-delivery statutes to ease prison overcrowding, they nonetheless established an episodic insolvency system.[31]

Massachusetts took a different approach. In 1714 it adopted a statute that permitted two or more creditors to file a bankruptcy petition with the governor and council against commercial debtors—merchants, traders, and shopkeepers—who absconded or otherwise avoided process. Three or more freeholders, armed with a blanket warrant, would then seize the debtor's property, sell it, and distribute the proceeds among the creditors in proportion to their debts, upon which the debtor would receive a discharge from further liability. Although the process was involuntary in the sense that debtors could not initiate it, it held out to debtors the promise of retaining a small portion of their property as an inducement to cooperate by disclosing their assets. By its terms the law expired after three years and was not renewed. New Hampshire enacted a similar statute in 1715 but repealed it after little more than two years. Massachusetts did not enact another bankruptcy statute until 1757. Although short-lived, the Massachusetts and New Hampshire statutes confirmed that the model for American experiments with bankruptcy legislation until well into the nineteenth century would be English—a system that harnessed coercive process to help creditors collect their due from unwilling commercial debtors whose reluctance to pay extended to subterfuge and evasion.[32]

This, then, is where the law of failure stood at midcentury: Brief, limited experiments with true bankruptcy discharges but only for the least cooperative debtors. Conditional access to insolvency process in the two largest colonies, with debtors' property distributed among their creditors, for debtors who owed less than £100. Occasional release from prison for indigent debtors who owned too little to turn over to their creditors and therefore too little to be worth keeping in jail, unless, of course, a creditor was sufficiently distrustful or vindictive to shoulder the expense of maintaining the debtor in jail himself. And nothing for the most entrepreneurial debtors whose credit had once been good enough to allow them to amass large debts. Whereas lesser, more marginal debtors always had at least some call on their creditors' compassion, it was this last group—commercial debtors—that ultimately would benefit most from the recasting of insolvency as economic failure.

The legal landscape changed dramatically after about 1755, coincident with the Seven Years' War. Wartime economic expansion, coupled with wartime economic risk, followed by postwar economic contraction, created the sort of fluid economy in which both success and failure could flourish. War creates winners and losers—military, most obviously, but also economic, social, and political. Part of the irony of war is that economic gain and loss do not necessarily correspond to military victory and defeat. The Seven Years' War—itself an expansion of the North American conflict against the French and their Indian allies that had resumed two years earlier—created new markets for military provisions and the means of transporting them at the same time that it closed old markets by embargoes and direct military action. It rewarded merchants who had the capital to engage in smuggling or privateering and punished those whose ships became spoils of war. The sharp rise in prices of foodstuffs and supplies brought profit to sellers and expense to buyers, while the movement of goods assured that everyone along the chain of commerce was both seller and buyer, so that even those who initially reveled in high prices were squeezed as they acquired goods for resale. Then again, not all prices rose—closing some ports to trade produced gluts of American exports in the ones that remained open. War also exacerbated the normal scarcity of money, driving up the cost of borrowing, enriching those with money to lend, and building pressure on colonial legislatures to issue paper money, which, as always, promptly depreciated, causing additional dislocation. And lastly, the vagaries of war—as military theaters moved around the world, each shift disrupting settled economic activities and creating new ones—magnified the normal vagaries of production, trade, and investment, so that economic success was never a guarantee against future failure.[33]

The economic uncertainties of war were prelude to those of peace. Postwar contraction of economies that had expanded to meet wartime needs and opportunities is a common enough phenomenon, captured well by one New York merchant's reference to "these times of profound Peace and stagnate Commerce." In the 1760s the entrepreneurs hit hardest by peace were those who misjudged its arrival and made large investments in the expectation of high profits from continued war-induced shortages and elevated prices. Everyone suffered from the worsening shortage of specie. The supply of hard currency had dropped sharply after the capture of Montreal in 1760—the sudden loss of military spending when war moved to the Caribbean stemmed the flow of specie into New York, Philadelphia, and other eastern ports. The postwar demands of British creditors for payment in specie accelerated the depletion. To make matters worse, tightened enforcement of British imperial policy, such as the long-ignored Molasses Act of 1733, together with high taxes by the colonies themselves to repay war debts and new parliamentary measures to bind the colonies more closely to Britain, notably the Currency Act of 1764, combined disastrously to block sources of hard currency, drain paper money from the economy, and prevent new emissions of paper currency. As the supply of money shrank, commercial transactions required hopelessly long credits or reverted to commodity money, taxes could not be collected, and debts could not be paid. The colonial economies could not function smoothly or profitably without an adequate circulating medium of exchange. The post-war recession deepened into a depression that, in Carl Bridenbaugh's colorful phrase, "deranged the entire credit structure."[34]

Debtors and creditors alike measured the derangement by the number of failures, which stretched from urban merchants to rural traders. Letters to and from merchants and lawyers in the 1760s sound a constant refrain of the scarcity of money and the consequent difficulty of collecting and paying debts. Debtors described in great self-justifying detail their unavailing efforts to collect from their own debtors, their inability to liquidate their assets except on credit, and their attempts to acquire cash in various currencies that they hoped their creditors would accept. The failure of even prominent merchants became commonplace, with news of each collapse spreading quickly through the chain of correspondence that undergirded the credit network. By 1765 merchants such as John Watts of New York could write, "Business is here very languid, the weak must go to the Wall, frequent Bankruptcys and growing more frequent."[35]

Shortly after the war began, several colonies experimented with new statutory schemes for discharging debts as well as debtors, the first concerted effort to do so. Within a two-year period, 1755 to 1757, New York, Rhode Island, and Massachusetts enacted bankruptcy systems that distributed insolvent debtors' assets among their creditors and discharged them from further liability on their debts. Connecticut followed suit in 1763. The experiments were, in varying degrees, short-lived or restrictive in their application, or both. Each one expired or was repealed, leaving behind at best mechanisms for distributing debtors' assets without relieving debtors themselves, and at worst nothing at all. All grew out of the same economic stresses generated by the Seven Years' War, and all foundered on the same shoals of creditor distrust. Their mere existence, however, marked a change in popular attitudes toward insolvency.

War made everyone familiar with risk, economic risk included. With the economic impact of war and its aftermath clear for all to see, it became harder to stigmatize insolvency as moral failure. Writers and aphorists in the 1750s continued to warn against the dangers of debt in moral terms, but their target was consumer debt, not commercial debt. When "Father Abraham," Benjamin Franklin's alter ego, railed against debt from the pages of *Poor Richard's Almanack*—"He that goes a borrowing goes a sorrowing," "when you run in Debt, You give another Power over your Liberty," "The Borrower is a Slave to the Lender, and the Debtor to the Creditor"—and admonished his listeners that they should "[r]ather go to Bed supperless than rise in Debt," he was exhorting them not to buy consumer goods on credit—"what Madness must it be to run in Debt for these Superfluities."[36]

What Father Abraham left unsaid—that commercial debt was different—other writers stated clearly. The anonymous author of *Debtor and Creditor* acknowledged the interdependence of commercial creditors and debtors when he likened "the Race of Commerce" to "our spiritual Race." Just as in the latter contest we "should not only press towards Heaven ourselves," but also "give all possible Assistance to others in their Labours therein," our goal in the race of commerce should be "not only our own private Advantage, but also that of the Body of which we are Members." In business "it is our Duty to look on every Addition to our Fortune as an additional Obligation on us to assist and forward the Designs of those who perhaps, are more indigent, tho' equally industrious." This commonality of interest did not mean forbearance for all debtors. Commercial creditors have "the highest Right . . . to expect punctual Payments," both on grounds of abstract justice and, more interestingly, of policy, "because it is the Interest of every united Body to cherish and encourage whatever tends to supporting their Strength and promoting their Union, to which . . . nothing is more essential than an extensive unburthened Trade." Unburdened trade did not mean trade without risk. "Commerce," after all, "is of a fluctuating Nature, and there is no Branch of Trade, but what has its Uncertainties." One could reduce risk but never eliminate it. While idle, extravagant, dishonest, or reckless debtors still had no call on their creditors' mercy, the debtor who "has in his Business applied all his Attention and Care, and in his Expences, both Œconomy and Frugality, but yet, through inevitable Misfortunes comes to Distress," the debtor who has engaged in "no wanton Projects, no improbable Schemes," the debtor who has used "rational Means for advancing his Fortune and answering Demands against him"—that debtor "has indisputable Claim to the Compassion and Forbearance of his Creditors." The hand of God was not absent from failure, but it was the nature of business that "[s]o many unforeseen Accidents happen, so many Casualties are we subject to under the Sun, that unless we take upon us to correct the Course of Providence, and alter the Chain of Incidents which is under God's Direction only, it is Folly in us to be unable to bear Disappointments, and cruel in us to make no Allowance for them in others." Under those circumstances, with commercial creditors and debtors partners in the same race, forbearance "is only granting to Others what we would expect for ourselves, and acting, in short, according to the golden Rule of Christ."[37]

In refusing to identify insolvency with moral failure, while nonetheless acknowledging the connection in individual cases, *Debtor and Creditor* was in step with its time. In arguing only for forbearance—in effect, only for negotiating extended repayment plans—it was not. Indeed, it had parsed the biblical parable of the unmerciful servant selectively, taking as its text only the one verse in which the debtor begged his creditor, "Lord, have patience with me, and I will pay thee all," while ignoring the very next verse, in which the creditor "was moved with compassion . . . and forgave him the debt" (Matthew 18:26–27). Other writers went farther.

The first published argument for outright bankruptcy discharges appeared in a brief, anonymously written pamphlet in 1755, the same year that New York enacted a bankruptcy statute, entitled *Some Reflections on the Law of Bankruptcy.* The author lamented that "Men who prove insolvent, are commonly branded as villains." While conceding that some insolvent debtors deserved the label, he observed that "a great many" were "Men of Probity and Honour" whose ruin stemmed from nothing more sinister than their "not being sufficiently instructed in the Nature of Trade." He asked why such unskilled, luckless debtors should be "deemed as Villains" simply because "God, who gives the good Things of this Life as it pleases him, has not given with so liberal a Hand to these Men as to others." Imprisoning them served no purpose other than to disgrace and demoralize them. Releasing them from jail without addressing their debts did no better. The insolvent debtor freed from jail by the poor debtor's oath remains "so sunk with the Weight of his Debts, he has no Heart to contrive or work for his relief," and so will do nothing. He imagines "that he is Nothing but a Slave to his Creditors; that he is like never to possess any Thing for himself or Family, and so the remaining Part of Life is lost (and worse than lost) to himself, his Creditors, and to the Publick." If, however, an insolvent debtor could "deliver up his Effects to his Creditors, and begin the World anew"—if, that is, he could receive a bankruptcy discharge—"he might be encouraged to Frugality and Industry, and do every Thing in his Power to make an Interest for himself, as every Thing that he should then acquire would be his own."[38]

The benefits of a bankruptcy discharge for debtors were obvious. It "delivers them from the Malice and Revenge of their Creditors," restores them to their families, gives them a fresh start in the world, and lifts from them the moral stigma of failure by acknowledging that "a Man might be a Bankrupt, and yet be a Man of Honour and Fidelity." For the author the benefits to creditors and to the public at large were no less apparent. Without a discharge to relieve them of liability, the terrible specter of debtors' prison impelled debtors to spend assets that could have gone to their creditors in increasingly desperate efforts to avoid it by pursuing "such Measures . . . as really bankrupts both [their] Faith and Fortune." Once imprisoned, insolvent debtors "spend their Creditor's Estates in Gaol" to support themselves and their families, until so little remains that they qualify for release as indigent debtors, leaving their creditors "at a greater Remove from their just Dues than ever." A bankruptcy discharge would dissuade debtors from wasting their assets in futile efforts to recover by rewarding them for throwing in the towel. Moreover, imprisoning insolvent debtors deprived the public of their skills, their labor, and their enterprise—qualities that should be harnessed rather than shackled. And when the debtor was "a Man of Skill and Experience in Merchandize" or "a Man of known Ingenuity, either in Literature or in any of the mechanical Arts"—the debtors who most clearly merited relief—the loss to society was particularly great. In sum, a bankruptcy act was "consistent with Reason, and agreeable to the Genius of our holy Religion." With reason, because the only claim a creditor has against a debtor's person is as a means of access to the debtor's estate, which, once gained, releases the hold on the debtor's person, regardless of the sufficiency of the estate. With religion, because God commanded it. The pamphlet closed with a recitation of the parable of the unmerciful servant and drew from it the merciful lesson that if creditors "are really governed by those Principles, they will rather discharge their insolvent Debtors, than punish and imprison them."[39]

The flurry of statutory activity that followed can hardly be attributed to one anonymous pamphlet. Taken together, however, the acts and pamphlets reflect the ambivalent, but nonetheless unmistakable, shift away from the reflexive equation of economic failure with moral failure that defined Samuel Moody's moral economy of debt. The trend was clear, even if the statutory manifestations were not. Consider, for example, Massachusetts, which enacted a bankruptcy statute in 1757, forty years after its first one expired. Like the earlier statute, the later one was limited to commercial debtors—merchants and traders—and allowed debtors to retain some of their assets as an inducement to their cooperation. It differed in allowing debtors as well as creditors to initiate proceedings and, just as significantly, in requiring the consent of a majority of creditors, measured both in number and by the value of their debts, to any discharge from continuing liability. Only creditors owed £10 or more counted. The Privy Council disallowed the act at the behest of British merchant-creditors the very next year before it could expire by its own terms, but not before forty-five merchants, partnerships, and trading firms had received discharges. Massachusetts tried again in 1765, when it enacted an odd hybrid of its two previous efforts—an involuntary procedure that, although not limited by occupation, offered discharges only to debtors who absconded or otherwise avoided process, who then returned and assigned all of their property to their creditors. Dissatisfied with its operation, the General Court repealed the statute a year later. The Privy Council disallowed the repeal nearly two years later still, in February 1768, but the act expired by its own terms barely a month after news of the revival reached Boston.[40]

New York cobbled together a bankruptcy system that lasted, at least intermittently, for fifteen years, from 1755 to 1770, although whether it did so by surviving or escaping Privy Council scrutiny is unclear. The "system," if one can really call it that, was a succession of acts, each of limited duration. The statutes offered discharges to commercial and noncommercial debtors alike but only at the petition of their creditors and only if they agreed to assign to their creditors everything they owned except their clothing and bedding. Three-fourths of the creditors, as determined by value, had to agree to the assignment. Their agreement bound dissenting creditors, thereby ending the power of holdouts to keep debtors in jail by paying the weekly fees—unless, of course, the holdout was a particularly large creditor. At least one creditor thought that the acts "made a damd many Great Rogues."[41] Other creditors, however, saw their advantages. For example, when the New York partners of the great Belfast mercantile firm, Greg, Cunningham & Co., learned that other creditors of an Albany debtor were pressing him for preferential payments, they advised him to "put them all in a [equal] footing by taking the Benefit of the Act, by which means you will prevent any Complaints and be able to do something for yourself Imediately," and offered their assistance—as long as "we don't find others are paid and not [us]."[42]

Rhode Island followed a different path. Beginning in 1756, it made full discharges available to insolvent debtors on their own petition, whether commercial or noncommercial, who assigned all their property, necessary clothing and bedding aside, to their creditors. However, the law applied only to debtors who were insolvent on June 1, 1756. The colony enacted a general bankruptcy law in 1771, also voluntary, which allowed debtors to retain up to 5 percent of their estates if they repaid at least three-fourths of their debts and if a majority of the creditors by number and value consented to the discharge, only to repeal it after nine months.[43]

Connecticut, the colony which the author of *Some Reflections on the Law of Bankruptcy* had most wanted to influence, did not enact a full-blown bankruptcy statute until 1763—the first time, other than an occasional usury statute, that the colony had passed debtor relief of any kind.

The episode, short-lived as it was, is a good illustration of the difficulty of conforming the law to changing attitudes toward insolvency.

Before 1763 the sole statutory procedure in Connecticut for distributing an insolvent debtor's assets among his creditors applied only after the debtor's death, when technically it was no longer the debtor, but the debtor's estate, that was insolvent. Except for the small matter of not having to deal with a live debtor, the procedure, which was first enacted in 1716, replicated standard bankruptcy process in every major respect—an application to a judge for the appointment of commissioners to whom creditors would present and prove their claims and who would recommend to the judge a proportionate distribution of the decedent debtor's estate among his creditors after first subtracting certain government claims and limited items of exempt property for the widow, if any. The procedure underscored the fact that the true problem of insolvency was not whether or how to distribute the property of insolvent debtors but what to do with the insolvent debtors themselves. The law could easily apportion an insolvent debtor's assets but only after death had removed the issue of the debtor's continuing personal liability for the debts. That changed, at least temporarily, because of the greed of a handful of New York creditors, who in October 1761 procured the arrest of John and Jabez Cable, two brothers who were traders in Fairfield.[44]

At the time of their arrest, the Cables had combined debts in excess of £3,300 New York money, a sum that was more than balanced by their assets, although not by their liquid assets. The rub, however, was not their technical solvency but rather that the debts for which they were arrested were not yet due—they were for inventory the brothers had bought on credit at various times within the preceding year, some as recently as two months, and that both brothers swore they had purchased on twelve months' credit. It appears that the creditors, perhaps alarmed by an attachment that John had levied against Jabez's property to secure a debt due him, had sprung a demand for payment on the brothers. Caught short, the brothers persuaded their father, George, to offer the creditors his bond for the payment of any balance if the creditors would take the goods back at their invoice prices and accept an assignment of the brothers' property. As part of the negotiations, one of the creditors, Jacob Townsend, through his agent, induced John Cable to release his attachment against Jabez so that Jabez could assign his property and accounts to another agent for the creditors, who in turn promised not to arrest either brother while he went to New York to fetch discharges from the creditors. The agents lied. They arrested the brothers and threw them in the Fairfield County jail. They seized the Cables' inventory and sold for £200 goods that had an invoice value of £500. The brothers made repeated offers to turn over all their property and promised full repayment of any balance if only the creditors would release them from jail. The creditors refused, declaring, according to the brothers, "that they will take none of our Estate only as it is taken by Execution and sold at the Sign Post and that when our Estates are all gone that they will keep us in Gaol and maintain us to the Day of our Deaths." Even William Samuel Johnson, who represented two of the creditors, described the creditors' resistance as "imprudent," although he did so only after the consequences of their imprudence had become clear.[45] Thus pushed to the wall, their assets wasted to the point of true insolvency by repeated auctions at fire-sale prices and by the expense of maintaining themselves in jail and their families outside, the brothers petitioned the assembly in April 1762 with a remarkable request—that the assembly appoint commissioners to apportion their estate among their creditors, upon which "our Persons may be released and discharged out of Gaol and that we may be treated as by Law Bankrupts at Home are." No such plea had ever been made in Connecticut.

Although Connecticut did not recognize formal equity jurisdiction, except for one brief and aberrant episode early in the eighteenth century, the assembly had residual equity authority, which it could exercise by granting equitable relief on private petitions or by conferring limited equity powers on lower courts.[46] After 1753 the assembly typically proceeded on petitions by constituting three of its members a committee with chancery authority to inquire into the matters alleged, a separate committee for each petition that survived the assembly's initial scrutiny. The committee would then conduct hearings and report its findings and recommendations to the assembly at its next session for action. The petitions presented a wide range of grievances, linked only by the petitioners having exhausted their legal remedies or never having had legal recourse in the first place—land titles, mortgages, leases, failed arbitrations, broken promises, pleas for new trials, fraud in all its myriad manifestations, to name but a few. The Cables appear to have been the first insolvent debtors to petition the assembly for relief. They were certainly the first to challenge the assembly to adopt British bankruptcy law.

The Cables' petition did not fall on unprepared ears. One of the leading men in the colony, Jonathan Trumbull—merchant, colony assistant, and later chief justice, deputy governor, and governor—had been desultorily drafting a bankruptcy bill at the assembly's request. Spurred into a semblance of action by the petition, the assembly instructed Trumbull to have a bill ready for it to consider at its next session in October. The issue thus addressed, the assembly postponed the Cables' petition to the same October session, which left the Cables, who presumably would have preferred individual relief to statutory reform, in jail for at least another six months. Trumbull, who was on the brink of insolvency himself, did not finish in time, so in October the assembly appointed a committee to investigate the Cables' allegations and submit its findings and recommendations the following May. Johnson seems to have sensed that the creditors were in trouble. He wrote to one of them that the Cables' memorial contained "great complaints of the cruelty of their creditors . . . , which should receive some answer," and expressed the hope that the creditors would supply reasons and supporting evidence for their actions.[47]

At the committee hearing in early January 1763, the creditors admitted that they had rejected John and Jabez Cable's repeated offers to sign over everything they owned in return for release from jail because they had hoped that George Cable would give the creditors his bond for full payment of the debts in exchange for a twelve-month letter of license for the brothers. In other words, they had pressured the father to ransom his sons by personally guaranteeing repayment of their debts. The creditors also claimed that they had suspected subterfuge in the sharp decline of the brothers' assets rather than the wasting expense of lengthy imprisonment. Their arguments impressed the committee, albeit not in the manner they had intended. In a rare official rebuke of creditors for overreaching, the committee concluded that since "neither Law nor Equity allows the holding the Person of the Debtor only as a Security for the Payment of the Debts that are Due," and since it appeared from the evidence that the Cables were prevented from paying their debts by "the Fraudulent Transactions" of their creditors, that therefore the creditors "ought in Equity to be holden and oblidged to take and accept of what is Left and that the persons of the Debtors be released and discharged from their Confinement." Although the committee stopped short of recommending a bankruptcy-style discharge of liability, the attention it focused on the complicity of creditors in dissipating debtors' assets to the detriment of everyone had far-reaching consequences.

When the assembly next met in May 1763, it declined to grant John and Jabez Cable the relief so strongly recommended by the committee— not because it disagreed but rather because it recognized that the Cables were not unique. Wartime prosperity had already given way to the economic constriction of peace. Foreclosures had risen, and merchants and farmers alike felt the consequences of glutted markets and depressed prices.[48] As their numbers climbed, the plight of imprisoned insolvent debtors called for statutory redress rather than ad hoc amelioration. The assembly answered the call by enacting Trumbull's bankruptcy bill. The statute permitted imprisoned debtors to petition the superior court for relief, regardless of whether they had been arrested on *mesne* or execution process. If granted, the relief required debtors to submit inventories of their assets and debts to the court, swear to the accuracy and completeness of the lists and that they had not made any fraudulent or preferential conveyances, and, after a hearing at which creditors could object, assign their estates to trustees, who would liquidate the estate and distribute the proceeds among the creditors that had proven their claims. In return, not only would insolvent debtors be released from imprisonment; their debts would be discharged as well. In other words, full bankruptcy relief. The one concession to the traditional moral economy of debt was that debtors whose estates could not repay at least three-fourths of the claims against them could be assigned in service to their creditors for up to seven years at the discretion of the court. Like British bankruptcy law, the Connecticut statute recognized that it could take years to liquidate an insolvent estate and so provided for annual distributions to creditors until the assignees had collected the entire estate and converted it to cash. Unlike British bankruptcy law, the Connecticut statute was voluntary rather than involuntary—that is, debtors could invoke it, but not creditors. Even more unlike British bankruptcy law, Connecticut did not restrict discharges to debtors who followed certain commercial occupations and whose debts exceeded a high minimum amount. In theory, any insolvent debtor could qualify. Connecticut's approach to failure was, in statutory form at least, egalitarian.[49]

The assembly repealed the act after eight months, even though by its terms it was to have lasted two years. Creditors did not like the act. They were not swayed by the preamble, which announced that the purpose of the act was to "benefit . . . creditors by preventing . . . debtors from wasting their estates, which ought to be applied towards payment of their debts." Not surprisingly, they objected most to the discharge, but they also complained that the act did not empower them to compel debtors to assign their assets and that binding the debtor in service was only discretionary. Creditors' lawyers, making the reflexive equation of justice with their clients' interests that so endears lawyers to the public, denounced the act for "the prodigious advantage [it] has given to debtors." Johnson mordantly captured the thrust of creditors' objections when he remarked of one ailing debtor that "[h]e is in a very declining state in every respect and will soon die or take benefit of our insolvent act, either of which events will be equally fatal to his creditors."[50]

The equation of insolvency and death may seem a bit overdrawn, but debtors were quick to play on the fears it represented. More than one debtor threatened to petition for relief under the act if his creditors crowded him. Samuel Gregory, for example, a justice of the peace in Fairfield County whose creditors included several prominent Boston merchants, made it clear that he had no intention of avoiding arrest but would "shelter himself under the insolvent act" if pressed by his creditors. Flexing his leverage, he proposed a composition—a negotiated exchange of assets for a discharge. Johnson, who represented several of the Boston creditors, argued vigorously against it but reluctantly and resentfully advised his clients to accept, "[a]s I am well acquainted with the fatal consequences of our insolvent act and know how miserably all estates have turned out which have been settled by it." Even when a debtor had not threatened to seek shelter under the act, Johnson nonetheless had to counsel caution, as when he recommended to one client that "I think it best to proceed gently for fear of our insolvent act, which makes shocking work amongst us and almost persuades all debtors to set their creditors at defiance by the facility with which it enables them to discharge themselves from debt or imprisonment." Johnson rued the tactics that had been used against John and Jabez Cable, "which were a principal occasion of the passing of that act which will cost New York thousands," and missed few opportunities to rail against the statute, "which is become a perfect protection for all debtors." Not surprisingly, when it was repealed he rejoiced that it will "do no more mischief."[51]

Johnson vastly overstated the disruptive effects of the bankruptcy statute. Nonetheless, during its brief life the law added a novel element to relations between debtors and their creditors, one that typified experiments with bankruptcy and insolvency legislation. The mere existence of the statute gave debtors a small measure of power in their dealings with their creditors. Much like the threat of delay through reviews and appeals, the threat of invoking the bankruptcy act could forestall litigation and perhaps make a nonlitigated resolution more likely. The power was not much, but it was all that some debtors had, and for a few of them it did make a difference. For Johnson and his clients any difference was unwelcome. And it remained so. A quarter-century later, as one of Connecticut's delegates to the Constitutional Convention, Johnson joined Roger Sherman in casting the sole state vote against what became Article I, Section 8, Clause 4, of the Constitution, which empowered Congress to establish "uniform Laws on the subject of Bankruptcies throughout the United States."[52]

When Connecticut next addressed insolvency, it was more solicitous of creditors than of debtors. As much as creditors had disdained the short-lived bankruptcy act, they soon learned to miss the way it had placed all unsecured creditors on an equal footing, so that their disappointment in being forced to swallow losses was at least tempered by the knowledge that their fellow creditors shared in the disappointment proportionately. Repeal of the act restored pride of place to the first creditor to serve process on the debtor, forcing other creditors to sue and take their place in line—a race that accomplished little beyond multiplying litigation. So in 1765 the assembly enacted an insolvency law that permitted insolvent debtors, acting in concert with a majority of their creditors measured in both number and value, to apply to the superior court for relief. The petition had to include complete inventories of the debtors' assets and debts, which the debtors had to affirm under oath as well as swear that they had not made any fraudulent or preferential conveyances. If no creditor raised a credible objection, the judges would then direct the debtors to assign their estates to trustees, who would liquidate the estate and apportion the proceeds among the creditors that had proven their claims. Creditors gained company for their misery—the dissolution of all prior attachments against the debtor's property, thereby forcing them to share the losses equally. Debtors gained nothing other than immunity from future arrest for debts that existed before the assignment. They remained liable for the balance of the debts, and creditors could seize any property they acquired in the future to satisfy them. The assembly allowed the statute to lapse in 1767. Thus did Connecticut retreat from bankruptcy to insolvency to nothing.[53]

Imperfect and short-lived as these statutes were, they nonetheless were the high-water mark of the law of failure before the Revolution. In the absence of consistent statutory procedures, insolvent debtors sought relief elsewhere. Insolvent commercial debtors turned to the private law of contract by negotiating agreements with their creditors. Other insolvent debtors, including commercial debtors whose negotiations had failed, appealed to the legislature for individual dispensations. The negotiated agreements took two forms, letters of license and private compositions—the one an expression of desperate hope, the other simply of desperation. The appeals to the legislature were petitions for equitable relief.

Letters of license were promises by creditors not to arrest a debtor for a specified length of time. They neither discharged nor apportioned debts. The relief they offered debtors was only temporary, but it was relief nonetheless. By suspending their legal remedies, creditors created breathing room for their debtors to make a last effort to regain solvency, whether by completing a mercantile undertaking, collecting debts due them, or liquidating assets. Because they were private contracts rather than legislative forms, letters of license could take any shape agreed upon by the parties. Creditors' forbearance rarely came free. Isaac DeLyon of Philadelphia secured a five-year letter of license in 1772 from twenty-six creditors when he assigned his inventory to a committee of five of them.[54] Their New York creditors offered Reuben Schuyler and Ahasuerus Teller, traders in Albany County, an eighteen-month letter of license, but only if they signed over their house and land and their debts due on notes and bonds.[55] Peter R. Livingston, son of the "lord" of Livingston Manor, had to transfer all of his land to his creditors in 1771 to obtain a letter of license for three-and-a-half years. An anonymous New York debtor who was keeping to his house to avoid arrest offered to pay interest on his book debts, which normally did not carry interest, asking only "a [mod]erate time allowed me to Collect in my debts" and liquidate his assets. A bolder, less chastened Samuel Hazard, a prominent Philadelphia merchant and entrepreneur, tendered his London creditors in 1755 nothing other than his vow "to do Justice to Every Body as Fast as [is] in my power" and observed that the alternative is "to Confine myself at Home till all is spent or to Flee to some remote part of the Earth." He may have been expecting the same lenience he had shown a debtor four years earlier, when he and other creditors had signed a three-year letter of license for Timothy Matlack solely because they judged him "an industrious man and Esteemed honest." Hazard's creditors, however, declined.[56]

Not surprisingly, creditors always had to consider the alternatives. Letters of license gave debtors time to regain the wherewithal to pay their creditors. They also gave them time to spend or lose more money, leaving even less for creditors to attach. Gerard Beekman, for one, resolved in 1755 never to consent to a letter of license unless the debtor gave security, "for I have suffered so much already by Granting Letters of Lysence."[57] On the other hand, at least one lawyer thought that bare licenses left debtors too vulnerable to their creditors when they expired, because "however honestly [the debtor] may have acted, . . . he may be too much discouraged to attempt any thing for the support of his Family lest his Future Industry and success should tempt his Creditors to fall upon him and take away the Little he may have acquired." Of course, letters were useless unless all creditors joined. A single holdout—just one creditor not willing to suspend the race for the debtor's assets—rendered the letter ineffectual, leaving the debtor in jail, if already arrested, or barricaded in his house to avoid process servers, if not. Thomas Moland, for example, languished in the New Gaol in New York—often "a week at a Time without the Benefit of a meals Victuals"—because one creditor refused his repeated requests to sign a letter of license. Moland's plight underscored the fact that, by their very nature and limitations, letters of license were available only to select debtors—those who could convince their creditors that their inability to pay was a short-term embarrassment rather than a long-term disability and that their assets, including money owed them, really were sufficient to cover their debts and lacked only time to convert or collect. Hence the debtor's appeal to James Beekman in 1765 that "I have Real and personal Estate to amount of above Double the Value I owe," reminding him that "you well know that hardly any trading person in this City could pay all the debt they owe were they Emediately pushed for it"—a dual refrain sounded throughout the period by debtors too numerous to count.[58]

If letters of license had an air of postponing the inevitable—the loss of everything—private compositions tried to manage the inevitable in a way that would allow debtors and their creditors to be quit of one another, however unsatisfactory the parting. They were a private form of bankruptcy relief in which debtors agreed to assign all or part of their assets— real property, tangible personalty, and accounts receivable—to one or more of their creditors on behalf of all the creditors, in return for which the creditors agreed to discharge them from further liability for their debts. The discharges could be conditional or unconditional. If the former, they commonly hinged upon an appraisal of the assigned property, or upon the property satisfying a certain minimum proportion of the debts, or upon the debtor's title to the property being confirmed. While letters of license were not for debtors without prospects, private compositions were not for debtors without assets. Debtors had to have property worth trading for a discharge. The property typically was of a kind that was difficult to value or liquidate, or legally unreachable without the debtor's cooperation—such as land where it was exempt from attachment or when cash was scarce and there were no buyers except on long credit, speculative stock with valuations that took flight in the investor's imagination, unpaid debts and accounts that ranged from the merely uncollected to the uncollectible. Like letters of license, private compositions were only effective if all creditors joined. Daniel King, for example, painstakingly reached provisional settlements first with his Salem creditors, then with his Boston creditors— save one, Samuel Abbot, who refused to participate despite King's repeated entreaties and reminders that if he continued to "Insist on things Impossable all I have Done with Others is in Vain and I must Keep House the rest of my Days."[59]

As private contracts, compositions took their shape not from law but from the negotiating skill and bargaining power of the parties. Samuel Hazard tried—unsuccessfully—to negotiate for the appointment of specific assignees "who wou'd not only do Justice to the Creditors but Treat my Character in a Freindly and not in an Ill natured manner." Thomas Preston's opening position with his London creditors was that they take his extensive land holdings in Pennsylvania and New York "out and out at what he thinks they are worth," which his creditors' Philadelphia agent thought was double their real market value. Josiah Whetmore of Middletown, Connecticut, was more successful, at least initially. Not only did he persuade his creditors to accept partial payment of what he owed them; he also convinced them to wait eighteen months for even that, the first twelve of which would be interest-free. Whetmore's bargaining edge rested on his skill at avoiding arrest and at placing his assets beyond the reach of his creditors. Unhappily for all, he died before he could enjoy the benefit of his negotiating success.[60]

Even when private compositions held together, they could embroil creditors in appraising and apportioning goods and accounts that often proved difficult to sell or collect. A year after receiving David Osborne's assets by assignment in the fall of 1761, his creditors were still trying to liquidate them. Johnson, who represented a number of the creditors, tried without success to sell Osborne's inventory himself. Acknowledging defeat, he gave the goods to a shopkeeper to sell on consignment, who after several months had fared little better. In the meantime Johnson sued to collect Osborne's accounts—rather hastily, it appears, without first approaching the debtors—only to discover that almost all of them were disputed and that many of them were more than set off by the debtors' counterclaims against Osborne, all of which left Johnson with little more than bills for court costs to show for his efforts. After a year Johnson could only complain that "I am very sorry I ever meddled with his accounts, as I know they will turn out infinitely worse than was expected."[61]

Letters of license and private compositions were difficult to negotiate and even more difficult to enforce. As private documents that rarely left any legal trace, how many succeeded is as impossible to determine as how many were signed in the first place. Anecdotal evidence in the form of numerous unrequited pleas from debtors suggests that they were often proposed but infrequently contracted. One suspects that they were more likely to be agreed upon when there were credible statutory alternatives, such as insolvency or bankruptcy acts, that one party or the other could threaten to invoke if negotiations failed, although the threat was doubtless weakened in jurisdictions where the statutory alternatives themselves required the consent of most of the creditors.

Petitions to the legislature demonstrate the depth of the ambivalence about insolvency. Whether voluntary or involuntary, insolvency and bankruptcy acts provided a remedy for anyone who met the qualifications of the statute. The conditions could be quite restrictive—occupational limitations, high minimum debt levels, various accountings and hearings, creditors' consent—but any debtor who satisfied them attained whatever remedy the statute mandated—release from jail, protection from rearrest, distribution of assets, retention of exempt property, discharge of debts. Once an insolvent debtor cleared the statutory threshold, relief rested on meeting the criteria, not on the debtor's moral worth. Petitions for insolvency or bankruptcy relief, on the other hand, were altogether different. Even if all the debtor asked for was to be allowed to proceed under the provisions of a statute that had expired, relief lay in the discretion of the legislature—whether to grant the petition in whole or in part, reject it out of hand, or fashion some other relief. How the legislature exercised its discretion turned on its assessment of the petitioner's worthiness, which rested far more on individual notions of what made debtors deserving or undeserving than on formal criteria. Hence the supplicating posture of petitioners, who understood that success turned on how pitiable they could make themselves appear. Claims of starvation were common, as were descriptions of families made destitute by the imprisonment of their providers. John Tabor Kempe, the attorney general of New York, heard them all. When New York's episodic bankruptcy system lapsed in 1770, he received numerous pathetic appeals from imprisoned debtors begging to be included in special legislative acts that gave discharges to the individuals named in them. Seven debtors imprisoned in the New Gaol in New York invoked "[t]he Extreamities of Hunger" and professed that "many and many a time have they wished for Death, in a more Sudden and Honnerable way amongst christians." Two other imprisoned debtors were not as concerned for themselves, but their families "are in a Deplorable Situation for want of their Assistance."[62]

The petitions are narratives of failure—chronicles of how and why the debtors came to their present pitiable condition, with emphasis on the qualities they hope will elicit legislative mercy. The Connecticut petitions, most submitted after the 1765 insolvency act expired, are a good example.[63] Philip Daggett of New Haven attributed his insolvency to "sundry Epileptic Fits, severe Turns of the Long fever, nervous fever, several Turns of the Billious Cholic and Loss of his Eyesight, and . . . Sickness and Death in his Famely and other misfortunes." Azariah Smith of Farmington had been "reduced to a state of Poverty Indigence and Extream Want" in his

old age, not "by Negligence or Inattention to his Business but by Meer Ca-
sualty Misfortune and uncommon Disappointments in his traid Traffick
and with Mankind and More Especially" by his marriage to Ruth Benton,
who has been "the Cause of all his Misfortune in the Close of Life and
from whom [he] has had the Good fortune to be divorced," although not
until he had bound himself to pay the debts she had contracted before they
married. Although already insolvent, Ebenezer Martin had taken the pulpit
of a parish in Ashford, believing that "the work would not only render
him useful to his fellow men, [but] that was the most likely way to render
him capable of discharging his debts." He has "ever since Indeavoured to
Live in the most frugal and Industrious methods he could devise," and his
ministry has been marked by "grate peace and harmony." But sickness, infirmity, and "a scanty maintainance" dashed his hopes. One creditor cast
him in jail until, "his Life being apprehended to be in dainger," the creditor relented and released him in return for securing the debt.[64]

Abijah Beach of Stratford described "great Losses at Sea," "bad markets abroad," and "a Variety of Casualties to which those engaged in
Trade are more especially liable"—a litany of woe that appeared verbatim
in other petitions from insolvent merchants. When pressed by his creditors, he managed to negotiate a two-year letter of license after eight
months of keeping to his house to avoid attachment. However, one creditor broke ranks and sued him, forcing him to become "a Prisoner in his
own house" for three years, leading "a Life of Inactivity, unprofitable to
himself, the Community and his Creditors," and using his dwindling assets to support his wife and "seven small Children."[65] Mary Bellamy's distress did "not arise from any Default Negligence or Indiscretion on her
Part, but from Unavoidable Casualties and mishaps." Her husband, a
trader, had died, leaving her burdened with numerous debts and eight
small children. For nine years she tried to pay his debts and continue his
business, but she failed and "Suffered a Long Imprisonment in the Common Gaol." Now her creditors had attached her again and threatened to
return her to jail, "which is terrible to human Nature in general and much
more to her sex." For herself she asked only to assign her property and be
spared imprisonment. Her deeper concern, however, was that, "in Case

she should be again married," she did not want her husband to become liable for her debts.[66]

Clement Minor was a trader in Stonington, who "(as he humbly conceives) in all his Trade Deal and Commerce with Mankind hath always ben justly esteemd and maintaind the Character of an honest Man and fair Dealer." In recent years, however, he has suffered "great and heavy Losses both by Sea and Land and also by Fire and such like enevitable Accidents." Many of his own debtors are insolvent. His creditors seized his land and threw him in jail, "by means of which confinement he is much impaired and decayed in his Health, being sixty years of age and labouring under much infirmity of body." He thought it "both unjust and unreasonable he should be thus doom'd and subjected, by the Inhumanity and obstinacy of a few of his avaricious, merciless Creditors, to languish out the wretched Remains of Life in a loathsome gloomy Prison." Seven years later his son, Clement Minor, Jr., was "Reduced to Very Low Circumstances" by "Misfortune in Trade and Business and More Especially by means of his Being . . . Unwarily Drawn in to be Bondsman for Other People."[67]

It was the rare petitioner who appealed to logic rather than sympathy. The Reverend Nathaniel Eells of Stonington stands almost alone. He passed lightly over "a Series of unforseen Difficulties, Disappointments and Losses" and admitted that "he cannot complain that his Creditors have been cruel or unreasonable with him, as the sums to them owing are their just due." However, his anticipated imprisonment would "answer no valuable end, as he never has nor proposes to withhold his Estate from his Just Creditors," and his estate should be divided equitably among his creditors, as "it cannot be Just to Suffer one Creditor to Receive full Satisfaction of [his] Estate, when so small a part of the Debts [he] owes can be paid by the whole Estate."[68]

If the petitions offer glimpses of falls from economic grace by people of means, the responses are distinguished by their restraint. Not once before the Revolution did the assembly discharge debts on private petition.[69] The closest it ever came—and then only reluctantly—was when it ordered specific performance of a private composition between John Herpin, a merchant in Milford, and his New York creditors, who had agreed to discharge his rather substantial debts if he conveyed all his assets to them. Herpin performed his part of the bargain, but his creditors stalled. The assembly directed the creditors to comply but only after equivocating for nearly six years.[70] Enforcing a private contract for a discharge is very different from awarding a discharge directly, which the assembly refused to do even when its own committees urged it to do so. The committee appointed to consider Abijah Beach's petition recommended a full bankruptcy discharge, but the assembly granted only the benefit of the long-lapsed 1765 insolvency act even though none of the creditors objected to a discharge. Seven months later, another committee made the same recommendation for Ebenezer Keeney and Judson Burton, merchant-partners in Derby, with the same result.[71] Not surprisingly, petitioners rarely asked that their debts be discharged, and they never asked after the assembly refused discharges to Beach, Keeney, and Burton. Instead, petitioners moderated their requests. They sought private insolvency acts that would release them from jail, appoint trustees to receive assignment of their property, and free them from future arrest. Or they prayed for orders to compel holdout creditors to join letters of license or for decrees granting them immunity from arrest for existing debts for a stated period of time.

The assembly granted some form of relief on somewhat more than half the petitions it received from insolvent debtors before the Revolution—25 of 44. There are no patterns to which ones it allowed and which it denied, or to whether it granted the full relief requested or something less. Indeed, there was enough randomness that petitioners may have felt as though they were addressing the oracle at Delphi—their supplications followed certain forms, but the outcomes were utterly unpredictable. The legislature would not even appoint a committee for Clement Minor, Sr., who owed nearly £6,000 and had begged to be released from jail, yet took pity on his son, who owed only £150 and had asked merely to be protected from arrest. The difference may have been that the father railed against his creditors while the son had the support of his, but other instances make clear that the concurrence of creditors was no guarantee of success. The assembly routinely deferred petitions for one, two, or even three sessions, but when moved by the spirit of equity it could, on rare occasions, act with alacrity. For Mary

Bellamy, the assembly commissioned a committee to report back later in the same legislative session to which she had submitted her petition. Whether impressed by her herculean efforts to pay her husband's debts or outraged that her creditors had imprisoned a widow with young children and then bartered her freedom for a release of her dower rights, the assembly quickly voted her the relief she had requested. And although one suspects that moral judgments influenced the decisions, only occasionally were they explicit, as when the committee appointed to consider Elisha Royce's petition recommended that he assign his remaining assets to trustees for his creditors and be released from jail, because "it doth not appear that [he] has been Extravagant in his method of living but is reduced by Misfortune in Trade."[72]

Only Rhode Island turned petitions for insolvency or bankruptcy relief into a more or less routinized system. The 1756 bankruptcy act had applied only to debtors who were insolvent on June 1 of that year, but its appeal was such that the assembly quickly settled into a pattern of receiving and adjudicating private petitions for bankruptcy discharges. The successful ones it rewarded with a special legislative act that instructed the superior court to appoint commissioners to oversee the assignment of assets and to issue a certificate of discharge. The process became sufficiently routine that the debtors learned to threaten their creditors with a petition if pressed too closely. When Samuel Abbot of Boston finally ordered his attorney to sue Joseph Nash of Providence for debts he had been trying to collect for at least two years, Nash loudly protested that "I can without Vanity Boldly Say that no man hath Exerted himself more than I have in Every Honest Measure I could take to fullfil my Contracts and pay My Debts," recited his many misfortunes, rhapsodized that "I do not Dispare of the Smiles of Providence Even in this Life so as Sooner or Later to be able to pay Every man his just due unless"—and here he slips in the threat—"driven by fatal Necesaty to what my Soul Obhores Namely to apply to the Legislater to Obsolve my Debts which without Necesity I don't belive to be Just." In all, the assembly heard 136 petitions before the Revolution, and 2,238 more before the practice ended in 1828—not quite turning equity into law, but close. Despite the flurry of legislative experimentation in the wake of the Seven Years' War, the Rhode Island petition procedure, which like all petitioned relief existed because statutory relief did not, was the closest thing to a formal bankruptcy system anywhere in the colonies on the eve of the Revolution.[73]

On a formal level the law of failure in 1775 was little different from the law of failure in 1750. Statutory insolvency or bankruptcy process remained elusive. Culturally and intellectually, however, much had changed. Creditors remained reluctant to cooperate rather than compete with one another, and their distaste for discharging their debtors continued unabated, but neither posture was as secure as it had been at midcentury. In the intervening decades creditors throughout the northeastern colonies had periodically learned to accept, however resentfully, partial payment from their debtors' estates with little or no expectation of ever recovering the balance. They had also encountered, for the first time, published arguments for bankruptcy relief and, as we shall see in the next chapter, against imprisonment for debt. For their part, debtors had discovered the comfort—cold, perhaps, but comfort nonetheless—of insolvency process in relieving them from imprisonment or the threat of arrest and in replacing the customary free-for-all over their financial remains with a more orderly distribution. Some had even experienced the cleansing of a bankruptcy discharge, of being reborn free of debt. For debtors the lapse or repeal of the insolvency and bankruptcy statutes did not diminish the demand for insolvency or bankruptcy process, as the subsequent petitions attest.

The Seven Years' War and its aftermath demonstrated to all how far tremors in foreign markets rippled through the colonial economies. One consequence was to demystify economic success and failure by clarifying economic cause and effect, which in turn pushed insolvency farther from moral failure and closer to simple economic risk. The accompanying flurry of statutes and petitions suggests a new willingness to create a law of failure that was something other than mere debt collection process. Samuel Moody's moral economy of debt—where whatever compassion might be shown for the debtor's person, the debtor's obligation remained inviolable and nondischargeable—no longer reigned unchallenged.

❧ 3 ❧

IMPRISONED DEBTORS
IN THE EARLY REPUBLIC

Creditor, hardhearted—
I know there is no music in your ears,
So pleasing as the groans of men in prison
And that the tears of widows, and the cries
Of famish'd orphans, are the feasts that take you.

John Pintard copied these lines into his commonplace book sometime between 1806 and 1809—recalling, no doubt, the "1 year, 3 weeks, 20 hours" he had passed imprisoned for debt ten years earlier. Although he had since returned to a state of at least modest comfort and even some distinction, Pintard nonetheless sprinkled his commonplace book with numerous observations on debt, poverty, prisons, lawyers, and adversity. Imprisonment for the crime—or was it the sin?—of insolvency scarred Pintard lastingly, as it did every other debtor whose letters or recollections survive.[1] For some debtors the scars were too grievous to acknowledge. Thomas Rodney—an officer in the Revolution, a member of the Continental Congress, and a judge of the Supreme Court of Delaware—kept voluminous diaries in which he recorded everything from the smallest slights to his dignity to intricate accounts of his dreams. Amid all the detail, however, there is a gap, which corresponds to the fourteen months Rodney spent imprisoned for debt in the early 1790s. When his journals resume, they depict a bitter, impoverished man, steeped in resentment and humiliation, but who referred only obliquely many years later to the key to his bitterness.[2]

These clues notwithstanding, the world of imprisoned debtors remains largely unexplored—not because debtors themselves were at all reticent about decrying their fate but rather because the world itself is so alien. The small literature on imprisonment for debt in early America rarely ventures inside the prison walls, tacitly acknowledging the difficulty of discerning what lies within. The task of this chapter is to penetrate those walls—to explore the world of imprisoned debtors and examine how that world both reflected and influenced changing attitudes toward debt, insolvency, and imprisonment for debt in the Revolutionary era.[3]

The only consistency among debt laws in the eighteenth century was that every colony, and later every state, permitted imprisonment for debt—most on *mesne* process, and all on execution of a judgment. That is, debtors could be imprisoned upon arrest for failure to pay a creditor before a formal adjudication that the debt was actually due, or they could be imprisoned for failure to pay the amount a court had found due. Once imprisoned, how a debtor had been arrested was immaterial.

Imprisoning one's debtor did little to assure payment of the debt. In tacit recognition of that, every colony north of the Potomac, with the possible exception of New Hampshire, permitted insolvent debtors to be bound to service to their creditors without their consent, typically for as long as seven years, the standard term for indentured servants.[4] As one debtor succinctly warned, "the gaol will pay no debts."[5] That, of course, did not deter creditors, who hoped that the rigors of imprisonment would induce debtors to disclose concealed wealth or to part with assets that were exempt from attachment or, perhaps, that family members might step into the breach—or who acted out of anger. Arrest did sometimes produce epiphanies, as when William Dudley paid a disputed debt after being dragged by a constable to the prison door in New York, "at which I was very much terrified of the thoughts of being committed to such a place."[6] In reality, however, the most common outcome was that creditors received little or nothing. Several factors compelled this result. First and foremost, of course, was the penury of imprisoned debtors. Family members did sometimes come forward, and debtors did sometimes volunteer otherwise unreachable assets, but most imprisoned debtors were insolvent. Second, even if a debtor had the assets to satisfy the creditor at whose suit he had been imprisoned, once other creditors sued—which they invariably did because only by suing could they take a place in line for a chance at the debtor's property—the debtor could not purchase his freedom simply by paying the first creditor in the queue and ignoring the rest. This necessarily meant that creditors, if they received anything, would receive less than the debtor owed them because only by agreeing to share in the deficiency could creditors begin to apportion whatever remained.[7]

The principal statutory mechanisms for freeing imprisoned debtors recognized this reality. Every colonial and state insolvency and bankruptcy statute turned on the principle of creditors accepting some proportionate loss of their debts in return for a share of the debtor's property. The details, of course, varied. As we saw in the preceding chapter, colonies and states differed on whether release was available through insolvency proceedings, which freed the debtor and distributed his assets among his creditors but did not relieve him of his obligation to pay the underlying debts, or through bankruptcy proceedings, which accomplished the same ends but also discharged the debtor from liability for unpaid debts. They differed on whether either proceeding, if available at all, was available to all debtors or only a few, and whether by free application to a court or only by special act of the legislature. They differed on whether debtors could invoke relief on their own or all or a certain portion of their creditors had to agree, and on whether creditors could be compelled to join or be bound by a composition. They disagreed on the consequences of a creditor refusing to join other creditors in fashioning a settlement and on how to determine priority among creditors in dividing up an insolvent estate. They also differed on the length of time a debtor had to be imprisoned before qualifying for discharge, on who was responsible for maintaining the debtor in prison, and on whether a creditor could hold a debtor in prison by paying his support. And these were just the major points of disagreement.

Disagreement or no, imprisonment for debt was an unquestioned piece of the cultural baggage of English immigration in the seventeenth century. It could hardly have been otherwise for a practice that had existed in England for three hundred years. This is not to say that English law on the subject was transplanted wholesale—rather, that the idea of imprisoning delinquent debtors was never in dispute. As a petitioner from Salem, Massachusetts, remarked in 1678, "it is every dayes way in every trading towne, for merchants upon neglect of payment, for to arrest theire debtors." The application of the idea varied among colonies, partly in response to differing conditions of labor, partly because of differing facilities for incarceration, partly because of the presence or absence of reform impulses—none of which touched the premise that imprisonment was appropriate for failure to pay one's debts.[8]

So accepted was the idea of imprisonment for debt in early America that opposition to it did not appear until the 1750s, although criticisms of the practice had circulated—utterly ineffectually—in England for at least a century. Even then, the opposition was not to imprisonment for debt but to keeping debtors imprisoned after they had turned all their property over to their creditors as long as some debts remained unpaid. As one anonymous writer noted, in explicit disclaimer of any broader opposition, "if it should be objected, as a Consequence from my Reasoning, that the Person of the Debtor can in no Case be taken and holden; I shall not allow the Consequence; for Reason supposes he may be taken and holden." Within a few years, however, the level and nature of public attention to imprisonment for debt changed.[9]

Toward the end of the 1760s, a genre of popular public literature that might best be described as "dueling broadsides" (or, for the more verbose, "dueling pamphlets") began to feature the plight of unjustly—as they claimed—imprisoned debtors. There was Hendrik Oudenarde, who wrote a stream of letters from the debtors' prison in New York protesting his arrest and confinement for failing to pay an arbitration award that he regarded as severe, but that he had attempted to pay nonetheless. Or John Wright Stanly, who wrote at least three pamphlets from jail in Philadelphia denouncing his former partner, Jonathan Cowpland, whom he claimed had defrauded him, for kidnaping him from Honduras and returning him to Philadelphia, where Cowpland arrested him for debt. Or Gazelena Rousby's broadside campaign against James Jauncey, who had imprisoned her husband for a debt due Jauncey from an estate, the executorship of which her husband had allegedly declined.[10]

In none of this literature is there any imputation that the debtor's insolvency represented moral failure. To be sure, one would not expect debtors to argue that their plight reflected their own moral shortcomings, but neither does one find their creditors replying that their insolvency was immoral. Instead, debtors and creditors alike agreed that the debtor's insolvency and consequent imprisonment were caused by elements external to the debt itself—for debtors, economic misfortune, a vindictive creditor, or perhaps a fraudulent partner; for creditors, the dishonesty or villainy of their debtors, character defects, to be sure, but hardly specific to debt. As one anonymous author wrote, "a Man's Misfortunes does not prove him a Rogue. Nor is Weakness, Inadvertency, or Imprudence, which all Men have more or less of, a Proof of Fraud, Dishonesty, or Extravagancy." Some debtors undoubtedly were rogues—such as the Maryland swindler imprisoned for debt in Philadelphia by Samuel House, who understandably preferred to let him "lay there and rot"—but one could not reflexively assume that they were.[11]

The redefinition of debt from moral delict to economic risk made the new literature possible. Reform emerges from dispute, not consensus. As long as debt and failure to repay were widely deemed immoral—that is, as long as condemnatory voices like Samuel Moody's remained prominent—there were no grounds on which to question imprisonment for debt. Once economic causes were admitted, however, people could begin to imagine different responses to indebtedness. The redefinition was, of course, imperfect and incomplete. But, as we saw earlier, it had begun well before midcentury and gathered momentum in the rapid expansion of production and trade during the Seven Years' War and, more urgently, during and after the Revolution. Not surprisingly, the redefinition applied principally to debtors who were themselves entrepreneurs in the changing economy. After all, the criticisms of debt that recurred in public debates over land banks, paper money, and commerce in the first half of the century all reserved their strongest opprobrium for the purchasers rather than the purveyors of consumer goods, even though both acquired the items on credit. Thus, when Americans began to question the efficacy of imprisonment for debt, their animating concern was the imprisonment of people who trafficked in credit rather than those who merely purchased on it.

For proof of this one need look only at the first American writing to criticize imprisonment for debt, a pamphlet published in Rhode Island in 1754 entitled *The Ill Policy and Inhumanity of Imprisoning Insolvent Debtors, Fairly Stated and Discussed.* Early in the pamphlet the anonymous author notes that "all Men are liable to Pain, Misery, and Death; to the Loss of Reputation, Credit, Estate, Friends, and every Thing that is dear and valuable in Life." Almost immediately, however, he makes it clear that the imprisonment for insolvency of "all Men" is not his concern; rather, it is that of "the Merchants and Traders, who are every Moment liable to Misfortunes." Why this is so becomes apparent as the analysis unfolds.[12]

The fundamental question for the author was whether, when a debtor was insolvent, "it is best for Society, that his Creditors receive a Proportion of their Debts . . . and his Person be sat at Liberty to seek new Employment; or that his Body be imprisoned for the Deficiency, until he pays the utmost Farthing, which is impossible?" What is best for society, he argues, is that "Manufactures are more encouraged, Trade and Business negotiated, Navigation and Commerce carried on with more Dispatch and Safety." In short "it is best for Society, that a Law of Liberty for Insolvent Debtors, should be Established in all Trading Communities." The emphasis throughout is on trade. Although the author nowhere explicitly excludes from his analysis what we might think of as "traditional" debtors, the exclusion is clearly implicit. It is the "Man in Trade and Business, who is both a Debtor and Creditor, and is therefore liable every Moment to Accidents, unforeseen Casualties, and Contingencies," who is in need of relief, not poor farmers or laborers. After all, he asks, "how often do we see the Bowl of Fortune, like the Bowl at Nine Pins, strike one Pin, which Pin strikes the next, who knocks down a third; all are shook, but some by Chance, stand out the Game." Are "those that stand, better Pins than those that Fall?" Might not "the Bowl of Fortune have happen'd on the standing Side first?" Not only does this capture the truism that creditors in trade or business are themselves debtors; it also expresses the commonality of interest between creditors and the debtors whose failures were economic rather than moral—which is to say, debtors who were also in trade or business.[13]

When the first pamphlets to question the efficacy of maintaining in jail debtors who were willing to relinquish their property appeared in the 1750s, the redefinition of debt from a moral to an economic offense was still in its infancy. Creditors needed to be reminded of the difference. An anonymous Connecticut writer observed in 1755 that, "as a Prison . . . in the Apprehension of Men, so much resembles the final Punishment of Wickedness, they imagine, that Man that is so unhappy as to be doomed in that Place, is not only become a Bankrupt as to his Fortune, but as to his Faith and Honour; and generally treat him as such." Lest one think that his caution applies to all debtors, the author makes clear that his concern is for the "Man of Skill and Experience in Merchandize, . . . who, by the Badness of the Times in Trade, or by the mere Providence of God, has been reduced."[14] Nonetheless, the redefinition was real enough that the biblical parable of the unmerciful servant, which forty years earlier Samuel Moody had invoked to illustrate the rigor of creditors' remedies, could now be offered to argue that imprisoning "honest Insolvents" violates "the Christian Religion"—the first time anyone had suggested in print that imprisonment for debt might not have divine sanction. Indeed, the parable was even recited to support the proposition that a bankruptcy law would be "agreeable to the Genius of our holy Religion."[15]

One can discern before the Revolution an occasional glimmer of recognition that whatever relief accrued to men of commerce from an economic construction of debt should apply equally to all imprisoned debtors. For example, another Connecticut writer, the pseudonymous Justinian, declared sweepingly in 1770 that "confinement for debt, when nothing to pay, is contrary to the foundation of law." He appeared to be speaking of all insolvent debtors when he wrote that "[i]t is difficult for the poor to command attention—their words make a despicable sound . . . The miseries of the poor are disregarded, and yet some of the lower rank, undergo more real hardship in one day, than those of a more exalted station, suffer in years." But the glimmer is just that—a fleeting glimpse. Even Justinian seemed to have had in mind a more limited class of debtors when he asked if "[m]en whose words are taken for £4 or 500 lawful money"—an unsecured amount well beyond the reach of debtors who were as impoverished before imprisonment as they were in prison—"must they be made drones?" A genuinely catholic opposition to imprisonment for debt lay far in the future.[16]

Strictly speaking, there were no debtors' prisons in America before the Revolution, and only two that even approximated the description in the first decades afterward. In physical terms, imprisonment for debt in America before the Revolution—and everywhere but Philadelphia and New York after the Revolution—meant something very different than it did in England. There, freestanding prisons exclusively for debtors, such as the King's Bench and Marshalsea prisons in London, were of long standing. In America, on the other hand, the closest approximation to a separate debtors' prison before the Revolution was a room set aside for debtors in a jail otherwise filled with criminals awaiting trial or execution. Even that degree of separation was unusual—where jails existed, it was much more common for debtors and criminals to be thrown together. Where jails did not exist, a room in the sheriff's house or an outbuilding sufficed.[17]

Descriptions of the physical conditions of imprisonment for debtors before the Revolution are few, although the complaints are many. Charles Woodmason, an Anglican minister traveling in South Carolina in 1767, described sixteen debtors crowded into a room measuring twelve feet square in the jail in Charleston, where "[a] person would be in a better

Situation in the French Kings Gallies, or the Prisons of Turkey or Barbary, than in this dismal Place." Before 1759, debtors in New York were held in the attic of city hall, which doubled as a prison. When overcrowded, some were moved to the sub-basement with condemned criminals. Sanitary conditions were so bad as to be remarked upon by people passing by on the street. A description of the county jail in Worcester, Massachusetts, in 1785, shortly before the county built a new, more commodious jail, probably typifies the jails of similar-sized counties before the Revolution. The Worcester jail was a small, two-story structure. On the first floor was one room, fourteen feet square, for criminals, plus a smaller "condemned room" and dungeon, "which are used only on Special occasions." Debtors were confined in a room on the second floor, about fourteen or fifteen feet square, which adjoined a smaller room commonly used for female prisoners. Although Massachusetts law required that criminals and debtors be housed separately, the sheriff reported "that upon some occasion he has been obliged to mix Criminals with Debtors, and at other times, Debtors with Criminals."[18]

The picture becomes a bit clearer after the Revolution when we turn to the two institutions in America that came closest to separate debtors' prisons on the English model—the New Gaol in New York and the Prune Street jail in Philadelphia. They are of particular importance for our purposes because the number and prominence of debtors imprisoned there prompted the national debate over bankruptcy legislation in the 1790s.

The New Gaol in New York stood in the northeast corner of the present City Hall Park, then known as the Commons or, more popularly, the Fields. Until rapid development transformed the area early in the nineteenth century, the location lay just beyond the northern edge of the settled part of town. Built in 1757–1758 in the style of domestic architecture that typified most public buildings before the 1790s, the prison was a three-story stone structure, "finished in a handsome manner, so as to represent marble." It was seventy-five feet wide and sixty feet deep, topped by a cupola and surrounded by a fence, with a central entry and barred windows. Initially home to debtors and criminals alike, the New Gaol became the debtors' prison after the Bridewell opened for criminals in 1775 a few hundred feet to the west on the other side of the almshouse, although it continued to house a few convicted misdemeanants and accused criminals awaiting trial for minor offenses. The building had fourteen rooms on its three floors, arranged on either side of a hall that ran the depth of the building on each floor. The middle and upper halls—the second and third floors—each had six rooms, which seem to have been occupied by merchants and skilled artisans, perhaps four or five to a room. The lower hall, or first floor, housed laborers and other less substantial debtors in more crowded conditions. Less privileged debtors slept in the common hallway. In the early nineteenth century, and perhaps before, truly common debtors—prostitutes, sailors, and the like—occupied a damp cell in the basement. A rumor that the jail was haunted, which if true would have added a nice touch of dread, turned out to be a fabrication by the wife of an imprisoned debtor, who published it to raise money for her husband's release.[19]

Descriptions of the Prune Street jail in Philadelphia are spare. It was a stone building at the corner of Prune (now Locust) and Sixth streets, forty-five feet long and fifty-five feet deep, built originally as a workhouse for the Walnut Street jail, which it abutted. The Walnut Street jail, which housed criminals, occupied the remainder of the block to the north of the debtors' apartments. The yards of the two were separated by a wall, which was not tall enough to prevent a certain amount of communication between debtors and criminals. As one writer put it, "Crime and poverty . . . were the tenants of the two apartments, separated by a courtyard."[20]

Conditions within the prisons were severe. "[T]his unhappy mansion," a "human slaughter house," "that dismal cage," a "loathsome storehouse" were but some of the descriptions of the New Gaol through the years.[21] Unlike criminals and paupers, debtors had to provide their own food, fuel, and clothing—supplied from their own resources, the generosity of family or friends, begging, or the beneficence of a local relief society—or they did without. Occasional statutes requiring creditors to maintain their debtors under certain circumstances or providing state assistance were few, sporadic, and often ineffectual. In general, what William Holdsworth, the encyclopedic historian of English law, described as "the strictly medieval view" of imprisoned debtors prevailed. In the harsh, uncompromising words of an English judge of the sixteenth century, a debtor in prison "ought to live of his own, and neither the plaintiff nor the sheriff is bound to give him meat or drink, no more than if one distrains cattle, and puts them in a pound." If the debtor cannot feed himself, he should hope for "the charity of others." If none is forthcoming, "let him die, in the name of God, if he will, and impute the cause of it to his own fault, for his presumption and ill behaviour brought him to that imprisonment."[22]

Pleas of starvation echoed in petitions and letters from debtors in every jail and prison across the decades. William Moore wrote from the jail in Poughkeepsie that for four days he had eaten nothing but a few scraps spared by fellow prisoners and found it hard to believe that there was "not Law parvided man not to starve to Deths in goal." Thomas Moland claimed that he had often "been a week at a Time without the Benefit of meals Victuals." Seven debtors in the New Gaol petitioned John Tabor Kempe, attorney general of the province, that they "are Really Like to perish To Death with Hunger, . . . And without Speedy Relieff, must Dye." Another debtor in the New Gaol, John Young, warned that he "must Inevitably perish for want of food and Raiment." Abel Butterfield, the former schoolmaster in Hardwick, Massachusetts, pleaded from jail in Worcester for food and clothing, "as he has lost his Right Arm [and] is almost naked." Andrew Fraunces, imprisoned in Newark, repeatedly begged William Duer for assistance. For three weeks, he claimed, he had known no "Comfort of Life except a Potatoe and a little salt meat." "[B]egging a bone to gnaw is all I have subsisted on." Duer, who was himself imprisoned in New York, could only reply that "I cannot do Impossibilities."[23]

Conditions could also be dangerous, whether because of violent prisoners or unhealthful quarters. For example, Hugh McEwan feared for his life in the New Gaol—"this Drery place of Exile"—at the hands of "a monster Confined amongst us" who had physically assaulted several imprisoned debtors, women as well as men, "who on account of their Confinement Can Not Run from his [murderous?] Desires." Accommodations in the Worcester County jail, never good under the best of circumstances, took a sharp turn for the worse on December 6, 1785, when eleven new debtors were imprisoned, further overcrowding the twelve who were already there, including some who had been imprisoned nearly a year, and one for a year and a half. With no space left in the one room set aside for debtors, the jailer put the new arrivals in an unheated garret. Bowed, perhaps, but not chastened, all twenty-three debtors petitioned the court of quarter sessions the very next day complaining of the cramped billet and lack of heat in winter, which made the garret in particular "by no means fit for any of the Human Race to lodge in."[24]

Scenes such as these prompted the formation of relief societies. Not surprisingly, the two largest and best known were in New York and Philadelphia—the Society for the Relief of Distressed Debtors (later renamed the Humane Society) in New York and the Philadelphia Society for Alleviating the Miseries of Public Prisons, organized within four months of each other in 1787 and modeled in part on similar societies recently founded in England. Smaller, somewhat ephemeral groups doubtless existed elsewhere, such as "the Committee of the Patriotic Society for the relief of distressed debtors" in Newark. The Philadelphia Society ministered primarily to criminals, and the Humane Society later devoted "a portion of its care to the resuscitation of persons apparently dead from drowning," but the purposes of both with respect to debtors were similar. Each distributed donated food and clothing, appointed visitation committees to inspect conditions in the prisons, and lobbied for various legislative reforms, although never to abolish imprisonment for debt itself. The Humane Society, for example, explicitly accepted imprisonment for debt as "a justifiable punishment of the debtor," limited only by the qualification that subjecting an imprisoned debtor "to the sufferings of cold and hunger, and the consequent hazard of his life, infringes that fundamental axiom in legislation that the punishment of an offence should always be in proportion to the degree of it." Its central mission was largely palliative—to "administer to the comfort of prisoners, by providing food, fuel, clothing, and other necessaries of life," and to "procure the liberation of such as were confined for small sums, and were of meritorious conduct, by discharging their debts." Of the two, it was the Philadelphia Society that left the most vivid images of the conditions of imprisoned debtors.[25]

The dominant impression of the debtors' prison conveyed by the records of the Philadelphia Society in the late 1780s is one of licentious chaos. It is almost as though the cautions of ministers earlier in the century that debt bred luxury and vice had proven true, and that as punishment for their sins debtors now lived in a purgatory worthy of Hieronymus Bosch. The debtors' prison observed by the visitation committees of the Philadelphia Society was one in which thugs levied "garnish" on new arrivals by forcibly stripping them of their clothes to sell for liquor, criminals scaled the wall separating the two sides to abuse and rob the debtors, turnkeys extorted favors from visitors, drunkenness and fighting abounded, men and women mixed indiscriminately, and prostitutes procured their arrests for debt to serve a captive clientele. The county grand jury charged that the jail had become such a "desirable place for the more wicked and polluted of both sexes" that newly released prisoners routinely signed "fictitious notes" and confessed judgment on them so they could return to the "scenes of debauchery."[26] Adding to the confusion, both Prune Street and the New Gaol were comparatively open. Visitors—whether family members, friends, creditors, messengers, vendors, or the like—came and went with relative ease. Charles Brockden Brown's fictionalized description of the Prune Street apartments a few years later is a bit tamer but evokes the same themes of dissolution:

> The apartment was filled with pale faces and withered forms. The marks of negligence and poverty were visible in all; but few betrayed, in their features or gestures, any symptoms of concern on account of their condition. Ferocious gaiety, or stupid indifference, seemed to sit upon every brow. The vapour from an heated stove, mingled with the fumes of beer and tallow that were spilled upon it, and with the tainted breath of so promiscuous a crowd, loaded the stagnant atmosphere.[27]

In truth, the inspectors of the Philadelphia Society may have been just as shocked by drunkenness, fighting, thievery, and prostitution among the unimprisoned lower orders elsewhere in the city. At least one imprisoned debtor tacitly assumed this in a long letter to the Society on the affront to polite moral sensibilities presented by conditions within the prison. The writer, an Irishman, described himself as formerly "in the Mercantile line" in Dublin. He claimed to have visited forty prisons in England and Ireland in the course of business and out of curiosity. Although none of those buildings "Exceeds that of Philadelphia in Neatness, and . . . Convenience," all of them separated men from women and debtors from criminals. Of the two pairings, it was the intermingling of men and women in the Prune Street jail that most offended the writer, as he was sure it would the Society. Men and women "being premiskesly [promiscuously] put together at nights, is to Every thinking person, Shocking, and must in Some measure Convay to the minds of Strangers, this must be a Country, where neither Religion or Desencey is observed." His principal concern was the lasting moral stain that attended the appearance of indecency, which he illustrated with the story of "[a] very honest Industress man [who] may from missfortunes be sent to Gaol for Debt." His wife then visits him and finds him placed, through no fault of his own, "alongside of sum Strumpet," which "Immediately Convays to herself, the worst Consiquences." She returns home angry and tells her husband's friends of his apparent debauchery. "[T]hey disspise him, will lend him no Aid to get out." She refuses to visit him, and the longer he remains in prison, "the more shee is Confirmed in her Opinion, so that perhaps this side of time may not Remove it."[28]

That there were women in debtors' prison is certain. How many or in what capacity is unknown. A visitor to the New Gaol in 1810 claimed to find it "swarming with females of loose character" imprisoned by brothel owners for small boarding debts when disease or age limited their usefulness. Fifteen years earlier, the turnkey of the New Gaol, Benjamin Haskins, spread the rumor that Margaret Frean "had kept a public Bawdy House" in Charleston, South Carolina, and that her room in the prison "was no better." He claimed that one of the married debtors "knew so much of [Frean's] Character that he would not permit her to board with him, nor to be in Company with his Wife." On the other hand, the other debtors roundly condemned Haskins as "an outlaw a Public Lyar and disturber of the Peace" who "in a malicious and wanton manner endeav-or'd to criminate the Character of almost every Prisoner on the Hall." Di-rect references to women imprisoned as debtors, such as Frean, are few—indeed, of the 130 debtors confined on one floor of the New Gaol from 1795–1798 for whom we have full names, she is the only woman. More common are mentions of wives staying in jail with their imprisoned husbands, although whether out of devotion or necessity is unknowable.[29]

The class-driven difference in moral sensibilities described by the Irish debtor appears elsewhere in the records of the Philadelphia Society. Whereas the debtors complained about the price of liquor, the inspectors objected to its presence. Petition after petition asked, "Is a poor Debtor from any Law oblidged to give the prison keeper half a Doller for a Quart of Spirits that they can get out of Doors for 18 pence," or protested that the keeper and turnkeys confiscated liquor that visitors attempted to bring to debtors and sold it to them instead.[30] The Society, however, denounced even the use of liquor as one of the "three great evils" that cried for re-dress, alongside the failure to separate men from women and debtors from criminals, and argued for its prohibition. It argued that by banning spirits altogether, "good order and Decorum would be Materially promoted . . . , and the Miseries of the prisoners themselves considerable alleviated"—a conclusion with which many imprisoned debtors doubtless disagreed. The Humane Society in New York was similarly censorious. In a memorial to the legislature in 1788, two of its founders argued that imprisoned debtors were "liable to become useless, if not pernicious, members of society, from the great danger they are in of acquiring habits of intemperance." The causal progression from liquor to idleness to vice was, of course, a com-monplace in the reform literature. Benjamin Rush, one of the founders of the Philadelphia Society, condemned "spirituous liquors" as "the parents of idleness and extravagance, and the certain forerunners of poverty, and frequently of jails, wheelbarrows, and the gallows." His famous "moral thermometer" linked mixed drinks to idleness and debt and hard liquor to crime and disease, finding the moral high ground of health, wealth, and happiness only in water, milk, and weak beer. The conviction that liquor was not simply an evil but the fundamental evil from which others flowed extended to the county grand jury in Philadelphia, which reported to the court of oyer and terminer in 1787 that the jailer's sale of liquor "by small measure" encouraged the intermingling of debtors and criminals. Tellingly, and in perfect illustration of the class basis of moral sensibility, the grand jury cited only one ill consequence of the intermingling—that "many worthy" debtors, "who have once seen better days, and have been reduced by misfortune, should not have the liberty of a place to receive the air, without being interrupted by wretches who are a disgrace to human nature."[31]

One senses that an earthiness or vulgarity of behavior that would have offended the inspectors if encountered outside the prison offended them more deeply inside. Perhaps it could not have been otherwise. The debtors they observed within the prison included "worthy characters" not unlike themselves, distinguished from them by economic misfortune rather than moral culpability, and subjected by the leveling effects of insolvency to behavior they had once shunned. Moreover, unlike the New York Humane Society, which existed solely to relieve "distressed debtors" (at least until it branched out to include near-drowning victims), the Philadelphia Society was first and foremost a prison reform society, which, as Michael Meranze observed, "fused Christian charity with political advocacy." It was founded and led by the mercantile and professional elite of the city—men such as Benjamin Rush, William White, Caleb Lownes, William Shippen, Thomas Wistar, John Swanwick, and Tench Coxe—whose commitment to devising public welfare institutions appropriate to an enlightened republic made Philadelphia the center of public experimentation in prisons, hospitals, asylums, and workhouses.[32] The Society was a moral reform movement intended, as it proclaimed, to "alleviate the Miseries of Prisons, by procuring in them that reform, in their Policy, so obviously necessary, before a reformation, can rationally be expected, in the morals or conduct of any Criminal confined in them." To this end it delegated a six-man "acting committee" to visit the prison weekly, report any "abuses" to the appropriate civil authority, and "examine the influence of confinement or Punishment upon the morals of the persons who are the subjects of them." All for the larger purpose, announced in the preamble to its constitution, that "the links which should bind the whole family of mankind together . . . be preserved unbroken and, such degrees and modes of Punishment may be discovered and suggested, as may instead of containing habits of vice become the means of restoring our fellow Creatures to virtue and happiness."[33]

Debtors were incidental to this scheme.[34] However, as long as their confinement intertwined with that of criminals, they were a necessary incident. Hence the identification of "the indiscriminate confinement of debtors and persons committed for criminal offenses" as one of the "three great evils which call for attention." Although the Society recognized that the failure to separate debtors and criminals "often subjects the innocent [debtor] to personal abuse and loss of property," its greater concern was moral. It noted instances "where debtors by mixing with the criminals have formed connexions which ultimately led to their being convicts themselves" and observed that "numerous connexions have been formed in this way to the total ruin of [many unfortunate prisoners, who have been compelled] to associate with men of infamous morals, whereby their principles have become corrupted." Inasmuch as some number of the imprisoned debtors were acquitted criminals whose debts were the charges for their own unsuccessful prosecutions, the Society may have thought them particularly susceptible to criminal instruction.[35]

The Philadelphia Society was not alone in this belief. The idea of prisons as schools of vice, which dominated prison reform for much of the nineteenth century, first appeared in the 1780s to describe the corruption of debtors by the criminals with whom they were confined. James Bland Burges, in a massive work that circulated widely in America, wrote that by so imprisoning debtors, "we do but encourage that vice which we wish to correct; . . . we nourish and mature those evil habits, which a different process might have eradicated." To a debtor the "sight of an hardened criminal, permitted to revel in the enjoyment of sensual gratifications, and mocking that legal authority so impotently exerted against him, must prove a dangerous example." For that reason, prisons are "not the school of virtue. Many have entered them with innocence; few have quitted them without contamination." On the other hand, occasional individuals insisted that the process of corruption ran in the other direction. Mary Weed, who succeeded her dead husband as keeper of the Walnut Street jail, is said to have complained "that the debtors in their apartments, from being able to overlook the yard of the prison, made her fear that their conversing together, swearing, etc. might corrupt the morals of her people"— that is, her criminal prisoners.[36]

Significantly, all mention of debtors disappears from the records of the Society after 1799, by which time debtors and criminals had been effectively separated from one another, even though men and women had not.[37] In fact, there is scant mention of debtors after 1792, when the Society noted that "they are induced to believe that [from] the attention paid by the Society to the Business for which they originally associated and from the success which had attended their labours, many of the evils which Existed in the prisons upon their first becoming the objects of the Care of the Society, are nearly or altogether removed." When contact between imprisoned debtors and criminals ceased, the debtors dropped from view. The Philadelphia Society for Alleviating the Miseries of Public Prisons evidently stopped its practice of paying the debts of persons imprisoned for "trifling" amounts and turned its attention exclusively to penal reform.[38]

To a limited extent the Board of Inspectors of the prison, authorized by statute in 1789 to supervise the keepers after lobbying by the Philadelphia Society, took up the slack. Indeed, the six—later twelve—inspectors, who were appointed by the mayor and aldermen, were often members of the Philadelphia Society. However, debtors surface only occasionally in the minutes of the inspectors' monthly meetings at the prison. Some of the entries are tantalizing, such as the reference to the necessity of putting the debtors' apartment "in decent order"; or the appointment of a committee to draft a memorial to the legislature calling for reform of the insolvent laws "to remedy the evil" of "the situation of the Prison wherein the debtors are confined"; or the frustration of the Board at its inability to remove the keeper of the debtors' apartment, who had "permitted and encouraged" "many disgracefull practices," all regrettably unspecified.[39]

As suggestive as these entries are, the most telling indication that debtors were as incidental to the concerns of the Board of Inspectors as they were to those of the Philadelphia Society is that none of the five committees appointed by the Board in the 1790s to draft rules, regulations, or memorials for or on behalf of the debtors ever appear to have completed their tasks.[40] On the other hand, their failure may have reflected futility rather than dereliction. When the governor, Thomas Mifflin, inspected the prison in 1791, he was struck by the "painful difference" between the "wretchedness" of the debtors' apartment and "the order, the industry, and the cleanliness" of the criminal side. Debtors "languish in the jail, without clothes, without food, and without fire," while criminals "enjoy every supply that is requisite to maintain life." He concluded that "to be a debtor, would seem to be more offensive to the laws, than to be a criminal; and to be unfortunate, must, sometimes, be more fatal, than to be vicious." Mifflin urged the legislature to make some provision for the material comfort of imprisoned debtors. Nothing happened.[41]

Conditions in debtors' prisons may have improved during the 1790s, but it is difficult to tell with any certainty. Cities and counties established or expanded, even if only slightly, prison limits or bounds into which debtors could be bailed, although the bonding requirements, which could be as high as twice the amount of the debt, discouraged the practice.[42] Andrew Fraunces, in one of his frequent pleas to William Duer from Newark jail for assistance, pleaded that he was "not only sick but naked, dirty and Lousy," but he may simply have been trying to render his plight more pitiable in the hope of eliciting compassion. Jonathan Wallace spent nearly three months in "a close and nauseous room" in western Pennsylvania, initially in leg irons, without the access to the jail yard usually given even criminals—but his description is in a broadside diatribe against the "infamy and abominable cruelty" of a man who may have been opposing him for public office. The Humane Society provided food to up to 170 debtors each year, yet the one mass escape from the New Gaol may have been prompted by hunger. On April 25, 1798, forty prisoners, most of them debtors armed with pistols and clubs, broke out at midday. Twenty-four escaped, of whom all but seven were recaptured within ten days. Five days after the escape, a letter appeared in the New York *Argus* captioned "Desperate Laws occasion desperate means, and it is an old adage, that hunger will break through stone walls." The author, "A Spectator," observed that most of the escaped prisoners were debtors "whose situation was desperate . . . [T]hey were in want of the common necessaries of life, and their situation is far preferable, should they be placed in the list of criminals"— he did not have to explain that the city fed imprisoned criminals but not debtors. The hunger behind the public spectacle of a bloody, violent jailbreak by men who until then had not been criminals may have been the spur to the Society for Free Debate, which the very next week donated sixteen dollars and "a most seasonable and large supply of beef, bread, etc." to the imprisoned debtors.[43]

Improved conditions or no, the debtors' prisons of New York and Philadelphia were most frightful during the yellow fever epidemics that swept through the mid-Atlantic states with distressing frequency. At those times, everyone who could afford to—and many who could not—abandoned the cities for the countryside from August until early November. Business came to a standstill. Courts canceled entire terms. Even in Boston debtors used the fever "as an Apology for not Coming in to pay their debts."[44] For imprisoned debtors, who could not join the exodus, fever season meant at the very least that the friends upon whose generosity they had relied for food or money had fled town. It also meant that they faced contagion in crowded, unsanitary surroundings, unable to escape. As one writer noted at the beginning of yellow fever season in 1800, "[i]t would be considered the most barbarous of all acts, if the goal of the city was on fire, for the goaler to flee from it with the keys in his pocket, and leave the prisoners to be consumed in the flames." Are not debtors in similar straits "in this sickly season—to be shut up in a prison in the raging of a mortal disease, when the tie of property will not bind those who can flee from it." The answer, of course, was yes. As Joseph Fay remarked of the 1803 epidemic, when rich and poor alike fled New York, "Humanity exerted herself in favor of every class of the community—except the debtors."[45]

Debtors imprisoned at Prune Street in the late summer and fall of 1798 followed the progress of the epidemic through newspapers and rumor. On September 18 they read that it had reached the criminal prisoners across the wall and that the jailer had abandoned his post. The contrast with the legendary plague season of 1793, when the warden worked tirelessly on their behalf and was, with his daughter, the only victims in the prison, would not have escaped them. The *Gazette*, while applauding the "efficient measures" that had been taken "for the relief of the poor and distressed of the city in general," lamented the "forgetfulness as to those who are confined in the Debtor's Apartment" and observed "that there is no description of people within the city whose situation more loudly calls for assistance." One of those debtors, Robert Morris, once the wealthiest man in America, wrote frequent letters to his partner, John Nicholson, describing the tightening circle of contagion in the rooms around him and expressing his fear that "Death will soon enter the door opposite to mine," even as the Board of Inspectors sent female prisoners to his abandoned, unfinished mansion a block away.[46]

A few days after yellow fever reached the New Gaol in New York in September 1798, Charles Young wrote the creditor who had sent him there—and who had himself left Philadelphia to avoid the fever—pleading to be released and offering security for his return. "You have arrested me in this place and cannot for your Judgment wish to Execute with Death." Young, whose creditors always suspected him of exaggerating his distress, wrote that he was "surrounded by Disease and Death" and that his wife, who was with him, "every Hour is surprized into Vapours and Despondency" by her surroundings. Two or three days later, some of his fellow inmates published a plea "to their Creditors and Fellow-Citizens," imploring their aid for themselves and their families. As "the destroying angel hovers over the city, with his Sword unsheathed," they reported that pestilence was "already among us . . . and threatens instant death to all."[47]

A few months later, with the spectacle of "the Mournful Hearse staulking continually with Sick and Dead" still fresh, keeper Alexander Lamb thought it a propitious time to petition the Common Council to restore the money for cleaning the New Gaol that it had withdrawn when it removed the last of the criminal prisoners to the Bridewell. Lamb, a compassionate man who often distributed food from his own table to the debtors, warned that "the Filth which will soon be accumulated therein will undoubtedly create some contagious Distemper that may endanger the Lives of the Prisoners confined and extend throughout the whole City." He was wrong. The Common Council rejected his petition.[48] The presumption that public authorities bore no responsibility for the care or maintenance of imprisoned debtors ran deep. Citizens could do as they wished, individually or collectively through relief societies. The state, however, owed debtors nothing—not food, not clothing, not heat, not sanitation. Thus, when the city of Philadelphia moved its criminal prisoners to a jail outside the city at the height of the 1798 epidemic to reduce contagion, it left its debtors behind in Prune Street, leaving to the fever the chore of relieving overcrowding in the debtors' apartments.[49]

All imprisoned debtors doubtless felt the closeness of confinement and the humiliations of dependence and penury. In times of plague, all knew that death was no respecter of persons. Only rarely, however, did prominent debtors experience the deprivation and degradation of ordinary debtors. The collapse of large-scale speculation schemes in the 1790s resulted for the first time in the imprisonment of large numbers of what one might call "wealthy debtors"—men who had fallen from great heights, whose successes had been measured by large ventures rather than by a good harvest, and who even in insolvency retained sufficient resources to raise their daily lot above that of ordinary debtors, even if their assets were in large part illiquid or unreachable. They were not the small debtors whose lives before imprisonment had been as impoverished as they were after.

The crowded conditions that typified imprisonment for most debtors did not affect wealthy debtors except in a relative sense—relative, that is, to the houses to which they had been accustomed. Most debtors in New York and Philadelphia lived four or more, and often many more, to a room. Reports such as eleven debtors in a single room in the New Gaol or seven women in a cellar room in Prune Street with two blankets among them were common. Wealthy debtors enjoyed—if that is the right word for accommodations that were still in a prison—rooms to themselves.

What made the disparity possible, of course, was money. Debtors rented living space from the keepers. Debtors with more money could rent more space.[50] When Robert Morris first entered Prune Street, he wrote that, "having no particular place allotted for me, I feel myself an intruder in every place into which I go. I sleep in another persons bed. I occupy other peoples rooms, and if I attempt to sit down to write it is at the interruption and inconvenience of someone who has acquired a prior right to the place." He tried daily "to get a room for a high rent," and finally succeeded after a week in renting a room he considered "the best in this house," which he then could outfit with "such furniture and conveniences as will make me comfortable"—three writing desks, a borrowed mahogany table and desk, an "old Windsor Settee and eight old Windsor chairs," a copying press, dozens of letterbooks and account books, six chests and trunks of papers, drawers and letter cases for correspondence and business papers from 1777 forward, maps, mirrors, a trunk of clothes, and a bed.[51]

Debtors of means could redecorate or even renovate their rooms. While still staving off his own imprisonment, Morris noted that another merchant, David Allison, had "fitted up a room in Prune Street where a dozen of them play cards from morning 'till midnight."[52] When John Pintard was arrested and imprisoned in Newark, he spent the first three weeks repairing his apartment—a project that began the day before his arrest and included papering and painting the room and overseeing carpenters. William Paine of Boston, who had "only" $140,000 in notes to pay debts half again as much, had the sympathy of his friends as he "furnished his apartments." It was reported in Philadelphia that in New York "a few capital bankrupts, . . . occupy alone, apartments furnished and decorated in a manner that vies with any drawing room in town," and that "when a recent bankruptcy took place, upholsterers were employed to cover the walls of the room in which lodgings were to be provided, with stout paper tarred, and this again with an elegant paper hanging—and that other measures were taken to render the apartment highly agreeable." A Polish traveler wrote of the former speculators imprisoned in New York in 1797 that "they receive their friends, live sumptuously, provide themselves the pleasures of music, gaming, etc. . . . Many times, while passing near the prison,

I have [seen?] those gentlemen strolling on the roof, laughing and talking, while a band of musicians played for them airs gay and tender by turn." Morris received cases of wine and entertained George Washington at dinner. Walter Livingston's brother paid the jailer the ample sum of £52 a year to make sure he would "not want for the comforts of life, as far as his confinement will admit."[53] Although poorer debtors may have resented such privilege, that was not necessarily so. For example, William Duer, the speculator whose failure in 1792 caused panic in the streets of New York and sent tremors as far as Boston and Philadelphia, was accorded a room to himself as a mark of "the good will of his fellow prisoners and in Consideration of his Long Confinement, advanced years, and Numerous Family."[54]

Wealthy debtors such as Morris and Duer spent large portions of each day trying to gain their release. One might think that poorer debtors did the same, but they did not. The reason for the difference was, once again, money. The statutory path to freedom in the 1790s rested explicitly on economic distinctions and implicitly on social ones. For example, under the New York Ten-Pound Act of 1789, two categories of debtors were eligible for gaol delivery—debtors who had been in prison for thirty days or more for debts that did not exceed £10, and judgment debtors imprisoned under writs of execution for debts that did not exceed £200 who assigned their property to their creditors.[55] Thus, the debtors who could be freed most easily were the ones who owed least—debtors for whom the meagerness of their indebtedness reflected that of their resources. The smallest debtors—the ones imprisoned for trifling amounts who had no business to transact or accounts to arrange or property to yield up—had only to wait thirty days, then take an oath to their insolvency and lack of any property other than a few exempt items, and they would be released back into the poverty from which they had been plucked by a constable. For these debtors the most pressing business each day in prison was not to arrange their release but to secure enough food to survive.

Wealthy debtors, on the other hand—the Morrises and Duers of the prisons—owed too much money to qualify for gaol delivery, a somewhat dubious distinction merited only by those whose success had been great enough to allow them to incur large debts. For them the duration of their imprisonment was uncertain. Their release rested on their ability to persuade their creditors to accept a composition or an insolvent assignment or a bankruptcy discharge, depending on which of those, if any, was available in their state. To accomplish any of these, given the complexity of the business affairs that had generated such indebtedness in the first place, took vast amounts of time. Duer was so busy trying to wheel and deal his way back to solvency during most of his seven years in prison that visitors required an appointment to see him. Morris found himself so inundated by "incessant tormenting applications" that he required visitors to be announced and admitted only with his permission. His greatest impediment, after imprisonment itself, was that his books, papers, and letterpress initially remained at his country home.[56]

The imprisonment of "wealthy debtors"—and the deaths of some of them—confounded the normal expectations of social and economic status and altered the political dimensions of debtors' relief.[57] In the wake of the financial collapse of the 1790s, the debate over debtor relief was recast as a debate on the merits of bankruptcy. In part this was because the sudden increase in the number of people imprisoned for their debts generated new calls for ending the practice, which, although never explicitly stated, necessarily raised the question of how else to deal with unpaid debts. In addition, the widespread popularity of speculative investment had helped speed the redefinition of debt from a moral delict to an economic one for which imprisonment seemed an inappropriately criminal punishment. Most important, however, the prominence of the speculator-debtors dovetailed with the traditional ambit of bankruptcy in England, where bankruptcy relief was only available to merchants, traders, and brokers whose debts exceeded a minimum that itself exceeded the typical indebtedness of farmers, laborers, and shopkeepers—in short, of most ordinary debtors. Thus, from the time late in 1797 that Congress first began to consider seriously the bankruptcy bills that had been proposed every year before then, it was clear that any uniform, national system of bankruptcy would apply only to these "wealthy debtors." From that point forward, ordinary debtors were left behind.

One person who took up their plight was William Keteltas, whom one historian aptly described as "an impecunious lawyer with a flair for dramatizing humanitarian causes." Whereas Keteltas's flair had once sent him to jail for contempt, his impecuniousness eventually landed him in the New Gaol. There he campaigned against imprisonment for debt through a newspaper he published from within the prison entitled the *Forlorn Hope*, which appeared for twenty-five issues during six months of 1800.[58]

From his very first issue Keteltas attacked the twofold "impolicy" of treating debtors as criminals and of treating them worse than criminals. In a pseudonymous letter to the editor, Keteltas contrasted recent reforms in criminal punishment with the position of imprisoned debtors. He noted approvingly that the "deep rooted prejudices in favour of the criminal code have been successfully attacked." The "child of depravity"—the criminal—is now "permitted by the humane legislator, to reflect in close confinement on his past errors, . . . so that when penitence and a confirmed continuance in the paths of virtue, through the benign influence of the laws, restore him to society," he will be prepared to walk the upright path of a responsible citizen. "Miserable debtors," on the other hand, "cannot even hope for a restoration to society." Of them, Keteltas asked, in a passage which captures his fervor,

How have you merited your unhappy situation? Are you then more criminal than the robber or manslayer? Is it the greatest of all crimes to have your labour and industry blasted? Must you then, because you are . . . stripped of your all by an act of God—must you indeed become outcasts from society, and compelled to submit to a Shylock's taking your heart's blood, even when you offered him the relics of your property, and evidenced your willingness to bind yourselves by a solemn engagement, that your future labours, if successful, shall be appropriated to the payment of his demand?[59]

The successful attack to which Keteltas alluded was the transformation of American criminal law and punishment after the Revolution. State after state accepted the reforming argument that the "sanguinary" British criminal code of corporal punishments and liberal executions had no place in a virtuous republic. The revised American criminal codes of the 1790s thus replaced whipping, ear-cropping, branding, and other physical penalties with prison sentences of specified lengths, calibrated to the seriousness of the crime. Within the prisons there were early stirrings of the idea that incarceration should uplift and reform rather than merely punish, an idea that took brief flight three decades later. Keteltas was fully aware of this revolution and of its implications for debtors. The shift to determinate sentences for convicted criminals left imprisoned debtors more disfavored than they had been before. The state had never assumed responsibility for clothing or feeding imprisoned debtors, as it had imprisoned criminals—a distinction the reforms did nothing to alter. Before the reforms, however, incarceration—which always was indeterminate—was reserved for accused criminals awaiting trial, convicted felons awaiting execution, and debtors. After the reforms the only prisoners who did not know when or how or even if they would be freed were debtors. As Keteltas understood, when imprisonment became a criminal punishment, imprisoned debtors saw themselves punished as criminals yet with none of the comforts afforded convicted criminals in terms of food, clothing, heat, or the knowledge of when they would regain their freedom. Faced with that prospect, some debtors in fact became criminals—most notoriously, John Young, a music publisher who, "distress'd in mind, harras'd with my cares, and the dread of again being confined," shot and killed a deputy sheriff who was trying to return him to debtors' prison.[60]

Nearly every issue of the *Forlorn Hope* drove home the unfavorable comparison between debtors and criminals. There were references to "the present dreadful penal code of laws against debtors" and reminders that "misfortune is no crime." There were didactic stories such as that of the convicted murderer, fed by "the benevolent laws of the Country," who refused even "a morsel of his allowance" to an imprisoned debtor, "an honest man whom he had once plundered" and whom he now cursed. There was a statutory analysis demonstrating "that a felon imprisoned for a term of years, is better off than a debtor" because the former is "liberated by law after being fed, clothed, and taught a trade, at the expense of the state," whereas the latter "is imprisoned for life, for being unfortunate, obliged to support himself and family . . . whether he has means or not, or starve, being left solely at the disposal of his creditor." There were unflattering comparisons of debtors imprisoned in New York with the inmates of the Bastille in Paris, noting that "the former rather exceeds the latter in misery." The conclusions were inescapable and hardly subtle: "why should the state nourish and protect the violators of its institutions (who are in that respect debtors to the public) and yet give up the necessitous man for a failure in a private contract?" "As the law now operates, . . . it is a greater crime to run into debt, however fair the prospect of paying, than to rob a man on the highway, commit a rape, or burn a house." Lest anyone doubt that the reforms that improved the lives of convicted criminals could neither in reason nor conscience be withheld from debtors, Keteltas reprinted a chapter from Cesare Beccaria, the Italian theorist whose writings shaped American penal reform, in which Beccaria asked "upon what barbarous pretence" the "honest bankrupt" was imprisoned and "ranked with criminals."[61]

The ultimate extension of these arguments, which Keteltas reached with little hesitation, was that imprisonment for debt was a form of capital punishment wielded by private creditors with the acquiescence of the state. In his first issue Keteltas announced that "[t]he suicides which have occurred in the debtor's jail in this state, shall be cited in future papers . . . and will be placed to the debt of the creditor." He printed numerous descriptions of imprisonment for debt as "a lingering death, (for you cannot starve a man in less than five days, while they put the murderer to death in as few minutes)." He published accounts of wasting deaths of ancient debtors under comments such as "a jury of Inquest sat on the body, and returned a verdict—death, precipitated by the oppression of a merciless Creditor!" His letter-writers asked, "Is not the killing of man in any way, with malice prepense, murder?" "What," one queried, "can the relentless creditors of Duer, Sylvester, and of the many others who have died under the infliction of their torture, expect from the throne of grace" when they pray with the words, "Forgive us our debts as we forgive our debtors?" In sum, "the creditor unconstitutionally possesses [absolute power] over the life, liberty, and property of the debtor."[62] "Unconstitutional" was an as-yet-unexplored term in 1800, and its application to the limitation of individual rights was particularly novel. From a position this advanced, it was perhaps inevitable that Keteltas came to oppose capital punishment altogether and concluded that "[s]ociety has no right to punish an individual with Death . . . [M]an should not assume the prerogatives of Deity, and deprive a fellow creature of his natural existence."[63]

The identification of imprisoned debtors as criminals did not exist in the reform literature in any sustained fashion before Keteltas's campaign.[64] After 1800 it became a central trope of the arguments against imprisoning debtors. For example, an anonymous Philadelphian argued in 1803 that insolvency laws "have been founded on the fiction of debtors being criminal," a fiction that served "no purpose, but to associate the idea of crime with misfortune." He observed that "Blackstone does not place insolvents or bankrupts, under the head of Crimes or Public Wrongs" and invoked the English reformer, James Bland Burges, for the proposition that imprisonment for debt "is unauthorised by Law and Magna-charta:—that the practice, is the offspring of Popery and Tyranny."[65] Those arguments took a long time to prevail, as arguments for reform generally do. New York did not abolish imprisonment for most debtors until 1831; Pennsylvania not until eleven years later. Keteltas was not more immediately successful in part because of the recasting of the debate as one on the merits of bankruptcy. That and gradual economic recovery in the first years of the nineteenth century returned debtors' prisons to their core populations—genuine indigents whose debts were as trifling as their assets. These were the debtors ministered to by the Humane Society, which did so with great compassion but without ever questioning whether imprisonment for debt should exist at all.

In that latter tradition of blinkered acceptance was a rival newspaper to the *Forlorn Hope*—the *Prisoner of Hope*, published in New York for nearly four months in 1800 by William Sing, himself once a prisoner for debt. Unlike Keteltas, Sing aspired to a more general readership by offering shipping news, "foreign intelligence" and "domestic occurrences," essays on literary themes, and advertisements. He intended the profits to supplement the funds of the Humane Society, which may explain the timidity with which he addressed the plight of imprisoned debtors. Where Keteltas published vigorous polemics, Sing published dolorous poems bearing such titles as "On observing one of the feathered Songsters warbling his notes on the top of the Prison" and "The Debtor Relieved," the latter of which referred to the mercy or charity of creditors, not to legal reform. Like the Humane Society, Sing never opposed imprisonment for debt. All he aspired to was to "pour a balm of comfort on the aching heart" of imprisoned debtors. He once refused to print a letter on imprisonment for debt because it was "couched in language too severe." Indeed, the only vitriol in the *Prisoner of Hope* was in Sing's attacks on Keteltas for refusing to cede the market and sell Sing the *Forlorn Hope,* which had preceded his paper by six weeks.[66]

The two newspapers swam in different currents of public thinking about debt, insolvency, and imprisonment for debt. Cruelty, deprivation, despair, and death comprised the lot of imprisoned debtors. Keteltas campaigned to banish them altogether; Sing was content simply to mitigate their effect. As we shall see, ideas about the proper place of debt in the dialectic of dependence and independence often reflected similar differences in aspiration. For reformers, of course, the solutions were self-evident. As Joseph Fay wrote, "[t]he prison itself would sooner convince men that imprisonment for debt is morally wrong, than all the logic that could be used on that subject." Therefore, Fay recommended, let "the most obstinate supporter of the present laws by some unforeseen accidents be involved in debt; let some exasperated creditor cast him into the miserable receptacle of debtors." There let him witness "the scenes of riot, drunkenness, debauchery and vice . . . Let him breathe the air of pestilence in summer, and no fire shall cheer him in the blast of winter." Thus imprisoned, he will "subsist on the scattered crumbs of charity, with just strength enough to drag about his emaciated body, and the weight of his miseries shall so exhaust the powers of his mind, that he shall have but just enough intelligence to understand how abject and wretched he is." He may "tell his sufferings to his keeper—but instead of sympathy he shall meet with curses." Finally, "[w]hen experience, the best teacher in the world, shall make him thus acquainted with the subject, . . . let him sit in the legislature on the grand question, to abolish the degrading system of slavery for debt." If he then votes against abolishing imprisonment for debt, "he is not a man but a fiend—he is the inveterate, irredeemable enemy of liberty." The very vividness of Fay's words suggests that by the time he wrote them, ten years after Keteltas campaigned in the *Forlorn Hope*, few people were listening.[67]

❦ 4 ❦

THE IMAGERY OF INSOLVENCY

Says John to his friend, "What is't to be free?"
"Why to live in a country by Congress' decree,
"The nation most free and enlighten'd on earth,
"For liberty here is secur'd from our birth."

John replied, "Is it so? well, we'll see in a crack,"
And without proof of debt, clapp'd a writ on his back;
Had him taken to jail, for the lawyers—he feed 'em,
And there left him to boast of his excellent freedom.

Forlorn Hope (April 19, 1800)

John Pintard was accustomed to celebrating the Fourth of July—"our National birthday," as he called it. He organized what became annual observances in New York and Newark, proudly anticipating that "in the process of time it will become a great national jubilee and distinguished as such in every part of the United States." In 1798, however, he was detained from the festivities by his creditors, at whose instance he had been arrested and confined to jail in Newark. While the town outside the prison walls celebrated with orations and a reading of the Declaration of Independence, Pintard, lacking a copy of the Declaration, made do with reviewing the Constitution in the involuntary privacy of his prison apartment. Later in the day "a complimentary deputation from the Citizens" arrived with a bottle of wine. In their company Pintard drank a few toasts and spun a tale of the celebration he might have organized with his fellow debtors within "the walls of this enchanted castle." He described a procession, of necessity not very long, bearing as its banner "a tatter'd pair of breeches . . . displayed on a constable's staff, with inverted pockets." Atop the staff, in place of a liberty cap—"for Liberty alas! has nothing to do within this walls"—was an empty purse.[1]

Pintard keenly felt the dependence of debt and the anomaly of that dependence in a republican society. In this he was not alone. The masthead of the *Forlorn Hope,* the newspaper published from debtors' prison in New York by William Keteltas, carried an emblem of a black slave clad only in a loincloth, on bended knee, with his hands clasped together and his head tilted upward in an attitude of supplication, chained by the wrists to a white man dressed in a tattered shirt and worn breeches, standing with his head bowed and his hands chained at his waist. Above them curled a banner with the words, "We should starve were it not for the Humane Society." Below them wrapped another banner with the defiant slogan, "LIBERTY SUSPENDED BUT WILL BE RESTORED."

These images evoke themes that sound with particular resonance in the Revolutionary era—themes of dependence and independence, of slavery and freedom. Debt sat uneasily within those pairings. From one perspective, it was the antithesis of republican independence—after all, if liberty and its attendant virtue rested on the independence that came from control of one's property or of the fruits of one's industry, how could one be in debt, yet free? From another perspective, debt represented opportunity, against which insolvency was merely the risk one took as an entrepreneur. Whether from one vantage point or the other, the imagery of insolvency found expression in the antipodean pairings of dependence and independence, slavery and freedom. That expression took one form before the Revolution and a quite different one after, as the nature of indebtedness changed in ways that, when mixed with the rhetoric and ideology of independence, created a new framework for the way people thought about debt and insolvency.

Orphaned as an infant, son of a merchant father, reared by a merchant uncle, Pintard came of age during the Revolution. His inheritance depleted by wartime inflation, he longed to establish his personal independence, but his first efforts were ill-conceived. Early in 1784, when he was twenty-four, Pintard explained to his friend and foster cousin, Elisha Boudinot, ten years his senior, the terms on which he would consider entering a trading partnership with a former Loyalist and prominent dry-goods merchant named Alexander Robertson, who had returned from exile with a plan to form what became the Bank of New York. Full of his own abilities and unschooled in the ways of the business world, Pintard expected Robertson to admit him to partnership for his services only, with but a small capital contribution. With the preening posturing of youth, Pintard declared to Boudinot that "I must decline exposing myself to a dependency which I will never submit . . . nor while within my own power to support myself will I basely stoop to feed on the crumbs that may fall from any rich mans table." For Pintard, independence was a public status as well as a financial one. He confessed to Boudinot his ambition "to become a capital merchant and . . . among the first characters of the place"—"not," he protested, "that I may riot in luxury but that I may have it in my power of being an useful and honorable member of society, and a credit to my name and family."[2] Eager to secure his position even before he had secured his fortune, Pintard pursued the activities and responsibilities expected of prominent citizens. He vigorously promoted the newly formed Tammany Society and was first secretary of the first fire insurance company in New York. He won election first to the Common Council as an assistant alderman and then to the state assembly. He became secretary of the New York Manufacturing Society, rose to leadership in the Masons, and cultivated intellectual opinion as trustee of the New York Society Library, founder of the American Museum, and literary correspondent of figures such as Jeremy Belknap, historian and founder of the Massachusetts Historical Society (the latter perhaps spurred by an idea of Pintard's).[3]

After some early, if modest, success in the East India trade, Pintard's efforts to assure his independence began to unravel in 1790. His letters to Boudinot referred darkly to "hours of gloom and despondence" and "the present bitter draught out of the cup of affliction." The immediate occasion of his distress was, in light of his later circumstances, the ironic one of having stood special bail for a debtor without realizing the extent to which it exposed him to personal liability.[4] Pintard weathered the crisis, but it clarified two personal values to which he clung in the years that followed. One was a religious belief in the redemptive value of adversity. The other was a strong sense of personal honor, with its component concerns for reputation, dignity, and integrity. Together, the two gave Pintard an introspection that, although sometimes Camille-like in its posings, nonetheless led him to record the sentiments and reflections that allow us to explore the mental world of debt and insolvency.

Pintard's greatest, albeit short-lived, commercial success was as a stockbroker, earning commissions by satisfying the speculative urges of investors in public securities through coffeehouse auctions and private sales, initially on his own and then in partnership with Leonard Bleecker, who, in one of those ironic coincidences that in retrospect seem almost a portent, was secretary of the Society for the Relief of Distressed Debtors, popularly known as the Humane Society. It was this path to his dream of financial independence that led Pintard into the employ of William Duer in 1791. Duer was a leading member of the cohort of merchant-speculators—the most prominent of which was Robert Morris—that had mixed public service with private profit in supplying the army and financing the Revolution, Duer as secretary of the Board of Treasury and Morris as superintendent of finance. Unlike Morris, whose desire to do well while doing good compromised but did not outweigh his public contributions, Duer struck a balance in which self-interest always prevailed and public benefit, although often real, was incidental.[5]

After the war Duer moved effortlessly into speculating in depreciated government warrants and certificates—veterans' pay notes and land warrants, state securities and currencies, indents, Loan Office certificates—and from there on to bank scrip, securities of the consolidated national debt, and land, although, like modern investors, he preferred the faster and potentially higher profits of trading in paper, that is, the more volatile game of making money with money. When Pintard joined him as his agent, Duer's principal speculative interest was bank stock and federal government six percents (federal debt instruments funded at 6 percent interest), which he purchased with the proceeds from secured loans and later, when he ran out of collateral, with funds borrowed from investors to whom he gave promissory notes at very high interest. Duer's goal, which he pursued in secret partnership with Alexander Macomb, Walter Livingston, Isaac Whippo, and others, was to corner enough stock and six percents to control the Bank of New York and perhaps the Bank of the United States, which were the depository banks for United States Treasury funds.[6] Duer's thirst for investment capital—a thirst caused by his insatiable appetite for stock and securities—drove him to borrow money at rates as high as 5 percent per month. And when his credit alone was not enough to persuade investors to part with their savings, he borrowed the credit of others by offering notes endorsed by reputedly creditworthy friends, partners, and other associates, Pintard among them. As more than one observer noted, "Usurious interest became frequent and almost fashionable."[7]

Duer's speculations pushed stock prices skyward, feeding the "scripomania" and "bancomania" that quickly engulfed investors large and small. Seduced by the promise of independence apparent in the rapid creation of paper wealth, his investors ranged from wealthy merchants to "shop keepers, widows, orphans, Butchers, carmen, gardners, market women, and even the noted Bawd Mrs. Macarty," all of whom gambled their savings in the curious belief that prices could only rise, never fall.[8] More historically minded observers surveyed the frenzied atmosphere and saw a speculative bubble ripe for bursting. Newspapers filled with references to the still-infamous South Sea Bubble, seventy years and an ocean distant. Although some, like John Adams, thought that "a few bankruptcies" would restore sense to investors, others feared that unrestrained speculation threatened the social and economic foundations of the republic. Seth Johnson, an astute analyst of speculative investment in general and of William Duer in particular, worried about the deranging, addictive effect of "scripomania" on nonmercantile, or amateur, investors. He recognized that the sudden riches realized by some lures others "of all ranks, from those regular habits of business thro' which, the acquirement of property tho' low is certain," enticing them to gamble. "Those who gain, play in hope of more, those

who lose, continue in hope of better fortune." Not only is their "industry
. . . destroyed by their thus neglecting their proper business, but many are
rendered unhappy and discontented." Tradesmen ask if they should continue "in the drudgery of daily and laborious attention to an employment
which gains me but a few dollars, while my neighbor, in one evening, or
with a dash of his pen acquires thousands." To Johnson, such ideas were
"subversive of private industry, happiness, and œconomy, and of consequence injurious to the public welfare." Duer himself understood the allure, even suspecting at one point that Pintard might have succumbed to it
by holding scrip rather than selling it as Duer had instructed. "There is
such a cursed Temptation in this Abominable Scrip," he wrote, "that a
Man's Honesty must be like adamant, to resist the Temptation of making a
Fortune . . . by sacrificing his Principal."[9]

Duer's world, and perforce Pintard's, collapsed around him in March
1792. Stock and securities prices dropped. After months of issuing promissory notes that vastly exceeded his ability to repay, Duer defaulted. Rumors of his debts reached as high as $3,000,000, equal to roughly
$40,000,000 today. William Duer, "the king of the alley," was insolvent.[10]
Driving another nail into his credit, the federal government sued Duer to
force him to account for $240,000 in Treasury funds that were missing ei-
ther because of his sloppy bookkeeping or his embezzlement when he was
secretary of the Board of Treasury, charges that his wiliness and close association with Alexander Hamilton had forestalled for three years.

Duer's failure triggered the first financial panic in American history.
As the bubble of his speculations burst, investors large and small saw their
investments—which for many had been their life's savings—evaporate.
Not surprisingly, they blamed Duer for their ruin. Amid rising threats of
violence, Duer realized that locking himself in his house, while it shielded
him from service of process, did not protect him from creditors who
sought revenge rather than redress. Accordingly, he allowed himself to be
arrested and imprisoned for debt. As Duer's agent, Pintard faced much of
the abuse heaped on his principal. Worse, while aggressively borrowing
investment capital for Duer and his partners, he had endorsed nearly
$1,000,000 worth of their promissory notes, thereby assuming liability for

payment—secondary liability, to be sure, but liability nonetheless. With an astuteness that had failed him when he endorsed the notes in the first place, Pintard now fled New York with his family a step ahead of the sheriff and made his way to Newark, where Elisha Boudinot gave him shelter. Years earlier, Pintard had contemplated removing to Newark "[i]f ever a kind providence should so far bless my honest endeavours as to enable me to retire . . . from the great hurry and bustle of a city life to the calm quiet of a country retreat."[11] Now his "country retreat" was a borrowed house that offered at best an imperfect haven from his creditors.

Assisted by the written promise of twelve prominent residents of Newark to stand bail for him in the event of arrest, Pintard managed to avoid imprisonment for five years. In that time he became a respected member of Newark society—not the highest of accomplishments, perhaps, but still a mark of his continued aspiration to be "an useful and honorable member of society." He entertained and was entertained, joined the militia, served on town committees, organized the Newark Fire Association, and was a founding officer of the Patriotic Society for Promoting Objects of Public Utility, a local betterment society under the auspices of which Pintard helped establish a public market, inspect the county jail, and collect money for yellow fever victims—all smaller-pond equivalents of his civic activities in New York before his fall. However worthy, though, they were scant distraction from Pintard's loss of independence. He yearned in vain for a letter of license, which, by allowing him to conduct business without interference from the creditors who signed, "would extricate me from obscurity . . . and enable me to appear in the world again, before despondency shall have destroyed the energy of my mind and faculties." Instead, unable to earn a living, Pintard's enforced leisure gave him ample time to read and reflect. Always an avid reader, he now became an inveterate diarist, which let him express privately the anguish he tried to conceal from others. The very first entry, which recorded an encounter with a minister he had known in New York, established the tone. The "sight of a respectable fellow citizen who had known me in my more fortunate (I cannot say better) days" left Pintard mute and moved him nearly to tears, but "[b]eing in the public street and amidst a throng of people coming out of church, I was obliged with great difficulty to suppress my feelings." Every subsequent entry reflected the same torment.[12]

Throughout his trials—and trials is how he saw them—Pintard wavered between vilification of his creditors (or, as he wrote in his diary, in defiance of the law of negotiable instruments, "the creditors of Mr. Duer, for I can never own them mine") and, if not quite Christian forgiveness, then Christian forbearance, the two poles linked by a religious sense of persecution. He referred to his creditors as "my adversaries" and railed against their "inhumanity." "The gratification that may arise from distressing me, is the only circumstance that seems to actuate some persons. God forgive them. I hope he will enable me to do so."[13]

Pintard's creditors were not a forgiving lot. Many shared the opinion of Seth Johnson, who, shortly after Pintard fled New York, wrote that "Pintard has gone off, without clearing up his character, and from all appearances he has been a perfect swindler." It was on execution of a judgment won by the most unforgiving of them, a New York merchant and president of the Marine Society named James Farquhar, that Pintard finally entered Newark prison—"this abode of human wretchedness"—in July 1797, barely a week after the Fourth of July celebration in Newark for which he had served on the organizing committee. There he remained until August 6, 1798, when he gained release under the state insolvency act. Two years later Pintard won final discharge of all his debts under the newly enacted federal bankruptcy statute, thus ending "8 yrs. 6 mos. 8 days thraldom."[14]

Near the end of his life, Pintard described the thirteen months of his imprisonment as "the most profitable part of my life, I had access to the best English authors, and read at the rate of fourteen hours the day." While his impaired hearing—allegedly the result of gunpowder explosions from an Independence Day celebration—encouraged his withdrawal into books, Pintard's sanguine recollection·was the luxury of a man whose failure had occurred early in life and who lived long enough to redeem himself. Early in his travails Pintard had remarked upon the happy fortuity of his "turn for books," noting "[h]ow many hours of keen anguish have they beguiled." While in prison he kept two journals, a Reading Diary of reflections on his reading and other matters and a Journal of Studies in which he recorded the number of lines of Greek, Latin, and English verse he read each day, as well as weather observations and other occurrences, not to mention a daily log of his exercise mileage—104 lengths of the prison hall to the mile.[15]

Pintard had a habit of noting "red letter days" in his diaries. The first was Independence Day, which appeared in 1797 as the day on which he was "disagreably interrupted in the celebration" by the writ that sent him to prison. In time, the list included the anniversaries of both his imprisonment (July 15) and his "enlargement from prison" (August 6), as well as his federal bankruptcy discharge (September 17). The practice, which was reminiscent of what David Cressy has described as "a calendar of layers as well as passages" in early modern England, grew from a self-conscious attitude of reflection that was rooted in Pintard's Christian faith. For Pintard, "the anniversary returns which commemorate the events and mysteries of our Holy religion, make a very forcible impression on my mind, and dispose my soul to more than usual attention and devotion." Secular anniversaries made a similar impression, particularly as Pintard grappled with his own loss of independence. By identifying the days in his life when the wheel of fortune took a particularly sharp turn and defining them as "red letter days" to be remarked upon annually, Pintard constructed personal lessons in history, reminders of humility.[16]

To the same end Pintard began a commonplace book several years after his bankruptcy discharge. Despite his return to respectability, he filled it with entries under "Poverty," "Prison," "Creditor," and, most prominently, eighteen passages on the redemptive and character-building effects of "Adversity"—among them a passage from Oliver Goldsmith's *The Vicar of Wakefield*, the protagonist of which was also imprisoned for debt—to remind himself that "Man little knows what calamities are beyond his patience to bear 'till he tries them."[17]

Years of such introspection bred a heightened sensitivity to the inequalities in dependent relations. As a young man during the Revolution, recently graduated from Princeton, Pintard had assisted his uncle, the resident agent to American prisoners of war in British-occupied New York, in visiting the jails and prison ships and distributing food, clothing, blankets, wood, and other provisions to the prisoners. He observed the deprivations of imprisonment. Early in his exile, while he still enjoyed a conditional freedom, he served on a committee in Newark "for the relief of distressed debtors," helping to provide "necessaries for the subsistence" of imprisoned debtors who were without resources of their own. He paid court costs to free a debtor—a stone-cutter who had "served with reputation" as an artillery officer during the war—but asked for anonymity as he did not wish the man's "feelings should be hurt by acknowledging any thanks to me," that is, by acknowledging any further dependence. With these examples fresh in mind, and perhaps with a fearful look into his own future, Pintard wrote in his diary that it was "really an abominable thing that man should be left so much at the mercy of his fellow creature, as the debtor is under the power of the creditor, who may cast him into goal and leave him there to perish." He disparaged the "sanguinary" debt laws of England as feudal in origin, "when the most trifling property of the proud baron was deemed more worthy of protection than the life of his vassal," and exclaimed that "[i]t is high time that the Rights of Man should be something more than a mere catch word."[18]

Later, while awaiting his federal bankruptcy discharge, Pintard read *A Vindication of the Rights of Woman* by the English feminist, Mary Wollstonecraft, "an extraordinary female." First published in England in 1792, Wollstonecraft's *Vindication* was excerpted in various American magazines the same year. Three complete American editions had appeared by 1795. It was, as Rosemarie Zagarri has observed, "the strongest and most reverberant statement of women's rights up to that time." Although he could not "concur with her in sentiments respecting the cohabitation of the sexes," he praised her for "inculcat[ing] precepts of independence, which if adopted, would elevate the female world." To Pintard, Wollstonecraft "vindicates her injured sex from the grovelling, contemptible sensual light in which they are generally considered [by] their tyrants men." "Why," he asked, "should the companion of mans life . . . be viewed only as an object to gratify brutal passion, or the pageant of his table, or the mere superintendent of his household." Instead, echoing Wollstonecraft, "[h]er education ought so to be conducted as to entitle her to his confidence and re-spect." "None but a weak mind need be jealous of improving female edu-cation, which must be attended with important consequences," not the least of which would be that the "intellectual improvement of the female sex, would likewise tend to excite superior emulation among men."[19]

Pintard's striking meditations on the dependence of women were not mere abstractions. In the early years of his exile, his mentions of his wife, Elizabeth Brasher Pintard, dwelt on her circumscribed social activity. He commented on her "becoming fortitude" in the face of what he regarded as "his" adversity when he declined an invitation to a ball in Newark—"a hard sacrifice for my consort who is passionately fond of dancing." While he did "not regret solitude much" for himself, "it is otherwise with my Cara sposa. She has been too much accustomed to gay life and gay com-pany to relinquish their charms without a sigh." In time, he recognized that she retained a freedom he had lost—the freedom to travel without fear of arrest. She became his emissary to his creditors, crossing the Hud-son to New York to negotiate for a letter of license and to persuade credi-tors to withdraw their federal lawsuits so that he could be released from prison if he received a state discharge. She was now his "dear friend and partner" whose "love and duty . . . has wonderfully consoled me thro' every stage of my afflictions." It was with this evolution of his wife's role in mind that, when Pintard read Wollstonecraft's *Vindication* in August 1800, he was moved to make a few extracts "for my dear Mrs. P's perusal." As he did, he reflected with regret on what she might have attained "had she been blest with the advantages of education, possessing natural abili-ties to qualify her for any profession."[20]

Pintard was not the first husband to recommend Wollstonecraft to his wife—Aaron Burr, for one, had done so seven years earlier. Indeed, her work had been widely read and discussed in America for eight years by the time Pintard read it.[21] Moreover, the concept of women's rights—whether political rights or, in Wollstonecraft's formulation, equality of educational opportunity—could not have been new to Pintard. Propertied women en-joyed the franchise in New Jersey for thirty years after independence. Pin-tard was also undoubtedly familiar with, and very likely heard, a Fourth of

July oration by his friend and patron, Elias Boudinot, in 1793, in which Boudinot, then a member of Congress, proclaimed that "[t]he Rights of Woman are no longer strange sounds to an American ear."[22] Nonetheless, Pintard's discovery of Wollstonecraft is striking. Pintard was profoundly conservative in matters of religion and morality. Yet he read Wollstonecraft's *Vindication* sympathetically despite having also read the recent memoir by her husband, whose account of her sexual libertinism dismayed so many of her supporters.

Some men—although not, it seems, Pintard—experienced insolvency as threatening their very masculinity. From his own imprisonment William Duer exhorted his insolvent partner, Walter Livingston, to "[s]ummons your Natural Manliness, and be governed by my advice." When Robert Morris wrote his partner, John Nicholson, that "[w]e must work like *Men* to clear away these cursed Incumbrances," he was reminding himself as well as Nicholson of the gendered implications of not doing so. A creditor, John Hook, confronted those implications directly when he wrote of his debtor confined within the prison limits of King William County in Virginia that "his distress has so unman'd him that he is now incapable of laying any kind of plan to extricate himself." The anonymous author of a pamphlet on insolvency felt compelled to proclaim that, despite insolvency, "We are men—the same as formerly."[23]

For these men, winners and losers alike in the grand game of business enterprise, the gender imagery of failure is inescapable. Some of them read Daniel Defoe. All of them would have recognized his allegorical figure, "Lady Credit," who, as Sandra Sherman has reminded us, embodies "the whimsicality of the market." Lady Credit is passionate, mercurial, seductive. She is, in Defoe's words, "a coy Lass," who "will court those most, that have no occasion for her."

> If you court her, you lose her, or you must buy her at unreasonable Rates; and if you do, she is always jealous of you, and Suspicious; and if you don't discharge her to a Tittle of your Agreement, she is gone, and perhaps may never come again as long as you live; and if she does, 'tis with long Entreaty and abundance of Difficulty.

The personification of credit as an inconstant female figure is emblematic of the fact that, as J. G. A. Pocock has observed, "masculine minds constantly symbolize the changeable, the unpredictable and the imaginative as feminine." In the speculative society so eagerly embraced by Duer, Morris, Nicholson, Pintard, and so many others, Lady Credit stands, again in Pocock's words, "for that future which can only be sought passionately and inconstantly, and for the hysterical fluctuations of the urge towards it." If merchant-speculators saw themselves as bold adventurers, their financial collapse when deserted by Lady Credit—a collapse attended by constricted lives, inability to provide for their families, and ultimately by imprisonment—left them weak, dependent, and thus, as they said themselves, "unman'd."[24]

The feminization of failure notwithstanding, it is impossible to imagine Pintard writing so sensitively about women without the intense experience of his own loss of independence. Not simply an awareness of his dependence, but of having fallen from the grace of independence. Pintard's sense of independence lost—his personal understanding of becoming, as it were, unfree—did not spring fully formed from his first threatened arrest for debt. Rather, it grew during the years he lived at large in Newark, attained its sharpest expression during his imprisonment, and ripened with a certain poignant wisdom after his release.

After his flight from New York, Pintard initially—and self-consciously—continued to fulfill the obligations of citizenship incumbent on independent gentlemen. "There is no man," he wrote after participating in militia exercises, "however humble his situation in life, but has it in his power to benefit society by showing a disposition to discharge all its duties, and thereby encourage others to do the same. This is the essence of Republicanism." Taken with the force of his own example, he wrote that "[a]ctions not words prove the good citizen" and exhorted himself in his diary, "Let us all endeavour more and more to excell in Republican virtues, and elevate the character of a free people, beyond all that the world has yet exhibited." Increasingly, however, the burden of his insolvency forced Pintard to admit his loss of independence. He gradually withdrew into the shelter of his books and his family. By October 1793 his world had constricted even more, as he decided not to risk leaving the county and resolved "not to absent myself from home least some accident, some arrests should turn up again." Shortly afterward, he went into hiding for two weeks to avoid being served with a particularly unwelcome writ. After that experience, during which a "truly mortifying" rumor spread that he had absconded, Pintard found it harder to maintain a facade of independence, whether to himself or others.[25]

That facade crumbled entirely in prison. One would, of course, expect prison to impress upon inmates the loss of their independence. Debtors, however, experienced imprisonment differently from criminals. For them, it was the end of a process that grew increasingly inexorable as their indebtedness turned to insolvency. In the months leading to his confinement in the Prune Street jail in Philadelphia, Robert Morris littered his letters with references to the fate that loomed ever larger before him—"it may not be long before we get among the Prunes," "I suppose you will soon hear of my being in Prune Street," the contents of a letter "point out the road to Prune Street" or "I read Prune Street in every line." Pintard thought of himself as imprisoned even before he was incarcerated. Three months before he took up residence in the Newark jail, he wrote of "my anxiety for enlargement," mused about what he would do "were I at large," wondered when "these pharaohs"—his creditors—"will at length let Israel go," and confessed that he was "solicitous for freedom." For debtors, independence was something they lost gradually rather than in the sudden closing of a prison door behind them. Thus, when Pintard celebrated American independence, it was as one who had watched his own independence slip away through insolvency and who recognized that liberation from prison would not restore it.[26]

Pintard's journal commentary on what he read while in prison is rather less impressive than the breadth of his reading. One critic described his literary analysis as "mundane and devoid of any penetrating insight"; another as "shallow and superficial."[27] His taste was catholic, almost indiscriminate— over 150 novels, histories, biographies, theological tracts, legal treatises, and volumes of plays, poetry, essays, and sermons. Most of Pintard's annotations are quite forgettable, but nine months into his imprisonment, his reading notes took a melancholy turn, with increasing references to his own dependent condition. Upon reading the English poet Ambrose Philips's "Splendid Shilling" with "sympathetic emotion," Pintard copied a long passage. It described a creditor's dun as a "Horrible monster! hated by Gods and men," served by a constable, whose "polluted hands," if clapped on a debtor's shoulder, conveyed him instantly to an "enchanted Castle,"

> Where gates impregnable, and coercive chains,
> In durance strict detain him, till, in form
> Of money, Pallas sets the captive free.

He read Dr. Dodd's "thoughts in prison," taking particular note of the solace Dodd found in books in "the present hour / Of gloomy, black misfortunes"—or, in Pintard's gloss, "the night of calamity against the gloom of despondence"—and of his condemnation of "the cruelty and hardship of intermingling unfortunate debtors with desperate felons." Reading *Hamlet,* where the prince of Denmark wonders, with Pintard's emphasis added,

> Who would bear, the whips and scorns of time,
> The *oppressors* wrong, the proud mans contumely
> The pangs of despised love, the *laws delay,*
> The insolence of office, and the spurns
> That patient merit of the unworthy takes,
> *When he himself might his quietus make*
> *With a bare bodkin?*

Pintard wrote that without his Christian faith he, too, "should more than once have been driven to the brink of suicide."[28]

These strands come together in the remarkable invention with which this chapter began. In his diary for July 4, 1798, Pintard first described the public observance of "our countrys natal day" in Newark—the reading of the Declaration of Independence, the town oration, an address to the young men—all performed "with much decorum on the part of the citizens." By way of contrast, Pintard's imagined celebration was not decorous at all. Indeed, it resembled nothing so much as it did carnival, with the debtors cast as lords of misrule. The commingled and inverted symbols of dependence and independence—the constable's staff, the tattered breeches substituted for a martial banner, the empty purse in place of a liberty cap—define an extraordinary spectacle in which the debtors hailed "the blessings of Freedom" from within "the walls of this enchanted castle," "Where gates impregnable, and coercive chains / In durance strict detain us," the latter image a paraphrase of the Philips poem he had copied two months earlier.[29]

Nowhere in this is there the slightest mockery of independence. Quite the contrary. Pintard's debtors, though dependent, valued independence for themselves individually and collectively for the nation. The objects of the mockery were those who mistook dependence as a reason to deprive debtors of their liberty. Lest anyone miss the point, Pintard apostrophized the tattered breeches, again adapting lines from his recent reading of Philips:

> A Galligaskins that had long withstood
> The winters fury, and encroaching frosts,
> By time subdu'd: what will not time subdue
> *Except relentless creditors.*

Pintard's celebration then turned serious, as he offered a series of "prisoners toasts," each accompanied by a "characteristic sentiment." The first, of course, was to the "22d Anniversary of American Independence." Then came the customary toasts to Congress, the president, and George Washington. The fifth toast was to Congressman Robert Goodloe Harper, "the Creditors and Debtors friend," with thanks "to his well meant, tho' fruitless endeavours to promote a statute of bankruptcy."[30] The sixth was to Congressman Joshua Coit and "the opposers of the Bankrupt bill," whom Pintard mocked with an adaptation of Marc Antony's refrain in *Julius Caesar*, "But, Brutus is an honorable man! / So are ye all, all, honorable men!!!" Then to John Howard, the English prison reformer, followed by one to "the Gaol: that last assylum of the oppressed and distressed."

The ninth and tenth toasts were to "our merciful creditors, God bless them," and to "our vindictive Creditors," with the request that God have mercy on the latter "and incline their hearts to mind this law: Forgive us our debts, as we forgive our debtors." The next pair were to "the Friends who have adhered to us in the hour of adversity" and to "Trencher Friends, the insects of a summers day"—"fat and greasy citizens" who, for "Fashion," gawk at the "poor and broken bankrupt"—followed by one to "our fellow sufferers in the prisons of the United States." The last three were to "Resignation," "Hope," and "the Grave"—the last with a footnote explaining that the prison adjoined a cemetery, the "daily contemplation of which, although it may not cheer the gloom of imprisonment, tends at least 'To teach the captive moralist to die.'" Three volunteer toasts brought up the train—one to John Gifford, "our humane keeper," another to the "sons of glee and harmony wherever assembled to celebrate this auspicious day," and a final one to "LIBERTY, Thou Goddess heavenly bright," with the sentiment that "A day, an hour of virtuous Liberty / Is worth a whole eternity in bondage."

The imagined procession and the toasts were not Pintard's private musings. He gave them to a printer, and they were republished in newspapers and even almanacs and city directories in Newark, New York, and Philadelphia, always under the heading "Newark Prison." Two years later, William Keteltas reprinted them in the first issue of the newspaper he published from the debtors' prison in New York.[31] Pintard's representation of the dependence of debt and the anomaly, indeed the immorality, of that dependence in a republican society thus gained wide circulation, as, one suspects, he intended. Eighteen months later, when Pintard traveled to Philadelphia to discuss the pending bankruptcy bill with its chief sponsor, James A. Bayard, it was as someone whose views on debt and dependence were well known.[32]

Embedded somewhere in those views was one on a dependent relation that Pintard mentioned only once in his public and private writings, but which elsewhere was a staple of writing and thinking about debt, dependence, and imprisonment for debt—namely, slavery. Pintard had appended to his first toast, "the 22d Anniversary of American

Independence," the sentiment "May its next revolution no longer find imprisonment for debt and personal slavery, solecisms, in the chapter of American rights and privileges." Although it had long been a common trope to liken debtors to slaves, Pintard's toast may have been the first published linkage of the abolition of imprisonment for debt with that of slavery. One should not, perhaps, make too much of the connection. After all, Pintard devoted significantly more reflection, albeit privately, to the dependent status of women, yet no one, Pintard included, ever joined calls for ending imprisonment for debt with summonses to improve the condition of women, even as they sometimes expressed business failure or insolvency in terms of being unmanned or more explicitly feminine references. On the other hand, it does appear that Pintard shared a large part of his stay in Newark jail—possibly including the day of the toasts—with a free black barber named David Simpson, who was also imprisoned for debt. However fleeting the reference, Pintard linked debt and slavery.[33]

In the dark but sometimes hopeful period between his release from debtors' prison and his bankruptcy discharge, Pintard designed a heraldic seal for himself. Its device was a palm tree, "whose property it is to surmount every obstacle that impedes its growth," with the motto *"Depressa Resurgo"*—"Bowed low, but I rise again." At the base of the tree lay "the anchor of Hope," with a shield bearing his initials and the further motto "Never Despair." He could not afford to have his design executed, but his "brother cousin," John Marsden Pintard—the cousin with whom he was reared in his uncle's household—had one fabricated in gold and presented it to him "as a Souvenir." After Pintard viewed the seal, he wrote, "Time must discover whether [it] will be characteristic of my fortunes." What mattered to Pintard was independence. It was to independence that he offered the first toast from his prison apartment. It was independence he resolved upon during his bankruptcy proceedings when he surveyed his future prospects, because "[c]ontingencies resulting from dependence on others, are too precarious to build upon." And it was independence that he sought after his bankruptcy discharge when he traveled to New Orleans to

assess the possibility of restoring his fortunes there—dependent, ironically, on letters of introduction from his friends.[34]

When Pintard traveled west in search of his lost independence, he
was following what was already an American tradition. Westward migration had been a part of American settlement from the beginning, when it
referred simply to New England west of Boston. Both the nature and scale
of westward movement changed dramatically after the Seven Years' War
removed the French and weakened their Indian allies as barriers to migration. Settlers poured across the Appalachians in mass defiance of the
Proclamation of 1763, which would have kept them east of the mountains.
Smelling profit, speculators formed land companies to lay claim to hundreds of thousands of acres and try to appropriate—they would have said
facilitate—the dreams of individual settlers by selling them land that in
many instances they were already working. British efforts to hold the
Proclamation Line by refusing to renew preliminary land grants to speculators or to ratify new ones and by limiting the establishment of government institutions in the backcountry had the unintended consequence of
encouraging illegal settlement by shielding squatters and making the region even safer for absconding debtors.[35] Prompted by the desire for land,
these early migrations produced the pattern of widespread land ownership
that, by the eve of the Revolution, defined America for many observers
and created the image of a free and virtuous yeomanry on which republican theorists rested both their calls for independence and their arguments
for the structure and government of the new nation.

For all that, traveling west was never more closely associated with independence than it was in the decades after the Revolution. The economic
dislocations of the 1780s and 1790s created large numbers of debtors who
saw opportunity in the West and who, more important, were now armed
with a vocabulary of independence to describe what they were seeking.
Even men whose pursuit of opportunity was not driven by debt linked the
West with independence. To take just one example, Jean-Baptiste Charles

Lucas emigrated from France in 1784, became John B. C. Lucas, and bought a small plantation on the banks of the Monongahela River near Fort Pitt in western Pennsylvania on the recommendation of Benjamin Franklin's son-in-law, Richard Bache, who advised him that land there was much cheaper than near Philadelphia. Within three years Lucas was writing panegyrics to the independent farmer. To one correspondent he wrote, "[t]he cultivator here enjoys his natural rights." Unlike in France, the farmer "is not condemned . . . to work all his life to satisfy the ostentation and fancies of the grand seigneurs, the intrigues and debauchery of the young clergy, the idleness and gluttony of the monks, the greediness and molestations of the financiers. In a word, he is not obliged to support his oppressors." Instead, he works "for himself and his family," and "all are alike as to the independence of their persons and of their lands."[36]

Lucas's example notwithstanding, the westward propulsive effect of debt cannot be overstated. Even when not trying to escape liability, more than one Virginia gentleman-planter took stock of his finances, assessed the mounting debts and sinking resources, and concluded that he could live comfortably at less expense in Kentucky. The lists of Virginia debtors compiled for British creditors after the Revolution to assist them in collecting pre-war debts under the terms of the peace treaty recorded that debtor after debtor had "gone to Kentucke" or, even more tellingly, was "presumed gone to Kentucke," as though the mere fact of a debtor's absence created a presumption of flight across the mountains. Private correspondence paints the same picture. James Mercer, whose father had once run a newspaper advertisement chastising his fellow planters for not paying the legal fees they owed him, urged his half-brother to sue for their debts quickly, for "[t]he Debtors will be gone to Kentucke very soon and good bye to all their Debts due here." Jonathan Meredith's agent in central Pennsylvania reported that a debtor had left town to avoid Meredith and his other creditors, and that his friends "either know not, or pretend to know not, where he is gone—either to Kentucke or South Carolina."[37] In Kentucky and wherever else they migrated, these debtors did not live as outlaws. They settled towns, opened stores, carved farms out of the wilderness, built plantations, bought slaves, traded, voted, socialized, worshiped, married, reared children, and died. Rather, they lived outside the practical reach of all but the most determined creditors. By uprooting their families and moving to distant places, they were trying to create the fresh start in life that would have been theirs had there been a bankruptcy law in force to discharge their debts. Since there was not, they substituted distance for discharge.

For some, the trans-Appalachian West was the second or third stop in their efforts to secure independence. Peregrine Foster, the aptly named youngest son of a politically prominent western Massachusetts family, first sought his fortune in the late 1780s in Rhode Island, where his two older brothers had attended college and where Theodore, the oldest, remained well-connected. However, the "unforeseen Revolution in Favour of Shayism and Wickedness" in the state "proved extremely unfortunate" to him. As his brother Theodore observed, "[t]his Wicked Paper Money System has the Property of Stripping a Man of all his Earnings after a Life of Industry, and vesting the Means of his subsistence in the Hands of Idlers, or Sharpers." Unable to pay his own debts, Peregrine found it increasingly difficult to collect the debts due him, even in depreciated paper currency, in part because of state debtor-protection measures but also because of anticreditor sentiment that one who sued to collect a debt "is only fit to fill the gibit, grace the Halter or be tarred and feathered."[38]

As Foster sank deeper into financial distress, he wrote his brother Dwight in Massachusetts that he wished "to live to see my Family more independent . . . than they now are." He resolved to go west and begin again in the Ohio valley. Debt was the cause: "My Business heretofore joined with a benevolent Disposition and too much confidence in the Honesty of those with whom I dealt perplexes me with the Collection or rather with an attempt to collect from a large number of People a small sum of Money heretofore dearly earned." His family tried to change his mind—his mother dispatched Dwight from Boston to dissuade him by arguing "the Dangers, the Inconveniencies, the Distresses the Losses he must probably suffer" and "the Immorality of exposing his defenceless Family"—but he remained firm: "I cannot tarry here and see myself exposed to Poverty and of consequence Infamy and neglect." In "the Western Territory . . . there will be

Doors open to Business of Importance to industrious enterprising and capable Men." Ironically, when Foster did resettle in the West—he got as far as Morgantown, in what is now West Virginia, before moving on to Ohio four years later—he found that his ability to join others who were "making Independent Fortunes" was inhibited by his "aversion to purchasing on credit." Years afterward, he was still entreating his brothers for assistance, but with his faith in the West undiminished, as "the only one who will hand the Name of the Family to future generations in a part of America which will . . . eventually form a very important part in the American History."[39]

Some who went west to restore their independence, like Foster, went with their families, intending to stay. Others, like Pintard, went alone, expecting to bring independence back with them from the frontier. One such pilgrim was Jonathan Wallace of Carlisle, Pennsylvania. Wallace had watched his "handsome" estate diminish "day after day" under the onslaught of executions occasioned by sureties he had given, until it was "in danger of being totally swallowed up." His family was "threatened with poverty and ruin." To secure them "against these impending evils, and if possible fulfill my engagements, and do justice to my creditors," he left his family "to shift for itself" and went to Kentucky. Eleven months there restored "the shattered remains" of Wallace's finances. He returned home to Carlisle, "bringing along with me considerable sums of money," and felt himself, once again, "a native freeman of America." Independence was fleeting. Another creditor arrested Wallace and held him in close confinement in the Cumberland County jail, where he felt the "stinging and poignant sensations which the iron hand of my oppressor and this horrid situation, were calculated to excite." Three months later Wallace regained the freedom that he so recently thought he had recouped by signing all of his property over to his creditor, "whose avidity and rapacity was now completely gratified, and after stripping me of all my estate, turned me naked among my enemies." Freedom, however, was not independence.[40]

The image of debtors as slaves was a common one before the Revolution, although almost exclusively in the tobacco regions of the

Chesapeake. For the most part, northern writers limited themselves to vague, metaphoric homilies such as the one Benjamin Franklin gave Poor Richard, "The Borrower is a Slave to the Lender, and the Debtor to the Creditor," or the passing observation by an anonymous Connecticut author that without a bankruptcy discharge an insolvent debtor "is Nothing but a Slave to his Creditors"—both of which, albeit pungently expressive, were nonetheless far removed from the stark imagery after the Revolution of the masthead emblem of the *Forlorn Hope*. In the plantation South, on the other hand, the immediacy of slavery made the image a vivid one, although in its own way it, too, was removed from William Keteltas's depiction.[41]

The great planters of the Virginia tidewater were an exceptionally self-possessed lot. With their exaggerated sense of their own independence and entitlement, they came closer than any class in America ever did to replicating an English gentry. Complete personal independence was the social ideal to which all planters aspired. So thoroughly did they do so, and so thoroughly did aspiration replace reality, that even a man as astute as St. George Tucker could look back long after events had proven him wrong and insist that "there was no such thing as Dependence, in the lower counties." One of the grand ironies of the period is that it was the tobacco planters who proclaimed their independence most ardently yet who were most deeply enmeshed in debt, for it was on the shoals of debt that their self-image of independence foundered.[42]

The problem was tobacco. Tobacco did not simply dominate the tidewater economy; it defined every significant element of life—the economy, the labor system, social relations and social structure, patterns of settlement, commercial life, government, identity, and more.[43] For our purposes, the two most important qualities of tobacco were that its cultivation required slave labor and that the length of time from planting to shipping was fifteen months. The former held forth an ever-present example of lifelong, hereditary dependence; the latter created the condition of perpetual indebtedness that planters instinctively analogized to slavery.

For much of its history in the tidewater, tobacco promised lavish profits. However, each year's crop had to be planted before the previous year's harvest had even been shipped for sale, let alone produced any return. The result was a gap in time between expense and income that was bridged by credit extended by the British merchants to whom the planters sold their tobacco. Tidewater planters thus always made purchases in anticipation of future profits. As their habits of consumption increased to keep pace with their self-image, their anticipations grew as well. This was supportable as long as profits increased, but tobacco prices declined steadily from the 1750s on with only occasional upticks. The great planters, who had constructed their entire world around the intricacies of tobacco culture, were too enmeshed in that culture to change. Their debts with British merchants grew longer and larger. When international financial crises in the 1760s and 1770s compelled the merchants to call in long-standing debts, the effect on the great planters was cataclysmic.[44]

Debtors and creditors in the Chesapeake—or, more precisely, Chesapeake debtors and their local and foreign creditors—lived in a state of mutual dependence possible only in a highly leveraged economy, where the fortunes of borrowers and lenders were so thoroughly intertwined that they often seemed more like partners. In commercial economies the road to wealth lies through credit. The road to ruin lies through debt. The enduring problem is that the two roads are identical until they diverge—a fork that is visible only in retrospect, and often only after it is too late to go back. Debt was a constant companion of the successful and unsuccessful alike; few planters after 1660 managed to avoid it. Planters purchased slaves with promises to pay for them at a future date. They shipped tobacco to British merchants on the understanding that the payment they ultimately received would be based on the market value of the tobacco when it arrived. They bought supplies and consumer items from British merchants and local traders by promising to pay for them with anticipated future profits. For many local transactions, including paying taxes, they used tobacco crop and warehouse receipts as a circulating medium, in denominations that reflected the amount of tobacco they had stored awaiting shipment to Europe. They bought tobacco from and resold goods to lesser planters who did not have their access to British markets, with all parties exchanging promises as well as goods. The flow of commodities, goods, and slaves within the Chesapeake and across the Atlantic thus rode on debt—that is, on promises that were, at least in theory, legally enforceable. There were other promises as well—promises to consign tobacco of a certain fine grade to one merchant-creditor rather than another, or to use cash for paying debts rather than buying slaves. These promises, however, were executory, which is to say unenforceable. Whatever force they had was moral rather than legal. Considering the pervasiveness of promises both enforceable and unenforceable, one young tobacco trader observed bitterly that "this may properly [be] called the Land of Promis without any intension of Performing."[45]

Debt, which had always been endemic to the plantation economy, mushroomed after about 1740, spreading beyond the great planters and reaching deeper into the social structure, trends that accelerated as the Revolution approached.[46] Reasons for the mounting indebtedness were varied. Droughts in 1755 and 1758 crippled tobacco crops. Prices rose because of the diminished supply but not enough to compensate planters with little or no tobacco to sell. Whenever the overall decline in tobacco prices was interrupted by a temporary increase, planters borrowed to buy more land and the slaves to work it, thereby expanding production and driving down the prices they had hoped to profit from—a consequence the House of Burgesses tried to prevent by levying and then raising a duty on imported slaves in attempts to limit production and debt by restricting the size of the labor force.[47] The near-absence of cash in the colony forced people to conduct even routine transactions on credit, thus driving up the effective cost of every purchase. Even failures did little to reduce indebtedness—the scarcity of cash limited the number of bidders and kept prices low when debtors' property was levied upon and sold at auction, leaving sizable deficiencies for which the debtors remained liable. Arching over all of these factors was the increasing, and increasingly insatiable, appetite for consumer goods—dubbed "luxuries" by those who disapproved of them.

The "consumer society" that emerged in England in the eighteenth century quickly spread to America. Imports of British manufactured items increased dramatically to all colonies, where they percolated throughout the social structure and even to the frontier, especially after the defeat of the French allowed people to think less of survival and more of comfort. Although the consumption of luxury goods rose throughout the colonies, the increase in—and consequently the burden of—consumer debt was particularly large in Virginia. There the great planters adopted an ethos of consumption as part of their self-presentation as an Anglicized country elite, and lesser planters emulated greater ones—all resting on the unstable foundation of a single export crop that was itself a luxury good, albeit an addictive one. Indeed, so completely did the purchase and display of luxury goods come to define their social identity that planters rarely curtailed their expenditures even as they slid toward insolvency. To have done so would have signaled their weakness to their creditors. More important, it would have been an insult to their honor, which required them to live large—graciously, to be sure, but large. Frugality was not a southern virtue.[48]

To complicate matters further, debt in Virginia was as much cultural as economic. The tidewater gentry before the Revolution perceived commercial relations with British merchants in highly personal terms. To the gentry, exchange was not merely an economic relationship. It was a form of "friendship" that summoned into play a planter's honor, virtue, and independence. Among themselves Virginia planters regarded extending credit, either directly or in the form of personal guarantees, as a gentleman's obligation. So deep did the sense of obligation run that John Robinson, speaker of the House of Burgesses and colony treasurer for nearly thirty years and to all appearances as wealthy as he was generous, seems never to have declined a request for a loan. When he died in 1766, the administrator's list of debtors of his estate—250 names in all—comprised a veritable social register of the planter elite. However, unbeknown to anyone, Robinson had performed his social duty with public funds. Over £100,000 of his "friendly" loans came from the provincial treasury, which, like his estate and many of his debtors, was now insolvent.[49]

Robinson's generosity was extreme, but whether large or small, credit among southern planters and gentlemen represented a form of patronage, and it was accompanied by an etiquette of debt that rested on complex perceptions of honor and personal autonomy. This oddly stylized understanding of local exchange relationships was grounded in values that were constitutive of the great planters' world. Perhaps the tidewater planters may be forgiven, then, for projecting those same local meanings onto their transactions with British merchants as a way of putting faces on distant markets and making them conform to local assumptions. The planters transformed their British correspondents into men who understood the meaning of honor and independence and who were as committed as they to constructing an ideal of reciprocal commercial friendships. Needless to say, this was not an image of themselves that the British tobacco merchants would have recognized. By constructing their transatlantic commercial relations in such intensely personal terms, tobacco planters were ill-prepared to understand how their spiraling purchases of consumer goods, the internationally disruptive economic consequences of the Seven Years' War, and falling tobacco prices could leave them so vulnerable. All they knew was that they felt betrayed when British merchants called in their debts, thereby shattering their treasured self-image of independence and demonstrating to them that the image had been an illusion and that they were, in fact, dependent.[50]

Virginia planters had feared that debt would be the vehicle of their dependence. For example, when the Virginia assembly in 1758 authorized the issuance of paper notes that would circulate as legal tender, London merchants complained vigorously to the Lords Commissioners for Trade and Plantations. Their protest brought to the surface sentiments that clearly had been roiling underneath. Peyton Randolph, the attorney general and one of the most influential men in the colony, published a response to the merchants' memorial in the form of a letter from Virginia. He admitted that Virginians were indebted to the merchants "in large Sums of Money" and continued in the following extraordinary passage:

We have had many of us for some Time past, great Reason to own the Thing is unhappily true in the first Instance, of our being indebted. Unhappily in as much as the Generality of Creditors are a Kind of lording Tyrants over their unfortunate Debtors, notwithstanding the undoubted Securities pledged, and the annual tribute paid in, of a very high tho' lawful Interest. And to this we do attribute . . . the Growth of many Innovations and arbitrary Charges . . . that have been and are every now and then brought to Account to keep the poor Dogs of Debtors deep in their Books, and render the Redemption of their Freedom impossible, by thus lowering the Produce of their Commodity, that they may continue under the Obligation of sending it to them alone, thro' Fear of more apparent Persecutions.

Here we have, in brief compass, every idea associated with debt that circulated in Virginia before the Revolution—dependence, servitude, tyranny, and, ultimately, the explanation that the growing burden of debt was rooted in a mercantile conspiracy. Thus, when Robert Beverley learned in 1764 that his principal British correspondent was tightening credit, he protested that "I dread very Much from the Appearances of this Day that [Virginia] will be condemned forever to a state of Vasalage and Dependance." Thomas Jefferson, after the Revolution, still believed that British tobacco merchants had conspired to deprive planters of their liberty by enticing them with credit, ensnaring them in debt, and then dropping tobacco prices until the debts became "hereditary from father to son, for so many generations, so that the planters were a species of property, annexed to certain mercantile houses in London."[51]

The overwhelming dependence of the Virginia economy on a single export crop made Virginians singularly vulnerable to the financial demands of their British creditors. The vulnerability became even greater in the 1760s when the Glasgow merchants that controlled much of the tobacco trade established stores in the Chesapeake from which their factors took over local tobacco purchases and sale of imported goods, thereby giving local arms to once-distant creditors. Thus, when British mercantile firms, bankers, and investors came under pressure, as they did in the financial crises of 1763 and 1772, their distress quickly spread to Virginia as British lenders shut off credit and called in their debts.[52] When their debtors did not pay—which they could not since wealth in the Chesapeake was embodied in land, slaves, and consumer goods rather than cash—

British creditors empowered their local agents to sue, which they did with a vengeance, or so it seemed to the debtors. British merchants began dunning their Virginia debtors at roughly the same time as Parliament imposed the Stamp Act and other unpopular and seemingly repressive duties. In such a charged atmosphere, private grievances merged with public ones—indeed, they seemed to arise from the same conspiracy—and the language of one spilled over to the other. By the early 1770s, as parliamentary efforts to raise revenue from the colonies continued and the insistent demands of British creditors spread deepening distress, planters conflated the debate over constitutional rights and liberties with that over private indebtedness. Their newly recognized financial dependence lent a personal context to country idioms of political discourse—power, bondage, liberty, rights, virtue, independence—investing them with even greater emotional intensity than they carried on their own.[53]

The loss of independence that attended their indebtedness gave planters an unwonted, and doubtless frightening, kinship with the slaves who produced the tobacco that had long been the source of their credit, both personal and financial. Some of their creditors were crude enough to remind them of the likeness, such as the young Scottish merchants in Norfolk who on election day in 1755 chose as their own mayor a slave named Will, and "seated him and drank to him as Mr. Mayor by way of Derision." But Virginia debtors, who could write of themselves as reduced to "Vasalage and Dependance," did not need others to remind them of the implications of their indebtedness.[54] Although planters probably could never make the cognitive leap required to imagine themselves as slaves, they clearly felt enslaved, both by their British creditors, whose duns threatened their personal liberty, and by Parliament, whose duns threatened their political liberties. Hence the spectacle, so anomalous to modern sensibilities as well as to contemporary British observers, of slaveholders denouncing British conspiracies to reduce them to slavery.

To be sure, slavery metaphors were not the exclusive preserve of slaveholders. Northern writers, too, could invoke the specter of British enslavement. John Adams, writing anonymously at the height of the Stamp Act crisis, proclaimed "We won't be their Negroes," and argued that

Providence never intended the colonists "for Negroes . . . and therefore never intended us for slaves."[55] But for Adams and most other northern writers, slavery was less immediate, even though the northern colonies were hardly free of slaves. For southerners it was a personal reality and an economic necessity. Thus, when the pseudonymous "An American" attacked parliamentary taxation in the *Virginia Gazette,* he wrote as a slaveholder addressing an audience of slaveholders, referring to "our masters in Britain," who were "as indulgent to us as we are to our poor slaves," and to British mercantilists turning Americans into "the slaves of Britain." These denunciations derived their personal immediacy to the tobacco-planting gentry from debt, which had already demonstrated to them how men who prized their independence above all else could be rendered dependent. Virginia planters did not rebel because they were in debt, but their indebtedness brought home to them the intolerable prospect of a dependence they had previously associated only with slaves.[56]

The problem of planter indebtedness did not, of course, disappear with national independence. The peace treaty expressly provided that British creditors would be able to pursue their pre-war debtors in American courts without hindrance and with no suspension of interest for the years of hostilities. Independence did not lift the fear of dependence from the planters. James Mercer, for one, invoked the image of "an army of Brittish Creditors" unleashed on America by the treaty and, betraying a gentry perception of how much property one needed to be independent, complained that "[a] man with only one thousand pounds in possession, may be free and independant, and refuse a thousand pounds and more. But if this Man is liable to lose the thousand pound, his all, to a Creditor, he then is at the mercy of his Creditor for his existance." Thomas Jefferson, for another, cautioned the wife of a young planter against taking credit from tobacco importers, because "long experience has proved to us that there never was an instance of a man's getting out of debt who was once in the hands of a tobacco merchant."[57]

Amid the planters' affirmations after the Revolution of their independence and their anxiety about losing it to their creditors, one thing is missing. No longer did they routinely liken the dependence of debt to slavery.

Instead, they retreated from the full implications of the argument they had used so freely before the Revolution. There were, of course, exceptions. Jefferson's famous comment in 1786, quoted above, that planters' debts were "hereditary from father to son . . . so that the planters were a species of property, annexed to certain mercantile houses," was redolent with slave imagery. It invoked the hereditary servitude of slaves, who legally were a "species of property" and as such were "annexed" to the land— indeed, in some states they were land, classified as real property. Of course, as Jefferson well knew, both as a lawyer and from bitter personal experience, debts became "hereditary" only when the debtor's heirs vol- untarily agreed to pay them; otherwise they extended only as far as what- ever assets the debtor left behind. His own lifelong struggle with debt had begun in 1774 when, as an executor of the estate of his father-in-law, John Wayles, he distributed the estate to the heirs—of which his wife Martha was one—before Wayles's creditors were repaid, thereby making himself liable for the debts. One can, of course, question the degree of volition in- volved when heirs could inherit land and slaves to which they were enti- tled and on which they relied for wealth and status only by assuming liability for debts that would otherwise have to be satisfied by selling off that selfsame land and slaves. For the most part, however, when, to borrow John Pintard's phrase, "the Rights of Man" became "something more than a mere catch word," slaveholders abandoned the imagery of slavery to ex- press the loss of independence that accompanied debt. Imprisoned debtors in the North, on the other hand, found the imagery compelling and took it as their standard.

The masthead emblem of the *Forlorn Hope* forcefully propels one into the intertwined themes of dependence and independence, slavery and freedom. One of the charges William Sing hurled against Keteltas in their brief press war was that Keteltas had squandered start-up capital for the *Forlorn Hope* by borrowing money "to pay for the frontispiece, where you have chained a black and white man together." Nothing in Sing's com- plaint explicitly criticized the pairing, although one might infer implicit criticism from the fact that it was the only reference to slaves or slavery Sing ever made in his newspaper. Keteltas, however, chose to treat Sing's objection as racial rather than financial. He replied that the law, not he, "chained a white and black man together." The emblem "is only a representation of the fact, that the law has indiscriminately confined the African and American in one common goal for debt." Reminding Sing of his own imprisonment for debt, Keteltas opined that "you have had your pride mortified as a man of wealth, to be confined with a poor negro." He proclaimed his conviction that "crimes and dishonor are not to be found in the color of a man's skin, but in the baseness of his heart, and wicked actions of his life."[58]

Keteltas had no qualms about making explicit a connection that hitherto had largely been implicit, and that certainly had never been rendered so graphically. Against the arresting imagery of the masthead emblem, the opening statement of Keteltas's declaration of editorial purpose in the inaugural issue—"The love of liberty is the strongest passion of the human soul"—almost pales.[59] Yet slavery and imprisonment for debt were inseparable, as the banner wrapped beneath the emblem with the slogan "Liberty suspended but will be restored" proclaims. The slogan did not curl around only one of the two chained figures. It embraced both. For Keteltas, liberty was a condition into which all men were or should be born, and to which all had a right to return.

The *Forlorn Hope* was unique.[60] Through satire, letters, reprinted excerpts, serialized columns, poems, anecdotes, and editorials, Keteltas deployed the imagery of slavery and dependence in a sustained attack on imprisonment for debt. The passion of his attack left no room for subtlety. For example, he printed a petition to Parliament from "the Sharks of Africa," who were incidental beneficiaries of the British trade in slaves. The sharks hovered around the slave ships, "these floating dungeons," and were "frequently gratified with rich repasts from the bodies of living negroes, who voluntarily plunge into the abodes of your petitioners, preferring instant destruction by their jaws to the imaginary horrors of a lingering slavery." They expressed their "utmost indignation" that some voices were calling for abolition of the trade, as well as their confidence that Parliament "will not suffer sharks to starve in order that negroes may be happy." To which Keteltas added the following debtors' gloss:

Blessed be the man! whose pencil drew
So strong a picture and so true—
The captive black, to grief a prey,
In anguish wastes his hours away,
From joys domestic rudely torn,
Compell'd his hapless fate to mourn
In fell despair—a picture dark!
Becomes thy prey—*despotic Shark!*
Sad emblem of our wretched fare,
Condemn'd a despot's pow'r to bear;
Alike our griefs—alike our case—
Let Shylock hold the fish's place,
We too, oft find, a gloomy grave:
For both alike, disdain to save.[61]

Keteltas wrote of debtors and their plight in terms that echo deeply in the literature of antislavery. Images abound of the absolute power of the creditor and of heartless creditors tearing families apart, images that require the reader only to substitute "master" for "creditor" to be transported into the world of plantation slavery. Keteltas argued that it was "an insult to common sense to say that we are a free people . . . when the law gives absolute power to one individual over another's life and liberty." He condemned "this feudal system of severity." He wrote that government had "left the debtor at the sole disposal of the creditor, subject to his caprice, folly, and vengeance." He printed the last will and testament of a debtor, who instructed his executors to sell his mortal remains to surgeons and lend the proceeds at interest to pay his debts—if, of course, his creditors consent, because his "body . . . by a law of this state, is the property of my creditors." He described the debtor "torn from the arms of an affectionate wife, and driven, in fetters, fifteen or twenty miles like an ox to the slaughter." He wondered if "the malignant creditor" could comprehend "the ruin and wretchedness" he caused when he "tear[s] a man from his family . . . and the tears of his wife and children are falling at your feet" and asked, "After depriving the wife of a husband, and the children of a father, what is their chance in a cold and hostile world?" He published the plaintive petition of two children to a creditor, begging him to liberate their father; their mother has died of a broken heart, and they cannot but acknowledge the creditor's "absolute power over [their father's] life, liberty, and property."[62]

The warmth of Keteltas's argument came in part from his anger at the gulf he saw between political aspiration and practice. He invoked the guarantee of the Declaration of Independence to life, liberty, and the pursuit of happiness, and asked "whether it would not be more just, humane, and beneficial to the debtor, the creditor, and the state also, to dispose of the debtor's person as a slave, the neat proceeds of such sale to be appropriated to the creditor." He printed the preamble to the New York state constitution, which also began with a claim of self-evident truths "that all men are created equal" and "are endowed by their Creator, with certain unalienable rights," alongside the text of the state statute permitting imprisonment for debt and pointedly asked how they could be reconciled.[63]

For Keteltas, the key was the meaning of independence. Like Pintard, he observed the Fourth of July. However, he never mentioned the day without a certain ruefulness. He reprinted Pintard's toasts and imagined debtors' procession in his first issue. Three months later he offered another story, of "a Countryman full of amor patria," who on the Fourth of July, "looking for some political society to keep the festive day, accosted a gentleman not full in the belief of the republicanism of the government of this state," and asked, "Pray, Sir, can you inform me where the republican societies meet, to celebrate the day?" The gentleman spied the "American flag then flying on the top of the debtors prison, (Oh what a burlesque)," and saw "a fortunate opportunity to set the man to reflecting," so he pointed him to the jail. The "countryman blind with enthusiasm, never perceived the grates, but took the goal to be a hotel, thanked the gentleman, and in great haste set off to celebrate the freedom and independence of 130, American citizens, confined for debt—

> Who fought and bled in freedom's cause,
> Who fought and bled in freedom's cause;
> And when the storm of war was gone,
> Enjoy'd a goal their valor won:—
>   Hail! Columbia, happy land.[64]

The closing verse suggests the bitter irony of independence for Keteltas. The immorality of imprisonment for debt was never greater than when the debtor was someone "who fought and bled in freedom's cause." Keteltas made the debtor whose will asked that his remains be sold an "old American Officer" who had sacrificed his fortune and risked his life in the Revolution, "supposing my country was about to be inslaved." For all he had given in "founding the American republic," he now hoped that his children will never inherit "all the advantages I have gained by my sacrifices." He left as his final wish that imprisonment for debt be abolished and debtors enjoy the liberty for which "the blood of our fathers was shed to secure to us and our posterity." In another instance, warning that "the period is not far distant, when we shall retain little more than the name and shadow of liberty in America," Keteltas wrote, "If you wish to see the virtuous patriot and soldier, who purchased the freedom and independence of his country with his blood, examine the hospitals, alms-houses, goals, and the public streets, where you will behold this ruined and despised class of citizens, swindled out of their pittance, by those to whom they looked for justice."[65]

Keteltas summoned the imagery of dependence and independence, of slavery and freedom, so frequently and so insistently that one is surprised to realize that he expressly joined the abolition of imprisonment for debt with that of slavery only twice in the six months the paper lasted. Once was the fleeting reference in Pintard's toast to "the 22d Anniversary of American Independence—May its next revolution no longer find imprisonment for debt and personal slavery, solecisms, in the chapter of American rights and privileges." The other was only slightly longer, but it made up in elegance and simplicity what it lacked in length. It appeared, appropriately, in the weekly issue that fell closest to Independence Day:

> Posterity will wonder, as the savage nations do, that a man should be confined because he could not pay his debts. That a law should have remained so long after we were separated from the British government, is still more astonishing—a law repugnant to reason, religion, and liberty. I flatter myself a few revolving years will bring about the emancipation of the African, until which, we cannot, with propriety, claim pre-eminence as the most free and enlightened nation.

The anonymous author of that passage—perhaps Keteltas—prefaced it with the statement "Imprisonment for Debt, I never believed consistent with a state of civil society, much less that high and improved state which republicanism contemplates." Herein lies the significance of the imagery of insolvency in the early republic—its place in "that high and improved state which republicanism contemplates."[66]

Much of what Keteltas wrote was, of course, polemical invention. Nor do we know anything of his possible encounters with blacks in jail—free or slave—other than the tantalizing fact that at one time "several negroes," who may or may not have been debtors, lodged among the merchants and skilled artisans on the middle hall of the New Gaol "to keep the place clean and light the Lamps."[67] The truth or accuracy of what he wrote are not germane to its importance. He was, to my knowledge, the only writer who, in comparing imprisoned debtors to slaves, intended to condemn slavery as well as imprisonment for debt rather than invoking the comparison simply to illustrate the debasement of imprisoned, and presumably hitherto free, white debtors. Examples of the latter use abound and grew naturally from long-standing associations of the dependence of debt with enslavement. For postwar pamphleteers such as Hugh Williamson, who announced that by indulging in foreign luxuries on credit "we are little better than slaves, degraded by national bankruptcy,

. . . constantly labouring in the soil for the benefit of another empire," slavery was the depth to which debtors should not sink. Others who inveighed against imprisonment for debt, rather than against the moral and political dependence of a nation of debtors, also summoned the specter of slavery solely to argue the injustice of subjecting debtors to the indignity and debasement of imprisonment. Joseph Fay railed against legislatures that valued liberty so little they permitted "a single exasperated creditor" to "treat his debtor worse than a criminal, confine him to a filthy cell, . . . thus actually purchasing . . . the positive, but *useless* slavery of a free citizen.—Slavery! not for a day, or a year—but for life!" Even writers who sought to describe the plight of unimprisoned insolvent debtors borrowed the imagery of slavery. Freeing debtors from prison but not from their debts "is worse than slavery! It is a mockery of liberty, the name, without the essence!" Creditors should not have "the power . . . to decide on the freedom or slavery of a debtor."[68]

With or without slavery, the imagery of insolvency was dependence. Witness the cautionary words of advice offered to Duer by a fellow debtor in Baltimore early in 1792, with their recognition that a man's entrepreneurial strivings for independence carried with them the risk of dependence:

From ill-placed Confidence I have been steeped in Poverty to the very lips, I have borne the proud Man's Contumely, and the oppressor's wrong; I have felt scorn, and Contempt; and even Insult with Impunity. In this State Poverty is one of the Greatest of Crimes, and of that offense I have been convicted above Seven long years . . . I hear of your prosperity, and rejoice at it. I know the activity of your Soul, and fear your Views, and Schemes are boundless. If Reports are true, that you have secured a Plumb, I sincerely wish, that you would set limits to your Desires. If you had drank deep, as I have done, of the bitter Cup of adversity, you would never Risk Independance again. May the voice of freindship take the liberty to intreat you to stop in time; and sit down, with so ample an Independance, in peace of Mind, and Body!

For Duer, the entreaty came too late. Within two months he was confined in the same prison from which Keteltas later published his newspaper. He remained there for seven years, leaving only to die in the nominal freedom of the prison limits. Keteltas, who published numerous death notices of real and apocryphal debtors, mentioned Duer's death at least twice. Duer's loss of independence, including the ultimate loss, thus became, literally, the stuff of *Forlorn Hope.*[69]

❧ 5 ❧

A SHADOW REPUBLIC

Q. Suppose you are a sensible, pious and moral man, and have no money, and are indigent, what will become of you?

A. You will be dispised by your relations, as a disgrace to them—By the Government as unworthy of confidence—and avoided by your former friends, for fear of being asked to assist you, though you have rendered every service to your country, friends and relations, when in wealth, and become poor in so doing.

Forlorn Hope (July 19, 1800)

O n Saturday evening, April 15, 1797, members of the Philadelphia Lyceum for Free Debate gathered at Oeller's Hotel on Chestnut Street to debate the question, "Is imprisonment for debt consistent with sound policy?" That same night, debtors imprisoned in the New Gaol in New York met to attend the appointment as wardens of two of their number, William Davis and John McCrea, by three judges they had elected themselves. The two locations resembled one another not at all. Where the assembly room at Oeller's was "a most elegant room . . . papered after the French taste, with the Pantheon figures in compartments . . . and groups of antique drawings," the New Gaol was "a loathsome store-house" with tubs for human waste in the stairwell. Yet the two audiences were more alike than their surroundings would suggest. In more fortunate times the debtors had enjoyed much the same privilege, position, and authority as the members of the Lyceum. They were entrepreneurs whose success creditors had rewarded with more credit. Most were merchants or skilled artisans who owed too much money to be released without the consent of their creditors—a perverse measure of their success before they fell. Chief among them was William Duer. They had, to be sure, lost their independence as well as their wealth, but their fall from financial grace did not mean that they had abandoned civility, order, or legality. Indeed, they affirmed their devotion to those values by governing themselves under a written constitution, which they enforced through an elected court and officers.[1]

The debtors' constitution was, in the most literal sense, constitutive of their polity. It imparted a corporate identity to the debtors such that their formal dealings with debtors on other floors or with the jailer were conducted collectively as members of the middle hall—the second floor of the jail, where they were confined—acting through their appointed representatives. By the authority of the constitution, the debtors elected officers whom they invested with executive or judicial authority over them, created a court that observed formal rules of procedure and jurisdiction, and uttered collective judgments about how members who transgressed the norms of the polity should be punished. In sum, the debtors attempted to recreate in miniature the constitutional order they had known before their imprisonment. They became, quite literally, a republic of debtors. Their efforts—indeed, their success—attest to the power of the values and ideals that had defined their independence in better days: respectability, gentility, even constitutionalism and the rule of law.

The chief instrument of the debtors' constitutional order was "the Supreme Court held at New York Jail." To be sure, there was irony in the title, as there was in the occasional use of "York Castle" in the captions of notices within the prison. Nonetheless, the debtors were in earnest. They were themselves the "court." It was the collective identity they assumed when they gathered formally. They intended the court "To preserve Cleanliness and Order," "To promote good Will, and Harmony, amongst the Prisoners," and "To punish those who infringe on the Laws of the

Police, or Endeaver to disturb the public Peace." Their goal was not unrestrained power. Like the framers of the recently ratified federal Constitution, the debtors understood that constitutional government implied limits. Only prisoners who consented to the constitution by signing it could be bound by it. No one could be charged with an offense that had not previously been enumerated as one of "the Laws of the State." Most important, the framers established precise rules of procedure for the court, "to prevent its becoming an Engine of private Oppression." All complaints were to be in writing, "the Offence particularly specefied," and signed by the complainant and three other debtors who "do Concur in the above application for calling a Court." To assure adequate notice, complaints were to be served on the defendant at least six hours before the time scheduled for trial.[2]

The constitution created an array of officers, some elected by vote of the members of the hall, others appointed by the elected officers. Chief among the elected officials were the three judges of the court, who, in a somewhat fanciful inversion, may have enjoyed the same life tenure as judges appointed under Article III of the federal Constitution—at least they seem to have served until they resigned, died, or were otherwise liberated. The judges presided over the meetings of the court and voted with the other members when action was required, by custom voting last. Lesser in stature, but important enough to serve by election rather than appointment, was the attorney general, who acted as prosecutor on complaints brought before the judges. At least one debtor, Joseph Brantingham, used the attorney generalship as a step up to the higher office of judge. Several of the elected officers began their service in one of the lesser appointive positions. Consistent with the importance of the offices and the consensual nature of the community, election as judge or attorney general required a three-fourths' majority of the members. Once elected, judges and attorneys general alike took an oath "upon honour that I will execute the trust reposed in me without fear favour prejudice reward or hope of reward." Also elected, although the margin required is unclear, was the sheriff, who issued formal notice for meetings of the court pursuant to warrants directed to him by the judges, collected fines, and administered the oath of office to the attorney general and presumably also to the judges.[3]

The judges appointed seven lesser officers—a clerk, two wardens, and four stewards. The clerk of the court kept the records, maintained custody of "the Book of Constitution" and presented it to new prisoners for their signature, and purchased paper, quills, and candles with fines collected by the sheriff. The judges also appointed wardens, two at a time, for terms of one or two weeks, whose primary duty was to assure that their fellow debtors kept their rooms and common areas clean. Wardens filed formal complaints against members who violated the sanitation regulations adopted by the membership and could themselves be prosecuted if they neglected to do so. Because their duties required them to make the rounds of the rooms, and because they had some part in securing accommodations for their fellow prisoners, the wardens were also responsible for notifying the clerk of new arrivals on the hall so that he could present the constitution to them for their signature and thus their submission and consent. Lastly, the judges appointed stewards who appear to have functioned as a constabulary. They were empowered "to Keep order on the Hall" and even seem to have had summary authority to remove disorderly debtors from the hall to the stairwell to cool off. In addition, the residents of each room on the hall selected a governor of the room whose duties were unclear but at the very least—and it was the very least—included emptying the room spittoon.[4]

At first glance it is tempting to dismiss the constitution, court, judges, officers, rules, and procedures as an elaborate entertainment concocted by the debtors for their own amusement and perhaps also to mock the people who had used those very same devices to strip them of their freedom. However, to do so would do them a disservice. Not a trace of mockery or jest peeks through the three years of records of the court. Quite the contrary. The records portray a sustained effort to maintain order in matters both mundane and larger, which if left untended could render life in crowded confinement intolerable.

The court perched atop the structure performed two complementary constitutional roles. It served as the guarantor of the rule of law within the debtors' quarters and acted as the embodiment of the "sovereign" debtors when they wished to speak with a collective voice. The emphasis on legal authority is evident from the beginning of the record. At the first recorded meeting, on October 29, 1796, the judges appointed Duer and Joseph Brantingham as wardens. Less than two weeks later, the two men were ordered to stand trial "for Neglect of Duty in their Office" in "suffering filth and dirt to remain in the Hall during the whole of the week." However, they did not receive the six hours' notice "required and pointed out by the Constitution" and so did not bother to produce any evidence in their defense. Instead, they pleaded in abatement of the complaint that it was improperly served. The court accepted their plea and dismissed the complaint.[5]

The legalism of the proceeding is striking. It demonstrates both a commitment to due process as a worthy end in itself and a ready acceptance of technical pleading as an appropriate means to that end. Pleas in abatement did not address the substance of the complaint. Rather, they argued that a technical deficiency in the way the complaint had been served should bar the prosecution. Guilt or innocence on the substantive charge was irrelevant. The debtors believed that imprisonment did not suspend the principle that defendants should be informed of the charges against them and allowed sufficient time to prepare their defense. After the complaint against him had been dismissed, thus reaffirming the principle, Duer moved that the judges be given authority to fine wardens for neglecting their duty. The debtors' attorney general, who had signed the complaint against the wardens, seconded the motion, which carried in a vote by the assembled debtors.[6] This is one of the first entries in the record, so it is not clear what sanctions had been available to the judges before. What is significant is that the motion and its approval demonstrated a willingness to address a common problem by enlarging the authority of a judiciary that was expected to, and did, observe the procedural requirements of due process.

One might argue that the episode simply reflects a collective concern about people leaving chamberpots in the hallway, but that would ignore the formality of the proceeding. The problem would not have required the means used to address it unless the means themselves had independent value—a value measured here by principles of legal and constitutional order. Procedural safeguards permit the expansion of judicial authority by establishing the limits within which it acts. Moreover, the same sense of procedural exactitude typified other cases, such as the appointment of a "Clerk pro Tempore" to record the court proceedings while the clerk himself was being prosecuted, or the recognition that a warden who had attempted to extort two glasses of gin in return for not reporting an infraction of the sanitation code should be removed from office but could not be punished further because "there was no Existing Law of the Hall Relating to the Case." These two incidents reflect two rather sophisticated elements of legal and constitutional authority—the principle that one should not participate in adjudicating one's own case, and the constitutional prohibition of ex post facto laws.[7] The judges also recognized that justice is substantive as well as procedural. Once, after convicting two wardens for neglect of duty, they set a low fine, "this being the first offence," then further reduced one warden's fine, "it having been proved that the principal neglect was on the part of" his colleague. The judges thus tempered punishment in two very discriminating ways—by recognizing past records of good behavior and by apportioning culpability.[8]

The role of the court as the embodiment of the sovereign debtors appears in the earliest dated document. On March 18, 1795, the judges called a meeting of the members "to consult which will be the most proper means of regaining our lost Priviledges which we conceive to be decreasing rapidly." No record of the meeting exists, but the debtors clearly saw themselves as collectively entitled to certain privileges. The following year, they appointed three of their number a committee to request of the new jailer, Thomas Hazard, "the Enjoyment of the Priviledges we had previous to his coming into office." The six privileges they requested facilitated their ability to maintain a modicum of gentility in their surroundings—matters of hygiene such as placing additional tubs in the garret and cleaning the garret regularly, a guarantee that visitors not be refused admittance to the jail or be "incomoded with the impertinent Questions of the Turnkey," and that the times for locking the doors to restrain the criminal-side prisoners be regularized so that the debtors "may not be disappointed in seeing their Friends by the Inconvenience." For the most part, Hazard complied.[9]

The debtors of the middle hall also acted in the same quasi-corporate fashion in occasional negotiations with fellow debtors of the upper and lower halls over merging their respective polities. They first attempted to bring the lower-status residents of the lower hall—laborers and other less substantial debtors—within their authority by declaring unilaterally, and rather condescendingly, that "Members on the lower hall shall be considered as under the Jurisdiction of this Court" if they signed the constitution. In effect, they offered to annex the first floor, which may or may not have had its own organization at the time. The lower hall declined the honor. Its "members" replied with a letter that was a ringing affirmation of the right of constitutional self-determination. They declared "that Each Hall has the power of instituteing regulations for its own Goverment." When "any Circumstance of Oppression or . . . for the Benifit or Wellfare of the members of the house Generally Should arise the members of the lower Hall are perfectly disposed to Join their weight and Influance if any they should have to obtain the desired End."[10]

Rebuffed from below, the debtors of the middle hall turned to their brethren of the upper hall a year later, this time in a manner that recognized their status as equals, with merchants and skilled artisans on both floors. There may have been some friction between the middle and upper halls. A member of the middle hall had once charged a fellow member with provoking a "Disturbance" between the two halls "to the Manifest Injury" of both. Now committees shuttled up and down the stairs for five days, finally hammering out a tentative agreement that "the Constitution shall Extend its Jurisdiction to the upper Hall." The various offices would be divided between the halls, and each would "regulate its own Police"— that is, sanitation—through its respective wardens. In the end the negotiations broke down over the question of whether the middle hall, which had more members, would always be able to elect two judges to the upper hall's one. The debtors on the upper hall wanted to leave open the possibility of reapportionment according to which hall contained "the majority of Members who have signed the Constitution."[11]

The complementary constitutional roles of the court—guarantor of the rule of law and corporate embodiment of the debtors—merged when the court confronted challenges to its authority. Duer had demonstrated his attachment to the constitutional order in 1795 when he filed a complaint against the attorney general for "having Endeavourd to excite a Combination . . . to subvert the authority of the Court." The prosecutor had convened "an irregular Meeting to usurp the Power vested in" the court and threatened debtors who refused to attend "with Arbitrary Fines."[12] The most revealing challenge came two years later, when Isaac Sherman posted a call for a meeting of the debtors that did not comply with the prescribed procedure for calling meetings. Sherman couched his challenge in explicitly constitutional terms. He declared that an "alarming" increase in the number of debtors "renders it not only Expedient but Requisite" for the members to reapportion living quarters within the hall and called on them "[t]o make such Alterations in our constitution as may be Judged conducive to the benefit of the whole consistent with good order Found on legality." Duer himself had attempted to relieve the overcrowding one month earlier by giving up the room he occupied alone "for the accomadation of the Prisoners on the Middel Hall." He and his fellow judges now responded swiftly. They charged that Sherman's planned meeting was "illegal" and had been called "in a Mode unauthorized by the Constitution and tending to disturb the Peace Order and Harmony of the Hall." They urged all "Friends to the Established Constitution and the preservation of the Public peace" to boycott the meeting. The record does not indicate what happened, but since there is no subsequent evidence of Sherman's proposals, it is clear that "the real Friends of the Constitution"—by Duer's lights—prevailed.[13]

The outcome of the dispute is less significant than the fact that Sherman sought to change the system by ratifying its basic principles. To legitimize his challenge, he appealed to the same values as the debtors' constitution itself—"the benefit of the whole consistent with good order Found on legality." He did not propose to overturn the constitution, only to make alterations in it. When he failed, he accepted its authority and comported himself accordingly, if that is not too much to infer from the fact that three weeks later he followed the constitutionally prescribed procedure in filing a complaint against two fellow debtors for breach of the peace.[14]

Sherman's submission illustrates the authority of the debtors' constitutional order. It also reveals a communal side to that order. Residence on the middle hall was, of course, involuntary. Membership in the constitutional order of the middle hall, on the other hand, was consensual. The debtors enforced common norms of behavior by formal procedures that relied for their efficacy on the voluntary submission and consent of the members. Their community drew strength from the fact that it was almost coextensive with the hall itself. The names of 161 imprisoned debtors appear in the records and file papers, which span thirty-four months, with full names for 130. Recorded votes indicate that the number of members at any one time ranged from twenty-one to forty-one, with a likely average of between thirty and thirty-five, which would mean that the membership comprised virtually all the debtors on the hall. Although the court did impose small fines—much of which went for paper, quills, and candles—its principal sanctions were those of any consensual community: censure by, and ultimately expulsion from, the group, softened by the prospect of readmission upon appropriate penance.

Communal sanctions work by enlisting the group in disciplining errant members. Censure, expulsion, and restoration evoke both Congregational church discipline and the mock seriousness of private gentlemen's clubs. For example, when the court dismissed Joshua Snow as warden and fined him "for Misconduct and Neglect of Duty," Snow took "the book of the Constitution" and erased his name from it in a fit of pique or perhaps anger. It was not an idle gesture. His signature had been his solemn pledge to support the constitution. The court now tried and convicted Snow for violating that pledge. After a two-day adjournment it sentenced him to "close confinement in his own Room, for one Month," during which "he shall not be permitted to walk the Hall except for the discharge of the evacuations of nature or a discharge from prison." In addition, Snow was "excommunicated from the Benifits of this constitution and declared unworthy the conversation of the Members of the Hall." His fellow debtors were enjoined not to speak to him "unless upon private Business, and that in his own Room." Moreover, Snow would not be permitted to sign the constitution again and thus return to formal fellowship until released from confinement and after making "a public concession . . . in open court to the satisfaction of all the members."[15]

Snow was not expelled from the hall—a punishment that would have required him to take up residence with his belongings in the stairwell—but the court removed him from the community of the hall just as effectively as if it had expelled him. The condition the court imposed for his return was the same act of contrition required of excommunicated church members for readmission to communion or of clubmen for return to sociability. As if to underscore the analogy, the court decreed that the sufficiency and sincerity of Snow's "concession" were to be determined by the community of debtors as a whole. Thus, it was the community—defined here as the debtors who had signed the constitution—that decided who could remain within it and whether offenders from whom it had withdrawn fellowship could be readmitted.[16]

At the same court session that sentenced Joshua Snow, Duer urged that the debtors appoint a committee to consider empowering the judges to remit or mitigate sentences. To assure that the committee on such a significant issue would be representative, he insisted that it should include members from each room on the hall. Two days later, the committee, which Duer chaired, presented three proposals, which linked mercy to contrition and made distinctions based on the gravity of the offense and the record of the offender. For a first offense, unless the sentence was expulsion from the hall, the judges could remit or mitigate the sentence if the defendant made "satisfactory submission." For subsequent offenses, with the same exception, mitigation depended on making the submission "in open court to the satisfaction of the Majority of the Judges and members." The most severe sentence, expulsion from the hall, required the concurrence of three-fourths of the members and could not be remitted or mitigated "unless the most Ample Submission be made by the offender in Open Court" and accepted by a majority of the judges and three-fourths of the members. The debtors adopted the recommendations unanimously.[17] Duer's committee did not invent expulsion from the hall as a punishment—instances appear almost from the beginning of the record. Rather, the committee put the punishment within a more explicitly communal framework, thereby strengthening a constitutional authority that rested, at bottom, only on the voluntary submission of individual members.

The record is full of cases that illustrate the debtors' dual commitment to community and constitutional order. One in particular, that of Newel Narine, can stand for the others. Narine wrote a short note to one Morison warning him of arrest if he came to the prison—Morison may himself have been a debtor whose creditors had threatened him with attachment. Robert Turner, a fellow imprisoned debtor, had been counting on property of his in Morison's hands to help him obtain his release. Frustrated by Narine's intervention, he filed a complaint against Narine for "haveing acted in an unbecomeing Manner" by sending the letter. The court tried Narine on the charge and found him guilty "by a Unanimous Voice of the People." With explicit reference to the resolutions on sentencing enacted seven months earlier, the court then took up the question of whether to expel Narine from the hall. By a vote of seventeen to five, the members banished Narine from their midst.[18]

Narine's trials did not end there. For seven weeks he lived in the stairwell. Indeed, the committees of the middle and upper halls would have stepped over him as they shuttled back and forth in their merger negotiations. Finally, as fall approached, Narine petitioned to be readmitted to the hall, reciting "the great injury of his health from the impure smell from the [waste] Tubs and the night air," the "approaching inclement season," and the fact that his trunks and baggage were obstructing the stairs. He admitted his "improper Conduct and behavor" and was restored to the membership by unanimous vote. The debtors could not banish errant members from the prison, but they could expel them from their community.[19]

The threat of expulsion was a potent one, as Thomas King discovered. King brought a complaint against James Devan for "disorderly behavior"—noisily disturbing the hall and using "very abusive Language." It appears that Devan was rather rowdily, and no doubt annoyingly, celebrating his imminent release from the jail. Devan pled guilty. As it was his first offense, the court, with Duer presiding, mitigated his punishment to a

first offense, the court, with Duer presiding, mitigated his punishment to a reprimand. King was not satisfied. He hired a lawyer, filed a civil action against Devan in the Mayor's Court of New York for the same incident, and had Devan arrested. Devan now found himself imprisoned not for debt but on a civil warrant for assault. He immediately charged King with "contempt and disrespect" of the judges of the debtors' court for attempting to relitigate their decision "in a foreign Court"—a term of art for a court in a different jurisdiction—in "open violent breach of his faith as a member of the Constitution." The debtors' court tried King, convicted him, and gave him twenty-four hours to withdraw his civil action against Devan upon penalty of banishment from the hall. Faced with expulsion, a contrite King acknowledged "the impropriety of his Conduct," withdrew the civil suit, and asked "to be restored as a member of the Hall."[20]

Thus did a court that existed only by the consent and sufferance of a group of imprisoned debtors assert its jurisdictional primacy over a real court of law with coercive process at its disposal. That it did so by pressuring an individual litigant rather than by directly confronting the rival court does not lessen the significance of compelling a member to choose between the authority of the community to which he belonged and that of the legal system that imprisoned him in the first place. By signing the constitution, debtors committed themselves to the norms of order, legality, and community it embodied. One could not easily withdraw from a community that rested in part on one's own consent.

Its legitimacy established by a constitutional mandate from a community of sovereign debtors, the court went about its business of "preserv[ing] cleanliness and Order" and "punish[ing] those who infringe on the Laws of the Police" with the kind of quiet routine that characterizes established institutions. It heard complaints against members who "Shamefully and ungentlemanlike" or "violently" abused the complainants "as well as the good Constitution."[21] It fined wardens for neglect of duty. It punished members who "did Quarrel and fight and make a Great noise in the Hall," thereby committing a breach of the peace. The judges dispatched the wardens to inform a debtor that he could not build a room that would obstruct the window in the common hallway. As routinely as it acted, the court could just as routinely not act, as when it dismissed a complaint against one Hutchinson, whose deficient grooming habits left him lice-ridden, when it discovered that Hutchinson, although resident among them, had not signed the constitution and thus, lousy or not, stood outside the jurisdiction of the court.[22]

The court was at its most court-like, which is to say its most legalistic, in the resolution of civil disputes. There it is readily apparent how thoroughly the debtors recreated legal norms within the prison walls. Early on, however, before the formal record book picks up, one catches a fleeting glimpse of a less formal, less legalistic way of adjudicating disputes—a single arbitration award rendered by the three judges of the debtors' court acting not as judges but as arbitrators.

The dispute arose from the grievance of Jacob Canter, who upon paying four dollars to David Beattie became a member of Room 5 entitled to board. Sometime after paying this "garnish," Canter was tossed out of the room, whether by Beattie alone or by his roommates in concert is unclear. Instead of lodging a complaint with the court, Canter and Beattie submitted the dispute to arbitration, presumably agreeing to abide by any award the arbitrators should make. The arbitrators met, took evidence, and, "upon a fair, liberal, and candid discussion of the different points relative to the dispute," made two findings. The first was that Canter owed Beattie four dollars for board "according to agreement," thereby affirming the validity of the contract between the two men. The second was that, after paying the agreed amount and becoming a member of the room, Canter was turned out of the room "without any Just cause or provacation, in a verry unwarrantable manner," before the money paid had been "expended for the benefit of the . . . Room"—thereby finding Beattie in breach of the contract. On the basis of these findings, the arbitrators ordered Beattie to return three of the four dollars to Canter, the one-dollar difference presumably being the value of the board Canter had received before his expulsion.[23]

Arbitration is the archetypal voluntary disputing process. Unlike litigation, it is consensual—both the agreement to submit to arbitration and the agreement to abide by the arbitrators' award are voluntary. Individuals who submit their disputes to arbitration do so together, rather than in the adversarial posture of plaintiff and defendant that characterizes litigation. The consensual nature of arbitration makes it well suited to resolving disputes within communities, where one goal of the process is to enable the disputants to continue communal relations, however contentious those might be. Yet during the eighteenth century, arbitration became increasingly legalistic and inflexible. Among other changes, awards came to look less like equitable decrees and more like judgments at law.[24] The award in the matter of Room 5 is such an award. The arbitrators broke the dispute down into its legal components—was there a contract, was it breached, and what should the remedy be—which is a very different way of parsing a dispute than asking what is the grievance and what can we do to resolve it. The arbitrators analyzed the dispute as judges would a contract action. The remedy they fashioned was a legal one limited to monetary damages. They did not attempt the quite different, equitable question of whether Canter should be reinstated as a member of the room. Thus did legal norms shape even less formal ways of resolving disputes within the prison.

The legalism of the arbitration anticipates that of the debtors' court. The rules for the form and service of complaints manifested a commitment to procedural due process. The limits on persons and offenses that were subject to the authority of the court demonstrated jurisdictional restraint. Members were not allowed to vote in cases to which they were parties. The court required witnesses to testify on oath. Refusal constituted contempt of court, punishable by a fine or, failing payment, by close confinement to their rooms. Perjury merited expulsion from the hall—after trial and conviction, of course—and the perjurer "Never again [to] be admitted on the Hall on any pretence whatever."[25] When the court discovered that a person who was charged with a criminal offense had been admitted to membership and allowed to sign the constitution, it did not expel him—his admission, although unwelcome, had not violated any rule. Instead, the court appointed a committee to revise the standards for admission to exclude similar persons in the future—a very lawyerly solution.[26]

As the arbitration between Canter and Beattie suggests, the most complex civil disputes involved living arrangements, as debtors jockeyed for scarce space. When James Smith came onto the hall, he signed the constitution but did not have a place to stay. William Baylis, who was about to be released, occupied a partitioned-off portion of Room 3, which he offered to sell to Smith for the "customary" price of thirty-three dollars. Smith accepted—there seems to have been some negotiation over the financing— but the other occupants of Room 3 barricaded the door against him "and forcibly resisted his entrance." They disputed Baylis's right to sell his "apartment," which they claimed for themselves. Smith petitioned the judges for redress, saying that while he "might have opposed force to force, yet being desirous to maintain the peace of the Hall, he prefers leaving" the matter to the court. When the court convened, the members addressed a series of procedural issues before turning to the testimony. They first decided that the parties to the dispute—Smith and his would-be roommates—would not be permitted to vote. They then agreed to use written ballots rather than the usual show of hands. Lastly, on the motion of one of the residents of Room 3, they decided that the roommates could be present during the testimony and examine the witnesses. The minutes of the subsequent hearing are unfortunately garbled, but it appears that the right to sell a room that one paid the jailer to occupy was not as settled or customary as Smith had been told. Nonetheless, and without recording its reasons, the court decided by a vote of eighteen-to-seven that Smith should be allowed to occupy the apartment he had purchased. Three days later, Duer proposed a formal discussion of whether debtors should be able to sell their rooms to one another and, if so, on what conditions. The record is silent on what, if anything, happened next. What the record reveals, however, is the court had decided the issue before it—Smith's right to the apartment—and had done so with careful attention to procedures that all agreed were important.[27]

The key to the success of the constitution and the polity built on it lay in the similarity between the norms of order and legality embodied by the constitution and those held by the debtors in more comfortable times before their imprisonment. When one of the wardens, William Arebeck, filed a complaint against Edward Jamison for overturning the waste tub in the stairwell—describing the act as "Destructive to good order, Decency and Gentillity"—he appealed to a standard of propriety that he assumed everyone shared, even though he himself could only sign the complaint with his mark. Similarly, when Margaret Frean charged that Charles Ellison's verbal abuse of her and of his wife "tend[ed] to disturb that Peace Harmony and good Order which ought to Subsist in any civilized Society," she invoked values that she did not consider abrogated by imprisonment. Ellison had called her "a damn'd infamous Bitch, a Damn'd Lyar a damn'd faggot a damn'd infamous Woman." Frean may have been accustomed to such insults—remember Benjamin Haskins's claim that she was a prostitute, for which he was barred from the hall—but Ellison's treatment of his wife is another, more revealing matter. After the debtors on the hall "are all gone to Bed," he would use "such insulting Language to his Wife by damning and cursing her" that he would disturb everyone else. Ellison may have been an abusive lout. On the other hand, just one month earlier, as a judge of the court, he had voted to expel John Jones from the hall for denouncing the wife of another debtor as "a damned whore," "a good for nothing durty Bitch," and "many other abusive and injurious expressions." So it may also be that the loss of independence, the close confinement in crowded conditions, the lack of privacy, the constant reminders of having been "unman'd" by failure, had taken their toll. In any event, by defending reputation, the debtors affirmed that the values of order and legality they had embraced in freedom remained as precious in confinement.[28]

The record sketches a world in which debtors recreated the constitutional order they had known before their imprisonment. To be sure, imprisoned populations elsewhere organized themselves and established authority structures. Debtors in the King's Bench prison in eighteenth-century London created a corporate college, the president of which also presided over a court, sometimes assisted by a jury. As an administrative body, the college was quite elaborate, but the court is largely a mystery. Criminal prisoners in the Walnut Street jail in Philadelphia formed "a secondary and inferior government . . . for their own convenience," but all we know of its jurisdiction is that it specified where prisoners could spit their tobacco juice. During the Revolution, captured American sailors held on British prison ships or in British prisons fashioned forms of corporate government and discipline. However, none of these approached the debtors of the New Gaol in the self-consciousness of their constitutionalism or the preciseness of their legalism.[29]

Why this was so is bound up with who the debtors were. A guide to the debtors' prisons of London noted that "[d]ebtors' prisons like the grave . . . level all distinctions"—a powerful statement but false, both in England and America.[30] The statutory path to freedom implicitly rested on social and economic distinctions, and the members of the middle hall owed too much money to qualify for easy release. Stray references make clear that most, perhaps all, of them owed more than £10, presumably a lot more. Under the New York Ten-Pound Act of 1789, debtors who owed more than £10 were not eligible for gaol delivery unless they assigned their property to their creditors, and even then only if the creditors agreed. If they owed more than £200—increased to £1,000 in 1791—they could not be released at all.[31] Only merchants or skilled artisans could accumulate debts that large. They were men for whom independence had been a reality, not just a hope or a promise.

Even within this group there was a status hierarchy. The leaders of the middle hall—the men elected judge or attorney general—were generally more distinguished and, before their failures, more successful than their fellow debtors. Of the 161 debtors whose names appear in the records and file papers, only twelve served as judge and four as attorney general, including one who served successively as both. The most prominent, of course, was Duer. Henry Bedlow, "a man of rich family and connections," was a judge, as were Thomas H. Brantingham, Abraham Fowler, and James Harrison, all established merchants. Brantingham had engaged in land speculation with Robert Morris, at least to the extent of purchasing 50,000 acres from him.[32] Christopher Duyckinck, although a judge, was not in the same financial league, but his sail-loft was a substantial operation. The only judge clearly below the social standard of his brethren on the bench was David Beattie, who appears to have been a grocer. The attorneys general were similarly prominent—Joseph Brantingham, son and mercantile associate of Thomas H. Brantingham, William Langworthy, the agent of Lord Grosvener in a mining venture, and William Mumford, a merchant whose debts were substantial enough to qualify him for a discharge under the federal Bankruptcy Act of 1800. The one possible exception, although perhaps not by much, was James Blanchard, who had held the lease on the city slaughterhouse.[33]

Men of substance—at least of former substance—were thus the acknowledged leaders of the middle hall. Their fellow debtors elected them to positions such as men of their station held in civil life. They presided over a constitutional order that emphasized legal authority and the rule of law. There is, of course, a certain incongruousness to their behavior. Viewed from one angle, one sees once-important men, now in disgrace, catching at straws to reassert their respectability, gentility, and authority. From this perspective, court and constitution become a shield against the squalor and vulgarity of their surroundings and against their fears of being "declassed" and "unman'd" by their dependence. On the other hand, it was an order that they regarded with the utmost seriousness. Whether chamberpots were emptied and the common hallway kept clean, whether quarrels could be stilled and disputes resolved—all were issues of consequence in the constricted world of imprisoned debtors. Thus, when the debtors concluded that the attorney general, "apparently lost To every sense of delicacy," was derelict in his duties, they initiated impeachment proceedings out of a conviction that his continuance in office was "big with danger to the very being of the Constitution."[34] Such language may seem rather grandiose for people who were, after all, imprisoned by legitimate legal process. But it is a measure of the extent to which constitutionalism was an essential part of their community, even as the opportunities created by the Revolution had collapsed around them. To be sure, the debtors' ability to govern themselves was constrained by their confinement. No legal authority conferred legitimacy on their actions. Nonetheless, the constitutional order they created was greater than the sum of their individual actions. It drew its legitimacy from the consent of the debtors and, with that legitimacy, withstood every challenge to its authority.

The values of constitutional order and the rule of law acted as a bridge between the community the debtors fashioned during their confinement and the communities they had lived in before. It was a bridge that, I suspect, the debtors needed. Their failure had been economic, not moral, and they refused to act as though they had forfeited any claim to the principles by which society outside the prison walls continued to live. When they learned that Congress had enacted the Bankruptcy Act of 1800—which, because of its limitation to merchants, brokers, and factors whose debts exceeded one thousand dollars, held out particular promise to the members of the middle hall—the debtors in the New Gaol celebrated with a festival, replete with "a rich repast of social conversation" and toasts "to celebrate the auspicious event," almost as though they were gathered at Oeller's Hotel. William Keteltas published the toasts in the *Forlorn Hope*. While joyous and even a bit defiant, the toasts nonetheless emphasized order and respectability. They exhorted debtors who qualified for the new act to "evince its propriety in obeying, fulfilling, and discharging all the duties required in it." They enjoined every debtor relieved by the act not to "consider himself discharged from his debts in his own mind"—notwithstanding his discharge at law—"until he has satisfied his creditors or spent the remainder of his days in his attempt to do so." They appealed to "wisdom and justice."[35] In both form and substance, the assembly resembled other social gatherings outside the prison walls of like-minded, reputable citizens whose toasts were published in other newspapers. Those other social gatherings were of the world from which the debtors of the middle hall came and to which they hoped to return. Though imprisoned, it was the norms of that world that they pledged to uphold.

❧ 6 ❧

THE POLITICS OF INSOLVENCY

A Countryman who had some money to spare, was told he might add considerably to his property by going to the city and deal in scrip;—full of this idea he came to New-York, and was recommended to a gentleman well known for his drollery; upon applying to the gentleman for his advice, after pausing a minute, his reply was, "My friend, my advice is, that you go home, and lay out your money in pigs, . . . because you will by that means, have at least a squeak for your money, which, upon my honor, is more than you ever will have for it if you part with it here.

Forlorn Hope (August 23, 1800)

Benjamin Franklin Bache viewed class with the eye of a thorough democrat. Reared in privilege but educated to an egalitarian regard for liberty by his namesake grandfather, he was the most ardent—and consequently the most reviled—Republican journalist of the 1790s. In January 1797 he published this anecdote in his newspaper, the *Aurora:*

A few days ago a sailor, passing down second street nearly opposite the city tavern, where a number of gentlemen were standing, met an oysterman crying "very good oysters." Well cried Jack if they be so very good let us have half a dozen of them. The oysterman stopped his barrow and opened the oysters which proved so agreeable to Jack's palate notwithstanding the coldness of the day he ordered the oysterman to open him another half dozen. On swallowing these he stepped off in great haste. The oysterman ran after him, hallowing to him to return and pay for the oysters, Jack turned short on his heel, with an air of importance, and exclaimed *damn your eyes have you not heard that I have stopped payment.*[1]

For a paper praised by its supporters as courageous and condemned by its opponents as scurrilous and seditious, the story, at a distance, seems innocuous, if clever. But it was not. City Tavern, across from which Bache's invention unfolded, was a traditional gathering place of Philadelphia's mercantile and legal elite, who had built it at great expense by private subscription in 1773 as an establishment where they could engage in learned, weighty, and genteel discussion—with suitable libations and comestibles as conversational lubricants—without having to endure the interruptions of the artisans, mechanics, laborers, and sailors who frequented other public houses in the city. It had lost some of its luster by Bache's time, particularly after Oeller's Hotel opened a few blocks away in 1791, but its association with social and economic privilege remained.[2] The men who socialized at City Tavern were men who could stop payment. Bache's sailor was not. Before one could stop payment, one first had to have the reputational and financial wherewithal—"credit" in the fullest sense of the word—to pay for one's obligations with promissory notes or bills of exchange, which then circulated in the economy until presented to the maker for payment. If the maker refused—that is, if he "stopped payment"—he effectively announced to the world his financial embarrassment and likely insolvency. Stopping payment thus required a substance that Bache's sailor did not have. All he could do was satirize the haughtiness of those who did. Indeed, whereas merchants and other businessmen who stopped payment were said to have failed, no one ever spoke of an indigent sailor or laborer as having failed. In eighteenth-century economic parlance, to "fail" meant to fall from entrepreneurial grace. Bache's sailor, and all whom he represented, never having ventured in business, could never fail—they simply grew poorer.

Bache disdained the commercial and political values he associated with City Tavern. Merchants were as rootless and as unburdened by loyalty as the promissory notes they put into circulation. They were "men who know no country but that where they can make money," who "carry their capitals, ships and our sailors to the country which will encourage them." In Bache's view "two classes or descriptions of men" exist in "all civilized nations." The first class "are labourers, men who produce by their industry something to the common stock of the community." They are farmers, mechanics, artisans, and the like. The second class "are such, as live on the stock of the community, already produced, not by *their labour*, but obtained by their *art* and *cunning*, or that of their ancestors." They are merchants, speculators, priests, and lawyers, who "get their living by thinking, not by labour, by the various arts which draw the productions of labour into their hands without working themselves."[3]

Of this "second class" Bache reserved special opprobrium for speculators. In this, of course, he was not alone. Even his publishing arch-nemesis, John Fenno of the Federalist *Gazette of the United States*, depicted speculators as rabid dogs that spread the fever of speculation to one another and to investors by biting them. Fenno's son and successor, John W. Fenno, took a similar view when he printed the suggestion that the state of Georgia, which was notorious for the corruption of its speculator-controlled legislature, should adopt for its state seal "the emblem of a man in the act of signing, with one hand, a scroll of paper, beginning with '*Know all men by these presents,*' and with the other pointing to large tracts of land in the moon." But where the Fennos satirized, Bache attacked the "clan of Land Jobbers" that have "monopolized" the public lands and by whose speculation "thousands are impoverished, and thousands more are on the threshold of becoming victims to this species of rapacity." Because of their importunities "our people are loaded with debts for purchase of land which will plunge multitudes in distress and ruin."[4]

Had Bache lived—he died of yellow fever in September 1798—he would not have been surprised that when Congress eventually enacted bankruptcy legislation in 1800, it applied only to his second class of debtors, like those who frequented City Tavern, not to his sailor or any other members of the first class. Every bankruptcy bill Congress took up in its first decade had made the same distinction. Indeed, whether bankruptcy should be available to anyone else seems never to have been considered. Nevertheless, the debate over bankruptcy relief in the 1790s was conducted in the language and imagery of dependence and independence, slavery and freedom, commerce and agriculture, vice and virtue, nationalism and federalism, as, one suspects, Bache knew it would be.

Article I, Section 8 of the Constitution empowered Congress "[t]o establish . . . uniform Laws on the subject of Bankruptcies throughout the United States." The clause had received scant discussion at the Constitutional Convention, where the only reservation expressed had been Roger Sherman's observation that English law prescribed the death penalty for certain acts of bankruptcy, "and He did not chuse to grant a power by which that might be done here." Not that Sherman was alone—his fellow Connecticut delegate, William Samuel Johnson, had as a creditors' lawyer before the Revolution denounced insolvency and bankruptcy legislation in Connecticut, which he said "makes shocking work amongst us and almost persuades all debtors to set their creditors at defiance"—but the Connecticut delegation cast the sole vote against the bankruptcy clause.[5]

This seeming nonchalance toward federalizing bankruptcy stands in sharp contrast to how large the issue of debt loomed in the 1780s—or, more precisely, the issues of debt, for the debts that cast such shadows over the decade were both public and private. Although different in origin, public and private debts were intertwined in public imagination and debate and were linked more formally by the medium of paper money. The public debt originated in the fact that "[t]he grand sinew of war is money."[6] The Revolution, like all wars, was fought on credit in the form of direct loans and, more important, of paper currency and scrip issued by the Continental Congress and state governments. These latter emissions comprised a system of "currency finance" in which Congress and the individual states issued bills of credit and loan certificates of various kinds to purchase supplies and pay soldiers on the promise to pay interest or to redeem them in the future in specie or, more commonly, by accepting them in payment of tax obligations. Currency finance was not a Revolutionary invention—

every colony in the eighteenth century used variations, with varying degrees of success, to finance public obligations and furnish a circulating medium of exchange—but the Revolution called forth its use on an unprecedented scale.

Paper currency maintained its value in direct relation to the confidence of those who held it that the issuing government would fulfill its pledge to withdraw the money from circulation. Those pledges proved impossible to fulfill in wartime. Massive emissions of new currency were required to sustain the war effort, thereby precipitating a sharp decline in the value of the currency in circulation. Depreciation was aggravated by inflation, as large-scale government purchases drove prices upward, prompting Congress to print even more currency. As E. James Ferguson observed, "Congress stuffed the maw of the Revolution with paper money." A delegate from Maryland reported in 1778 that the printing "press is at work, . . . near a million a week is now made, and yet our Demands are greater then we can answer . . . [and] would expend the mines of Chili and Peru." By the end of the war, Congress had issued some $200,000,000 in Continental currency, which had fallen in value from near par with specie to considerably less than a hundredth of the value of specie. The states had emitted a similar amount. In addition, Congress had sold about $60–70,000,000 in loan certificates to investors and borrowed perhaps $12,000,000 from European sources.[7]

Private debts were only slightly less daunting. The war had created economic opportunity for merchants, farmers, and artisans. It had strengthened the domestic economy, promoted internal improvements, and encouraged manufacturing. At the same time, however, it had disrupted foreign trade, which was the linchpin of the entire economy. Peace did not undo the disruption. The West Indies, which had been a major market for New England foodstuffs, timber products, and other supplies before the Revolution—a trade that allowed the island planters to commit all of their slave labor resources to raising a single cash crop, sugar—was largely off-limits afterward, when American-built ships no longer qualified as British bottoms. Other markets did not immediately present themselves, with the result that prices declined and the American economy contracted more or less steadily throughout the 1780s. Meanwhile, the fledgling domestic manufacturing enterprises that had taken shallow root during the war were undermined when British merchants seeking to reassert their dominance flooded the American market with higher-quality, lower-priced goods and pressed commercial credit on coastal import merchants to enable them to feed the pent-up demand for consumer items. The tentacles of credit followed the goods from importers to wholesalers to retailers to consumers, from the ports to the backcountry. Exports fell, imports grew, income and wealth declined.[8] Soon denunciations of luxury appeared in private correspondence and public print that differed little from those that had circulated before the war. The complaint of New York merchant Thomas Stoughton to his partner that "the Country is impoverished by Luxury" was a common one. Writers such as Hugh Williamson argued that "we are nearly ruined by foreign luxuries . . . [T]he property of our citizens is daily mortgaged to strangers and foreigners, and the inheritance of our children bartered away for fineries and fopperies."[9]

With this last comment, it is easy to see how issues of public and private debt often converged. Thomas Jefferson linked the two explicitly when he wrote from Paris to a friend in Virginia that Americans' failure to repay their debts—by which he meant both public debt incurred during the Revolution and pre-war private debts still owed to British creditors—had discouraged European merchants and investors. He believed, however, that "good will come from the destruction of our credit." Nothing else could "restrain our disposition to luxury, and the loss of those manners which alone can preserve republican government." As credit itself cannot be prevented, its "ill effects" could be "cured" by "giving an instantaneous recovery to the creditor," thereby "reducing purchases on credit to purchases for ready money. A man would then see a prison painted on every thing he wished but had not ready money to pay for."[10] Given Jefferson's own lifelong habit of purchasing fine wines and other foreign luxuries on credit, it would be easy to dismiss his opinion as posturing. But, as is often the case with Jefferson, one must separate his words from his deeds, as he himself did. The combination of depreciating paper currency and mounting private indebtedness threatened to undo the independence so recently won.

Although the importance of paper currency and the credit it represented to trade and economic development was widely understood, the inevitable tendency of unsupported or undersupported paper money to
depreciate created an equally inevitable host of economic and political
problems. Depreciation constituted a form of taxation, transferring wealth
from the individuals who accepted paper to the government that issued it.
Depreciation also conferred a measure of debt relief when coupled with
state tender laws, which required creditors to accept paper at face value in
satisfaction of debts. Some creditors accepted the loss as a patriotic obligation. The elder James Otis, for example, a leader of the revolutionary
Massachusetts provincial congress, continued to accept paper money from
his debtors at par even when it had depreciated to 200:1 out of what his
grandson later rued as "a false and mistaken principle of Patriotism." Others thought that only Tories and scoundrels took advantage of patriotic
creditors, as when George Skillern of Virginia complained that "Torys
and such like Miscreants paid all their Debts with it," while refusing to accept paper money themselves, "so that the most Zealous whigs ware the
only persons who ware well punished for theyr Loyalty." Robert Morris
complained that "there are cursed Rogues that want to pay Debts and purchase Lands with less than the Value." Still others treated depreciation as a
variable to be considered in negotiated commercial settlements. One
Rhode Island debtor wanted credit for his forbearance in not discharging
his debt in depreciated currency when "he had it often in his power" to do
so "but did not think it Right to settle it in a mode so incompatible with
Justice." He offered to pay the principal if the creditor would forgo the interest. George Read of Delaware observed that many debtors who repaid
pre-war debts in depreciated currency split the depreciation loss with their
creditors as "acts of Justice to suffering Creditors" and that the practice
had become customary in the postwar years "when both parties have been
such as were disposed to do equal Justice."[11]

The instability of paper currency in the 1780s generated several responses, all of which ultimately influenced the public debate over bankruptcy legislation in the following decade. The most immediate response
was proposals to charter banks, which could issue bank notes as a form of

private currency that would be backed by something more substantial than the traditional hope-and-a-prayer of government issues. Ideas for a bank circulated publicly as early as 1780 and quickened when Congress appointed Robert Morris superintendent of finance in 1781. From the beginning, calls for a bank emphasized the importance of public credit and a stable paper currency to commerce and industry.[12] Thus, when Morris procured a charter for the Bank of North America in 1781, the venture had widespread backing among merchants, as did similar banks organized or incorporated in New York and Boston in 1784 and Baltimore in 1790.

However, the identification of the Bank of North America with commercial interests in general and with Morris in particular proved its undoing, despite a spirited defense by as pedigreed a radical as Thomas Paine. Led by William Findley of western Pennsylvania, agrarian interests attacked the bank as an undemocratic concentration of wealth and succeeded in revoking its local charter. Findley gave voice to the anxieties of agrarian republicans about what they saw as commercial manipulations of the familiar economic order. He argued that the bank was, in essence, impersonal corporate capital that existed "for the sole purpose of increasing wealth." As such, "the personal responsibility arising from the principles of honour, generosity, etc., can have no place." Instead, "like a snow ball perpetually rolled, it must continually increase its dimensions and influence." Such an institution, "having no principle but that of avarice, which dries and shrivels up all the manly, all the generous feelings of the human soul, will never be varied in its object: and, if continued, will accomplish its end, viz. to engross all the wealth, power, and influence of the state." Contrary efforts by bank proponents such as Pelatiah Webster to portray commercial credit as a republican virtue—"credit is a most valuable thing in society, it gives hearts ease, it gives wealth, 'tis a nurse of every social virtue, it makes a soil suitable for the growth of public spirit and every public virtue"—were unavailing.[13]

A second response, corollary to the first, was the enactment of state tender laws, which required creditors to accept paper currency at face value in payment of debts, no matter what the actual depreciated value of the currency. Paper money as legal tender for public obligations such as taxes was familiar enough before the Revolution, but as legal tender for private debts was both novel and controversial. Although often cast as debtor relief measures, tender laws generated more complex reactions, largely because debtors were themselves often creditors, which made any tender law a double-edged sword. In addition, hostility to a state tender act varied with the rate of depreciation. Tender laws in states with reasonably supported paper currency did not encounter nearly the opposition they did in states with notoriously devalued currency. Initially, tender laws seemed an unavoidable, if drastic, solution to the problems debtors faced in how they were to repay pre-war and wartime domestic debts when the only currency available, when any was available at all, was depreciating paper. Thus, the first tender acts were ancillary to state issues of paper money during the Revolution. Legislatures did not set out to "defraud" creditors. Rather, they sought to bolster the value of the only currency they had. Not that legislators did not understand the effects of tender laws—while the Connecticut assembly was debating whether to repeal its tender act, one member reportedly rode home to offer repayment to his creditor "at nominal sum, of a considerable Debt," while he could still do so in depreciated paper.[14]

The difficulty, of course, lay in attempting to legislate the value of something that had no intrinsic worth. As Pelatiah Webster observed when Pennsylvania enacted a tender law in 1780, "It is not more absurd to attempt to *impel faith* into the heart of an unbeliever by *fire* and *faggot,* or to *whip* love into your mistress with a *cowskin,* than to force *value* or *credit* into your money by *penal laws*." Others argued that when "base money is declared to be legal tender—the diligent man is plundered for the benefit of the indolent and extravagant—industry languishes, for property is not safe—the orphan is defrauded, and the most atrocious frauds are practiced under the sanction of law." To some, "the rage for defrauding creditors by making paper money a legal tender" was proof that "men have not virtue enough to bear a government that is perfectly free"—an argument that became a standard Federalist figure in the ratification debates at the end of the decade.[15]

Still others linked tender laws to even greater losses of freedom. Providence Quakers called the Rhode Island tender act "a wide and fatal Door of Injustice and Oppression" and petitioned the Rhode Island assembly to repeal it. They began their appeal not with debt but by referring to a petition they had previously addressed to the assembly on "the iniquitous Trade to Africa for Slaves," which they considered "a national Evil, tending to draw down the divine Displeasure." The Friends were petitioning again because they were "fully persuaded that the same Principles of *Truth* and *Justice*" applied to the tender law. They warned of the "Prospect of *Injury* to many—perhaps *Ruin* to some"—creditors who could not or would not avail themselves with their own creditors of the legislatively sanctioned stratagems used against them by their debtors. The implication that creditors could be enslaved by their debtors inverted the pre-war image of Virginia planters enslaved by their creditors. But when one remembers that creditors were also debtors and that financial ruin—and hence loss of independence—could come from lower down the chain of indebtedness as well as from above, the analogy was apt.[16]

A third response was the rapid spread of speculation. In 1780 the Continental Congress asked the states to tax some of the national currency out of circulation at the sharply devalued rate of one silver dollar for every forty paper Continental dollars. Although this proportion still overvalued Continental currency, it turned depreciation into speculative opportunity by encouraging investors with access to specie to buy up congressional bills of credit at steep discounts and cash them in at a profit. Particularly industrious speculators could take further advantage by capitalizing on the fact that depreciation was a market condition, which perforce varied in different markets. Continental currency that traded at one rate in one city thus might trade at an entirely different rate in another, and in that difference lay profit. In this manner, William Barton argued, depreciation "gave rise to a spirit of speculation, by which every man endeavoured to advance his own fortune, at the expence of the community."[17]

The "spirit of speculation" became even more fevered at the close of the war when soldiers were sent home with settlement certificates as their pay. Speculators, sometimes in partnership with army officers, quickly bought up most of these certificates for as little as ten or fifteen cents on the dollar, which was about the same rate at which shopkeepers accepted them in credit for store goods.[18] In short order, and aided by a decline in prices that limited the appeal of trading opportunities, speculative activity spread to every kind of government issue that contemplated future redemption, whether land warrants or debt certificates. Within just a few years, a very large proportion of the state and national public debt was held by speculator-investors who had bought warrants, certificates, and indents from the original holders at steeply discounted prices, with the result that people began debating issues of debt equity long before controversy swirled around Alexander Hamilton's plan for funding the public debt in the 1790s. When the Pennsylvania legislature took up a bill to fund the state debt in 1785, Pelatiah Webster described a moral balance, with "the *soldiers*, who served us with *fatigue and blood* . . . , and other *virtuous citizens*, who *furnished the public*, in the greatest public exigence and distress, with *cash and other supplies*" on one side and "the *stock-jobbers* and *speculators*" on the other, leaving no doubt which side he found wanting. Not only was it unjust to tax the state, which necessarily included the original holders, to pay larcenous profits to speculators; funding would give public sanction to an activity "very ruinous to the public, as it affords *enormous profits without any earnings.*" Advancing an argument that others took up more urgently in the next decade, Webster wrote that nothing "can be worse than *public laws or institutions*, which tend to draw people from the *honest and painful* method of *earning* fortunes, and to encourage them to pursue *chimerical ways* and *means* of obtaining *wealth* by *sleight of hand, without any earnings at all.*" Of course, Webster's arguments against speculation were like trying to hold back the tide. As prospects for a stronger national government increased, so, too, did speculation in the public debt. In the words of one major investor as he joined a venture to buy up public issues, "the establishment of the new Constitution . . . must necessaryly give value to the securities of the United States."[19]

Alongside the "spirit of speculation" in the 1780s was a renewed acquaintance with failure. The decline of prices, the scarcity of cash, depreciation, competition from British manufactures, the obstacles to establishing export markets when no longer part of the British empire, and efforts by British commercial creditors to collect pre-war debts all contributed to a wave of business failures after the Revolution. What Thomas

M. Doerflinger so aptly described as the "fabric of adversity" that faced merchants became even more densely woven. The brief postwar boom that was typical of the first months of peace triggered a rush of merchants and traders to ports like Philadelphia, all eager to profit in the commercial frenzy, and all capitalized—and often undercapitalized—on credit. There were half again as many merchants in Philadelphia after the war as there were before. Reality intruded in the form of a postwar depression. The glut of imports drove prices down, while the drain of specie to Britain pushed the price of bills of exchange and the cost of credit up, causing trade to stagnate. Many of the newcomers, as well as many of the less nimble established merchants, failed, often at the rate of more than one a month in Philadelphia. Thomas Stoughton reported similar distress in New York, where, like Philadelphia, the "Commercial Situation daily grows more precarious and dangerous." He predicted that British merchant-creditors "will have reason to remember the year 1784, we have neither produce or Money to discharge our Debts," adding for emphasis, "happy is the Man of honest Principles who has nothing to do with dry Goods or exposes himself or friends to the Collection of Debts in this Country."[20]

Following as they did so closely on the heels of the steep rise in mercantile activity, the business collapses deepened the understanding of failure as the downside of entrepreneurial risk. This made failure the potential common fate of all merchants. In these circumstances merchants recognized the value of asserting mercantile control over failure, much as the law merchant rested on the principle that matters of commerce were best adjudicated by men of commerce under procedures that accommodated the demands of commerce. For merchants, the attempt to control the consequences of failure took two forms—one voluntary, the other not. The former was the private composition—a negotiated settlement between a commercial debtor and his creditors in which the debtor agreed to assign his assets to his creditors or pay a prorated portion of his debts in return for a discharge. The latter was a bankruptcy law, which Pennsylvania enacted in 1785.

The Pennsylvania statute was a true bankruptcy act. It offered the holy grail of debt relief—a discharge of unpaid debts—but only to commercial debtors. Unlike standard insolvency laws, the Pennsylvania bankruptcy law followed English practice by limiting its application to merchants, traders, brokers, bankers, factors, and the like, and only upon petition by creditors who were owed a certain large minimum amount—£200 under the Pennsylvania statute. Enacted in response to the economic distress, the law announced its commercial purpose in the preamble. It was "necessary and proper as well as conformable to the usage of commercial nations"—thus assuming as fact an identity as a commercial nation that was hotly disputed in the debates over national bankruptcy legislation in the next decade—"that persons using merchandise"—that is, merchants, traders, and other businessmen—who "are unable to pay their debts should be compelled speedily and without delay to surrender up their effects for the use of their creditors" so they could be "liberated . . . to support themselves and their families."[21]

Albert Gallatin later argued that the Pennsylvania bankruptcy law, which expired in 1793, was "productive of nothing but fraud," even as he acknowledged strong support for it among "many respectable merchants," particularly in Philadelphia.[22] It is difficult to know what to make of his allegation. Commercial debtors had to lay bare their financial souls by submitting to being examined under oath about their assets and accounts. If the bankruptcy commissioners felt they were not sufficiently forthcoming, they could be cast out of the proceedings and returned to the vagaries of civil process, which included arrest and imprisonment. If the commissioners believed they were lying, they could be referred to the court of oyer and terminer for prosecution for perjury. While under a commission, they were, in an important and humiliating sense, commercially dead in that they could no longer transact business for themselves but instead had to stand aside while a committee of their creditors acted for them.

If Pennsylvania's bankruptcy system was "productive of nothing but fraud," it was fraud on a large scale: creditors filed 172 petitions against 184 debtors between 1786 and 1790. More likely, the system facilitated a more orderly management of the consequences of large-scale commercial failure in the mercantile hub of the state, Philadelphia, which may have been reason enough for Gallatin to oppose it. The vast majority of the debtors, 145, did business in Philadelphia or the surrounding county. Twenty more were based in other counties in eastern Pennsylvania along the Delaware and Schuylkill rivers. Only four were from the western part of the state, including one who had recently moved to Pittsburgh from Philadelphia, and the petitioning creditors for all four were from Philadelphia.[23] Some number of the petitions, probably few, were collusive in the limited and hardly wrongful sense that they were filed by "friendly" creditors—often family members—against cooperative debtors, thereby turning an involuntary process into a semblance of a voluntary one. Clement Biddle, a Philadelphia broker, agreed to let a bankruptcy commission issue against him on the advice of his creditors so he could "Close my old affairs" and "go on with more security in my present business." An indeterminate number of petitions were filed by nominees chosen by their fellow creditors at formal creditors' meetings to initiate proceedings on behalf of all of them, which indicates that the decision to throw a debtor into bankruptcy was not necessarily that of a single exasperated creditor, but at least sometimes was reached by groups of creditors after conferring with one another, and perhaps also with the debtor.[24]

The availability of bankruptcy process in Pennsylvania made its absence elsewhere more conspicuous. New York, whose capital city was the only commercial center comparable to Philadelphia, changed its insolvency system with breathtaking frequency in the 1780s. For a brief time, New York offered a full bankruptcy discharge to debtors without regard to occupation or the amount of their debts, but only to debtors in prison on the date the law was enacted in 1784 or on the dates of the several renewals of the statute. The pendulum swung back two years later when the legislature replaced this modified bankruptcy system with an insolvency one that was little more than a gaol-delivery statute for small debtors who did not owe more than £15. Later in 1786 a new statute permitted debtors joined by creditors who were owed three-fourths of the debtor's outstanding debt to petition for an assignment of the debtor's estate, with the carrot of a full bankruptcy discharge at the end of the process, but within a few months the assembly repealed the discharge provision, returning the process to an insolvency system. A year later it repealed the entire act.

Amid this inconstancy, Richard Harison, a leading lawyer in New York, lamented that "[u]nfortunately we have no Bankrupt Law in the State of NY, nor any Provision to oblige a Debtor . . . to yield up his Estate for the General Benefit of all his Creditors." His lament was for creditors, not debtors. Without a bankruptcy law to compel recalcitrant debtors to turn over their property for division among all their creditors, there was no way for creditors to control failure and limit its consequences. Without a bankruptcy law to prevent debtors from making preferential payments to some creditors and not others and to force creditors to cooperate rather than compete, there was no way for creditors to protect themselves from one another.[25]

While Pennsylvania and New York fashioned legislative responses to failure, the tightening coil of indebtedness created a rather different crisis in Massachusetts. Debtor-creditor relations had long been more hostile in Massachusetts than elsewhere. As the Revolution drew to a close, the largest Boston merchants resumed their pre-Revolutionary alliance with the legislature. Together they repudiated the paper money schemes that had financed the war and pursued monetary policies that benefited the merchants in international markets. Alone among the new states, Massachusetts required that all taxes and private debts be paid in specie. The legislature then aggressively levied new taxes to retire the public debt. It compounded the distress—and doubled the debt—by appraising the state's wartime currency at par rather than revaluing it to reflect at least some of the depreciation that by early 1781 had reduced it to 75:1, as even the Continental Congress had. When the postwar depression arrived, the legislature and its mercantile backers persevered. The demand of coastal merchants for specie to satisfy their foreign creditors echoed across the state, as debt collection suits flooded the courts and imprisoned debtors crammed the jails. Particularly hard hit were the farmers of Worcester and Hampshire counties, where lawsuits for debt more than tripled over pre-war levels and where debt actions embroiled nearly a third of the adult males of each county. These debtors were at the end of the chain of credit that ran from British merchants to Boston wholesalers to inland retailers and other commercial intermediaries. Desperate, they responded with the weapons they had learned to use against Great Britain. They met in town meetings and county conventions, from which they petitioned the legislature in Boston for paper money, tender acts, stay laws, and tax relief. When rebuffed, they closed the courts and took up arms.[26]

Shays's Rebellion, easily the most traumatic event of the Confederation period, was quickly put down. As is well known, it gave urgency to the growing effort to replace the Articles of Confederation with a more effective national government and was firmly in the minds of the delegates to the Constitutional Convention when they convened in Philadelphia a few months later.[27] For purposes of the law of failure, what is most interesting is what was missing. Despite their resentment of courts as instruments of creditor oppression, none of the insurgents called on the legislature to create a voluntary bankruptcy system to cancel unpaid debts and give debtors a fresh start in the quest for economic independence. Nor did any of the merchants who urged the state to loose the militia on the rebels demand a bankruptcy system—voluntary or involuntary—to manage the division of debtors' property among their creditors. On one level, these omissions are easily explained. Since no bankruptcy system could exclude land from the debtor's assets to be distributed to creditors, one could hardly expect farmers to demand debt relief that came at the cost of their livelihoods. And merchant-creditors faced the enduring dilemma of abandoning their hopes for full repayment in return for partial satisfaction—that is, of placing their collective self-interest ahead of their individual self-interest, particularly when the legislature was already so compliant.

On another level, the omissions suggest the persistence of traditional values and class assumptions, which continued to influence attitudes toward debt. Farmers could not opt out of the credit economy. Nor did merchants want them to. Boston merchants had reacted to the postwar competition from British factors by turning farmers into consumers, thereby expanding their domestic market. They did so through the genius of advertising, first by offering manufactured items and other consumer goods for sale at enticingly low prices for cash, then in exchange for various commodities, and finally, by late in 1784, on credit at seemingly affordable terms—all toward the end of increasing sales by blurring the distinction between luxuries and necessities. This helps explain why Shaysites directed mob action against prominent local retailers as well as against the courts.[28] As depression deepened and debtors found themselves unable to pay in the hard currency demanded by their creditors, both sides invoked the traditional moral economy of debt. Shaysites petitioned not to be relieved of their debts but for reforms that would permit repayment on less destructive terms. Creditors replied with lectures on frugality, luxury, virtue, and the sanctity of obligations. The legislature attributed the scarcity of money to "our own folly" in spending "immense sums . . . for what is of no value, for the gewgaws imported from Europe"; "we greedily adopted the luxurious modes of foreign natures"; "we have indulged ourselves in fantastical and expensive fashions and intemperate living"; as "the difficulty in paying debts increased, a disregard to honesty, justice and good faith, in public and private transactions become more manifest," which can only be redeemed "by recurring to the principles of integrity and public spirit, and the practice of industry, sobriety, economy, and fidelity in contracts." The inclusive "we" was, of course, rhetorical. Debtors were the ones without virtue, not the merchants who had so aggressively purveyed credit for their own profit and who now could not conceive of applying a mercantile process such as bankruptcy to ordinary debtors.[29]

These were the debt issues that roiled the 1780s and underlay the bankruptcy clause of Article I, Section 8. The clause itself merited little attention at the Constitutional Convention. The first mention of empowering Congress to enact bankruptcy laws came in a brief exchange over the full faith and credit clause. The Articles of Confederation had required the states to accept the validity of—in constitutional terms, give full faith and credit to—each other's judicial decisions. The Committee of Detail proposed enlarging this to include acts of the state legislatures as well. James Wilson of Pennsylvania and William Samuel Johnson of Connecticut, two prominent lawyers at a convention overrun by lawyers, explained that just as court judgments in one state should be accepted as the bases for legal proceedings in others, so, too, should the acts of each state's legislature, "for the sake of Acts of insolvency etc." Upon which Charles Pinckney of South Carolina moved to commit the provision to the Committee, with the additional proposition "To establish uniform laws upon the subject of bankruptcies, and respecting the damages on the protest of foreign bills of exchange." What prompted Pinckney to raise these new issues is unknown. There is no record of any delegate even uttering the word "bankruptcy" before this. South Carolina did have a bankruptcy system of sorts, which in important details was unlike any other. A colonial-era holdover, it discharged only those debts owed to creditors who accepted a dividend from the debtor's estate. The only protection offered the debtor against creditors who refused to settle for less than their full due was a twelve-month stay of their collection actions. In other words, the South Carolina discharge was so limited as to be largely illusory. Whether Pinckney was seeking to assure full-faith-and-credit acceptance of South Carolina's limited bankruptcy system, or to empower Congress to impose a true bankruptcy system, or something else altogether is open to conjecture. In any event, subsequent discussion on the motion did not mention Pinckney's addition. When the matter returned to the floor five days later, the expanded full faith and credit clause and the newly created bankruptcy clause—minus any mention of foreign bills of exchange—were taken up and voted on one after the other, although the final draft of the Constitution placed them in widely separated articles.[30]

As Wilson and Johnson intimated, insolvency drove the extension of full faith and credit to acts of the legislature. Alone among the states that had some form of insolvency process, Connecticut granted insolvency relief by legislative act rather than judicial decree. Although the Connecticut assembly was rather sparing in its grants of relief, many of the petitioners were merchants and traders who, if granted an act of insolvency or the lesser boon of temporary freedom from arrest, could travel less nervously to meet with their creditors in neighboring states and do business there if those acts conferred extraterritorial protection through the wonders of full faith and credit.[31] For its part, Pennsylvania had already dealt with issues of comity in insolvency on the question of whether a debtor who had been released from jail in New Jersey under that state's insolvency act could plead the New Jersey discharge to set aside a judgment entered against him by a Pennsylvania court for the same debt—in other words, asking Pennsylvania to accept the New Jersey discharge as its own in bar of further proceedings on the debt. Lawyers for the debtor, one Andrew Allen, argued that the full faith and credit clause of the Articles of Confederation meant that the New Jersey discharge "may be carried about by the D[efendant] to every State in the union as an impenatrable suit of armour to defend him from all future attacks upon his liberty for a cause of action then existing." The creditors' lawyers, one of whom, Jared Ingersoll, later served with Wilson in the Pennsylvania delegation to the Constitutional Convention, replied that the New Jersey discharge was a mere "Municipal regulation," "a local order confined to a limited district," which only released Allen from the Essex County jail and shielded him from further arrest in New Jersey but did not determine the underlying debt or how Pennsylvania could proceed. The presiding judge of the court of common pleas for Philadelphia County, Edward Shippen, agreed. If the New Jersey order had discharged the debt, he stated, full faith and credit might have required Pennsylvania to follow suit, but an order discharging a debtor from jail in one state did not discharge him from a different jail in a different state. In a passage with which Wilson surely would have been familiar, and Ingersoll clearly was, Shippen wrote that "Insolvent laws subsist in every State in the Union, and are probably all different from each other; . . . and they have never been considered as binding out of the limits of the State that made them."[32]

While the delegates were meeting in Philadelphia, Ingersoll was preparing to argue—or perhaps had recently argued, the precise timing is uncertain—a case that squarely raised the issue of what effect a full bankruptcy discharge in one state should have in another. For a brief period in 1787, Maryland had a bankruptcy statute. A debtor, one Hall, a resident of Maryland, had received a discharge under the statute. His creditor, one Millar, who lived in Philadelphia, had not seen the notice of Hall's intent to seek the benefit of the act, which was published as the statute required in the *Maryland Gazette,* nor had Hall listed Millar as a creditor in his schedule of debts—oversights that meant that Millar had not had the opportunity to share in the division of Hall's estate. When Hall next set foot in Pennsylvania, Millar had him arrested for the unpaid debt. Ingersoll, representing Hall before the Pennsylvania Supreme Court, argued that the full faith and credit clause of the Articles of Confederation required Pennsylvania to recognize the Maryland discharge. He also contended that the same result was compelled "from general principles; . . . from the reason of the thing, and from the mischievous consequences of a contrary position," because without it, "perpetual imprisonment must be the lot of every man who fails; and all hope of retrieving his losses by honest and industrious pursuits, will be cut off from the intemperate bankrupt." While he and his fellow delegates were mulling the bankruptcy clause, Ingersoll obviously could not have known that the court would agree with him when it ruled in January 1788. Still less could he have known that Chief Justice Thomas McKean would skip lightly over the full faith and credit clause and instead base his opinion on the "general principles" Ingersoll had argued. Nonetheless, Ingersoll was one of the most astute lawyers in the country and doubtless knew he had made an argument that was likely to persuade. He also doubtless knew that it was an argument that could justify a uniform law of bankruptcy.[33]

Although never discussed openly—or at least not so openly as to leave tracks in the historical record—the idea that bankruptcy raised issues that were better addressed on a national level rather than through the mechanisms of interstate comity seems to have taken at least tentative root during the convention. The lawyers and judges in the two Pennsylvania cases, and through them some of the key delegates to the convention, clearly recognized the problems inherent in applying state insolvency and bankruptcy rules to debtors and creditors who lived in different states. Credit, like commerce, could not be contained within state boundaries. Full faith and credit helped somewhat, but it could harm out-of-state creditors by imposing on them state bankruptcy discharges that stripped them of their claims without their participation in the process. As Wilson remarked at the Pennsylvania ratifying convention, "Merchants of eminence will tell you that they can trust their correspondents without law; but they cannot trust the laws of the state in which their correspondents live." Federal "uniform Laws on the subject of Bankruptcies," which subjected debtors and creditors to the same rules and procedures regardless of where they lived, would be more in keeping with the interstate nature of commerce and the credit relations on which commerce rested. James Madison recognized this in the one mention of the bankruptcy clause in *The Federalist,* when he wrote that the "power of establishing uniform laws of bankruptcy, is so intimately connected with the regulation of commerce, and will prevent so many frauds where the parties or their property may lie or be removed into different States, that the expediency of it seems not likely to be drawn into question."[34]

Madison's mention of frauds notwithstanding, it is evident that the purpose behind empowering Congress to establish uniform laws on bankruptcy was to protect debtors—albeit not all debtors—as well as creditors, a dual purpose recognized by at least some participants in the ratification debates.[35] English bankruptcy law, on the other hand, which Madison seems at least dimly to have had in mind, focused more on protecting creditors from the evasive malfeasance of commercial debtors, even to the extent of criminalizing certain statutorily enumerated acts of bankruptcy. An involuntary system, it grew out of sixteenth-century attempts to deal with the creditors' bête noire, the fraudulent or dishonest debtor, by making various acts taken to avoid creditors felonies punishable, like all felonies, by death. Widespread recognition by merchants that failure could result from misfortune as easily as immorality, together with pressure from writers as sharply persuasive as Daniel Defoe, prompted Parliament to enact statutory distinctions between honest and dishonest bankrupts in the early eighteenth century. However, the frequent difficulty of distinguishing between the two contributed to the continued divergence of judicial and mercantile understandings of what bankruptcy law should accomplish. Judges, whose business was adjudicating issues of individual civil and criminal behavior, were more concerned with punishing fraud, while merchants, whose business was business and who necessarily included debtors as well as creditors, were more interested in Madison's "regulation of commerce." The limited evidence of the Constitutional Convention suggests that the framers had in mind the latter.

After this seemingly uncontroversial beginning, the question of national bankruptcy relief languished. Proposals for "uniform Laws on the subject of Bankruptcies" arose and died in each Congress from the very first one through the 1790s. Despite repeated efforts, Congress failed to enact even a temporary bankruptcy law until 1800, and a permanent one not until 1898. The apparent ease of including the bankruptcy clause in the Constitution was misleading. After all, "bankrupt" was still a term of opprobrium, even for people who otherwise welcomed the expected benefits to commerce and credit that the new government would bring. Oliver Ellsworth, one of the Connecticut delegates to the convention, asserted that anyone who favored paper money and tender laws "effectually advertises himself a bankrupt" as well as an opponent of the Constitution. An unnamed Massachusetts satirist lumped "bankrupts" with "paper-money gentry," "land-jobbers," "state-leeches," "idlers," and even unreconstructed Tories.[36]

Moreover, where Madison had skipped lightly over the clause, Antifederalist writers saw something rather more sinister, even conspiratorial. The anonymous "Federal Farmer" argued that even if uniform bankruptcy laws were practicable—which he thought unlikely given "the extent of the country, and the very different ideas of the different parts in it, respecting credit, and the mode of making men's property liable for paying their debts"—a federal bankruptcy power was nonetheless an interference "with the internal police of the separate states, especially with their administering justice among their own citizens." Such a power threatened to extend the reach of the federal judiciary—always a concern of the Antifederalists—by drawing "almost all civil causes" into the federal courts.[37] The equally anonymous "Deliberator," ignoring the distinction between bankruptcy and insolvency, claimed that the clause meant that "[n]o state can give relief to insolvent debtors, however distressing their situation may be." A third dissenter, "Aristocrotis," addressed James

Wilson as a "political hackney writer to the most lucrative order of the bank," the "only person fitted by nature to organize the government upon true despotic principles," and satirically urged him to "make some provision for the relief of your insolvent brethren" by procuring Congress to constitute the future capital "a Sanctum-Sanctorum, a place of refuge for well born bankrupts, to shelter themselves and property from the rapacity of their persecuting creditors."[38]

Despite the strenuous efforts of Federalist polemicists to stigmatize all Antifederalists as "knaves, harpies, and debtors," the lines of division were not nearly so neat. When asked to identify who favored and who opposed the Constitution, George Bryan, a judge on the Pennsylvania Supreme Court, readily placed various groups in one camp or the other—merchants, lawyers, ministers, "Monied Men," sailors, Tories, commercial artisans, even women (who "all admire Gen. W.") for, with farmers and "Men of Letters" against—but not debtors or creditors. Perhaps recalling his own mercantile failure and bankruptcy before the war, he wrote that "Creditors were influenced in favor of it by their aversion to paper money;—yet some were opposed to it," and that "Debtors are often Creditors in their Turn" and just as averse to paper money. His son Arthur pointedly captured the contradictions when he wondered how the eminent John Rutledge, who represented South Carolina at both the federal constitutional and state ratifying conventions, could "agree to that article of paying debts" when he bought his own bonds at steep discounts and laughingly stiffed his creditors.[39]

Against this background it should not be surprising that bankruptcy was politically problematic from the beginning. One early exchange illustrates why. Midway through the first session of the First Congress, the House appointed a committee of three strongly Federalist lawyers—Fisher Ames of Massachusetts, John Laurance of New York, and William Loughton Smith of South Carolina—to draft a bankruptcy bill. Nothing happened. Eight months later, Thomas Hartley of Pennsylvania renewed the call for a bill, saying that "some steps should be taken to show that Congress had the credit of the country in view." It was Smith who objected first, arguing that the "present situation of the country . . . was such as to render a general law on this subject a more intricate and perplexing business than the gentleman was aware of"—the wealthy young cosmopolitan educated at the Middle Temple while others fought the Revolution condescending to the soldier ten years his senior who had only recently read law in central Pennsylvania. Smith said he "thought it most prudent to defer the business till the public debt should be funded, and banks established," allegedly because without a funded debt and banks "it was difficult to conceive how arrangements could be made to facilitate the payment of debts, or the operation of such a law." Theodore Sedgwick of Massachusetts seconded Smith's observations and added that although England "had enjoyed a degree of tranquillity and domestic happiness unknown for a century before" since adopting its "present system of bankruptcy," the "obvious difference in the circumstances of the two countries, with respect to commercial transactions" made bankruptcy not yet ripe for discussion, at least not until "there appeared to him to be a greater facility in recovering debts." Hartley agreed to let his motion be tabled.[40]

Smith, Sedgwick, and Hartley did not disagree on the desirability of national bankruptcy legislation. Nor did they disagree on the importance of promoting commerce. But Smith and Sedgwick were more astute than Hartley. For them, the most urgent issue was funding the public debt. Indeed, Smith and Sedgwick, together with Laurance and Ames, were among the most vocal supporters of Hamilton's funding plan when Congress began debating it a few days later. Taking up the question of whether private debtors might escape their obligations would have complicated an already contentious debate on the nature of obligation itself. One could not easily claim that the credit, reputation, and commerce of the nation rested on the repayment of public debts in full while also asserting that business would be served by allowing commercial debtors to repay their private debts only in part. The two issues had to be separated. Moreover, southern planters, whose support was needed if funding was to pass, were vigorously resisting the demands of their British creditors that they repay their pre-war debts. This was not the time for supporters of funding to propose a bankruptcy law that would further empower creditors and expose land to execution.

Then there was the matter of commerce itself. Southern Antifederalists embraced trade but not commerce, which many associated with stockjobbers and other speculators rather than with merchants. They saw the displacement of state by federal commercial authority as simply trading subordination to British merchants for subordination to northern merchants. George Mason had warned against this at the Constitutional Convention when he proposed that federal commercial legislation should require a two-thirds majority in each house until 1808—a date that would have symbolically linked restrictions on federal commercial power to the prohibition on federal interference with the slave trade.[41] Amid such suspicion, a bankruptcy law, which in its English form was quintessentially commercial legislation, would not pass easily. However, the power of speculation was such that by the end of the decade it was almost inevitable that a bankruptcy law would pass.

The "spirit of speculation" that William Barton decried in 1781 was even more pervasive ten years later. Investors had welcomed first the prospect, then the reality, of a national government as an invitation to speculate on scales previously unimagined. The advent of such massive speculation—whether in bank stock, government securities, or land—transformed indebtedness in fundamental ways. Agricultural debt had a seasonal quality to it. Farmers and planters borrowed for current needs or wants with the expectation of repaying after the harvest. That the expectation was often only a hope did not change the seasonal, and therefore cyclical, nature of the process, which was the same whether the obligation lay on the books of a local shopkeeper or existed as credits extended by an English tobacco merchant. Speculative debt, on the other hand, was utterly independent of the natural calendar. It was detached from the land and had no connection with the production or exchange of goods, whether agricultural or manufactured. The financial world of the speculator was thus built more completely on promises than that of any merchant—promises to buy up land warrants or scrip that, in essence, he would resell at prices that would enable him to repay his investors at the promised times and promised rates of interest.

Moreover, to a far greater extent than routine extensions of commercial credit, speculation sorted debtors into large and small, each with different kinds of indebtedness and different reasons for borrowing. Speculators such as Robert Morris and William Duer dealt in sums that far exceeded the capital resources of even the greatest American merchant—sums that they accumulated in the form of loans from thousands of investors, some for large amounts, others for small ones. Speculators stood at the center of a financial vortex. Their competition for capital drove up the interest rates they had to offer to investors, which in turn attracted investments from ever-widening circles, both demographically and geographically. As a result, when they failed, the effects of their failure rippled outward, often engulfing those who had loaned them money. The correspondence of the great speculators as they slid into insolvency brims with letters from investor-creditors who had loaned amounts that, although small to the speculators, were large to them and who were now pleading for at least partial payment to stave off their own creditors or even hunger.

The rise of speculation as the investment of choice in the 1790s had several consequences. The most obvious one is that the two financial crises of the decade were triggered by the collapse of speculation schemes—the bursting of Duer's speculations in bank stock and government securities in 1792 and the failure of large land ventures in 1797, many of which involved Morris. The resulting economic distress far surpassed any that had occurred before. For the first time numerous prominent men found themselves imprisoned for their debts or fugitives from their creditors. Their presence in the pool of insolvent debtors confounded the normal expectations of social and economic status and altered the political dimensions of debtors' relief. A less obvious consequence is that the debate over debtor relief was recast as a debate on the merits of bankruptcy. The reasons for this are twofold. One is that the sudden increase in the number of people imprisoned for their debts generated new calls for ending the practice, which necessarily raised the question of how else to deal with unpaid debts. The other is that the identity of the speculator-debtors dovetailed with the traditional ambit of bankruptcy in England, where bankruptcy relief was available only to merchants, traders, and brokers, whose debts exceeded a minimum that itself exceeded the typical indebtedness of farmers, laborers, and shopkeepers—in short, of most ordinary debtors. Together, these two factors made discussion of bankruptcy inevitable.

As Harrison Gray Otis surveyed the wreckage of the Panic of 1792—once-wealthy friends and others "roused from the gilded dream, and presented with splendid ruin"—he asked his wife "why do mankind eternally sigh to explore the latent charms of affluence, regardless of the dangers and the stress?" The answer in part, as Otis well knew, was the addictive allure of speculative profits, which required nothing more of investor-creditors than passive loans and the belief that prices only rose, never fell. For William Duer, this belief was simple enough to maintain. His determination to corner the market in bank stock and government securities required ever-increasing sums of capital as his own purchases drove prices upward. To feed his speculations, he borrowed from a widening circle of people to whom he gave promissory notes at whatever interest was necessary to induce them to part with their money, while pointing to the rapid rise in prices as proof of the promised wealth. The stock and securities that were the objects of Duer's speculations were novel abstractions to unsophisticated investors—which is to say, to most people. Prices of land and goods could stagnate, but the sharp, almost magical rise of these new instruments promised quick, easy, sure profits. The faster and higher they rose, the more intense the desire to partake. Months before the bubble burst, observers commented on the frenzied, gambling-like atmosphere. Seth Johnson reported from New York in August 1791 that "[t]he rage of speculation is arrived to an alarming height," such that "[i]t is difficult to stand or breath in the Coffee House room at the time of sales." He predicted that the "greatest sufferers" would be the "new adventurers"— novice investors—who enticed "by the prospect of gain risqued their all in a business they were unacquainted with." To Johnson's eye, they exhibited all "the anxiety and eagerness attendant on deepplay"—gaming. Similarly, Thomas Jefferson, who wrote from Philadelphia that "[s]crip and stock are food and raiment here," likened speculation to rolling dice, saying that "the credit and fate of the nation seem to hang on the desperate throws and plunges of gambling scoundrels." One of those "gambling scoundrels," Alexander Macomb, wrote after his own failure that "[t]his damn'd Speculative concern appears more like gambling than anything else," although we should probably not mistake his regret for an epiphany. Amid this mania, Congress appointed a second committee to draft a bankruptcy bill in November 1791. One of its members was Elias Boudinot, the older brother of John Pintard's friend and soon-to-be protector. The committee was still deliberating when Duer defaulted and took refuge in the New Gaol the following March.[42]

The panic triggered by Duer's failure was literal as well as economic. Benjamin Rush recorded in his diary that a "gentleman just arrived from New York says that he scarcely entered a house in which he did not find the woman in tears and the husband wringing his hands," and that "Men are often seen to weep in the streets." Henrietta Maria Colden reported to John Laurance, one of the committee preparing the bankruptcy bill, that "speculators are daily boxing in the streets, Cursing and abusing each other like pick pockets, and trying every fraud to prey on each others distresses." Rush also heard that "Fighting and boxing are common at the Coffee house" and noted two similar incidents in Philadelphia.[43] The first notes Duer defaulted on were the promises he had made to repay the money he had borrowed so aggressively by sending his brokers, whom one correspondent described as "little better than robbers," into "every house where they thought there was money." This was not the capital he had raised from merchants and traders in secured loans, which he also defaulted on, but was money raised "principally among the middling and poorer classes of people." These were the shop keepers, cartmen, draymen, butchers, oystermen, gardeners, market women, widows, orphans, and prostitutes, remarked on by numerous observers, whom Duer's agents persuaded to part with their hard-earned savings by promising interest as high as 60 percent a year and assuring them that the promissory notes they received in return were "perfectly safe."[44] They were, in other words, unsophisticated investors who, in an economy with few investment opportunities for people of their limited resources, did not understand that interest rates reflected risk and who naively believed that a promise was a guarantee.

When Duer failed, taking their dreams and their savings with him, their panic was real. Five hundred people mobbed the streets and stoned the jail, breaking windows and street lamps. Although the rioters included a few merchants, after the fashion of Revolutionary-era mobs, they were the exception. Whereas Duer's larger creditors threatened litigation, his smaller ones, who did not have the resources to ride out the legal process, threatened violence. It was "the lower class to whom he owes money" that talked of dragging Duer from jail and hanging him—with the single colorful exception of Pierre de Peyster, a merchant who cornered Duer with a brace of pistols and told him he must duel or pay, saying that "he might as well lose his life as his money." In the end their talk was simply that, but at the time, as one nervous party wrote, "whether it will all wind up without bloodshed God knows."[45]

The specter of violence notwithstanding, what most alarmed observers of the panic was the rapid spread of failures. Within days of Duer's collapse, numerous other prominent merchants, brokers, and traders—all involved with Duer—stopped payment, shut themselves in their houses to avoid arrest, fled the city, or followed Duer to jail in a remarkable display of how large speculative schemes, which grew on the promise of independence, in reality made participants dependent on one another in what Colden referred to as "the whole fabric of Speculation." As Jefferson reported to his son-in-law in Virginia, Duer's failure "soon brought on others, and these still more, like nine pins knocking one another down, till . . . the bankruptcy is become general, every man concerned in paper being broke." The distinction of the bankrupts also impressed. Colden's very first observation on the panic was that "the most opulent men in this City are wholly ruined." Rush remarked on the "bespoke carriages" of the failed brokers and, ever the clinical observer of human behavior, recorded that he had "not heard of one instance of Insanity, and only one suicide," which, to his seeming relief, "was a Frenchman." From the beginning, the more perceptive commentators recognized that the wave of failures would reach Boston and Philadelphia, where there had been heavy investment in Duer's schemes. Others thought the collapse so great "as to affect . . . private Credit from Georgia to New Hampshire." Even people who had not invested with Duer felt the consequences of his fall. Construction projects ground to a halt, laying off workmen, and prices of produce from the countryside plummeted because of the sudden, sharp constriction in private credit. As Seth Johnson noted with some awe, "Such a revolution of property perhaps never before happened."[46]

Amid the crisis, people knew of the possible bankruptcy bill. Some speculated on how it might help. When a report circulated that Alexander Macomb, one of Duer's principal partners and creditors, had put real estate worth £70,000 beyond the reach of his creditors by transferring title to his brother in Canada just before entering debtors' prison, Samuel Blodget expressed the hope that such fraudulent conveyances "might be rendered null provided the Bankrupt Law now Pending in Committee is passd this Session of Congress." John Pintard assured a creditor from his refuge in Newark that he considered himself "still in honor bound to make good these debts . . . notwithstanding any release I may obtain from an Act of Bankruptcy." However, no bill left committee. The largest obstacle was Duer himself.[47]

Duer personified the panic. He was "the Prince of Speculators." "He alone has been the source of all the misfortunes which are now experienced." "Well may this Town exclaim cursed be the house that gave the world a *Duer*." When the *Boston Gazette* blamed the debacle on "a set of Swindlers, who ought to be in Simsbury Mines," everyone knew who the chief swindler was.[48] Even Duer's closest associates, who were roundly denounced themselves, pointed accusing fingers at him. When Duer asked his partners to "[d]istinguish between an Unfortunate, and a guilty Person," they did, although not as he had wished. Macomb, who concealed assets, made fraudulent and preferential transfers, and bought on credit until the day he stopped payment, and who was criticized for not admitting his complicity "like the man of honor or honesty," denied his own responsibility and instead condemned "this damned Duer." Walter Livingston, who fled to his country estate and boasted to his son-in-law that before leaving the city he had hidden assets so that "Ex post Facto Laws will not effect it," accused Duer of "endeavoring to despoil" him.[49] Duer did not, of course, speculate alone. But the panic nonetheless bore his face. Any bankruptcy law that released him, as any bankruptcy law would, would have sparked outrage. Moreover, Duer did not want bankruptcy relief. Although notoriously unrevealing in his correspondence—he preferred oral communication for its greater security—there is no indication that he ever advocated a bankruptcy law, even during his seven years' imprisonment. Instead, he was determined to speculate his way out of insolvency and back to wealth through various land schemes. A bankruptcy discharge would have stripped him of the wherewithal to do so.

There matters lay until fall. In late November Congress reconstituted the committee to draft a bill, adding William Loughton Smith, who evidently thought the issue riper then than he had thirty months earlier. Why he thought so became apparent twelve days later, when 148 of his fellow South Carolinians, merchants and traders all, petitioned the Senate for a bankruptcy law "for their relief." Within days Smith presented a bankruptcy bill to the House, which after two readings referred it to the Committee of the Whole, where it quietly died.[50] No copy of the bill survives, but Jefferson's objections to it do. His "Extempore thoughts and doubts," as he labeled them, briefly outlined the issues that shaped the debate over bankruptcy for the remainder of the decade. They also reveal the depth of the antipathy to the kind of speculation that had precipitated the recent panic.[51]

Jefferson, who during the panic had deplored the "stockjobbing speculations" that drained capital from "commerce, manufactures, buildings and agriculture," seemed pleased that the bill followed English law in excluding "the buyers and sellers of bank stock, government paper etc." from its application.[52] But he was alarmed by whom the bill did include. Where British law expressly exempted "*farmers, graziers, drovers,* as such, tho they buy to sell again," the American bill did not, which implied that agrarian debtors who traded on the side would be swept together with merchants. Where British courts adjudicated shoemakers, blacksmiths, and carpenters as bankrupts "if the materials of their art are bought," Jefferson questioned whether "the body of our artists desire to be brought within the vortex of this law?" In addition to fearing for the artisans themselves, he argued that principles of master-servant law might make a bankrupt of a master who employed an artisan as a hired or indentured servant or as a slave for his own benefit, if the servant in his spare time made anything for the master's neighbors. Jefferson also objected that the bill would invoke federal intervention too readily by treating any move across state lines as an act of bankruptcy, even though the debtor remained subject to legal process under the full faith and credit clause. He deeply disagreed with the power given to commissioners to "enter houses, break open doors, chests, etc." to search for assets, asking rhetorically, "Is that spirit of independance and sovereignty which a man feels in his own house, and which Englishmen felt when they denominated their houses their castles, to be absolutely subdued, and is it expedient that it should be subdued?"—thus echoing James Otis's argument against writs of assistance before the Revolution.[53]

To Jefferson, these reservations paled next to what he saw as the most threatening part of the bill—that it permitted the land of bankrupt debtors to be seized and sold. In his notes to Madison and letters to others, Jefferson cast the issue as federal trespass on state prerogative—he considered land title solely a matter of state law—but his true objection was not one of constitutional theory. It was that the failure to exclude agrarian debtors who engaged in some trading would "render almost all the landholders South of [Pennsylvania] liable to be declared bankrupts," and thus subject to losing their land to their creditors. The bill placed "landed and farming men . . . in danger of being drawn into it's vortex."[54] This led Jefferson to his peroration, which is worth quoting in full:

> Is Commerce so much the basis of the existence of the U.S. as to call for a bankrupt law? On the contrary are we not almost merely agricultural? Should not all laws be made with a view essentially to the husbandman? When laws are wanting for particular descriptions of other callings, should not the husbandman be carefully excepted from their operation, and preserved under that of the general system only, which general system is fitted to the condition of the husbandman?

Although a common trope for Jefferson, this was the first time that anyone assigned bankruptcy to a side along the ideological divide between commerce and agriculture in the new nation. From that moment forward, bankruptcy ceased to be about debtors and creditors and became instead part of the struggle for the soul of the republic.

The same minuet of apparent action followed by deliberate inaction recurred in the Third Congress and the Fourth, with committees appointed and bills reported and ignored.[55] Insolvent debtors like John Pintard might lament "the impossibility of settling [their] affairs without a Statute of Bankruptcy," but the drumbeat of denunciations of speculators continued. James Sullivan, the attorney general of Massachusetts, regarded it as inevitable that "[w]hile there are stocks transferable by their constitution, there will be stockjobbers," and argued that it was a business like any other—"reputable and honourable" when conducted "with truth, sincerity, and fairness," and "contemptible and dangerous to society" when practiced with "chicane, cunning, deceit, and fraud." But few shared his opinion. Hugh Henry Brackenridge—novelist, lawyer, and, later, judge—censured speculators for seeking profit in manipulation and chance rather than productive labor. His Princeton classmate, Philip Freneau, addressed speculators as "Base grasping souls" and devised titles of nobility to reward speculators, starting with "the order of the Leech" and ascending to the "Order of the Golden Fleece," with their lordships to be addressed as "Their fulnesses," "Their Rapacities," "Their Hucksterships," or "Their Pirate-ships," according to their rank. More mildly, a writer in Charleston cautioned bank directors against discounting notes for speculators. Another in New York hoped that the bankruptcy bill then languishing in Congress would relieve honest debtors but leave no loopholes for cunning manipulators like Duer to escape through.[56]

The denunciations continued because speculation itself did, primarily in land. Land schemes were hardly novel, but the scale was. New opportunities abounded. The cession of state land claims to the federal government, the promised withdrawal of the British from the frontier, the diminished threat from Indian tribes, the extension of internal transportation networks, and the availability of easy credit and surplus settlers opened the trans-Appalachian West. Large, unsettled tracts in Maine and upstate New York also beckoned. Thomas M. Doerflinger has described the surge in land speculation as "an escapist flight from trade, a way to build up a fortune without enduring the drudgery and risks of day-to-day commerce."[57] It drew on the already mythic lure of land on the vast and, to European eyes, unoccupied American continent. Fueled in part by loans from the city's three banks, Philadelphia speculators led the way in buying up enormous tracts of land. While some invested wisely—carefully evaluating prospective purchases for quality and location, limiting their borrowing, meticulously organizing and supervising settlement—most allowed themselves to be swept along by the seeming certainty of easy, immodest profits that speculative fever generates. Many bought land sight unseen in amounts greater than they could afford. Then, with no patience for the laborious task of selling lots to individual settlers, they gambled on quick resale to other speculators. Not surprisingly, most failed. Ironically, given that virtually all of these schemes contemplated eventual agrarian settlement, the speculation that set in motion the failures that led to the Bankruptcy Act of 1800—which southern planters vigorously opposed— was not agricultural at all. It was spawned by those same planters' insistence on locating the national capital on the Potomac.

Like all "public" works of the era, Washington, D.C., was a feat of government-licensed private enterprise. It was also an invitation to speculation. To build a city from nothing and to finance the construction of government buildings, the commissioners of the nascent Federal City sold lots on the condition that purchasers build on them to prescribed specifications within a certain time. James Greenleaf, a persuasive young merchant-speculator from Boston, purchased three thousand lots in September 1793, to be paid for in annual installments without interest. He quickly joined with Robert Morris and John Nicholson of Philadelphia to buy another three thousand lots on similar terms and made them partners in the ones he had already bought. Within three months their partnership controlled 40 percent of the building lots in the future capital. Greenleaf, who had traded in Amsterdam and was married to a Dutch baroness who did not yet know that he had deserted her, promised to secure loans from Dutch bankers to finance the speculation. However, the French invasion of Holland intervened and diverted Dutch capital to the widening war in Europe. What little money Greenleaf did raise he used to pay his own obligations, which Morris and Nicholson did not learn of until later. He also drew large sums on Morris's credit by bills of exchange, which Morris did not discover until presented with the bills for payment.[58]

Faced with installment payments and no cash, and finding few purchasers for their Washington lots, the three men formed the North American Land Company in February 1795 to hold six million acres of land they owned or claimed individually from their other speculations in Pennsylvania, Virginia, Georgia, Kentucky, and the Carolinas. The scheme was to consolidate their speculations, raise the capital they needed to pay their creditors by selling stock in the diversified company to European investors, and share in the anticipated profits from the sale of the land, which would appreciate in value as they improved it and peopled it with settlers drawn from America's rapidly growing population. However, Greenleaf, whose resources were never as great as he pretended, was dilatory and evasive in fulfilling his commitments. He also misappropriated money that was to have paid part of an installment due in Washington and defaulted on notes that Morris and Nicholson had endorsed for him. In exasperation, and in an attempt to gain control of their fates, Morris and Nicholson bought out Greenleaf's interest first in the Federal City venture in July 1795, then in the North American Land Company a year later. As they, too, were strapped for cash, they paid him with promissory notes backed by the Washington lots or the company shares as collateral—an arrangement that assured that they would never be free of him.[59]

Although not by design, the speculation came to resemble a giant pyramid scheme, as Morris and Nicholson scrambled for new investors to raise cash to pay promised dividends to old investors and to meet their other obligations, which included interests in numerous other land companies. Morris dispatched a small army of agents—among them his son-in-law, James Marshall, younger brother of the future chief justice—to Europe to sell stock and land and to obtain loans secured by the company shares, with scant success. He corresponded tirelessly with possible investors in Europe and America, singing the praises of his lands after the timeless fashion of all promoters: "This country continues in the most flourishing and thriving state of any in the world." The "Lands are amongst those of the best quality that can possibly be had." "[E]very Stroke of an axe gives additional Value to the Land." The "price of our Lands . . . will continue rising every year for a Century or more, and the profit to those who can lay out the Money and keep the Lands will be certain and great."[60]

Morris's pitch concealed a rising desperation. He and Nicholson had made massive land purchases on credit in the expectation of quick sales, which did not materialize. The North American Land Company represented only a portion of their holdings. European investors looked on American land schemes with suspicion. Pressed for cash, Morris and Nicholson financed their purchases with millions of dollars' worth of their notes, which they cheerfully cross-endorsed for each other and which creditors readily accepted because, after all, if a financial colossus like Robert Morris was not creditworthy, who was? As their fortunes declined, their notes—referred to as "M & Ns"—traded at increasingly steep discounts and became objects of speculation themselves, even as they remained a heavily depreciated medium of exchange.[61] To complicate things further, their land titles were rarely clear. Imprecise surveys, no surveys, unextinguished Indian titles, competing claims from other speculators, unissued patents, unmet conditions, squatters' claims, mortgages and other encumbrances, litigation claims, creditors' attachments, government liens, tax assessments, mechanics' liens—in short, every title defect known to law—made their land both difficult to sell and difficult to hold on to. In addition, much of the land turned out to be worthless dirt that swindlers as entrepreneurial in their own way as Morris and Nicholson were in theirs had passed off on the partners. Then their notes started falling due. Nicholson alone turned away so many demands for payment that the notary who recorded the protests began using printed forms, with Nicholson's name preprinted as well.[62] The result was a cloud that began to settle over their affairs as early as 1794 and that grew to envelop everyone with whom they did business, which is to say almost every investor of consequence in the country.

The outbreak of war in Europe in 1793 triggered a rash of mercantile failures in London, many of whom were Morris's correspondents on whom he had drawn bills of exchange that they now could not honor, which meant that the payees now looked to Morris for satisfaction. Men of lesser means than Morris whose bills also were returned could not stay afloat and so failed themselves. A French trader in Philadelphia warned a countryman that "bankruptcies are multiplying" to such an extent that "[i]t seems that men and the elements have conspired against our unfortunate city." As the European conflict widened, the sharp constriction of credit available in Europe combined with French predations on American shipping to disrupt American commerce, drive the cost of money even higher, and expose the precariousness of land speculation schemes built on pyramids of credit. Morris and Nicholson were only the largest of many speculators who had issued large quantities of commercial paper backed by the land they claimed to own.[63]

By December 1796 business failures were epidemic. Benjamin Rush counted 150 failures in six weeks in Philadelphia and sixty-seven people imprisoned for debt in two weeks. Among them was James Wilson, whose extensive speculations had been a continuing distraction from his duties as an associate justice of the United States Supreme Court, to which he had been appointed in 1789. His confinement was brief, but it worried Morris, "for W-l-ns affair will make the Vultures more keen after me." The biggest, most prominent speculators were no longer immune from the indignity of arrest and imprisonment. Indeed, the rumor that Morris himself was in prison circulated in New York and Boston. As Morris wrote to a Baltimore creditor, "People are ready to tear one another to pieces." Morris's and Nicholson's notes, held by virtually everyone and said to total $10,000,000, were trading at one-eighth of their face value. With money so scarce, interest rates rose so high that hundreds of people called in low-interest loans and withdrew their money from banks to lend it through brokers at 30 percent and higher. They were the profiteers to whom Morris referred when he wrote of the "vultures who are preying upon the general scene of distress" and for whom "no premium for the use of their money is enough nor any security sufficient." A "spirit of speculation infected all ranks."[64]

Not everyone regretted the distress. Theodore Sedgwick, for one, was "not sorry that the bubble of speculation has burst" and even found satisfaction "in the reflection that the sins have been confined wholly to the Jacobins"—the label that Federalists used as an epithet and Republicans adopted with pride. Other Federalists were not as severe. Robert Goodloe Harper of South Carolina, an investor in the North American Land Company, rose in Congress to say that "the state of the country called for" a bankruptcy law, but again nothing resulted, although this time it took a vote rather than neglect to table the bill. Congress's ritual of reporting bankruptcy bills then refusing to consider them kept insolvency law in a state of suspense. Only Connecticut, Rhode Island, and Maryland permitted bankruptcy discharges, and then only on special petition to the legislature, which meant that relief was random. Pennsylvania, which had let its bankruptcy statute lapse in 1793, withheld enacting a new one because of the prospect that Congress would act and preempt the field. However, with Philadelphia bearing the brunt of the failures, the deliberateness of Congress's inaction pushed the Pennsylvania assembly to take up a bankruptcy bill limited to commercial debtors imprisoned for two months or more. Morris recommended it to Nicholson, but it did not pass.[65]

The paper pyramid collapsed in 1797, when speculators could no longer find takers for their notes or forestall their creditors. Morris and Nicholson gave up control of their Washington lots to the trustees of the Aggregate Fund, which they formed with their creditors in the Federal City project to try to save the lots from foreclosure by the city commissioners. Beset by dozens of lawsuits, they evaded arrest for months by sequestering themselves at their country estates outside Philadelphia. Within the year, however, virtually every major speculator was in jail—first Greenleaf, then Morris, and finally, late in 1799, Nicholson. Wilson abandoned the Supreme Court and was imprisoned first in Burlington, New Jersey, then in New Castle, Delaware, and lastly in Edenton, North Carolina, where he had fled to avoid arrest. He died there from malaria and a stroke, reportedly raving deliriously on his deathbed about arrest, bad debts, and bankruptcy. Jefferson reported to Madison that "the prison is full of the most reputable merchants, and it is understood that the scene is not yet got to its height." For six months Morris and Greenleaf occupied adjoining rooms in Prune Street, much to the distaste of Morris, who wrote Nicholson that "I do not want to be under the same roof with such a scoundrel lest it should fall to crush the guilty and the innocent be involved in the same fate." Greenleaf's custom of "indulging himself with a rapid ride, on a fine horse" in the prison courtyard each morning while Morris exercised more soberly by walking doubtless did not lessen the distaste. Sedgwick, who referred to Morris and Greenleaf as "the great destroyers," declared to Rufus King in London that "there is hardly a County in any of the Eastern States where there are not *monuments* of the prevailing mania"—meaning imprisoned speculators. He described the bursting of the "Bubble of Speculation" as "a very happy circumstance, though vast numbers, and among them many worthy people, are involved in ruin by it," and condemned the "rage to get rich, without industry or economy," although he did seem to regret the threefold increase in debt actions in his home district in western Massachusetts.[66]

Newspaper attacks on speculation intensified, but with the added twist for some publishers of blaming George Washington, who had speculated in land himself. Benjamin Bache charged in the *Aurora* that the "lands of the United States have been monopolized by a clan of Land Jobbers, and a few desperate speculators have engrossed the territory to their private emolument [by which] thousands are impoverished, and thousands more are on the threshold of becoming victims to this species of rapacity." Under Washington's leadership "our ears are dinned with the tales of bankruptcy, the ruin of our commerce, and the distress of our citizens." As an object lesson to speculators, Bache printed a brief notice, captioned "Chinese Speculation!," of the public bastinado of a merchant in China whose failure ruined millions. He also reprinted a speech attributed to a man pilloried for forging a deed, who contrasted his fate as "a poor old man publicly disgraced for attempting to make a penny out of fifty acres of Vermont rocks" with the "great rogues" in "gay coats, mounted on naggish horses, who . . . wear silver spurs, and white beaver hats, and . . . talk of [their] millions of acres." He asked "what is the difference, as to sin, between a man, who forges a deed and sells land under it, and a man, who sells lands, to which he knows he has no title?" and advised his onlookers that "if you must speculate in lands let it be in millions of acres; and if you must be rogues, take warning by my unhappy fate and become great rogues."[67]

Many of those imprisoned could have been released under state insolvency laws, which varied in detail but which shared the common requirement that the insolvent debtor assign all but a small amount of exempt personal property to his creditors. Although some eventually did so, most of the major speculators refused. Insolvency acts freed them from jail, not from their debts. Entrepreneurs to the bitter end, they were not willing to purchase their liberty at the cost of the lands that had been their downfall but that still represented their hope. Stripped of their land, they would never have the means to repay their debts and return to wealth. The loss of independence, which they could pretend was temporary as long as they held on to their land, would become permanent.

On November 27, 1797—after Greenleaf's imprisonment but before Morris's—Robert Goodloe Harper rose once again in Congress to move the appointment of yet another committee to prepare a bankruptcy bill. The scale of the crisis made the proposal both more pressing and more controversial. Joshua Coit of Connecticut questioned "whether such a law be expedient." Abraham Baldwin of Georgia noted that the issue had bedeviled every previous Congress and argued that "Our country . . . was so extensive, and our interests so various, that no system of bankruptcy . . . could be formed to suit all its parties." In a concession to the political delicacy of the matter, the House appointed a committee of sixteen members, one from each state, not to draft a bankruptcy bill but rather to consider the threshold question of whether a committee to draft a bill should be appointed. The committee's discussions were contentious. A divided committee agreed to recommend that the House appoint another committee to draft a bill, but when Harper returned to the floor to report why, two dissenting members of his committee—Coit and John Nicholas of Virginia—sharply raised procedural objections. Albert Gallatin, who was not on the committee but who opposed bankruptcy legislation of any kind, supported them. Harper beat a tactical retreat, then returned two days later to present his report. Though brief, the report merits close attention.[68]

Harper, whom John Pintard later apostrophized in his Independence Day toasts as "the Creditors and Debtors friend," acknowledged that one could expect little agreement on the efficacy or even the desirability of a bankruptcy system. Indeed, "[s]uch doubts and difficulties have presented themselves forcibly to the committee." Nonetheless, "this institution is greatly desired by the mercantile part of the community, on which it is calculated more peculiarly to operate." It would have "beneficial effects in the support of mercantile credit, the prevention of fraud, the restraint of imprudent and destructive speculation, and the relief of honest industry, reduced to distress by the vicissitudes of trade." Only by drafting and then debating a bill could Congress determine whether the obstacles were insurmountable. If they were, then the states, knowing that Congress had found a uniform federal system impracticable, "will no longer be prevented, by expectations from that quarter, from attempting local establishments for themselves." Despite significant dissent, the House named a five-member committee to report a bill.[69]

There the matter languished, even as Federalist editors declared bankruptcy an issue of liberty. To John Fenno and others, that England had a bankruptcy law while America did not was "a reproach to us, as a free people, that the maxims and edicts of monarchical and even despotic governments should . . . be more favorable to personal liberty (the most inestimable of human blessings) than those of our boasted republican institutions." Without a discharge, insolvent debtors made "their own dwellings a prison for months or years," "banish[ed] themselves to some foreign country," or "crouded in an unwholesome prison at the mercy of creditors, lawyers, and sheriffs." The House, however, was diverted by impeachment proceedings against Senator William Blount of Tennessee and by lengthy and acrimonious debate on whether to expel one of its members for assaulting another. The delay also reflected opposition, as Pintard, in jail but still informed, noted when he followed his toast to Harper—"Thanks to his well meant, tho' fruitless endeavours to promote a statute of Bankruptcy"—with one to "Mr. Coit and the opposers of the Bankrupt bill."[70]

The landscape changed seismically six weeks after the committee was appointed, when Morris surrendered himself to jail. That Morris could fall so far was, for many, inconceivable. Public perception had changed little since Arthur Bryan had written ten years earlier that "Morris I think can't fail—if he does ruin on Thousands will [result]—I would hope that he would rather decay away than be Bankrupt." Thus, when Congress finally took up the bankruptcy bill in earnest in December, it did so in the shadow of "the great man" himself, pacing the prison courtyard two blocks away. For the first time the debate was substantive. It was also explicitly ideological. Drew McCoy, the only modern historian to take more than cursory notice of the debate, has described it as "a focus for the clash between predominantly Federalist optimism about America's advance to a higher stage of social development and Jeffersonian fears about the republic becoming a corrupt and over-commercialized society."[71]

Speakers for the most part ignored the technical details of the bill's fifty-nine sections. After some early procedural delays, opponents of the bill sat by while proponents discussed such matters as the recapture of fraudulent conveyances and whether discharging debts incurred before the act violated the constitutional prohibition on ex post facto laws.[72] When the real debate began, it addressed the threshold issue of whether the nation required a bankruptcy system at all—a debate made possible by widespread agreement on the nature of bankruptcy itself. No one questioned that bankruptcy should apply only to large-scale commercial debtors. That it should was simply assumed.

The limitation of bankruptcy relief to commercial debtors was of long standing and deeply rooted in English law. It remained so even after the Revolution, when conformance to English law was a choice rather than a condition. Although New York fleetingly offered discharges without regard to occupation, the norm was otherwise. The Pennsylvania bankruptcy statute, which lasted eight years, applied only to commercial debtors. When the Senate considered a motion to draft a bankruptcy law in 1790, William Maclay of Pennsylvania was equivocal on the value of such a law but certain that its "proper field" was "the Trading part of the community." Pintard thought of a bankruptcy statute as the power "to coerce mercantile engagements." Federalist and Republican newspapers alike made the same identification of bankruptcy with merchants. Some did so implicitly, as when Bache reprinted an assertion from the *Boston Chronicle* that war with France would spread "poverty amongst the tradesmen and bankruptcy among the merchants in general." Others did so explicitly, as when Fenno noted approvingly that European bankruptcy laws excluded all but merchants "on an idea that no one, excepting those who are engaged in commerce, ought to be under circumstances to need such a remedy." Everyone else, "whose expectations are not connected with the hazard incidental to commerce"—that is, farmers and tradesmen—"ought to order his affairs in such a manner, as that he can see his creditors with confidence, and justice."[73] In other words, bankruptcy statutes applied only to commercial debtors because only they could not avoid economic risk. Only they could fail. All other debtors merely grew poorer, their insolvency the result not of risk but of their reach exceeding their grasp. This was, to be sure, an oddly narrow understanding of economic risk, excluding as it did the hazards and chance that could rain economic ruin on farmers, tradesmen, and other nonmerchants. Moreover, it treated noncommercial debt as somehow avoidable and hence nonpayment as somehow culpable. Nonetheless, in claiming a unique exposure to economic risk, merchants appropriated bankruptcy to themselves as well.

The principal antagonists in the debate were Albert Gallatin and James A. Bayard—the former the leading Republican in Congress, the latter an ambitious young Federalist. Others who spoke at length were Samuel Sewall and Harrison Gray Otis of Massachusetts for the bill, and Abraham Baldwin of Georgia and William Gordon of New Hampshire against. "No commercial people," Bayard declared, "can be well governed without" a bankruptcy law. Commerce ran on credit. "Debts of great magnitude must be contracted; and the most honest and prudent man may, by accidents and misfortunes incident to commerce, be deprived of the means of making good his engagements." Agrarian societies did not require bankruptcy "because credits of so great an extent are not given, nor are persons engaged in pursuits liable to so many unforeseen accidents." If an "honest merchant, from the loss of his ships, or other unforeseen misfortunes," should be unable to repay his debts in full, no one would contend that he should be "imprisoned to the end of his life, and therefore lost to his family, his friends, and his community." Rather, it is "reasonable" that his creditors should divide his property among themselves proportionally—a distribution dictated by "common justice"—and set him "at liberty to begin the world anew." A fresh start will "inspire a man with activity in making a future provision for himself and family." Without a discharge "all his hopes are blasted, and he has no motive for industry or frugality, and he is lost to himself and the world."[74]

Gallatin acknowledged the advantages of a bankruptcy system. By giving assignees control of a bankrupt debtor's property, it "check[ed] the career of a debtor, who might be supposed to be either insolvent or to have an intention to defraud his creditors." It did justice to creditors by dividing the debtor's property among his creditors "without distinction as to the nature of their debts." It released "unfortunate debtors" beset by "accident, or other unforeseen event" from future liability. Such a system, he conceded, which applied only to people "who follow the business of buying and selling," was "proper" and "generally useful" in a nation that was "in a considerable degree commercial." But Gallatin understood the complexities of debt and credit better than Bayard. Whereas Bayard thought one could distinguish clearly between commercial and noncommercial debtors, Gallatin knew otherwise. "Go into the country," he said, "and you will scarcely find a farmer who is not, in some degree, a trader. In a grazing part of the country, you will find them buying and selling cattle; in other parts you will find them distillers, tanners, or brick-makers. So that, from one end of the United States to the other, the people are generally traders." A bankruptcy system that did not recognize this would reach too far into the countryside and sweep in too many debtors. Moreover, it would singularly disadvantage such debtors. Rural traders, Gallatin argued, held much of their property in land, which was notoriously illiquid and could be sold quickly, if at all, only at a "sacrifice." In addition, lacking the access to bank credit of their urban counterparts, they were more likely to mortgage their land to raise money. The consequence "would be that many honest men, who are perfectly able to pay all their debts, and have a handsome surplusage, if time were given them, would be made bankrupts, and have their property taken from them and sold for much less than would satisfy the demands of their creditors." State laws that limited or barred the seizure of land for debts "would fall to the ground," to the ruin of many "who at present believe themselves in comfortable circumstances."[75]

William Gordon took Gallatin's analysis a step further and argued that, even if one could distinguish between commercial and noncommercial debtors, the bill did not limit the consequences of bankruptcy to the former. Credit was, after all, a chain. Under a commission of bankruptcy, the assignees of the debtor's property were charged with collecting debts due to the bankrupt debtor. Country traders who owed such debts could find their property attached and their bodies imprisoned with no relief, "since they are deprived of all the benefits derived to larger traders from the bankrupt law, from the smallness of their concerns." Their only recourse would be to sue their debtors in turn. Noting Bayard's argument that honest merchants should not have to suffer jail and the loss of their liberty, Gordon remarked that rural traders to whom the bill would not apply "certainly . . . are as much entitled to our commisseration as those who trade on a larger scale."[76]

Samuel Sewall, for one, was not concerned by the potential plight of country traders, whom he and others described as "the medium between merchants and farmers." If they cannot pay their debts, he "would not only have their personal property sold, but also their land, and let them suffer the loss, however great it might be." In a stunningly modern free market analysis, he stated that if this meant "that we shall not then see so many country traders as at present, this will be no disadvantage to the community, as the larger stores deal more advantageously for the public. A number of men who now carry on business of this kind might be more usefully employed." Sewall "was willing, therefore, that the diminution of this kind of traders should be one of the effects of this law."[77]

Sewall's severity reflected his resolution of a fundamental confusion in the justifications for a bankruptcy system—a confusion that was a direct result of taking English law as the model. For all the talk about rescuing honest merchants from the consequences of economic misfortune, the bill itself followed the English statute in defining acts of bankruptcy, which were prerequisite to a debtor being adjudicated a bankrupt, as certain enumerated actions taken by the debtor "with intent unlawfully to delay or defraud his or her creditors." Bayard himself stated that "[t]he great principle of this law" was that "its energies cannot be called into operation, except in cases of fraud. A man can do no act which can make him a bankrupt without a fraudulent intent." Thus, alongside the "honest merchant" brought low by "unforeseen misfortunes," Bayard placed the fraudulent debtor—the former a beneficiary of the law, the latter a target. Recent experience, he said, offered many examples of "men going on in speculative schemes, by means of fictitious credit, imposing upon the community, and amassing property by contracting debts to an immense amount, without an intention to pay, and ultimately failing, to the ruin of thousands of individuals." Despite having the means to pay, they have "held their creditors at arm's length, and bid them defiance. Every process known to the laws of this country has proved ineffectual to obtain justice." A bankruptcy law, however, would have enabled creditors to stop such perfidy and force the debtors "to make a just distribution of their property," by which "many families might have been preserved from beggary." Sewall, on the other hand, did not care about a fresh start for the honest merchant. To him, "the main principles of the bankrupt system are to avoid the extension of fraud." In a dig at Gallatin and Gordon, he invoked as a prime example of the fraudulent debtor "the country trader" who "divides his property among his neighbors, who are either his creditors, or pretend to be so, and the creditor in the city perhaps never hears of the transaction until all the property is divided."[78]

Amid the discussion of fraud, no one addressed how a law nominally aimed at fraudulent debtors could benefit honest ones. Even Bayard seemed at times to regard the two objects as mutually exclusive, as when he asserted that "if a man go on in the straight path of integrity, he is at all times out of the power of his creditor under this law." Otis pointed the way to an explanation. He claimed that "great inconveniences had arisen for want" of a bankruptcy system. "Misfortune, enterprise, speculation, and a spirit of over-trading, have involved thousands in ruin," with the consequence that the "compassion due to real misfortune is diminished by the number of its victims," while "the disgrace that should attach to fraudulent bankruptcy is relieved by the influence of the delinquents." Failure fell unequally on its victims: "Men fail for millions; and, though these great leviathans of speculation, after having sunk in the ocean for a time, may rise again and revel on the surface, yet the widows and or-phans, the fair merchants, industrious tradesmen, and credulous friends, who are involved in the same whirlpool, rise no more." To prevent these injustices, "we should give to creditors a control over the property of their debtors, so as to stop the fraudulent in their career, and we should rescue the honest but unfortunate insolvent from the oppression of a vin-dictive creditor."[79]

Otis was a close observer of failure. When he was a young man, his father and uncle had failed in quick succession. In 1792 he feared that Pin-tard had absconded with securities he had given him to sell. As the Panic of 1797 unfolded, he wrote numerous letters to his wife describing the an-guish of their friends. A young cousin was James Wilson's widow. When Morris finally submitted to jail, Otis described for his wife "a dreadful scene of distress" in which "Mrs. M was almost frantic, and flew upon the Person who was his bail . . . and would have committed violence but was prevented." He knew that Morris "will now probably moulder away a few remaining wretched years in prison, and her joys and comforts have prob-ably forever vanished."[80] Otis understood the human and financial costs of failure. He knew that the costs fell on good people as well as bad, on the culpable as well as the unfortunate. He knew that some creditors could be vindictive and some debtors fraudulent. He was also a lawyer, with an imagination constrained by a lawyer's respect for English law. If English bankruptcy law was an involuntary system obsessed with fraud—creditor-driven in every respect—an American law should be as well. By promot-ing a bankruptcy system in which creditors alone had the power to initiate proceedings, Otis and his colleagues placed on creditors the responsibility for policing themselves as well as their debtors. Filing a bankruptcy peti-tion against a debtor would thus serve either to "stop the fraudulent in their career" or to "rescue the honest but unfortunate insolvent from the oppression of a vindictive creditor," as circumstances required.

Gallatin and other opponents were not as trusting of creditors. To their eyes the bill gave creditors too much power by defining fraud too broadly, going so far as to infer fraud from inability to pay. If creditors could thus transmute innocent failure into fraudulent default—a reverse alchemy of gold into lead—there would be no limit on the power of creditors to seize their debtors' land. They also distrusted some of the debtors themselves. Gordon, for example, said that "he did not think it was owing to the natural operation of commerce, that a number of persons are now in jail." Rather, it was "from a spirit of speculation which had raged to a great extent in this country; which has driven the merchant from his counting-house to speculate in land, and produced a sort of mania among the people of the United States." Jails are thus "crowded with persons anxiously solicitous" for a bankruptcy act. Gordon did not think a law for their relief served "the public good." Gallatin, a land speculator himself, noted how easily speculators could manipulate the proposed system. Despite their contribution to the general economic distress, land and stock speculators were not included within the list of persons covered by the act. Thus, they "may laugh at their creditors." But if they saw any benefit in it, they could qualify for the act simply by engaging in trade "for a short time, and then become bankrupts."[81]

Lurking behind these issues was another, which received only passing mention but which became more important in the next session. Bayard argued that a "great advantage of this law will be that it will generalize, by an uniform system through the United States, the most important law of any society—the law regulating the relation of debtor and creditor." As a matter of justice and for the benefit of commerce, a "general system" was desirable so that "a trader at one extremity of the United States might always know what are the laws at the other, where he may have concerns." Even opponents of the act recognized uniformity of law as a value in itself—Abraham Baldwin rhapsodized that the "contemplation of uniformity on any subject excites pleasing sensations"—although they argued that uniform laws required uniform circumstances not found in the diverse

economies of the United States. But Bayard had in mind more than certainty and predictability of legal relations. Uniformity to him was a means,
not an end. He believed, indeed he hoped, that a uniform national bankruptcy law would "unite and naturalize the United States, and . . . cement
together the different parts of the Union and connect more closely the nation with the Federal Government." This was why he regarded a bankruptcy act as "among the greatest national objects."[82]

No one took up Bayard's challenge. After Bayard finished speaking
that day, the bill lost by three votes in a chamber in which his party held a
narrow majority. Although the vote was mostly along party lines, neither
side held firm. Gordon, who thought a bankruptcy system would produce
"more evil than good," was a Federalist. So was Dwight Foster of Massachusetts, who voted against the bill even as he noted in his journal that
most of those he voted with were "Jacobins." One "Jacobin" who voted
for the bill was Blair McClenachan, a Philadelphia merchant-speculator
who earlier had fraudulently transferred assets to his children, had recently been imprisoned for debt, and who sought refuge under the state insolvency act after Congress adjourned. Another was Edward Livingston
of New York, whom a Federalist newspaper denounced as "a *beardless
lawyer* . . . rendered odious by his conceit and pert loquacity," deeply in
debt himself, but who championed the act despite the likelihood that it
would not apply to him. Nonetheless, Bayard's remarks represented the
first time since the ratification debate that anyone had linked bankruptcy to
the extension of federal authority. Within a few months, bankruptcy,
which was already part of the ideological divide between commerce and
agriculture, would become part of that between nationalism and federalism as well.[83]

When Bayard reported yet another bankruptcy bill to the next Congress on January 6, 1800, John Pintard and Theodore Sedgwick had different responses—one personal, the other political. Pintard, who had long
despaired of such a law, rushed to Philadelphia to lobby Bayard, "who
speaks encouragingly of the fate of the Bankrupt bill." Sedgwick, who was

Speaker of the House and who also thought that the bill would pass, wrote his old friend Henry Van Schaack that the bill "will be of public benefit, the circumstances of the country absolutely demanding it." For Sedgwick, however, the "public benefit" had nothing to do with promoting commerce, relieving honest merchants, or punishing fraudulent debtors. Instead, a bankruptcy law would promote the authority of the government "by submitting to it all the relations of creditor and Debtor, and the active agency of commercial interests and passions" and, more important, "it will render it absolutely necessary to spread out the national judicial by a creation of new districts and Judges, and instituting the offices of justice or some thing similar to it." Underscoring the connection, the committee that produced the bankruptcy bill and the committee appointed to draft a judiciary bill consisted of the same five Federalists. One Republican congressman referred to the judiciary bill as "the eldest child of the bankrupt system."[84]

Sedgwick was not known for his charity toward the failings of others. He had long denounced the evils of speculation and the rage to get rich "without industry or economy." He had watched the collapse of Morris, Nicholson, Greenleaf, Wilson, and others before his eyes in Philadelphia without remorse. However, by 1799, when he somewhat grudgingly lamented that "in too many instances, ruined speculators commence zealous patriots," he had ceased to stigmatize debtors for their moral and political failings and concentrated instead on the potential for political gain. With Federalists now in a clear majority, Sedgwick thought they should act in concert to expand the judiciary "so as to render the Justice of the nation accessible to the people, to aid the national economy, to overawe the licentious, and to punish the guilty." Thus would the government be strengthened and "the efforts of the Jacobins against it" repressed. Sedgwick repeated his assessment of the political benefits of a bankruptcy system in numerous letters as the bill wound its way through Congress. Although he recognized the commercial advantages of bankruptcy relief, his eyes remained firmly fixed on the political. He fairly rejoiced as he saw the bill "every day more and more assuming the complexion of a party measure," which he thought would assure its passage. When the bill passed to its third reading, he wrote to Rufus King not of the commercial advantages of the act but of its fit with Federalist proposals to enlarge the judiciary and extend a national network of turnpikes—all of which he saw as essential to expanding the authority of the national government. Whereas Bayard and Gallatin had debated the commercial or agrarian character of the republic, Sedgwick addressed questions of power and national authority.[85]

The change in emphasis meant that this time no one discussed the social or economic desirability of a bankruptcy system or whether the commercial development of the country merited one. Instead, they parleyed over amendments and votes. Bayard reported to his father-in-law that "we have been labouring very hard to carry . . . our Bankrupt Bill. The Antis have discovered that it will add strength to the federal compact, and they make every exertion to defeat it." To counter the opposition, "we have been obliged to intrigue and ingratiate in order to gain strength." He regretted the compromises they had to make—"Accommodation has been the worst instrument we have made use of. Gentlemen have been indulged with amendments which have half spoiled the Bill"—"[b]ut we are determined to have it on any terms we can get it."[86]

Part of the difficulty was that the Federalists, though nominally a majority, were themselves deeply divided. Sedgwick—by his own description a highly partisan "ultra federalist"—had been elected speaker by only one vote when southern Federalists threw their votes to the Republican candidate. The party itself was already well down the path of self-destruction that would lead to its rout in the election that fall. Sedgwick clearly recognized the divisions over bankruptcy. He predicted that every Republican except Edward Livingston, "who has conflicting motives," would vote against the bill because it would bind "commercial men" to the government, defuse opposition to the government by debtors—whom he described as "the most active and clamorous description of persons"—and, "more than any measure the government can adopt," require expanding the judiciary. He also identified the issues that divided his own party. A national bankruptcy law would undermine the attachment laws common in New England, "which from habit and education, have more favor than their merit entitles them to." In Virginia it would subject land to the payment of debts in certain circumstances "and may form a precedent for the further extension of the principle" in others.[87]

The vulnerability of land in bankruptcy was a key issue in the discussion of commerce and agriculture. Opponents could, and did, debate whether the country needed a bankruptcy law. They could not, however, legitimately debate whether land should be included in a bankrupt debtor's assets to be distributed among his or her creditors. To exclude land would enable debtors to conceal assets in plain sight simply by buying land, thereby frustrating almost every purpose served by a bankruptcy system. Shielding land meant forgoing bankruptcy. Creditors had long regarded land as a source of wealth—albeit often a uniquely constrained one—for the repayment of debts. Those seeking the greatest security for their loans would require mortgages of their debtors, thereby circumventing some or all of the formal restrictions that applied to creditors trying to attach a debtor's land to satisfy an unsecured debt. A number of states, primarily in the South, barred creditors from seizing debtors' land at all unless they held a mortgage. Others limited creditors' access to their debtors' land, with or without a mortgage, by imposing valuation requirements and other measures designed to prevent distress sales at artificially low prices. Whereas traditional republican ideology regarded land as the foundation of political independence, commercial advocates saw it as a source of financial independence. A Virginia writer, calling for ratification of the Constitution, argued that Virginians remained "in the chains of British slavery" because state laws shielding land drove capital elsewhere, even though "[w]e have the best mortgage to offer, which is immense and fruitful lands." Virginians thus "have enjoyed none of the great advantages, which independence promised us. . . . For this axiom is certain, *nothing is lent to those that have nothing, and credit is offered, at its lowest rate, to those that offer the best securities.*" Otis echoed this argument in the bankruptcy debate when he asserted that there was "plenty of money in the coffers of the rich, and in the city banks," hoarded by "moneyed men" who were "afraid of trusting it in the country, under the present laws for the recovery of debt" and who would lend it to the "honest trader" at "fair and legal interest" if the law "will secure their money to them, by a lien upon all the estates of their debtors." Bayard was even more emphatic. To him, protective land laws were vestiges of aristocracy on the order of primogeniture. They struck so deeply at "the root of commercial credit" that "[c]ommerce, and a law like this, cannot live and flourish on the same soil."[88]

Despite his hopeful belief that the bill was becoming "a party measure," Sedgwick knew that a number of his fellow Federalists—primarily from the South, but two or three from New England as well—were likely to vote against it. This made Sedgwick and other proponents particularly eager to placate John Marshall, the respected and influential Virginia Federalist. At Marshall's insistence, the acts of bankruptcy that triggered proceedings were limited, and the all-important question of whether the debtor was bankrupt or not, on which the entire process turned, was left to a jury rather than a judge if the debtor so demanded. Sedgwick thought the latter concession would prove "inconvenient embarrassing and dilatory," but it was "the whim of General Marshall—with him a *sine qua non* of assent or dissent to the measure." Sedgwick knew that the "friends of the bill" had to submit or lose.[89] Another concession, although to whom is unclear, was that the act was only temporary—it would expire after five years.

Sedgwick was not prepared to lose. He pushed the bill to a vote on February 21, when several opponents were absent. After eleven Federalists defected to create a tie, he cast the deciding vote in its favor. Pintard, who had been following the progress of the bill from newspaper accounts and an occasional letter from Bayard, recorded the event, "which has so long tantalized expectation," cautiously noting that the bill "has yet to pass the ordeal of the Senate." The Senate, after narrowly defeating an attempt by its southern members to stipulate that the act "shall not be construed to extend to farmers, graziers, drovers, tavernkeepers, or manufacturers," approved the bill without amendment on March 8. John Adams signed it into law on April 4.[90]

Reactions were vigorously mixed, as one would expect of a law so closely contested. Pintard excitedly recorded the "*Glorious News.*" The debtors imprisoned in the New Gaol, as we have seen, joyously celebrated the news with a series of toasts to "this Godlike act." Their newspaper, the *Forlorn Hope,* which in its first issue had touted a bankruptcy system as "essential to the interest, honour and happiness of a free people," printed the entire text and declared that "Mercy now covers the judgment seat of our land—it is the dawn of a brighter day to many honest, but unfortunate citizens." No longer would the honest debtor "be incarcerated in a jail, and left as an outlaw to every species of degradation and misery."[91] The *Aurora,* on the other hand, denounced the law as a Federalist plot to extend the power of the federal judiciary and create "a patronage of nearly 250 offices great and small." Anthony New made the same charge to his constituents in Virginia, reporting that the law transfers to the federal courts "a great portion of the jurisdiction now held by the State Courts, . . . greatly increases Executive patronage, and may be made to extend to almost every description of citizens." He paired the bankruptcy act with the pending judiciary bill as examples of the Federalists' "favorite scheme of consolidation." Thomas T. Davis, a Kentucky Republican who also voted against the bill, told his constituents that the law was "replete with principles incompatible with a republican government" and warned that it would extend "British influence" by putting "American merchants in the power of British merchants" and "the merchants of Kentucky in the power of the merchants of Philadelphia and Baltimore." John Fowler, also of Kentucky, suspected that the law "will be little more than a machine for extending the influence of the executive administration" and "an instrument to injure the incautious agriculturalists."[92]

Sedgwick himself was disappointed, even though he thought the act was "of considerable importance." Nonetheless, it was "far from being such a one as I wished," largely because of the concessions to Marshall. Caleb Strong, Sedgwick's moderate fellow Federalist from western Massachusetts, was also critical. He believed that increasing the power of the federal judiciary without increasing the number of courts would "diminish the attachment of the People" to the government by subjecting backcountry debtors and creditors to the "intolerable inconvenience" of traveling to distant courts. Contrary to Sedgwick's conviction that the act would strengthen the government, Strong maintained that "every unnecessary

Extension of the judiciary Powers of the U.S. weakens the Government, as in the Opinion of the People it invests with it the Idea of Inconvenience if not Oppression." He also thought the law, which lacked the English sanction of capital punishment, "would produce more Fraud than it would prevent" because "a law without an effectual Sanction will do more hurt than good."[93]

The proof, of course, would be in the application.

❧ 7 ❧

THE FACES OF BANKRUPTCY

At a late sale of Bankrupt's effects a *pillow* was put up to auction. The auctioneer recommended it strongly, by saying that it must be a good one to sleep on, since he could sleep on it, who *owed so much.*

Gazette of the United States (November 14, 1798)

One wonders if John and David West smiled. While appraising the contents of Thomas Dawes's house in Boston on December 16, 1801, for the bankruptcy proceedings against him, they dutifully listed every book in his library. Shelved among the 234 volumes were two of ironic relevance, "Davis's Law of Bankrupts" and "Goodrich on Bankrupts." Unfortunately, all we know is that they misspelled the authors' names. The creditor who petitioned Dawes into bankruptcy listed Dawes's occupation as "underwriter or marine insurer." But he was not, except in the most conveniently nominal sense. Dawes was a lawyer and a judge of the Massachusetts Supreme Judicial Court. His career as an insurance underwriter consisted of participating in a handful of policies with a local broker on four days scattered across seven weeks.

The proceedings against Dawes moved quickly. Eleven creditors proved debts of $123,326.53, one of the largest totals among the 290 bankruptcy commissions issued in Massachusetts. On January 23, 1802, John Davis, the federal district judge for Massachusetts, discharged Dawes from all liability for his debts. Two days later, the eleven creditors released their claims to the household items—books included—none of which had ever left Dawes's possession. They received nothing on their debts. Nor, it would appear, had they expected to receive anything. Every debt but one proved against Dawes originated in promissory notes given by his wife's brother, the notorious speculator James Greenleaf, to him or to another brother, Daniel Greenleaf, who had immediately endorsed them to Dawes. The notes came into the creditors' hands by direct endorsement from Dawes or, twice, from others to whom Dawes had endorsed the notes. The one exception arose from land that Greenleaf had sold to Dawes, which Dawes in turn sold by a deed in which he improvidently warranted that the title was good, leaving him liable for damages when the title failed, as it inevitably did because of Greenleaf's previous derelictions. None of the eleven attempted to collect from Greenleaf, who, although insolvent, was not petitioned into bankruptcy until a year later in Pennsylvania. On the other hand, they were under no legal obligation to try, as Dawes's endorsements made the debts his. After his discharge Dawes remained on the bench. He also served as a commissioner overseeing his fellow bankrupts in 120 subsequent bankruptcy proceedings, perhaps to augment his income.[1]

The Bankruptcy Act of 1800 did not apply to lawyers or judges. It extended only to merchants, bankers, brokers, factors, underwriters, and marine insurers, who owed a minimum of $1,000 and who had committed one or more of the acts of bankruptcy enumerated in the statute "with intent unlawfully to delay or defraud his or their creditors"—absconding, hiding, keeping close to avoid arrest or service of process, procuring their own arrest or the attachment of their property, concealing property from execution, making a fraudulent conveyance, escaping from jail after being arrested for debt, or remaining in jail for more than two months after being arrested for debt. Bankruptcy proceedings were involuntary. They could be initiated only by a creditor who was owed at least $1,000 and who posted a bond, payable to the debtor, to guarantee prosecution of the petition.[2] Debtors could not petition themselves into bankruptcy. Thomas Dawes was not a merchant, banker, broker, factor, underwriter, or marine insurer. Nor were the proceedings against him really involuntary. So what was he doing in bankruptcy?

The answer to that question reveals the ambiguities, complexities, opportunities, and deficiencies of America's first national bankruptcy system. On its face the 1800 Act differed little from the English bankruptcy statutes on which it was modeled. Both were involuntary. Both spoke of protecting creditors from the evasive malfeasance of debtors. Both limited their application to debtors in specific commercial occupations who amassed fairly high minimum levels of debt. Both provided for criminal penalties for debtors who concealed or withheld assets or information or who lied under oath during the proceedings. Indeed, so similar were they that when Thomas Cooper wrote the first American treatise on bankruptcy in 1801, his chapter on the Act consisted of nothing but its text with citations in the margins to the English statutes that were authority for forty-seven of its sixty-four sections.[3] In application, however, the two differed sharply. Although in form involuntary, in substance the 1800 Act could also be wielded by debtors. English law had this potential as well— although largely unrealized, despite a widespread and essentially groundless belief that debtors routinely perpetrated sham bankruptcies to defraud their creditors.[4] In America, on the other hand, many of the filings were clearly collusive or cooperative, the result of insolvent debtors enlisting sympathetic creditors to sue out commissions of bankruptcy against them. Some may have been fraudulent, but there is little evidence or contemporary complaint that any were. Sometimes the collusion was between the debtor and a single creditor to pry loose a discharge from other, more reluctant creditors. Sometimes, as in Dawes's case, it encompassed all of a debtor's major creditors and used bankruptcy as a collaborative process to give the debtor a fresh start with his property intact rather than as an adversarial one to squeeze from the debtor what they could. On the other hand, many, perhaps most, of the filings were just what they appeared to be—last-resort efforts by frustrated creditors to salvage something from recalcitrant debtors. As varied as the filings were the debtors themselves, who ranged from the once-powerful to the obscure. Collectively, their experience reveals whether it was the fears or the promise of the Act that prevailed.

At least one person saw an immediate potential for profit in bankruptcy. Barely eight weeks after John Adams signed the Bankruptcy Act of 1800 into law, Robert Fields, an attorney in Boston, published *A Practical Treatise upon the Bankrupt Law of the United States*. Fields's "treatise"—a fifty-nine-page, step-by-step guide to the bankruptcy process, from initial petition to final dividend—was little more than a compilation of practice forms adapted from English bankruptcy form books, lightly interspersed with commentary. Whatever the legal merit of the volume, in marketing it "to the Gentlemen of the Profession, and others who may be concerned in prosecuting Commissions" under the Act, Fields at the very least displayed the kind of entrepreneurial spirit that many thought bankruptcy protected. He was also timely—the pamphlet came out the day before the Act went into effect. It may only be coincidence that significantly more bankruptcy petitions were filed in Massachusetts than in any other state. Thomas Cooper entered the market next with *The Bankrupt Law of America, compared with the Bankrupt Law of England*, published a year later, most of it written while he was in jail for sedition. A more treatise-like five hundred pages, including 103 practice forms adapted from English sources, the comparison was nonetheless rather one-sided—except for the text of the Act, Cooper dwelt almost entirely on English statutes and case law, perhaps because he wrote the book "for a country where the law may be considered as an experiment" and sought authoritative guidance. Indeed, although skillful in his legal analysis, Cooper gives no sign of ever having observed an American bankruptcy proceeding.[5]

Cooper's circumscribed writing conditions mirrored the limitations under which everyone labored in trying to understand the Act. There was no American law of bankruptcy to use as a guide. Only in Pennsylvania did lawyers and judges have any familiarity with operating under an established bankruptcy statute, from the eight-year experiment after the Revolution. To fill the interpretive gap, Fields and Cooper looked to English law—a natural source given the formal derivation of the Act and the reflexive intellectual anglophilia of American lawyers—but this does not mean that American bankruptcy law was simply English bankruptcy law writ small. Indeed, some lawyers well-versed in English law treated the Act as an American original, or at a minimum as something that did not require reference to English law to understand or apply. In May 1800 an anonymous interlocutor submitted thirty-six questions about the Act to five of the most prominent lawyers in New York—Aaron Burr, Robert Troup, Richard Harison, Brockholst Livingston, and Cornelius S. Bogert. Burr made only a cursory reply, but the others gave thoughtful, concise answers to each question. With only two minor exceptions, each man ignored English precedent and based his responses on straightforward construction of the statutory language. When not certain of an answer, they stayed within the statute rather than turn to English law for guidance.[6]

Procedure under the Act was relatively simple and quickly became sufficiently routinized that printed forms replaced handwritten ones. To begin proceedings, a creditor who was owed at least $1,000 by a debtor in one of the enumerated commercial occupations who had recently committed one or more of the stipulated acts of bankruptcy petitioned the federal district judge for the state or district in which the debtor lived to issue a commission of bankruptcy against the debtor. After the petitioning creditor proved his debt by a sworn affidavit and posted the required bond, the judge issued a commission to two or, more usually, three "good and substantial persons" to act as commissioners of the bankrupt. The men appointed commissioners were politically connected lawyers and merchants, a very small number of whom received most or all of the commissions in each jurisdiction—a practice that promoted efficiency and uniformity in the proceedings by creating, in effect, permanent commissions.[7] Once sworn, the commissioners oversaw the process. Their powers were both administrative and adjudicative. They made the all-important initial determination of whether the debtor was in fact a bankrupt. They took possession of the debtor's property and ordered its inventory and appraisal. They could issue summonses, arrest warrants, and contempt citations. They could imprison uncooperative witnesses. They conducted the debtor's examinations and determined whether he (or, once, she) had complied with the Act. They judged the validity of creditors' claims. When the judge awarded the debtor a discharge, it was on the commissioners' recommendation.

To receive that discharge, the debtor had to submit to a minimum of three examinations under oath within forty-two days—a number borrowed from English law—and there make full disclosure of his property and accounts, including the details of any recent transfers. Creditors could attend the examinations, produce witnesses and documents, and question the debtor. If the debtor or any creditor disagreed with a ruling of the commissioners, the aggrieved party could ask the judge for a jury trial to determine the facts in dispute. Similarly, a debtor could contest the commissioners' finding that he was a bankrupt by putting the issue to a jury—this was the provision insisted on by John Marshall. The debtor could be freed from jail if imprisoned for debt and was shielded from arrest during the examination period. Conversely, he could be jailed for contempt for refusing to be examined or for not answering questions completely and imprisoned for two to ten years if he committed perjury. After the final examination, if two-thirds (in England, it was four-fifths) of the creditors—measured by the number of creditors and the value of their debts—with proven debts of at least fifty dollars were satisfied that the debtor had laid bare every relevant detail of his finances and were willing to consent to his discharge, they signed a document to that effect. If the commissioners, or a majority of them, agreed and were themselves satisfied that the debtor had complied with the requirements of the Act, they in turn signed a certificate of conformity, addressed to the judge. With two exceptions, these requirements were procedural, relating to the examination and the disclosure and assignment of property. The exceptions were colluding with a real or pretended creditor in claiming a fictitious debt, and the charmingly moralistic one of amassing gambling losses before going bankrupt—shades of the old moral economy of debt. If the judge found everything in order, he is-

sued a certificate of discharge, which relieved the debtor of all further liability for any and all unsecured debts incurred before he became bankrupt—not just those of the creditors who consented to the discharge or
who proved their debts before the commissioners.

Unlike modern bankruptcy law, the discharge did not end the proceedings. When the commissioners declared the debtor a bankrupt and
scheduled the examinations, they also published notice for his creditors to
meet to prove their debts and to elect one or more of their number as assignees of the bankrupt's estate. Only creditors who were owed at least
two hundred dollars could vote. The assignees, who typically were one or
two of the larger creditors, managed the estate as trustees for all the creditors. Their primary responsibility was to collect all debts and other property owed or belonging to the bankrupt—by litigation, if necessary—and
thus maximize the amount available for distribution among the creditors.
They had full authority to liquidate the estate by selling the debtor's real
and personal property at auction. The statute directed them to render an
account and make a first dividend, or distribution, from the debtor's estate
to the creditors in proportion to their debts within five to thirteen months
after the commission issued, and a second distribution eighteen months
after the date of the commission—a schedule borrowed from English law.
The second distribution was supposed to be the final one, upon which the
estate would be closed. In reality, however, some estates remained open
and under active management by the assignees for years and even decades
after the debtor had received his discharge. To be sure, those estates were
exceptional, but since two-thirds or more of the debtors received their discharges before the earliest date permitted for a dividend, it is clear that
discharge and distribution were separate events, both in law and practice.
By way of contrast, under modern bankruptcy law debtors are discharged
from liability only after their assets have been distributed to their
creditors.[8]

Bankruptcy did not strip debtors of everything they owned, although
it came close, nor did it cancel all of their debts. It left the debtor with a
small amount of exempt property—"necessary" clothing, beds, and bedding for himself and his family. Until the discharge the commissioners or

assignees could give the debtor an allowance from the estate for his family's "necessary support." Like English bankruptcy law, the statute also gave debtors a small percentage—capped at relatively low dollar amounts—of the net estate collected by the assignees, graduated according to the size of the dividend allotted to the creditors. Seemingly compassionate, the gesture was limited by the fact that the allowance was discretionary rather than as of right unless the creditors received at least half their claims, a threshold reached by fewer than one in ten bankrupts' estates. For the most part, if bankrupt debtors were left with anything after their discharges, it was by grace of their creditors, as it was with Thomas Dawes. As for the debts, a bankruptcy discharge did not affect debts that were secured by mortgages or liens on the debtor's property, at least not to the value of the security, nor did it erase debts owed to the state or federal governments. The former doubtless explains why so little real property appears in bankruptcy inventories—debtors whose finances were so shattered as to be in bankruptcy were likely to have mortgaged their land to the hilt in their efforts to stay afloat. Their secured creditors would thus decide the fate of their encumbered property in state courts without reference to federal bankruptcy proceedings.

These were the procedural outlines of the Act. What most surprises is the extent to which it created, in practice if not in law, a voluntary bankruptcy system. Other scholars, looking only at the statute, have dismissed the Act as copied more or less wholesale from English involuntary bankruptcy.[9] Consequently, they have missed its significance. The genius, however awkward and halting, of the system created by the Act was that it operated on two levels. It encompassed both the coercion of involuntary bankruptcy, which disciplined recalcitrant debtors and forced them to disgorge their assets to their creditors, and the relief of voluntary bankruptcy, which encouraged debtors to cooperate with one or more creditors to secure the discharge that would enable them to start afresh in the economy. Admittedly, the Act did so by indirection. After all, it was, on its face, a design for an involuntary system. However, the immediacy with which debtors, creditors, and their lawyers recognized the voluntary potential of the process, together with the assertions of the drafters that the Act was necessary to protect entrepreneurial debtors, strongly suggests that the latent voluntarism of the process was deliberate.

The difference between a voluntary system and an involuntary one is not simply whether it is the debtor or creditor who files the petition to initiate proceedings, although that is the formal distinction. In a fuller sense, it is whether an insolvent debtor and some or all of his creditors cooperate to reach a common end. The goal can be as narrow as obtaining a discharge for the debtor, without regard to whether creditors recover anything, or as expansive as trying to do some justice for all by everyone agreeing to submit to a collective procedure that treats creditors equally, apportions the losses, and results in a discharge, and, if everyone cooperates, does so more efficiently and expeditiously than regular legal process. The Bankruptcy Act of 1800 had many faults, not least of which was its limitation to comparatively wealthy debtors, but it was a milestone in the law of failure.

In truth, there is little direct evidence that American bankruptcy proceedings were often voluntary, although there is enough to know that they could be. For example, Thomas Clark, an auctioneer in Boston, asked Nathan Frazier, the largest of his sixty creditors, "to make me a Bankrupt" so that "my Creditors may make the Most of my Property." Frazier obliged two days later. A Connecticut creditor was sufficiently concerned that his debtor, John J. White of Hartford, might try to engineer a friendly petition that he requested the federal district court clerk to notify him if White "should attempt any proceedings under the Bankrupt Act," which White in fact did.[10] Indirect evidence, however, abounds: Proceedings in which suspiciously few creditors, sometimes only one or two, bothered to prove their debts. Others in which the petitioning creditor was a close relative, often a father. Still more in which the creditors received nothing at all on their debts, which one suspects they often knew would be the case. The few instances in which the creditors elected as assignee not one of their own, but a lawyer who was owed nothing except, perhaps, a fee for brokering the proceeding. The act-of-bankruptcy affidavits that record scenes seemingly staged to meet the statutory criteria. The number of debtors who engaged in the barest minimum of commercial activity to bring themselves under the statutory occupational umbrella. The fact that the overwhelming majority of proceedings were concluded within the minimum statutory period without contention or disagreement. Or that debtors rarely contested the commissioners' finding that they were bankrupt. Or that creditors seldom disagreed enough to ask for arbitration or trial of their claims. Or that the impressive criminal penalties available under the Act—up to ten years' imprisonment for perjury or for deliberately omitting assets from the required disclosure to the commissioners or conveyance to the assignees—appear never to have been applied. Any of these, by themselves, would be equivocal. Taken together, they indicate a bankruptcy system that debtors as well as creditors could invoke—one substantively, the other formally.

Dawes's bankruptcy is a case in point. Procedurally correct in every respect, its purpose was not to save his creditors' property or to stop the depredations of a fraudulent bankrupt. Rather, it was to shield him from secondary liability on notes he had endorsed for Greenleaf, who had shamelessly appropriated his credit in the first place by securing the endorsements. Dawes was, to be sure, in financial distress, although how much is unclear. The signs of a cooperative process are legion. Dawes made token appearances at the first two examinations and was not asked to make the required statement under oath until the third one. Neither the commissioners nor his creditors formally questioned him at any session. The fact that all eleven creditors traced their claims to Greenleaf suggests that they were not a random group of people to whom Dawes owed money. In adversarial bankruptcies, creditors typically rushed to prove their debts at the first opportunity. All of Dawes's save one stayed away from the first examination—an occasion fraught with potential ignominy because it was when the bankrupt made his formal surrender to the commissioners. The one creditor who attended was his oldest friend, Rufus Amory, after whom Dawes had named his son. The two had read law together as clerks for John Lowell twenty-three years earlier. Creditors typically named one of themselves assignee. The position could be onerous and paid only expenses, but an assignee who was a creditor had an incentive to maximize the bankrupt's estate that a noncreditor did not. Dawes's creditors chose Edward Gray, a lawyer who was not a creditor but who may have negotiated the proceedings and who certainly moved them along. Of the 241 bankruptcy proceedings in Massachusetts that resulted in a discharge, only ten did so faster than Dawes's. Then, of course, there was the matter of the creditors releasing their claims to Dawes's household property, which by law could have been theirs, and the likelihood that they knew they would receive nothing on the debts they had proven. The bankruptcy proceedings benefited Dawes, not his creditors, at least not economically.[11]

Numerous other bankruptcies present patterns of cooperation, some more transparently than others. Creditors who petitioned their debtors into bankruptcy immediately after receiving promissory notes from them may have been sandbagging their debtors, but it is more likely that the transaction occurred to qualify the creditor to file the petition. The petition against William Allis, a Boston merchant, was filed by an attorney whose claimed debt was a demand note Allis had given him just the week before. It is, of course, possible that the attorney suddenly realized his imprudence, panicked, and hastily invoked the law. But if the object was to collect a debt, a lawyer-creditor would presumably be more likely to sue for his own recovery rather than initiate a bankruptcy proceeding in which he would have to share with others—unless the real objective was to procure a discharge for Allis. Moreover, the proof of trading—testimony that Allis had sold "a box of Chocolate" on the date of the petition—is suspiciously well-timed, not to mention easily the most frivolous commercial transaction in the records. There is no way to tell if the petition was Allis's idea or that of his creditors, but both sides embraced the proceedings, even Joshua Davis, a Boston merchant who carried half of Allis's debt and stood to lose the most.[12]

The presumption of cooperation is stronger when the petitioning creditor claiming a debt on which the ink had barely dried was a close relative of the debtor. For example, Louis Devotion sold English dry goods at his shop on Union Street in Boston. When his finances collapsed, he hid first at the schoolmaster's house and then at the store of his friend and fellow merchant, Joshua Snow, who had recently obtained his own bankruptcy discharge, where Devotion was arrested and imprisoned on several writs of attachment. While in hiding, he had executed a demand note to his father, who endorsed it to his brother, Jonathan, a merchant in Windham, Connecticut. When it became apparent that Devotion's creditors were not going to release him from jail, Jonathan, who was now formally a creditor, petitioned him into bankruptcy, which forced the creditors to submit their claims to the commissioners and permitted the commissioners to order Louis's release. Devotion eventually won a discharge. His creditors received nothing, not even the satisfaction of maintaining him in prison.[13]

Ebenezer Holbrook was a small retail trader in Braintree, Massachusetts, who failed awash in equally small debts. Most of the notes and accounts proved by his creditors—forty-seven in all, owed to nineteen persons, including his laundress—were for twenty-five dollars or less; many were under ten dollars. All but a handful were less than one hundred dollars. Some of the debts arose from failed litigation, including fees for his own attorneys, but most were for labor, supplies, and loans. Holbrook executed a demand note to his brother, Nathaniel—who had previously paid various accounts on Holbrook's behalf—that was just large enough to meet the threshold required for petitioning creditors. Within three weeks Nathaniel sent a deputy sheriff to serve a writ on Holbrook so that he could commit an act of bankruptcy by bolting the door, an act conveniently witnessed and later attested to by another brother. Holbrook's estate eventually yielded his creditors eleven cents on the dollar, which was more than two-thirds of the other bankrupts' estates in Massachusetts did. His creditors may have been disappointed, but they were not defrauded. Holbrook and his family had simply found a way to make his bankruptcy voluntary.[14]

When family members petitioned one of their own into bankruptcy, it is, of course, difficult to determine whether they did so vindictively or compassionately. Both are possible. In Massachusetts fully one-eighth of the petitions were filed by close relatives of the debtor. The motives of most are equivocal, but the ones filed by fathers against their sons bear the mark of one generation helping fallen members of the next to their feet. Benjamin Beale, Sr., was a successful lawyer in Quincy, Massachusetts. His son, Benjamin, Jr., was a less successful merchant who was able to finance his ventures only by relying on his father's credit. His father lent him money and co-signed his notes as surety. Finally, after two traders in Albany arrested Benjamin, Jr., and refused to release him from jail, Benjamin, Sr., paid the notes on which he was surety, petitioned for a commission of bankruptcy against his son, installed his nephew or cousin as assignee, and briskly engineered a discharge of nearly $11,000 in debts—three-fifths of which were due him—within two months, without a dividend. Shearjashub Bourne, Sr., who was chief judge of the court of common pleas in Boston, regularly lent his son money—by his own account, twenty-three times over eight years. Then one day he took out a writ against his son for the accumulated debt, returnable to his own court, and the very next day petitioned for and received a commission of bankruptcy against him. As the only creditor eligible to vote, he elected himself assignee and eventually gathered all of $2.50 in assets. Needless to say, there was no dividend. William Lang, Jr., of Salem was not content to remain an auctioneer with his father. He branched out as a factor, selling goods at auction imported on consignment. His father tried to keep him afloat by lending him money and credit but to no avail. When his father petitioned him into bankruptcy, he did so to force his son's thirty-five other creditors to accept his failure, not to avoid any payment at all. Lang's estate paid six cents on the dollar, more than three-fifths of the other bankrupts' estates in the state. John Read, Sr., a lawyer who had retired to a gentleman's life in Roxbury, had paid over $5,000 to his son's creditors. He was quick to recognize, and almost as quick to seize, the opportunity presented by the Act. The commission of bankruptcy he took out against his son—only the third one issued in Massachusetts—enabled him to cut his losses and his son to discharge a nagging and rather large debt to the Union Bank.[15]

The senior Read was not the first to recognize the voluntary potential of the Act. The New York lawyers asked for their opinions shortly before the Act went into effect explicitly described the steps that debtors who had already failed should take to qualify themselves for inclusion under the Act, since the acts of trading and acts of bankruptcy had to occur after the effective date of the Act. Although one of the five, Richard Harison, noted that "collusion"—his word—was grounds for voiding the proceedings, another, Robert Troup, who served on the second bankruptcy commission empaneled in New York, shortly afterward counseled a client how to conceal the collusion. Harison himself later gave detailed advice on how to initiate a "friendly" bankruptcy for an upstate merchant, even opining that cooperative debtors could prove their debts by affidavits executed in New York rather than having to travel to Albany, where the proceedings and the commissioners would be. He was serving on three bankruptcy commissions at the time.[16]

One did not have to be a lawyer to recognize the voluntary potential of the Act. The debtors who toasted the Act in the New Gaol presumably would not have done so had they thought its benefits uncertain or attainable only at the whim of hostile creditors. Instead, they spoke of "the comfort received from this ray of light" and of how "Justice and mercy have embraced each other," as though they fully expected debtors "entomb'd in the different Prisons in the United States" to emerge "under this law, as gold tried in the fire."[17] John Pintard knew that the Act promised salvation even before it passed. Once it became law, he lost no time in enlisting a sympathetic creditor to petition for a commission against him. His case is a good illustration of how a debtor and a creditor could join to pry loose a discharge from other, more reluctant creditors.

Pintard was, as we have seen, a close observer of debtor legislation. When he read that the New Jersey legislature had passed an insolvency act, he wrote in his prison journal that it was "the first ray of hope that has reached me in six years," exulting that "I am all sensibility and life," and immediately laid plans to take advantage of it. He worked on his accounts and inventories, consulted lawyers on whether an insolvency discharge in New Jersey would protect him from prosecution in other states, and petitioned for his release. Although initially blocked by a particularly angry creditor—"my unrelenting persevering persecutor James Farquhar"—Pintard received a state insolvency discharge in May 1798 and turned over to assignees what little property he had, mostly uncollectible claims against others. He remained in jail eleven weeks longer until other creditors could be persuaded to withdraw their opposition to a federal habeas corpus petition. Once freed, however, Pintard discovered the limits to his freedom. While on a visit to Boston with his cousin, he heard that Farquhar had sued out a writ against him there. Rather than test the extraterritoriality of his New Jersey insolvency discharge, Pintard hastened back to the relative safety of Newark.[18]

Three days after Pintard learned that John Adams had signed the bankruptcy bill into law, he asked a friend to inquire if Farquhar would consent to a bankruptcy discharge. While awaiting an answer, he studied the text of the Act with two other friends—one a judge—and spent five days pouring over an English bankruptcy treatise. Farquhar eventually sent word that he would oppose any discharge. Brockholst Livingston— one of the five New York lawyers then parsing the Act—advised Pintard to wait until others could test it. After more than a month of agitated study and reflection, Pintard wrote in his journal that Farquhar's "implacability" would likely prevent him from reaching the two-thirds threshold required for a certificate. Nonetheless, he dispatched other friends and, ultimately, his wife to entreat Farquhar, who eventually relented and promised her "not to persecute me more." Galvanized by Farquhar's change of heart, Pintard met on July 13 with John Blagge, a merchant against whom the first bankruptcy commission in New York had been issued one month earlier. That evening, he asked Alexander Macomb, William Duer's surviving partner, to be "my prosecuting creditor" and declared in his journal, "Have concluded to place myself within the operation of the act."[19]

Over the next ten days, Pintard moved to New York "for the purpose of availing myself of the benefit of the Bankrupt Act," arranged for two friends to stand bail for him should he be arrested, and strategized with Livingston, who "says that it is absolutely necessary that I should commence business, and act publicly as a broker, [so] I can be implicated as within the purview of the Bankrupt Act. I shall make my arrangements accordingly."[20] From Livingston he went to Leonard Bleecker to ask him "to give me some business to transact," then enlisted another friend to inform the sheriff that if a writ should issue against him—meaning a writ from a hostile creditor rather than a friendly one—he would surrender at the sheriff's office with his bail "to prevent unpleasing apprehensions . . . of being arrested in the public streets." On Wednesday, July 23, Pintard "commenced business" as a broker by placing an advertisement in the *Commercial Advertiser* and appearing at the coffeehouse for an hour, where he sold some stock for Bleecker. He gave his commission—fifty-eight cents, "the first fruits of my industry for above eight years"—to the Missionary Society for Propagating the Gospel. The next day he met Abraham Skinner, the secretary to the bankruptcy commissioners, and called on Macomb "to arrange the process of the writ to bring me within the purview of the Bankrupt Act, conceiving that I have done business, bona fide and sufficiently public to render me amenable."

Pintard returned to his sister-in-law's house on Broadway that evening to await the writ Macomb promised to take out in the morning so he could commit the required act of bankruptcy by avoiding it. One day of keeping close stretched into two when Livingston, who was handling the paperwork, took ill, which delayed the writ and left Pintard in "anxious suspense." It was late Saturday afternoon when the deputy sheriff attempted to serve Macomb's writ and was turned away by the housekeeper as planned, while Pintard remained upstairs. The act of bankruptcy thus accomplished, Pintard paid a visit to Livingston, who told him that "if my case does not fall within [the Act] that he does not see how it is possible that any person in my situation can be relieved by the Bankrupt Act." Livingston nonetheless thought Pintard should confer with Robert Troup and Alexander Hamilton because the bankruptcy commissioners "are very exact and difficult in construing the Bankrupt Act." Indeed, the commissioners had just terminated the proceedings against Blagge because his petitioning creditor had failed to prove an act of bankruptcy to their satisfaction.[21]

As the next day was a Sunday, when debtors could travel without fear of arrest, Pintard called on Troup, who "gave me a very friendly reception," then left the city to stay with an uncle in New Rochelle, there to await the next steps in his carefully orchestrated "involuntary" bankruptcy, or, as he called it, "the experiment I am making." As he so often did, Pintard spent his time in reflection. He visited a hundred-acre neck of land on Long Island Sound—"an elegant position for a gentlemans seat"—which "in my golden days I had given orders to purchase," but which now belonged to a farmer. In his diary he resigned himself to his fate—"If not an oak, which towers on high and resists the storm, I am like the humble osier which plies and yields to the sweeping tempest." On Wednesday, July 30, Pintard received word from his wife that the federal district judge, John Sloss Hobart—a founder of the Humane Society thirteen years earlier—had appointed commissioners on Macomb's petition who were meeting that morning "to decide whether my case comes within the Bankrupt Act." He was to remain in New Rochelle "untill further orders." Mindful of Blagge's misstep, Pintard's lawyers submitted affidavits from seven different people attesting to his acts of trading and of bankruptcy. Mrs. Pintard surprised him in person the next evening, when she arrived from the city with the news that the commissioners had declared him a bankrupt and scheduled the statutory examinations. She also brought "kind notes" from Livingston and Troup. To his diary Pintard confided, "I flatter myself that a period to my long calamities is fast approaching. I bow with humble gratitude before an all gracious providence for this signal instance of mercy." Pintard returned to the city on Saturday, August 2, prayed at Trinity Church the next morning for God "to grant a favorable issue to the process of law . . . that I may be restored once more to society and my dear family," and surrendered to the commissioners on Monday.

Pintard's bankruptcy proceedings may have been cooperative, but that did not mean that they were not at all adversarial or that a discharge was certain. His first examination by the commissioners and creditors, which he described as "painful and excruciating," lasted three hours. A week later he noted with some alarm that two of his commissioners had jailed another bankrupt for hiding a few silver spoons, which a suspicious creditor had dug up in his cellar.[22] On August 21, Pintard began making the rounds of his creditors to ask them to sign his certificate. He bravely started with Farquhar, his largest and most hostile creditor, without whose signature he could not reach the necessary two-thirds in value, shrewdly calculating that if Farquhar relented, other creditors would follow suit. Farquhar, who had been adamantly opposed as recently as the day before, signed, although not before making "very bitter and severe reflections." Pintard then approached Benjamin Moore, who, as he had hoped, signed after seeing that Farquhar had. So Pintard continued for three weeks. Some creditors signed, some refused—including one of his in-laws— some said they would consult their lawyers. Pintard worried about the holdouts—most of them smaller creditors who were needed for their numbers rather than their amounts—and enlisted various friends to plead his case with them. It was during this period that he read Wollstonecraft, oddly enough to "dissipate gloomy reflections and unavailing retrospect."

Twenty creditors proved debts totaling $65,246.87 against Pintard. Most of the debts were for notes Pintard had endorsed for Duer or executed himself in the weeks before they both failed in 1792. The two largest debts by far—roughly $15,000 each—were owed to Macomb, to settle accounts left over from Duer's speculations, and to Farquhar, on a court judgment he had won against Pintard in New Jersey on the same speculations. By his own account, Pintard owed just over one million dollars, all but a few hundred of which rested on his extravagant endorsements eight years earlier. The difference between the enormous sum Pintard legally owed and the comparatively piddling total proved against him measures a number of things, at least one of which was a major shortcoming of the Act. Unlike modern bankruptcy law, which requires individual notice of the proceedings to creditors, the Act of 1800 permitted publication notice in a single local newspaper. Creditors would thus know of the proceedings and the opportunity to prove their debts only if they read the paper or if someone told them. This may explain why the overwhelming majority of creditors who proved their debts in bankruptcy were commercial creditors, whose business it was to keep track of their accounts and investments and who had the legal and informational resources to do so. Distant creditors without local agents and smaller creditors who did not read the notices or have reason to talk to one another could easily have their debts discharged without ever learning that they had a right to share in any dividend—if, of course, they had shown up and proven their debts. Even when they received notice, distant creditors were at a disadvantage because of the difficulty and expense of engaging someone to represent their interests at the examinations they could not attend themselves. One suspects also that some number of creditors simply decided that the likelihood of recovering anything from the bankrupt debtor was too low to justify the time, expense, and aggravation of making a claim.

This left as the creditors who proved their debts in bankruptcy those who wanted to help the debtor obtain a discharge, those who thought the debtor might have some property to distribute, and those whose anger or outrage drove them to pursue the debtor without regard to the cost or likelihood of recovery. Pintard's creditors included some of the first and third, and perhaps of all three, groups. Maneuvering continued to the bitter end. Dissenting creditors successfully challenged three of the signatures on a technicality, forcing the three creditors to sign again. Pintard, afraid that he would fall short, personally solicited a painter and a doctor to prove the only debts that were for services and that had nothing to do with Duer. After intense lobbying by his friends, Pintard reached the two-thirds threshold with not a single creditor to spare. But for Farquhar, he would not have met the value requirement. As soon as Hobart signed his discharge, "kindly congratulat[ing] me on the favorable issue," Pintard made the rounds of his friends to thank them, then "met my little woman . . . and imparted the glad tidings of my restoration to freedom." Fully aware of how close his "experiment" had come to failing, Pintard took pains to list in his journal the names of his "humane" consenting creditors and his "unfeeling" objecting ones. He asked God to "enable me to retribute the goodness of the former" and prayed that the latter may "never want in case of necessity that mercy which they denied to me." Ironically, three of Pintard's humane creditors later became bankrupt. None of his unfeeling ones did.[23]

Pintard's case is a reminder that even "voluntary" bankruptcies could be contentious. Involuntary bankruptcies could be even more so. For example, several of Joseph Callender's ninety-one creditors demanded jury trials on their claims. One, whose claim the commissioners rejected because it rested on an admittedly usurious note, extorted a settlement by filing legal challenges that delayed what turned out to be a 36 percent dividend, a level attained by only one in eight bankrupt estates in Massachusetts. The standoff lasted for fifteen months, until the other creditors agreed to allow the debt and share the dividend with him. The assignees, commissioners, and creditors of Gurdon Miller of New London squabbled for nearly four years, as the assignees disputed debts and fought with the commissioners over whether claims should be removed to federal court. A Boston creditor who petitioned a local wine merchant, Thomas Dennie, into bankruptcy very much against his will, was left responsible for a sizable bill of costs for six commissioners' meetings when Dennie obtained a writ of supersedeas from the federal circuit court of appeals ordering the proceedings to cease.[24]

Creditors could be as distrustful of one another as they were of debtors. And with good reason. Creditors and their lawyers often maneuvered for advantage over one another. When William Meredith, a young lawyer in Philadelphia, sought advice on how to structure a land transfer by a merchant to some of his creditors so that the property could not be reached by other creditors in subsequent bankruptcy proceedings, he was only doing the bidding of his clients, who were the merchant and the creditors who sought the preference. Creditors were quick to pounce on any evidence that the debtor had illegally paid one creditor but not others, or that the debtor had tried to conceal property in plain sight by transferring title to solvent nominees. They also contested each other's claims, forcing them into arbitration. Joseph Bacon's assignee questioned him closely on why he had assigned an account to a creditor using a backdated receipt the day before he closed his store in Boston after confiding that he could not pay his debts. The assignee also investigated whether Bacon's delivery of a quantity of cotton to another creditor had been to pay off one debt or to secure future payment of a second—if the latter, the assignee could reclaim the cotton for Bacon's other creditors. Samuel Buel, who won a small court judgment against William Ladd days before Ladd was petitioned into bankruptcy, repeatedly directed the commissioners to people he suspected of holding Ladd's property for him—none of whom were, as it turned out. Zadock Pomeroy's creditors demanded that the commissioners examine one of their number under oath on the same suspicion.[25]

When Thomas Walter, a merchant in Boston, conveyed a ship and its cargo to a relative, his creditors immediately, and correctly, feared that he was trying to move assets beyond their reach. Until then, they had been content to give Walter time to try to recoup his fortunes and repay them. However, one creditor, Joseph Smith, who two years later was petitioned into bankruptcy himself, upset the balance by suing out a writ of attachment, which appears to be what triggered Walter's gambit. Now several creditors—although, curiously enough, not Smith—petitioned for a commission of bankruptcy on the ground that the transfer was a fraudulent conveyance and therefore an act of bankruptcy. Walter denied the allegation and demanded a jury trial. Despite having as his lawyer a congressional champion of the Act, Harrison Gray Otis, Walter lost the verdict. The jury found the transfer to be fraudulent and declared it void. Walter continued to resist. At his first examination the commissioners reprimanded him for his lack of cooperation and candor. Eventually, four dozen creditors received nine cents on the dollar, but Walter's recalcitrance delayed his discharge for ten months, nearly three times the median time and longer than all but 15 percent of the discharges granted in Massachusetts.[26]

At least Walter won a discharge. Others charged with concealing assets did not. For example, Benjamin Alley, a trader in Lynn, north of Boston, was poised to receive a discharge after nine months of proceedings. The commissioners and two-thirds of his ninety creditors had signed his certificate. At the last moment, however, two dissenting creditors—his relatives, no less—sued to block the discharge, claiming that he had defrauded his creditors by concealing unspecified goods and chattels and by collecting debts on his own and not turning them over to his assignees. Alley denied the allegations, demanded a jury trial, and lost. There would be no discharge. However, the assignees had already auctioned off his property, so his creditors received a 15 percent dividend anyway.[27]

Alley's case was unusual. Few discharge decisions wound up in litigation. Indeed, Alley's appears to have been the only one that did in

Massachusetts. That does not mean, however, that all bankruptcy proceedings progressed smoothly or resulted inevitably in absolution for the debtor. One in six commissions issued in Massachusetts did not produce a discharge. Of the ones that did, although most freed the debtor from liability within six months, one in nine took a year or more before enough creditors could be persuaded to consent. Other states were more or less stringent, but in none was a discharge a foregone conclusion.[28] As the number of sharp interrogatories in the files attests, creditors, assignees, and commissioners all had the power to discomfort the debtor with questions, doubts, accusations, and demands, which, if not answered adequately, could delay or derail the proceedings. Even when debtors and creditors had agreed on a discharge—whether at the outset in a collusive petition or later, while gathering creditors' signatures—the commissioners could demur. Even when no one objected, the judge could deny a discharge on his own authority, as Oliver Wolcott once did simply to make a point when commissioners had submitted sloppy paperwork for his approval.[29]

Two key decisions lay in the discretion of the commissioners— whether to declare the debtor a bankrupt, and whether to declare that the bankrupt had complied with the requirements of the Act. The former allowed the proceedings to continue, the latter enabled them to conclude. Debtors rarely contested the first, and never the second. At the beginning of the proceedings, commissioners were much more likely than debtors to question the petitioning creditor's proof of debt or the sufficiency of the acts of bankruptcy and trading alleged. If not satisfied, they would rule that the debtor "was not a Bankrupt." Creditors who wished to persevere would then have to petition for a new commission and hope they could muster more persuasive proofs.[30]

Once the requisite number and value of creditors had signed their consent to the certificate of conformity, the commissioners' concurrence, however likely, was not assured. The commissioners for Peter Blight, a Philadelphia import merchant who had amassed debts of nearly one million dollars, blocked his discharge for more than three years, longer than all but one of the discharges granted in Pennsylvania. From the very first meeting, many of Blight's creditors had suspected him of concealing assets, falsifying accounts, making fraudulent conveyances, and generally withholding information. His answers to interrogatories were often vague and forgetful. At one point the federal circuit court of appeals ordered him arrested for perjury, although the warrant may not have been served. Despite Blight's record of evasion and deceit, 151 of his 220 creditors consented to a discharge, perhaps in the knowledge that the assignees had collected enough to pay one-fifth of the debts—an unusually high dividend. The commissioners, however, disagreed. Swayed by the evidence rather than the creditors' wishes, they refused to certify that Blight had complied with the Act. Blight eventually won a discharge but only after a marathon seven-day trial in which his lawyer, Alexander J. Dallas—himself a member of fifty bankruptcy commissions—convinced a jury, at least five of whose members had previously consented to the discharge of their own bankrupt debtors, that Blight "hath made a full and true Discovery and Disclosure of all his Estate and Effects and in all Things conformed himself to the Directions of the Act."[31]

Blight obtained his discharge only by clearing a very high hurdle. Other bankrupt debtors in his position did not even try. For example, Robert Crommelin of New York had obtained an insolvency release under state law by promising key creditors that he would pay them in full if they would consent to his release. To ease their doubts, he gave them promissory notes. Once released, he entered into a retail partnership with John Betts, dipped into the new partnership assets to pay some of his individual notes, and slid back into insolvency—this time with Betts in tow. The partners hatched a plan to float their debts, then graduated to a plan to use the new bankruptcy law to their advantage. They would buy goods on credit, then "sell" them to their existing creditors to pay old accounts or transfer them to their endorsers as security. They expected that this diversion would buy them time until yellow fever season, when they could join the exodus of the well-to-do from the city without attracting notice. Fate intervened in the form of arrest warrants and a bankruptcy petition. Crommelin and Betts recognized an opportunity. Betts confided to a widow that "tho' they had failed they had taken damned good care to save enough to live upon." "The Bankrupt Law," he said, "was in their favor, . . . they meant to get rid of their old Business as well as new and do Business again in the same store." The commissioners learned of these stratagems at their last meeting. Crommelin had already testified to numerous transactions that did not appear in their accounts, many of them preferential transfers to creditors after they had stopped payment on their other obligations. The deceptions exposed, the commissioners rejected a discharge. Crommelin and Betts did not contest the decision. Instead, they appear to have negotiated a settlement with their creditors four years later. Unfortunately, we do not know what assurances Crommelin gave this time.[32]

Whether the proceedings were genuinely involuntary or only nominally so, the reality of the financial distress is reflected clearly in the fact that failure was a common experience of debtors and creditors alike. In Massachusetts, one in every twelve petitioning creditors was himself petitioned into bankruptcy within, on average, eight months. In New York, nearly one-fourth of the bankrupt debtors were themselves creditors who consented to the discharge of other bankrupt debtors, either before or after their own proceedings. In Pennsylvania and Connecticut, at least one in ten were. Although the assignees of bankrupt debtors rarely pursued their duty to collect assets to the point of seeking commissions against other debtors—I know of only one instance—they did not hesitate to join other creditors in filing claims against a bankrupt's estate in hope of obtaining even a small dividend for the creditors they represented. Numerous files contain proofs of debts filed by assignees, some of them contested as far as arbitration or even litigation between debtor's and creditor's assignees. Indeed, the unparalleled success of John Palmer's bankruptcy, which produced payment in full with interest for all his creditors, occurred because his assignees tenaciously litigated contract claims against the assignees of two other bankrupt debtors. The judgments they won were never paid in full, but they established Palmer, a merchant and agent in Philadelphia, as a creditor entitled to a dividend, which yielded enough to create a surplus in his own smaller estate.[33]

The commonality of debtors and creditors appears most poignantly in the account summaries prepared by bankrupt debtors or their assignees. When Jabez Perkins, a retail merchant and West Indies trader in Norwich, Connecticut, tallied up his losses, he attributed one-quarter of them to the failure of various debtors, the rest to shipwrecks and privateers. In one of the very few bankruptcy proceedings in upstate New York, Jacob Huistis's assignee reported that he had collected less than $16 and that most of Huistis's debtors "had absconded or were insolvent or both." Bankruptcy files in every state list as assets Robert Morris's and John Nicholson's notes, every last one of them worthless. Thomas Clark, an auctioneer in Boston, was owed nearly $19,000 by 133 debtors on book accounts and promissory notes. When his assignee listed the debtors and their debts, next to the names of sixty-one of them, who together owed four-fifths of all the debts due Clark, he wrote his assessment of the likelihood of repayment— "Bankrupt," "doubtful," "Poor," "very poor," "good for nothing," "absconded," "no value," "supposed of no value," "deceased, value uncertain," "very dubious." All told, seventeen of the debtors were already in bankruptcy, while three listed as "doubtful" or the like soon joined them. Joshua Blanchard, a Boston wine merchant, divided his seventy-one debtors into three categories—"Good," "Dubious," and "Desperate." His appraisals were accurate. His assignee was able to collect nineteen of the twenty-eight debts listed under "Good," one of the fourteen described as "Dubious," and none of the twenty-nine labeled "Desperate." Similarly, the assignee for Comfort Sands, a merchant and large-scale land speculator in New York, identified each of two dozen debtors who owed Sands nearly $70,000 as "Bankrupt," "Insolvent," or "Lives in Ga.," which meant the same thing.[34]

Failure could be a shared experience in other ways as well. When Pintard returned to New York to pursue a discharge, he ran into the father of former friends of his, Richard Yates, who was now "a poor broken spirited old man, ruined in his fortunes by the failure of his sons-in-law Carlisle and George Pollock." All three men followed Pintard into bankruptcy.[35] Other examples of sons or sons-in-law dragging their fathers or, in one instance, mother into bankruptcy abound. When they failed together, it was only because they had been partners. In Philadelphia, John Field, Sr., received a discharge from the same three commissioners who had certified one for his son eighteen months earlier. John Miller, Sr., followed his son into bankruptcy six months later. Thomas Murgatroyd and Richard Tittermary were petitioned into bankruptcy with their sons and partners, although for some reason Robert Tittermary won a discharge two months before his father did. Sometimes the roles were reversed. Nicholas Coverly, Sr., a printer in Boston, preceded his son, a trader across the river in Charlestown, into bankruptcy by five weeks. The commissioners who recommended his discharge denied one to his son. A commission issued against George Keith, Jr., a trader in Marshfield, Massachusetts, eleven days after his father received a discharge. The father's financial distress stretched back to the Revolution; the son's less than two years.[36]

Jonas Prentice, Jr., had a more complex relationship of finance and failure with his father, although both met the same end. Bankrolled by his father, who lived in New Haven, Prentice began business as an apothecary in New York in 1796 in partnership with a doctor. When the partnership dissolved after eight months, the doctor sold his share to a third party, who in turn sold it to Prentice's father, presumably so Prentice, Sr., could keep his son in business. Father and son ran the store for a year, during which time the father seems to have used it as a bank, sometimes withdrawing, sometimes depositing assets. The business failed in November 1797. Within a year, the son was arrested for debt and imprisoned in New York for thirteen months. Upon his release in 1800, he struggled to make ends meet as a broker, dealing in medicines. Failing at that, in July 1801 he was once again arrested for debt by several creditors, including his father. Jonas Prentice, Sr., may have sued his son to facilitate a later bankruptcy petition, but the fact that he left his son in prison for four months before seeking a commission against him suggests that collecting the sums he had advanced to set his son up in business was more important. If so, the senior Prentice certainly needed the money—thirteen months after his son received a discharge, he was petitioned into bankruptcy himself in Connecticut.[37]

Susannah Kneeland lived above her dry-goods store on Cornhill Street in Boston, which specialized in fabrics of various kinds. She ran the shop successfully for ten years after her husband died in 1792, leaving her with two young children. That all changed when her son, William, came of age, and she let him sell similar merchandise out of her store. They kept their inventories separate, but she endorsed a number of his notes. William's inability to pay compromised his mother. When they became insolvent, but long before they could become destitute, her family stepped in and arranged coordinated bankruptcy proceedings against them: separate commissions issued on the same day to the same commissioners on the petitions of different creditors, the same assignees—one of them a relative— the same dates of discharge, and nearly the same dividend dates. Her creditors negotiated the discharge of the mortgage on her property, returned her church pew to her, and allowed her to repurchase her furniture on relaxed credit terms. There is no indication that they treated William with similar generosity. Indeed, they pressed her assignees to file a large claim against his estate. Susannah's debts were almost twice William's. Her estate eventually repaid creditors sixty-four cents on the dollar; William's paid fifty-two cents. She continued in business at a smaller store nearby.[38]

Bankrupt debtors did not have to be relatives or partners to be bound to one another by failure. For example, Nathaniel G. Ingraham blamed all of his troubles, which were many, on Nathaniel Olcott. Olcott, a broker and land speculator, disappeared from his home in New York on October 6, 1800. A few days earlier, he had confided to his wife that he "did not know how he should get through with his business" and that "he must leave her." When he left his house that afternoon, he told her that "he did not know whether he should return again that evening or not." By the next morning, rumors were circulating in the coffeehouses and on the street that Olcott had drowned. When Ingraham, who had wide-ranging interests in land speculation and in West Indies and European trade, heard the reports, he declared to everyone within hearing that he was "a ruined Man" and that Olcott had "robbed" him of nearly $40,000, "which was every cent he was worth in the world." Three days later, another broker, Samuel Beebe, petitioned for a commission of bankruptcy against Olcott, who had yet to surface. The Bank of New York was particularly interested in finding him. In the months before his disappearance, Olcott had persuaded a teller at the bank to advance him some $118,000 on notes and postdated checks drawn by others that he swore were good, leaving collateral worth, at most, $25,000. Some of the paper represented loans that he had secured with his own promissory notes and that in fact would not be good if he did not repay them. At a cost of $2,500, including a reward of $2,000, the bank tracked Olcott to Pittsburgh, where it had him arrested on a criminal fraud warrant and returned to prison in New York—the Bridewell, not the New Gaol.

Ingraham was petitioned into bankruptcy in December. Olcott's failure may have triggered his, but shipping losses prepared the way. As for the money he claimed Olcott had "robbed" him of, he described that to the commissioners as a loan to Olcott at 3 percent interest monthly. Olcott testified that Ingraham had given him the notes to sell for a brokerage commission of half a percent. In fact, by his reckoning, Ingraham owed him $25,000. The commissioners, who summoned and resummoned Ingraham for six examinations—twice the statutory number—because of his evasiveness, denied him a discharge. One week later, the same three commissioners recommended one for Olcott. Ingraham eventually received one as well. Quite apart from whatever claims they had against each other, their lists of their debtors and creditors read like rosters of failure, with names of past insolvents and present bankrupts.[39]

Congress repealed the bankruptcy act in December 1803, eighteen months before it would have expired on its own. Born in controversy, the Act died in mere disagreement, with little of the ideological contention that had roiled its enactment. Supporters argued that the Act was an experiment that should be allowed to run its course, although they had not called it an experiment when they had debated its passage. If there were failings, amendments would correct them. Opponents united against the Act overwhelmingly—the vote to repeal was ninety-nine to thirteen—but for disparate reasons, some of them contradictory. From a party perspective, repeal seemed inevitable. The Act had passed over virtually unbroken

Republican opposition in a House with a Federalist majority barely large enough to weather the defections. The Federalists had been swept from office a few months later and by the Eighth Congress were outnumbered nearly three-to-one. The turnover on both sides of the aisle was so complete that only twenty-three of the representatives who voted on repeal had been in the Sixth Congress when Albert Gallatin and James A. Bayard debated the nature of the republic so vigorously. Only four members who had voted for the Act remained, all of them New England Federalists— two now voted to repeal, two missed the vote. However, the party shift alone cannot explain repeal. Republicans had held a two-to-one majority in the Seventh Congress but could not overcome opposition to repeal led by the ever-eloquent Bayard, who had recently lost reelection and would soon leave the House. Moreover, of the thirteen votes against repeal, only three were Federalists. Every other member of the party once led by Theodore Sedgwick, who by now was a judge of the Massachusetts Supreme Judicial Court, supported rescinding the act that owed its existence to his vote.

When the issue of repeal first arose in January 1803, no one any longer insisted that the United States was an agrarian society unsuited for a bankruptcy system. Indeed, when Bayard proclaimed the country "a great commercial Republic," even John Randolph of Virginia, who had voted against the Act three years earlier, agreed, asking only "to take care of the agricultural interest." By the same token, only Bayard, who had thrown the presidency to Thomas Jefferson by switching from Aaron Burr, still spoke of the centrality of credit to commerce and the consequent importance of a uniform bankruptcy law to merchants, but his influence was barely enough to postpone the vote to repeal the Act until after he had left the House.[40]

Critics of the Act were emphatic but vague. Members on both sides referred to the Act as "extremely defective." They alluded to its "existing evils" and "injurious provisions" without specifying what they were. Seth Hastings, a Federalist from Worcester County, Massachusetts, "believed that there had never been a law which had produced more iniquity and fraud," but did not elaborate. Randolph claimed that he "knew by experience that it had been in many instances ruinous; that many planters had been *choused* out of their property by the operations of this very law"—a tantalizing, but unfortunately unverifiable, assertion since no bankruptcy records from Virginia have survived. Hence Bayard's remark that "I have heard much of the evils attending to its execution, but I have never seen them."[41]

Two of the most vocal opponents of the Act, Hastings and Thomas Newton, Jr., a Republican from Norfolk, Virginia, both first-term congressmen, were also the most muddled in their arguments. At one juncture, within the space of a few minutes Newton protested first that the Act too readily permitted fraud, then that its deterrents to fraud were too severe. Hastings condemned the Act as so "entirely for the benefit of the debtor" that it should be renamed "an act for establishing an uniform system of fraud throughout the United States," while at the same time stating that he would vote to retain it if it were amended "to extend the benefits . . . to all classes of citizens." Taking up the theme of inequality, Newton claimed that the Act was "in principle anti-Republican" because it distinguished "between citizen and citizen in the dispensation of justice." However, he rejected Hastings's solution. With tortured logic, he argued that this "partiality cannot be remedied" because, under English law, "the words 'bankrupt, trader, and merchant,' are synonymous"; hence the Constitution, which permits "uniform laws on the subject of bankruptcies, . . . forbids us . . . from extending the provisions of a bankrupt law, to either the farmer, planter, mechanic, or any other class of citizens other than a trader or merchant." Perhaps Hastings and Newton were simply being disingenuous. Each expressed a strong preference for state insolvency laws, which did not carry occupational restrictions. Hastings had also asserted that he would favor a bankruptcy law if the bankrupt's property remained liable for his debts, which would, of course, eliminate the discharge and turn the Act into an insolvency law.[42]

When the new Congress took up repeal in November, the House disposed of the matter in one day of desultory debate, perhaps because the outcome was now assured. The Senate was more closely divided, but there, too, the speeches lacked the vigor of the enactment arguments.

Some members of the House complained that the law "enlarged the sphere of the Federal courts," others that it was an "extension of the Executive power." Ironically, many of the latter had created the "Executive patronage" they now denounced by voting the year before to take the power to select commissioners from judges and give it to the president. Still others argued that the Act, "however good in theory," was fatally weakened by the lack of the "sanguinary" punishments for fraud present in British law, even as they described American merchants as "probably the most honest . . . in the world." More interesting was the criticism—unheard of three years earlier—that creditor control of the process was illusory. The creditor's petition "was merely a nominal act" performed by a creditor "who was the friend of the bankrupt." The resulting voluntary proceedings operated to the advantage of debtors and the detriment of creditors. It created a "ten-fold temptation to fraud." It undermined "the morals of the mercantile world" by allowing merchants to incur risk with impunity and by exciting "a spirit of the most prodigal expenditure." It enabled a discharged debtor to "live in the greatest splendor, even ostentatiously displaying his property, without rendering it liable to seizure." Thus, "[e]vils infinitely greater had been inflicted by inconsiderate and fraudulent debtors taking refuge in the provisions of the bankrupt law than from all the inhumanity exercised by merciless creditors over unfortunate debtors." A far cry from what Samuel L. Mitchill, a Republican congressman from New York, once referred to as "a great experiment in the commercial and political world."[43]

All of this, of course, was rhetoric, not fact. None of the notorious figures whose failures occasioned the Act had been encouraged in their speculations by the promise of a then-nonexistent discharge. Nor had passage of the Act triggered a flood of petitions on behalf of debtors eager for relief, Pintard notwithstanding. In fact, in every state the number of commissions built slowly, then held steady or even declined over the life of the Act. Only in Philadelphia did the likelihood of repeal produce a surge in filings. Hardly the profile of proliferating fraud. In the end what seems to have united those who favored a bankruptcy system and those who opposed it was not a common set of verifiable reasons but rather the conviction, as Manasseh Cutler wrote afterward, that "the existing law was so radically deficient as not to admit of amendments"—a conviction that seems to have rested on little more than anxiety that debtors were using bankruptcy to escape obligations they could have repaid.[44]

Later critics of the Act contended that creditors had too often received little or nothing from the estates of their bankrupt debtors. Dividend information is sparse, but the observation was undoubtedly true, even though Bayard had claimed that "it is no uncommon thing to have dividends."[45] In Massachusetts nearly 40 percent of the estates yielded no dividend at all. On the other hand, one wonders why creditors would expect anything. Proponents of the Act had justified it on two grounds—as a means of empowering creditors to stop the evasions of fraudulent debtors and as a shield to protect honest debtors from vindictive creditors. Simply as a matter of probability, some of the debtors in bankruptcy must have defrauded their creditors, but direct evidence is exceedingly rare. There was also little reason to believe that creditors would petition their debtors into bankruptcy—whether involuntarily or cooperatively—while the debtors still retained enough property for a decent dividend. At the level of debt required to be a petitioning creditor, commercial creditors and debtors were more than just creditor and debtor—they were partners in the debtor's business. Not legally, of course, but economically. If the debtor prospered, so did his creditors. If the debtor failed, his creditors lost as well. As long as a failing commercial debtor remained in business, his creditors could hope for a recovery and future repayment. A creditor who petitioned his debtor into bankruptcy renounced that hope. The petition represented his acknowledgment that he would never recoup his investment—the debt—let alone realize any profit on it. All that remained was for creditors to apportion the loss. A bankruptcy dividend offered at most a small recovery, which from the creditor's perspective was a large loss. Small wonder that creditors did not petition their debtors into bankruptcy while the debtors still had the wherewithal to offer hope.

For their part, commercial debtors had little incentive to solicit a petition until most or all of their property and credit was gone. There is a difference between failing and admitting that one has failed. Bankruptcy—the legal status of being declared a bankrupt—was an admission of failure, a concession that the debtor had lost the game of commerce. Since a discharge did not leave debtors with sufficient capital to begin the game again, despite the absolution provided by a fresh start, debtors had no incentive to stop playing—to admit failure—until they had nothing left with which to play, at which point there was nothing left for their creditors. For commercial entrepreneurs the path out of insolvency was the same that led them into insolvency, only with better luck. If they did not believe that, they would not be entrepreneurs. That is why William Duer continued his speculations from prison.

Robert Morris, for one, knew that his creditors would never receive anything—not because he had hidden his assets but because he had none to hide. Still imprisoned after two years, he consulted a lawyer about the Act when it passed, but from his questions it is clear that he did not expect his creditors would consent to a discharge. Nor did he seek one. While trying to broker some bills of exchange "to help out the means of subsistence," he wrote his son from jail that he feared his creditors might find out. He knew that he ran "the risque of being made a Bankrupt" if they did, an end he hoped to avoid. When John H. Huston, whom he owed nearly $300,000, petitioned him into bankruptcy in July 1801, it truly was involuntary. Eventually, eighty-six creditors, several of them bankrupts themselves, proved debts of three million dollars against Morris. They were the determined ones. Most of his creditors did not bother. One lawyer reported that the creditors he had spoken with "will not even prove their debts." He told a creditor who sought his advice from Baltimore that Morris's estate "has been so entangled and mortgaged, and the amount of his debts are so great, that it is the general opinion there will not be one penny in the pound." After three months of questioning Morris before the commissioners, his creditors concluded that his remaining property would not even cover the costs of the proceedings. So they gave up. Morris received a discharge, without opposition, on December 4, 1801. The next morning he wrote his son, who had just won election to Congress as a Federalist from New York, "I now find myself a free Citizen of the United States without one cent that I can call my own."[46]

CONCLUSION

The Bankruptcy Act of 1800, like bankruptcy itself, looked both forward and backward—it marked a beginning as well as an end. While seeming simply to transplant long-standing English principles of involuntary bankruptcy, with its undercurrent of checking criminal or fraudulent behavior, in substance the Act created a framework within which commercial debtors and creditors could cooperate in sorting through the fallout of failure. Its very passage was testimony to the eclipse of the moral economy of debt as a religious imperative, as well as witness to its rebirth in a secularized form. The Act was forged in the ideological debates that defined Revolutionary America—issues of commerce and agriculture, vice and virtue, slavery and freedom, dependence and independence, nationalism and federalism—but it settled none of them. It addressed the fundamental question of whether and how a society should forgive its debtors, but the answers it offered were merely provisional. Every subsequent generation, including ours, confronted the question for itself. The next federal bankruptcy law—the Bankruptcy Act of 1841, which lasted barely a year before being repealed—elicited similar anguished discussions of lost masculinity, dependence, enslavement, the evils of speculation, and the importance of independence, as did several unsuccessful bills in between. Divers failed attempts later, the Bankruptcy Act of 1867 passed narrowly in the absence of southern representatives, who were barred from the first Reconstruction Congress. It survived eleven years but only in frequently amended, and therefore uncertain, form. Bankruptcy did not become a permanent part of the American legal landscape until 1898, and even then the laws were overhauled at forty-year intervals. For nearly a century after the Act of 1800, whatever relief was available in the long lacunae between federal enactments was a matter of state law. Recent debate as the twentieth century yielded to the twenty-first over "reform" of the bankruptcy system featured explicit calls to restore the "stigma" of bankruptcy so that insolvent debtors will heed their moral obligation to pay their credit card bills, although there is no evidence that bankruptcy has ever lost its stigma and abundant empirical proof that individuals file for bankruptcy for reasons of genuine financial distress untouched by the fraud or irresponsibility alleged by modern moralists.[1]

The fundamental dilemma of bankruptcy law has always been whether it is about death or rebirth. Is it a system for picking a debtor's bones in a more orderly fashion? Or is it an economic and social safety net that allows debtors to return to the world? The fact that it is both has never slowed debate that it should be primarily one or the other. As we have seen, the terms of that debate, as well as of the threshold debate on whether debtors should be relieved at all, changed dramatically during the course of the eighteenth century, as commercialization and leveraged economies multiplied the risk of failure and as people began to question imprisonment for debt. But the change was complex. Even when insolvency became associated more with economic risk and less with moral weakness, it was still labeled "failure," with all the doubts and emotions evoked by the term. Insolvent debtors did not have to believe that they had failed morally to feel dependent or unmanned. Nor did the ideological dimensions of the debate require a belief in the immorality of debt to be divisive.

Robert Morris, like all the "capital bankrupts" of the 1790s and like the Bankruptcy Act itself, rejected the central tenet of Samuel Moody's moral economy of debt—that insolvency was moral failure. A few days after Morris was imprisoned, he assured his son in Albany that "my Health is good, my Spirits not broke, my Mind sound and vigorous"—hardly someone bowing under the weight of his moral failure. None of his letters betray the slightest sense that his failure was anything other than economic. To Morris, his only failure was his failure to hold on to his success, a conviction he retained to the end. In his will he expressed "my regret at having lost a very large fortune acquired by honest industry which I had long hoped and expected to enjoy with my family during my own life and then to distribute it amongst those of them that should outlive me." Fate, however, "has determined otherwise." Even John Pintard, for all his religious devotion and lachrymose introspection, did not see moral failure in his "misfortunes," as he always referred to them. If there was moral responsibility, it lay in "all those who despitefully use me and evilly intreat me." All Pintard sought—other than a discharge, of course—was the "Christian humility" to enable him "to forgive and pray" for his persecutors. For his part, he had "ever endeavoured to act on the strictest principles of honor and honesty." He never once thought that he had done otherwise.[2]

This is not to say that insolvency had been drained of all its moral content. Far from it. Bankruptcy debates of the nineteenth century rehearsed many of the moral arguments so familiar to the eighteenth.[3] But the location of moral culpability had been refined. Cotton Mather's early perception that commercial debt was different from ordinary debt ripened, in the Bankruptcy Act of 1800, into a national statement of the "principle" that release from debts was a boon reserved for capitalist entrepreneurs, while simpler debtors should, by implication, remember the sanctity of their obligations. However much men of commerce might dun their own debtors, the Act of 1800 decreed that for them, and them alone, the hazards of the market trumped moral obligation. The Act was thus a declaration that the new nation was, emphatically, a commercial republic.

However, by separating large-scale entrepreneurs from their lesser commercial brethren, the Act defined citizenship in this commercial republic too narrowly to benefit either commerce or the republic. As first drafted, the bill that became the Act applied to commercial debtors who owed as little as $200, which would have made bankruptcy process available to a much broader, and perforce more egalitarian, swath of the economy by sweeping in even small and middling shopkeepers. If, as Robert Goodloe Harper had argued, a bankruptcy system would have "beneficial effects in the support of mercantile credit . . . and the relief of honest industry," the lower debt threshold presumably would have increased the "beneficial effects" to commerce. Yet it was Harper, toasted by Pintard as "the Creditors and Debtors friend," who proposed instead a minimum debt of $5,000, a staggering sum that, had it been adopted, would have excluded roughly 40 percent of the debtors who in fact received discharges. The figure agreed upon, $1,000, was still substantial. In addition, the Senate rejected an amendment that would have forced large creditors to share control of the bankrupt's estate with small creditors by allowing creditors owed only $50, rather than just those owed at least $200, to participate in choosing the assignee. Membership in the commercial republic envisioned in the Act would be limited to the select few.[4]

Benjamin Bache's sailor who stopped payment to the oysterman would have recognized the class implications of these discriminations. Theodore Sedgwick, Jr., who thought that "Mankind are selfish mercenary and sordid," certainly did. While apprenticing in a law office in Albany, he wrote his father about a more democratic bankruptcy law then under consideration by the New York legislature. The younger Sedgwick—who upon his death was described by the great James Kent as "an amiable, benevolent Man, but below par in Intellect, and not entirely Sound"—conceded that a bankruptcy law "may be a useful measure in a commercial country," but "to extend it to all Masses in the community would stagnate all business and industry, promote speculating contracts further the cause of vice and corruption and in fact make the whole State a bankrupt." It was not a privilege to be accorded the "rabble," as he described them. Yet the chasm between the elite commercial debtors favored by the Act of 1800 and Sedgwick's "Masses" was not empty. It was occupied by, among others, large numbers of artisans who were every bit as entrepreneurial as their mercantile betters and at least as important to the developing economy, but who courted success and risked failure without the safety net of a bankruptcy discharge. They were among the beneficiaries of the many failures of the 1790s, which, as Gordon S. Wood observed, "contributed greatly to the democratization of American society" by opening up opportunities in business and commerce to new men "who by the traditional standards of rank were very ordinary indeed"—and who were excluded from the Act.[5]

Concerned only with the mercantile elite, the Act of 1800 was, in a sense, a last expression of a dying Federalist order, even as it embraced the thoroughly modern concept of economic risk. The mass of citizen-debtors who remained liable for their debts may have bridled at their lot, but they did not clamor to be included within the Act. On the contrary, it was their representatives who argued for repeal—a reminder that the Act occupied contested ground. The traditional restriction of bankruptcy to elite merchants hinted at aristocratic privilege and so made bankruptcy untenable in the new democratic politics that erupted from the election of 1800. Moreover, evidence such as the fact that Methodist church discipline associated insolvency with "scandal" and allowed members to be expelled for failing to repay their debts suggests that the rapid spread of evangelical religion among southern whites may have encouraged a "re-moralization" of debt, despite the continued firm conviction of commercial entrepreneurs that failure was an economic state, not a moral one. Not until the Act of 1841, which opened bankruptcy to anyone who applied without regard to occupation, were these strands even briefly reconciled.[6]

Just as the Act itself straddled the old and the new, so did the debtors to whom it applied, who often gestured toward the old moral economy while standing firmly in the market. Early in his exile, John Pintard wrote to a creditor in Boston that "I shall consider myself still in honor bound to make good these debts" and pledged to repay them "notwithstanding any release I may obtain from an Act of Bankruptcy." Among their toasts to the Bankruptcy Act of 1800, the debtors celebrating in the New Gaol declared that no debtor relieved under it should "consider himself discharged from his debts in his own mind, until he has satisfied his creditors or spent the remainder of his days in his attempt to do so." Later, in the repeal debate, James A. Bayard argued in defense of the law that "though a man might be discharged from his contracts, the sense of moral obligation was not impaired." "[I]n *foro conscientiæ*"—in the court of conscience— "he was still answerable." Shortly afterward, an anonymous Philadelphia writer justified discharging debts by saying that were he insolvent he would labor "all my life . . . to do justice" to his creditors because he was "bound in duty, strengthened by honour, to fulfill every contract I have ever made." This was the ideal—that despite the legal absolution of a discharge, debtors retained a moral obligation to repay their debts.[7]

The reality was rather different. Pintard, for example, never repeated his promise nor did the creditor remind him of it when he sought a discharge. Other debtors also proclaimed their honor or character, typically when there was reason to doubt it. From his refuge in the New Gaol, William Duer answered charges that he intended to withhold property from his creditors by avowing that he would submit to poverty rather than "sacrifice Character"— this from a man who continued to speculate while in prison. One month after publishing notice of his financial distress and asking for "indulgence" from his creditors, James Greenleaf assured correspondents in Boston that he was "a Man of Honor" who "shall never allow you to tread on unsafe grounds." Whether he sent copies to Robert Morris or John Nicholson, whose funds he had misappropriated when they were partners, is unknown. Peter Stephen DuPonceau grew so disgusted with Greenleaf's evasions that he gave up on a debt after six years of attempting to collect it and sarcastically assured Greenleaf "that I have no witnesses to your repeated promises to pay me upon your honor." Morris pledged "my Honor" that he would pay the judgment Samuel Clarkson had won against him if Clarkson stayed execution, but when Clarkson tried to remind him of his pledge, Morris turned him away from Castle Defiance without letting him in. Daniel Thuun promised "upon [his] honor" to repay a debt, even shaking the creditor's hand "very cordially . . . in token of [his] gratitude" for the creditor's "liberal conduct" toward him, then reneged after he consulted a lawyer.[8]

These promises illustrate how completely the moral economy of debt had lost its religious underpinnings by the end of the eighteenth century, at least for commercial debtors. The redefinition of insolvency from moral failure to economic risk did not eliminate debtors' legal obligations to repay their debts. Rather, it secularized the foundations of the moral obligation to repay, which now rested on "honor" and "character," and changed the general understanding of how the law should treat failure. That said, there is something formulary and anachronistic about these invocations of honor. A modicum of integrity between debtors and creditors is certainly desirable, as it is in all human relations, but the law of debtor and creditor neither presumes nor requires it. In a commercial economy, honor is no substitute for a good security interest. Indeed, as the examples of Pintard, Greenleaf, Morris, and the others suggest, debtors trumpeted their honor only when they had lost all their credit, both financial and reputational. Yet the use of the term even in this deracinated sense is revealing.

"Honor" meant different things in Revolutionary America. In the highly stylized meaning lived by southern planters and gentlemen, honor had little place in commercial relations. As applied to debtors and creditors, honor there referred less to the debtor's moral obligation to pay and more to the creditor's social obligation to lend, be it money in the form of direct loans or credit in the form of standing surety. Refusal to endorse a fellow planter's note, no matter how prudent or responsible the decision, tore a social fabric woven in part of gift exchanges and honor. The only "debts of honor"—that is, debts that must be paid, whatever the sacrifice—recognized by southern gentlemen were gambling debts. Moreover, southern honor had a material base. A man's personal honor was supported by his property, land in particular. Southern objections to bankruptcy laws were in part a defense of honor against the mercantile notion of land as simply another commodity, as one source of wealth among many. Indeed, southern hostility to bankruptcy—the southern colonies and states never experimented with insolvency or bankruptcy relief with the urgency that their northern counterparts did—may have been a symptom of the region's inability to maintain its colonial economic supremacy after independence.[9]

Honor of a slightly different kind was a key element of national political leadership in the early years of the republic. There it was a reputation for honesty, integrity, and bravery, supported by social and financial worth—credit in the broadest sense of the term—that enabled elite politicians to wield power in the chaotic, highly personalized, newly democratic politics of the period. As Joanne B. Freeman has shown so well, northern and southern politicians alike were obsessed with reputation and well-versed in the code of honor that protected it, differing only in their readiness to resort to the violence of dueling. However, property was not as central to this understanding of honor, and debt played little role at all.[10]

For both, honor was a gendered concept. Only white men could have honor, which perforce meant that honor was an element of masculine identity. To lose one's honor was to be unmanned, to be rendered feminine and dependent or, worse, enslaved. The masthead of the *Forlorn Hope* illustrated this powerfully. Failure, too, could be constructed in gendered terms, as we saw in the figure of Lady Credit. That it could also impart a sympathy for other dependent populations, as when Pintard discovered an appreciation for Wollstonecraft and William Keteltas argued for the abolition of slavery, only underscored its feminization. Conversely, commercial success not only conferred independence; it also affirmed manliness. It represented personal victory in economic competition—the modern businessman's boast of money being a way of keeping score. When pursued to provide a competency for one's family, success supported patriarchal authority. It is here that these understandings of honor—particularly that of the southern gentry and that invoked by Pintard and other commercial debtors—intersect. When Morris told Alexander Hamilton shortly before he entered Prune Street that "I have lost the confidence of the World as to my pecuniary ability but I believe not as to my honor or integrity," he was deluding himself. By his own terms he had failed in an obligation of honor. After a few days in jail, he wrote his son in Albany that his imprisonment was "brought on me by a desire to provide too amply for a Family whose happiness is my greatest enjoyment"—that is, his failure was also a failure of his patriarchal duty.[11]

Morris can be forgiven his self-delusion. He embodied the contradictions and uncertainties about the place of failure in the new republic. With his burning desire to dominate, to monopolize, to control the economy, and the resources to make him think he could succeed, he was the archetypal large-scale capitalist entrepreneur. His reach, if not his grasp, surpassed mere personal independence; it aspired to power and dynastic wealth. The American economy did not see his likes again until J. P. Morgan and John D. Rockefeller, Sr., nearly a century later. For Morris, debt was a legal obligation, not a moral one. By issuing his infamous notes, he embraced debt as the engine of his vast speculations. Debt was investment; it was opportunity. Morris did not cloak market relations in sentiment, except when it suited his purposes. With his command of finance, his cold appreciation of economic risk, and his refusal to moralize failure, Morris was the most modern economic figure of the early republic. Yet he grounded his pursuit of political leadership, and hence public respectability, on decidedly eighteenth-century norms of civic honor that required him to deny his entrepreneurial instincts. He proclaimed "his disregard of money" even as he spent it lavishly to maintain the luxury and hospitality necessary to prove himself a disinterested republican aristocrat.[12] In so doing, he embraced a set of social and political values that saw in economic failure a failure of character—in particular, a failure of the character required to be deemed a republican aristocrat—despite his constant denial that his own failure diminished either his honor or his integrity.

If "the great man" himself could waver, it should not surprise us that lesser strivers could be ambivalent as well. After all, Americans had staked their claim to political independence on their superior character and virtue. As long as economic failure retained a whiff of moral failure, legislative efforts to confer absolution on insolvent debtors and send them back into the market to make a fresh start in the quest for economic independence—a quest that has been a driving theme in American history—could only be temporary and equivocal. Thus, in one sense, the solution to the struggle over the place of failure in the early republic was to deny that it had any place at all. The unreality of that answer was as apparent to those who had failed as it should be to us. Today when individuals fail—although not when corporations do—the ethic of personal responsibility remains powerful enough that we may wonder about the social consequences of their failure, but we rarely question the economic and political structures that undermined their independence by creating a world in which mere subsistence often requires husbands and wives to work, leaving families vulnerable when they lose a wage-earner to death, illness, injury, divorce, or unemployment. An almost religious belief in the moral neutrality of the market deflects such questions by making failure individual rather than structural. Two hundred years ago the stakes were, if anything, higher. Then, when the foundational belief of free Americans was in independence, whatever weakened independence reflected upon the republic itself. Hence the unease over failure and the difficulty of creating a legal framework for something so redolent of dependence. The solution eludes us still.

NOTES

ABBREVIATIONS

AAS   American Antiquarian Society, Worcester, Mass.

Annals of Congress   *The Debates and Proceedings in the Congress of the United States,* 42 vols. (Washington, D.C., 1834–1856)

BA1800-CT   Records of the United States District Court for Connecticut, Bankruptcy Act of 1800, Record Group 21, National Archives—Northeast Region (Boston), Waltham, Mass.

BA1800-MA   Records of the United States District Court for Massachusetts, Bankruptcy Act of 1800, Record Group 21, National Archives—Northeast Region (Boston), Waltham, Mass.

BA1800-NY   Records of the United States District Court for the Southern District of New York, Bankruptcy Act of 1800, Record Group 21, National Archives—Northeast Region (New York), microfilm 933

BA1800-PA   Records of the United States District Court for the Eastern District of Pennsylvania, Bankruptcy Act of 1800, Record Group 21, National Archives—Mid-Atlantic Region (Philadelphia), microfilm 993

BPL   Boston Public Library, Boston

CCR   J. Hammond Trumbull and Charles J. Hoadly, eds., *The Public Records of the Colony of Connecticut, 1636-1776,* 15 vols. (Hartford, Conn., 1850–1890)

CHS   Connecticut Historical Society, Hartford

CSL   Connecticut State Library, Hartford

DHRC	Merrill Jensen, John P. Kaminski, Gaspare J. Saladino et al., eds., *The Documentary History of the Ratification of the Constitution*, 15 vols. (1–6, 8–10, 13–18), (Madison, Wis., 1976–)
HBS	Baker Library, Harvard University Graduate School of Business Administration, Boston
HSD	Historical Society of Delaware, Wilmington
HSP	Historical Society of Pennsylvania, Philadelphia
LC	Library of Congress, Washington, D.C.
LVa	Library of Virginia, Richmond
MdHS	Maryland Historical Society, Baltimore
MHS	Massachusetts Historical Society, Boston
MoHS	Missouri Historical Society, St. Louis
NYCMA	New York City Municipal Archives, New York
NYHS	New-York Historical Society, New York
NYPL	New York Public Library, New York
PCA	Philadelphia City Archives, Philadelphia
PHMC	Pennsylvania Historical and Museum Commission, Harrisburg
PrU	Firestone Library, Princeton University, Princeton, N.J.
TJP	Julian P. Boyd et al., eds., *The Papers of Thomas Jefferson*, 28 vols. (Princeton, N.J., 1950–)
VHS	Virginia Historical Society, Richmond
WMQ	*William and Mary Quarterly*

INTRODUCTION

1. *Forlorn Hope* (New York), Apr. 7 and Apr. 19, 1800.

2. Samuel Moody, *The Debtors Monitor, Directory and Comforter: Or, The Way to get and keep Out of Debt, In Three Sermons* (Boston, 1715), 1–2, 6–7. The text was 2 Kings 4:1–7.

3. See Alice Hanson Jones, *Wealth of a Nation to Be: The American Colonies on the Eve of the Revolution* (New York, 1980), 127–154; Jackson Turner Main, *Society and Economy in Colonial Connecticut* (Princeton, N.J., 1985), 46–47; Deborah A. Rosen, *Courts and Commerce: Gender, Law, and the Market Economy in Colonial New York* (Columbus, Ohio, 1997), 34–55.

4. See Christine Leigh Heyrman, *Commerce and Culture: The Maritime Communities of Colonial Massachusetts, 1690–1750* (New York, 1984), 69–70, 235–238; Bruce H. Mann, *Neighbors and Strangers: Law and Community in Early Connecticut* (Chapel Hill, N.C., 1987), 11–46; William E. Nelson, *Dispute and Conflict Resolution in Plymouth County, Massachusetts, 1725–1825* (Chapel Hill, N.C., 1981), 23–24; William McEnery Offutt, Jr., *Of "Good Laws" and "Good Men": Law and Society in the*

Delaware Valley, 1680–1710 (Urbana, Ill., 1995), 93; Rosen, *Courts and Commerce*, 82–85.

1. DEBTORS AND CREDITORS

1. *Aurora, or General Advertiser* (Philadelphia), Jan. 2, 1797.

2. The *Oxford English Dictionary* traces the first use of "credit" in the sense of "reputation" to Abraham Fleming, *A Panoplie of Epistels* (London, 1576), 175: "Such as have the name and credite of wise men."

3. George Fisher, *The American Instructor: Or, Young Man's Best Companion*, 10th ed. (Philadelphia, 1753), 382. For examples of credit swindles, see Gerard G. Beekman to Abraham Rawlinson and William Preston, June 6, 1755, in Philip L. White, ed., *The Beekman Mercantile Papers, 1746–1799*, 3 vols. (New York, 1956), 1:251–254; and *Aurora*, June 14, 1799. Daniel Defoe devoted a chapter to reputation in *The Complete English Tradesman in Familiar Letters: Directing Him in All the Several Parts and Progressions of Trade* (London, 1726). For a good discussion of credit and reputation in England, see Craig Muldrew, *The Economy of Obligation: The Culture of Credit and Social Relations in Early Modern England* (London, 1998), 148–157.

4. Gerard G. Beekman to William Beekman, June 6, 1752, *Beekman Mercantile Papers*, 1:143–144; Perkins, Buchanan & Brown to Thomas Adams, Mar. 7, 1770, Adams Family Papers, sec. 6, VHS; Perkins, Buchanan & Brown, "Circular Letter to their Friends in Mary Land," Mar. 31, 1770, Adams Family Papers, sec. 6, folder 7. Their alarm was well-founded—the firm went bankrupt three years later. See Julian Hoppit, *Risk and Failure in English Business, 1700–1800* (Cambridge, England, 1987), 101.

5. Mark Pringle to Lubbock Colt & Co., Feb. 14, 1797, Mark Pringle Letterbook, 1796–1798, at 124–127, MdHS; Harrison Gray Otis to Thomas Dickason, Jr., Nov. 14, 1794, Harrison Gray Otis Letterbook, 1788–1807, at 182–183, Harrison Gray Otis Papers, MHS; [Pelatiah Webster], *An Essay on Credit, in which the Doctrine of Banks is Considered, and some Remarks are made on the present State of the Bank of North-America* (Philadelphia, 1786), 3.

6. William Black to James Mercer, Dec. 24, 1771, James Mercer Papers, 1760–1771, VHS; *Gazette of the United States* (Philadelphia), Apr. 17, 1798. Webster published the charge in his newspaper, *The Minerva, & Mercantile Evening Advertiser* (New York), Dec. 10, 1796. Letters by Dallas and Webster in rebuttal and response appeared in the *Aurora*, Jan. 3, 1797.

7. Thomas Stevenson to Timothy Hurst, Oct. 4, 1765, Logan-Dickinson-

Norris Papers, box "Correspondence before 1800," folder "Misc. 1765," HSP; George Meade, *You have probably heard before now . . .* [Philadelphia, 1785].

8. T. H. Breen, *Tobacco Culture: The Mentality of the Great Tidewater Planters on the Eve of Revolution* (Princeton, N.J., 1985), 93–106; John Moore to Richard Harison, Mar. 8, 1787, Richard Harison Papers, box 1, folder "Correspondence, 1782–1787," NYHS.

9. Debtors sometimes kept books in which they recorded payments to their creditors. Although book accounts, they did not create book debts. They figured in litigation only as an affirmative defense of full or partial payment of the creditor's claim. For a detailed examination of book accounts and their suitability to traditional economic relations, see Bruce H. Mann, *Neighbors and Strangers: Law and Community in Early Connecticut* (Chapel Hill, N.C., 1987), 11–27.

10. This paragraph and the two that follow draw on J. Milnes Holden, *The History of Negotiable Instruments in English Law* (London, 1955); William Holdsworth, *A History of English Law*, 16 vols. (London, 1903–1966), 8:113–176; Herbert A. Johnson, *The Law Merchant and Negotiable Instruments in Colonial New York, 1664–1730* (Chicago, 1963); James Steven Rogers, *The Early History of the Law of Bills and Notes: A Study in the Origins of Anglo-American Commercial Law* (Cambridge, 1995); and A. W. B. Simpson, *A History of the Common Law of Contract: The Rise of the Action of Assumpsit* (Oxford, 1975), 88–125.

11. Judges in both England and America gained authority to chancer, or lower, the sum won by a creditor on a conditioned bond from the face amount to the amount of damages actually proved. In England the shift began as a matter of Chancery practice early in the seventeenth century and entered law through the Statute of Fines and Penalties in 1697. See Simpson, *History of the Common Law of Contract*, 118–119; An Act for the Better Preventing of Frivolous and Vexatious Suites, 8 & 9 Will. 3, ch. 11 (1697). In the American colonies it seems to have crept into common law practice early in the eighteenth century.

12. The drawer's liability to the drawee-acceptor could be offset in whole or in part by a preexisting debt owed by the drawee to the drawer. Thus, if A drew upon B in favor of C for £100 and B owed A £100, B's acceptance of the draft and payment to C satisfied B's debt to A by virtue of the setoff.

13. Antony Carroll to Denis Carroll, Dec. 8, 1795, Anthony Carroll Letter-book, 1795–1796, NYHS.

14. Local custom determined the rate of surcharge. In Pennsylvania and New York it was 20 percent. See John Tisdall, *Laws and Usages respecting Bills of Ex-*

change, and Promissory Notes, Compiled from the best authorities, By John Tisdall, No-
tary Public of Belfast, with such alterations and additions as may render this treatise more
useful to the citizens of Philadelphia, by W. F. Esq. of Philadelphia (Philadelphia, 1795),
33; Antony Carroll to Denis Carroll, Dec. 8, 1795, Anthony Carroll Letterbook;
Antony Carroll to James Carroll, Dec. 20, 1795, ibid.

15. For purposes of the present discussion, we need not puzzle through the
question of when different written credit instruments became fully negotiable rather
than merely assignable, such that a person who received an instrument in good faith
through an appropriate transfer—a bona fide holder in due course—took it free of
any defenses that might have arisen from the underlying transaction.

16. For an insightful analysis of the implications of the relationship between the
maker's reputation and the value of a note, see Randall McGowan, "From Pillory to
Gallows: The Punishment of Forgery in the Age of the Financial Revolution," *Past
and Present*, no. 165 (1999): 107–140.

17. This statement is shorthand for foreclosure procedures that required more
than a creditor's whim to carry out, but that need not be discussed here.

18. Seeing sureties as products of a commercial economy clarifies the role they
played in relations between debtors and creditors. Sureties had no place in book accounts, which relied on a creditor's willingness to extend credit to people who did not expressly promise to repay the debt. As used in commercial transactions, sureties'
assurances replaced the unplighted trust that had underlain book accounts. At the same
time, however, sureties had interests of their own to protect that differed from those of
the debtors and creditors whose transactions they warranted. To illustrate this divergence of interests, watch William Samuel Johnson, a lawyer in Connecticut before the
Revolution, try to walk a tightrope between his clients and a relative: Johnson's uncle
was surety on a large debt owed by Edward Ward to several creditors. Johnson warned
his uncle that he was about to sue Ward for the debt on behalf of the creditors, so "that if
you are not effectively secured you may take care to secure yourself immediately."
Armed with this intelligence, Ward's sureties induced him to transfer all his property to
them so that they could liquidate it while he avoided arrest. The time thus bought was
critical. Ward's creditors had to sue him first. Ward himself lost either way. His sureties,
however, protected themselves by gaining control of his property, which they could use
in place of their own to satisfy their contingent liability to the creditors. See William
Samuel Johnson (hereafter WSJ) to Nathaniel Johnson, Nov. 22 and Dec. 22, 1762,
Feb. 7, 1763, WSJ to Theophilacte Bache, Dec. 3, 1762, WSJ to Ann DeVisme, Jan. 24
and June 24, 1763, William Samuel Johnson Papers, Letterbook 12, CHS. Johnson

decried the same tactics as "astonishing artifice and chicanery" when another debtor and his sureties used them on him. See WSJ to Walter and Samuel Franklin, June 24, 1763, ibid. For a discussion of the relationship between debt obligations and economic development in this period, see Mann, *Neighbors and Strangers*, 11–46.

19. WSJ to John Hancock, June 25, 1764, Johnson Papers, Letterbook 13.

20. On Johnson generally, see Elizabeth P. McCaughey, *From Loyalist to Founding Father: The Political Odyssey of William Samuel Johnson* (New York, 1980); George C. Croce, Jr., *William Samuel Johnson: A Maker of the Constitution* (New York, 1937); and E. Edwards Beardsley, *Life and Times of William Samuel Johnson* (New York, 1876), all of which pass lightly over his legal career. Johnson's distinction before the Revolution was more parochial. He was a leading member of the Connecticut bar, represented the colony in London, and was a judge of the superior court.

21. For example, see WSJ to Rev. [Solomon] Palmer, Dec. 20, 1762, Johnson Papers, Letterbook 12; WSJ to John Jones, Dec. 20, 1762, ibid. Johnson cautioned the creditor, John Jones of New York, that the debtor, Solomon Palmer, might not be able to repay the debt immediately because he had understood Jones to be content to continue to collect the interest.

22. See Samuel Blodget to Samuel Abbot, Oct. 9, 1756, Papers of Samuel Abbot, Domestic (Inland) Letters, box 1, HBS; John Kidd to Rawlinson & Davison, Aug. 27, 1752, John Kidd Letterbook, 1749–1763, HSP; Benjamin Parke to Thomas Hawthorn, Mar. 19, 1798, Meredith Family Papers, box 8, folder 6, HSP; Thomas Wright to Thomas Hawthorn, July 10, 1798, ibid., box 9, folder 1; Charles Hall to Thomas Hawthorn, July 25, 1798, ibid., box 9, folder 2. A year later, Hawthorn, a dry-goods merchant, was himself insolvent, in part, he claimed, because of the insolvencies of so many of his debtors. See Examination of Thomas Hawthorn, Nov. 20, 1802, in "Thomas Hawthorn," BA1800-PA, reel 15.

23. WSJ to John and Jonathan Simpson, June 15, 1751, Johnson Papers, Letterbook 6; WSJ to Ebenezer Storer, June 17, 1751, ibid.; Gerard G. Beekman to William Beekman, July 20, 1763, *Beekman Mercantile Papers*, 1:442–443; Frederick Rhinelander to Ephraim Kirby, Apr. 3 and Aug. 16, 1790, Frederick and Philip Rhinelander Letterbook, 1789–1793, NYHS. Kirby's reports were the one-volume *Reports of Cases Adjudged in the Superior Court of the State of Connecticut* (Litchfield, Conn., 1789).

24. WSJ to Seth Low, Oct. 3, 1766, Johnson Papers, Letterbook 13; Benjamin Pollard to Samuel Span, Dec. 4, 1787, June 9, 1788, Benjamin Pollard & Co. Letterbook, 1787–1792 (photostat), LVa; WSJ to Nathaniel Marston, [July 28, 1763], Johnson Papers, Letterbook 12; WSJ to Sidney Breese, [June 23, 1763], ibid.

25. WSJ to Edward Graham, Mar. 16, 1751, Johnson Papers, Letterbook 4; WSJ to Edward Graham, Mar. 28, 1751, Letterbook 5. The debtor later absconded. WSJ to Edward Graham, Apr. 25, 1751, ibid.

26. By way of contrast, actions on bonds and witnessed promissory notes—instruments whose validity depended only on their formal sufficiency—received one trial only, with no reviews or appeals. *CCR*, 6:559, 7:15, 195–196.

27. WSJ to Henderson Inches, [Dec. 3, 1753], Johnson Papers, Letterbook 8; WSJ to William Peters, Apr. 25, 1751, Letterbook 5; WSJ to Edward Graham, June 5, 1752, Letterbook 7; WSJ to Joseph Haynes, Sept. 29, 1752, Letterbook 8; WSJ to William Livingston, Apr. 17, 1763, Letterbook 12; WSJ to Stephen Forman, May 12, 1763, ibid.; George Washington Campbell to G. & C. Lindenburger, July 1, 1803, Letterbook, 1803–1811, George Washington Campbell Papers, box 4, LC; James Mercer to John Francis Mercer, May 1, 1784, Mercer Family Papers, sec. 29, VHS.

28. WSJ to Thomas Greene, Nov. 20, 1752, Johnson Papers, Letterbook 8; WSJ to James McEvers, Mar. 25, 1752, Letterbook 7; WSJ to Rudolphus Van Dyck, June 5, 1752, ibid.

29. WSJ to Gerard G. Beekman, Dec. 30, 1752, Johnson Papers, Letterbook 8; WSJ to Charles Apthorp, Nov. 7, 1752, ibid.; WSJ to James Jauncey, Oct. 15, 1752, Letterbook 12; Henry Rowland to Daniel Turner, Apr. 16, 1764, Logan-Dickinson-Norris Papers, box "Correspondence before 1800," folder "Misc. 1764." The classic analysis of the "repeat player" phenomenon is Marc Galanter, "Why the 'Haves' Come Out Ahead: Speculations on the Limits of Legal Change," *Law and Society Review*, 9 (1974): 95–160.

30. Gerard G. Beekman to Solomon Townsend, July 9, 1763, *Beekman Mercantile Papers*, 1:441. When Edward Bromfield and Francis Burroughs of Boston lost patience with their book debtor, Daniel Shelton of Stratford, Connecticut, they instructed their attorney to give Shelton a choice between being sued or executing a bond to pay the balance due in six months. Edward Bromfield and Francis Burroughs to Nathaniel Foote, n.d. [1695], Connecticut Archives, Private Controversies, 1st ser., 4:260, CSL. Lawrence Reade of New York, "being willing . . . not to trouble" Jedidiah Stow of Middletown, Connecticut, proposed deferring Stow's debt of £40 if Stow would give a bond with security. Stow, however, "declined procuring any security . . . for so small a sum" and offered instead his plain, unsecured note of hand, which Reade's lawyer accepted as "the best I could [do]." WSJ to Jedidiah Stow, June 23, 1752, Johnson Papers, Letterbook 6; WSJ to Lawrence Reade, July 26 and Aug. [ ],

1752, Letterbook 8. For a detailed discussion of the procedural advantages of written credit instruments over book accounts, see Mann, *Neighbors and Strangers*, 34–41. Lawyers often pointed out the advantages to clients and urged them to adjust their accounts and have the balance secured by interest-bearing specialties. For example, see WSJ to James Rivington, July 20, 1765, Letterbook 13; Eugene Hanley to Thomas Hawthorn, Jan. 2, 1798, Meredith Family Papers, box 8, folder 2.

31. *CCR*, 7:514. The legislation permitted debtors sued on written obligations to turn the creditor's action at law into an equitable inquiry into the factual circumstances of the transaction by raising a defense of usury.

32. A *capias* bypassed the defendant's property and went directly to his person, after which point the procedure was the same as on an attachment.

33. WSJ to William Coventry, Oct. 14, 1762, Johnson Papers, Letterbook 12. Laurel Thatcher Ulrich attributes the seventeen-month imprisonment of 79-year-old Ephraim Ballard in Augusta, Maine, in 1804–1805 to such a calculation. See Ulrich, *A Midwife's Tale: The Life of Martha Ballard, Based on Her Diary, 1785–1812* (New York, 1990), 265–274.

34. For example, see WSJ to Edward Graham, Apr. 25 and Oct. 26, 1751, June 5, 1752, Johnson Papers, Letterbooks 5–7; John Pintard to Elisha Boudinot, Nov. 20, 1790, Bayard-Boudinot-Pintard Papers, NYHS. The following advertisement from the *Aurora* illustrates the bind in which absconding debtors left their bail: "The Person who has lately absconded and left two of his nearest relations responsible for him as special bail . . . is informed, that if he will return and exonerate his bail, they will overlook his past conduct . . . His bail flatter themselves he will not hesitate to return and surrender himself, when he is informed that they will both be subject to imprisonment, if he does not relieve them. If they do not hear of or from him in one month from this date, they will be under the necessity of pursuing and advertising him throughout America and Europe. They will render his character so infamous, that he will not be able to find a resting place, and they will use every power which the laws of all civilized countries have provided for the relief of bail, to arrest him and bring him back to this state." *Aurora*, Sept. 28 and Sept. 30, 1799.

35. In both instances Johnson retreated and advised the creditor to wait a while longer before suing. See WSJ to John and Jonathan Simpson, June 25, 1751, Johnson Papers, Letterbook 6; WSJ to James McEvers, Mar. 25, 1752, Letterbook 7. Johnson eventually did sue Thompson. See WSJ to John and Jonathan Simpson, Sept. 1, 1752, Letterbook 8.

36. Solomon Kidder to Samuel Abbot, Apr. 25, 1766, Papers of Samuel Abbot,

Domestic (Inland) Letters, box 2; Henry Drinker to [ ], Dec. 17, 1784, Henry Drinker Letterbook, 1762–1786, Henry Drinker Papers, 1756–1869, HSP; John Pintard to Elisha Boudinot, Nov. 20, 1793, Bayard-Boudinot-Pintard Papers.

37. Samuel Hazard to John DePeyster, Mar. 10, 1752, Samuel Hazard Letter-book, 1749–1758, PrU; WSJ to John and Uzal Ogden, Oct. 13, 1762, Johnson Papers, Letterbook 12. See "An Act to establish an uniform system of Bankruptcy throughout the United States," 2 Stat. ch. 19 (Apr. 4, 1800), §1, in *The Public Statutes at Large of the United States of America, from . . . 1789, to . . . 1845* (Boston, 1845), 2:19–36.

38. Samuel Hazard to Stephen Heaven, Dec. 15, 1757, Hazard Letterbook; Daniel King to Samuel Abbot, May 12, 1763, Papers of Samuel Abbot, Domestic (In-land) Letters, box 1; Petition of Abijah Beach, Apr. 6, 1772, Connecticut Archives, In-solvent Debtors, 1st ser., 1:81.

39. WSJ to Ann DeVisme, June 24, 1763, Johnson Papers, Letter-book 12. A writ of execution ordered that either the person or property of the judgment debtor be seized. A writ of *capias ad satisfaciendum*—known to the cognoscenti as *"ca. sa."*— could be levied only on the judgment debtor's person. Jurisdictional custom deter-mined which one was used, as it did writs of attachment and *capias ad respondendum*. Colonies and, later, states that used *ca. sa.* issued separate writs of *fieri facias* and, sometimes, *levari facias* against the judgment debtor's property—personal property with the former, real and personal property with the latter.

40. Robert Morris to John Nicholson, Nov. 20, 1797, Papers of Robert Morris, Private Letterbooks, 1794–1798 (3 vols.), 3:85–86, LC. Morris and Nicholson referred to Nicholson's refuge as "Castle Defence." See Morris to Nicholson, Aug. 31, 1797, ibid., 2:534. Their affairs were so involved that they kept close to avoid both *capias* and *ca. sa.*—initial process and execution process.

41. For Morris's descriptions of lurking creditors and "Myrmidons," see Robert Morris to John Nicholson, Nov. 24 and Dec. 4, 14, 15, 1797, Private Letterbooks, 3:99, 121, 149–150, 151–152. For his advice to Nicholson and his vow "to Shed innocent Blood" if necessary, see Morris to Nicholson, Oct. 3 and Dec. 29, 1797, ibid., 2:602, 3:174. Morris described his criteria for whom to let in and whom to see only through a window in Morris to Nicholson, Sept. 6 and Nov. 1, 1797, ibid., 2:544–545, 3:51. The glazier episode is in Morris to Nicholson, Sept. 29, 1797, ibid., 2:596. One particularly irate creditor, "a Frenchman," did not appreciate being held at a distance and threat-ened to shoot Morris through the window. See Morris to Nicholson, Jan. 22, 1798, ibid., 3:227.

42. John Nicholson to Samuel Nicholson, July 21, 1797, John Nicholson

Letterbooks, 1795–1798 (7 vols.), 7:285–287, HSP. "The Hills" was the nonrueful public name of Morris's country house. For the legal advice that persuaded Nicholson to return to his own house, see Morris to Nicholson, Sept. 2, 1797, and Morris to Theophile Cazenove, Sept. 6, 1797, Private Letterbooks, 2:540, 545–546.

43. Robert Morris to John Nicholson, Jan. 9, 1798, Private Letterbooks, 3:209–210. For other such calculations, see Morris to Nicholson, Sept. 20 and 28, 1797, ibid., 2:573, 594. In the same vein, Morris advised Nicholson on whom he might safely admit. See Morris to Nicholson, Sept. 21, 1997, Jan. 17, 1798, ibid., 2:575, 3:219.

44. John Pintard, Diary, Newark, Nov. 16, 1793, John Pintard Papers, box 2, NYHS; Robert Morris to John Nicholson, Sept. 4, 1797, Private Letterbooks, 2:542; Morris to Nicholson, Oct. 30, 1797, Robert Morris Papers, box 3, NYPL. On some Sundays Morris would walk five miles to a tavern near Germantown, the Butcher's Arms, where he would transact business. See Morris to Nicholson, Sept. 24 and Oct. 15, 1797, Private Letterbooks, 2:581–582, 3:3–5.

45. See Walter Livingston to William Duer, June 30, 1792, Robert R. Livingston Papers, ser. 6, vols. 1761–1885, NYHS; John Nicholson to James Gibson, July 21, 1797, Nicholson Letterbooks, 7:290; Nicholson to William Moulder, July 22, 1797, ibid., 7:295; Robert Aitken to Nicholson, Aug. 8, 1797, Gratz Collection, case 8, box 5, HSP; Morris to Nicholson, Oct. 11, 1797, Private Letterbooks, 2:626.

46. WSJ to Peter Remsen, Mar. 27, 1752, Johnson Papers, Letterbook 7.

47. Benjamin Pollard to Samuel and John Span, June 10 and July 9, 1791, Benjamin Pollard & Co. Letterbook; WSJ to Sidney Breese, Nov. 4, 1763, Johnson Papers, Letterbook 12; James Mercer to John Francis Mercer, Sept. 9, 1783, Mercer Family Papers, sec. 29.

48. John Vining to John Dickinson, Apr. 23, 1768, R. R. Logan Collection, box 1, folder 5, HSP; Robert Morris to William Cranch, Nov. 13, 1795, Robert Morris Papers, box 2, NYPL; Daniel Ramsay to Benjamin Lincoln, June 20, 1788, Benjamin Lincoln Papers, MHS; [ ] to [James Beekman], Mar. 1, 1765, Beekman Papers, Box 15, NYHS.

49. See Demand on Isaac Pratt, June 25, 1788, Personal Papers of Samuel Barrett, BPL; James Cebra, *James Cebra, Respectfully offers his services to such as may think them useful, particularly in the collection of debts . . . June 23, 1790* [New York, 1790]. The *Aurora* ran the following advertisement under the heading "Debts Collected and Accounts Adjusted": "Merchants or Tradesmen wishing to engage with a trusty person occasionally to collect debts, may be accommodated by applying at the office of this paper." *Aurora*, Jan. 24, 1799.

50. Polite or not, for lawyers it always was a business, as one Virginia debtor noted when he complained about a lawyer who was dunning him, "D—n the Fellows Conscience he has added 6/8 for a Fee for writing to me." George Mercer to Thomas Adams, n.d. [1771], Adams Family Papers, sec. 6.

51. John Pintard, Commonplace Book, n.d. [ca. 1806–1809], 106, Pintard Papers, box 1; Thomas Preston to John Kidd, July 8, 1760, Hildeburn Papers—John Kidd Section, 1751–1791, HSP; Benjamin Pollard to Samuel Span, Dec. 4, 1787, Benjamin Pollard & Co. Letterbook; Robert Morris to John Nicholson, Dec. 15, 1797, Private Letterbooks, 3:152.

52. Robert Troup to Thomas and John Cooper, Aug. 24, 1798, Meredith Family Papers, box 9, folder 4. On "lumping it," see William L. F. Felstiner, "Influences of Social Organization on Dispute Processing," *Law and Society Review*, 9 (1974): 63–94.

2. THE LAW OF FAILURE

1. Cotton Mather, *Fair Dealing between Debtor and Creditor. A very brief Essay upon the Caution to be used, about coming in to Debt, and getting out of it* (Boston, 1716), 25; *Debtor and Creditor: or, A Discourse on the Following Words, Have Patience with me, and I will pay thee all* (Boston, 1762), 4.

2. For general overviews, see Stanley L. Engerman and Robert E. Gallman, eds., *The Cambridge Economic History of the United States*, vol. 1: *The Colonial Era* (Cambridge, 1996); and John J. McCusker and Russell R. Menard, *The Economy of British America, 1607–1789* (Chapel Hill, N.C., 1991).

3. John Winthrop, "A Modell of Christian Charity," in Malcolm Freiberg et al., eds., *Winthrop Papers, 1498–1654*, 6 vols. (Boston, 1929–), 2:292. On Winthrop, Cotton, Sanderson, and credit, see Mark Valeri, "Religious Discipline and the Market: Puritans and the Issue of Usury," *WMQ*, 3d ser., 54 (1997): 747–768. Winthrop's English Puritan contemporaries also discussed the charitable potential of credit. For example, see Henry Wilkinson, *The Debt Book, or . . . the Civil Debt of Money or Goods, and . . . also the Sacred Debt of Love* (London, 1625). On Hull, see Margaret Ellen Newell, *From Dependency to Independence: Economic Revolution in Colonial New England* (Ithaca, N.Y., 1998), 103–104.

4. Samuel Moody, *The Debtors Monitor, Directory and Comforter: Or, The Way to get and keep Out of Debt, In Three Sermons* (Boston, 1715), 9–10. On religious metaphors of debt in pre-Reformation England, see DeLloyd J. Guth, "The Age of Debt, the Reformation, and English Law," in DeLloyd J. Guth and John W. McKenna,

eds., *Tudor Rule and Revolution: Essays for G. R. Elton from his American Friends* (Cambridge, 1982), 69–86.

5. Moody, *The Debtors Monitor*, 21–25, 80–82.

6. Ibid., 28–29, 35–36.

7. Ibid., 19–20.

8. Ibid., 52–53, 66–69.

9. Samuel Willard, *Promise-Keeping, A Great Duty* (Boston, 1691), 5, 15–18.

10. Mather, *Fair Dealing*, 2–3, 13.

11. Ibid., 4–5. Mather's text was Romans 13:8—"Owe no Man any thing, but to Love one another."

12. Mather, *Fair Dealing*, 6, 17.

13. Ibid., 9, 15–16, 18.

14. Ibid., 18–19, 20–21.

15. Ibid., 8.

16. Willard, *Promise-Keeping*, 19–20.

17. Moody, *The Debtors Monitor*, 69; Mather, *Fair Dealing*, 18–20, 23–24. Note Mather's invocation of Giles Corey's defiant response to the *peine forte et dure* when accused of witchcraft at Salem twenty-five years earlier, an episode in which Mather acted ignominiously. See David Thomas Konig, *Law and Society in Puritan Massachusetts: Essex County, 1629–1692* (Chapel Hill, N.C., 1979), 174, and Perry Miller's famous judgment of Mather's role in *The New England Mind: From Colony to Province* (Cambridge, Mass., 1953), 191–209, esp. 204.

18. Mather, *Fair Dealing*, 25–26. Mather later discussed the procedural rules for church discipline at greater length. See his *Ratio Disciplinae Fratrum Nov-Anglorum: A Faithful Account of the Discipline Professed and Practised; in the Churches of New-England* (Boston, 1726), esp. 148–149. For an analysis of church disciplinary procedure and how it changed in the eighteenth century, see Bruce H. Mann, *Neighbors and Strangers: Law and Community in Early Connecticut* (Chapel Hill, N.C., 1987), 140–155. Although the disciplinary process did occasionally address questions of contract, debt, land title, or business ethics, people used it most often to correct drunken, lewd, or slanderous behavior, as well as assorted theological or ecclesiastical irregularities. See Emil Oberholzer, Jr., *Delinquent Saints: Disciplinary Action in the Early Congregational Churches of Massachusetts* (New York, 1956), 43–163, 186–215; William E. Nelson, *Dispute and Conflict Resolution in Plymouth County, Massachusetts, 1725–1825* (Chapel Hill, N.C., 1981), 30–34.

19. See Newell, *From Dependency to Independence*, 72–180.

20. See [Edward Wigglesworth], *A Letter from One in the Country to his Friend in Boston, containing some Remarks upon a late Pamphlet, Entituled, The Distressed State of the Town of Boston* (Boston, 1720), in Andrew McFarland Davis, ed., *Colonial Currency Reprints, 1682–1751*, 4 vols. (Boston, 1910–1911), 1:415–442; Paul Dudley, *Objections to the Bank of Credit Lately Projected at Boston* (Boston, 1714), in Davis, *Colonial Currency Reprints*, 1:239–261; Philopatria [Thomas Paine], *A Discourse, shewing, That the real first Cause of the Straits and Difficulties of this Province of the Massachusetts Bay, is it's Extravagancy, and not paper Money* (Boston, 1721), in Davis, *Colonial Currency Reprints*, 2:279–300. See generally Newell, *From Dependency to Independence*, 127–155; Elizabeth E. Dunn, "'Grasping at the Shadow': The Massachusetts Currency Debate, 1690–1751," *New England Quarterly*, 71 (1998): 54–76. On the idea of "competency," see Daniel Vickers, "Competency and Competition: Economic Culture in Early America," *WMQ*, 3d ser., 47 (1990): 3–29.

21. On English bankruptcy law, see William S. Holdsworth, *A History of English Law*, 16 vols. (London, 1903–1966), 8:229–245; Julian Hoppit, *Risk and Failure in English Business, 1700–1800* (Cambridge, England, 1987), 18–41; W. J. Jones, "The Foundations of English Bankruptcy: Statutes and Commissions in the Early Modern Period," *Transactions of the American Philosophical Society*, 69, pt. 3 (1979): 1–63; M. S. Servian, "Eighteenth-Century Bankruptcy Law: From Crime to Process" (Ph.D. diss., University of Kent at Canterbury, 1985). On changing economic thought in the period, see Joyce Oldham Appleby, *Economic Thought and Ideology in Seventeenth-Century England* (Princeton, N.J., 1978).

22. Scattered other statutes limited the range of debtors that could be imprisoned for their debts, set conditions for their release, prescribed the circumstances under which creditors had to bear the expense of imprisoning their debtors, and allowed debts contracted in specific agricultural commodities to be repaid over several harvests—this last a periodic Virginia enactment that at times applied only to solvent debtors. On the predominantly local character of credit relations in the seventeenth century, see Konig, *Law and Society in Puritan Massachusetts*, 82–88; Mann, *Neighbors and Strangers*, 17–18; James R. Perry, *The Formation of Society on Virginia's Eastern Shore, 1615–1655* (Chapel Hill, N.C., 1990), 116–143; Darrett B. Rutman and Anita H. Rutman, *A Place in Time: Middlesex County, Virginia, 1650–1750* (New York, 1984), 205–211; James Horn, "Adapting to a New World: A Comparative Study of Local Society in England and Maryland, 1650–1700," in Lois Green Carr, Philip D. Morgan, and Jean B. Russo, eds., *Colonial Chesapeake Society* (Chapel Hill, N.C., 1988), 133–175, esp. 171.

23. William H. Browne, C. C. Hall, and Bernard C. Steiner, eds., *Archives of Maryland*, 72 vols. (Baltimore, 1883–1972), 1:66–70; F. Regis Noel, *A History of the Bankruptcy Clause of the Constitution of the United States of America* (Gettysburg, Pa., 1918), 43; John Russell Bartlett, ed., *Records of the Colony of Rhode Island, and Providence Plantations, in New England*, 10 vols. (Providence, R.I., 1856–1865), 3:7–8, 10–11. Another historian described the Rhode Island statute—also wrongly—as "the earliest American colonial bankruptcy law," but this overlooks the fact that it did not discharge debtors from continuing liability for their debts. Charles Richard Morgan, "The Legal Origins of the Bankruptcy Act of 1800" (M.A. thesis, University of Virginia, 1973), 25. It is true that legislators, lawyers, debtors, and creditors did not always distinguish between insolvency and bankruptcy before 1800, but this is one instance where the modern clarity of the distinction must be read back into an earlier period if we are to make any sense of the law of failure.

24. Peter Boss to [ ], Oct. 15, 1764, VHS.

25. William Samuel Johnson (hereafter WSJ) to James McEvers, Oct. 23, 1762, William Samuel Johnson Papers, Letterbook 12, CHS. As it turned out, the officer could not find DeForest, and negotiations went forward without his knowing that McEvers had attempted to arrest him. WSJ to James McEvers, Nov. 18, 1762, ibid.

26. Robert Morris to Benjamin Harrison, Jr., Jan. 18, 1798, Papers of Robert Morris, Private Letterbooks, 1794–1798 (3 vols.), 3:248, LC; Samuel Abbot to Henry Daggett, Oct. 20, 1772, Papers of Samuel Abbot, Inland Letterbook, 1771–1776, HBS.

27. Occasionally the divide was explicit. A Maryland statute of 1708 distinguished between poor and insolvent debtors by making both eligible for release from jail after sixty days—the former upon taking the poor debtor's oath, the latter upon relinquishing their assets. The statute lasted for three years. "Poor" debtors were those worth less than £5. *Archives of Maryland*, 27:337–342.

28. Ellis Ames, Abner C. Goodell, and Melville M. Bigelow, eds., *The Acts and Resolves, Public and Private, of the Province of the Massachusetts Bay*, 21 vols. (Boston, 1869–1922), 1:330–333. Massachusetts repealed the statute in 1725, alleging abuses by debtors, but periodically revived a similar procedure at various times over the next six decades. See Peter J. Coleman, *Debtors and Creditors in America: Insolvency, Imprisonment for Debt, and Bankruptcy, 1607–1900* (Madison, Wis., 1974), 40–41, and Robert A. Feer, "Imprisonment for Debt in Massachusetts before 1800," *Mississippi Valley Historical Review*, 48 (1961–1962): 252–269, esp. 254–256. For a brief period, from

1733 to 1737, Massachusetts permitted debtors to be bound in service to their credi-tors. *Acts and Resolves*, 2:656–658.

29. The Rhode Island oath was available to judgment debtors worth no more than $10, but only with the consent of the creditor on whose writ they were impris-oned and upon giving the creditor a promissory note to pay the amount of the execu-tion plus interest within two years. "An Act relating to Bail on Mesne Process in civil Actions, and for the Relief of poor Prisoners for Debt," *The Public Laws of the State of Rhode-Island and Providence Plantations . . . 1798* (Providence, R.I., 1798), 224–232. Only rarely was a colony or state a debtors' haven in fact rather than reputation. Creditors are notorious for their resentment of even the slightest impediment to prompt repayment in full.

30. *Archives of Maryland*, 27:337–342, 36:596–597, 38:368–372, 39:130–138, 299–300; William W. Hening, ed., *The Statutes at Large, Being a Collection of All the Laws of Virginia*, 13 vols. (Richmond, Va., and Philadelphia, 1809–1823), 3:385–389, 4:151–167; James T. Mitchell and Henry Flanders, comps., *The Statutes at Large of Pennsylvania, from 1682 to 1801*, 16 vols. (Harrisburg, Pa., 1896–1911), 4:171–184, 211–215. See S. Laurence Shaiman, "The History of Imprisonment for Debt and In-solvency Laws in Pennsylvania as They Evolved from the Common Law," *American Journal of Legal History*, 4 (1960): 205–225, esp. 210–213. The best guide to the myriad statutes throughout the eastern colonies and states is Coleman, *Debtors and Creditors*, which, despite occasional inaccuracies, is remarkably reliable.

31. *The Colonial Laws of New York from the Year 1664 to the Revolution*, 5 vols. (Albany, N.Y., 1894–1896), 2:669–675 (Oct. 29, 1730), 753–756 (Oct. 14, 1732); 3:312–318 (Dec. 17, 1743), 694–700 (Apr. 9, 1748), 822–828 (Nov. 24, 1750), 866–872 (Nov. 25, 1751), 924–930 (Dec. 12, 1753), 1019–1025 (Dec. 7, 1754); 4:10–16 (Dec. 23, 1755), 103–104 (Nov. 27, 1756). See Coleman, *Debtors and Creditors*, 107–108.

32. *Acts and Resolves*, 1:726–729, 2:74; Albert Silliman Batchellor, H. H. Metcalf et al., eds., *Laws of New Hampshire, 1679–1835*, 10 vols. (Bristol, Concord, and Man-chester, N.H., 1904–1922), 2:192–196, 291.

33. For an excellent discussion of the economic impact of the Seven Years' War, see Cathy Matson, *Merchants and Empire: Trading in Colonial New York* (Baltimore, 1998), 265–276. The classic account is Virginia D. Harrington, *The New York Mer-chant on the Eve of the Revolution* (New York, 1935), 289–315.

34. John Watts to George and John Riddell, Sept. 18, 1764, in John Watts, *Letter Book of John Watts of New York, 1762–1765*, New-York Historical Society, *Collections* (New York, 1928), 61:286; Carl Bridenbaugh, *Cities in Revolt: Urban Life in America*,

1743–1776 (New York, 1955), 252. On the postwar depression generally, see Bridenbaugh, ibid., 250–255; Thomas M. Doerflinger, *A Vigorous Spirit of Enterprise: Merchants and Economic Development in Revolutionary Philadelphia* (Chapel Hill, N.C., 1986), 168–180; Harrington, *New York Merchant*, 316–351; Matson, *Merchants and Empire*, 276–298.

35. John Watts to William Baker, Aug. 11, 1765, *Letter Book of John Watts*, 368.

36. [Benjamin Franklin], *Father Abraham's Speech To a great Number of People, at a Vendue of Merchant-Goods; Introduced to the Publick by Poor Richard* (Boston, 1758), 13–15.

37. *Debtor and Creditor*, 4, 6–10.

38. [N.N.], *Some Reflections on the Law of Bankruptcy: Wrote at the Desire of a Friend: Shewing, That such a Law would be beneficial to the Publick, and analogous to Reason and our Holy Religion* (New Haven, Conn., 1755), 4–5.

39. Ibid., 2–3, 6–11.

40. *Acts and Resolves*, 4:29–44, 777–781, 883, 924–926. The number of discharges is from Coleman, *Debtors and Creditors*, 46.

41. *Colonial Laws of New York*, 3:1099–1106 (July 5, 1755), 4:182–183 (Feb. 26, 1757), 345–348 (Mar. 7, 1759), 526–533 (May 19, 1761), 747–748 (Dec. 20, 1763), 928–929 (Dec. 19, 1766); Gerard G. Beekman to Samuel Fowler, Jan. 11, 1768, in Philip L. White, ed., *The Beekman Mercantile Papers, 1746–1799*, 3 vols. (New York, 1956), 1:515.

42. Greg, Cunningham & Co. to John McComb, Feb. 19, 1765, Greg, Cunningham & Co. Letterbook (Sept. 22, 1764–Sept. 24, 1765), 203, NYHS. This is not to suggest that the firm regarded bankruptcy process with enthusiasm. In other instances it opposed debtors' attempts to seek discharges. See Greg, Cunningham & Co. to Waddell Cunningham, Jan. 21, 1765, ibid., 161–162.

43. *Laws and Acts of His Majesties Colony of Rhode Island, and Providence Plantations, June, 1756* (Providence, R.I., 1756), 24–29; *Laws and Acts of His Majesties Colony of Rhode Island, and Providence Plantations, August, 1771* (Providence, R.I., 1771), 50–59; *Laws and Acts of His Majesties Colony of Rhode Island, and Providence Plantations, May 1772* (Providence, R.I., 1772), 16.

44. "An Act for the Equal Distribution of Insolvent Estates," in *CCR*, 5:577–578. The act was amended in 1760 to expand the authority of executors and administrators to liquidate the estate and to specify that the exempt property should be the same household goods that were shielded from execution process. Ibid., 11:379–380. Except where noted, the following account rests on Petition of John and

Jabez Cable, Apr. 28, 1762, and Report of Committee, Jan. 4, 1763, Connecticut Archives, Insolvent Debtors, 1st ser., vol. 1, CSL.

45. WSJ to James McEvers, Nov. 17, 1763, Johnson Papers, Letterbook 12.

46. The one exception was a court of equity created by the assembly in 1715 at the petition and expense of Nathaniel Clark for the sole purpose of adjudicating some fifty debts allegedly due to the estate of a Huguenot trader and goldsmith, René Grignon, all the evidence of which had been lost in a fire. *CCR*, 5:533, 538–539. For a discussion of the court, see Mann, *Neighbors and Strangers*, 138–139, 155–161. Creating sources of equitable relief without conferring formal equity jurisdiction was a compromise peculiar to the New England colonies. See George L. Haskins, *Law and Authority in Early Massachusetts: A Study in Tradition and Design* (New York, 1960), 130, 182, 212–218; Peter Charles Hoffer, *The Law's Conscience: Equitable Constitutionalism in America* (Chapel Hill, N.C., 1990), 49–53; Konig, *Law and Society in Puritan Massachusetts*, 58–60; Stanley N. Katz, "The Politics of Law in Colonial America: Controversies over Chancery Courts and Equity Law in the Eighteenth Century," in Donald Fleming and Bernard Bailyn, eds., *Perspectives in American History*, (Boston, 1971), 5:257–284, esp. 263; Barbara A. Black, "The Judicial Power and the General Court in Early Massachusetts, 1634–1686" (Ph.D. diss., Yale University, 1975), 151–162.

47. *CCR*, 12:67; WSJ to James McEvers, Oct. 12, 1762, Johnson Papers, Letterbook 12. On Trumbull's financial difficulties while drafting the bankruptcy bill, see Glenn Weaver, *Jonathan Trumbull: Connecticut's Merchant Magistrate, 1710–1785* (Hartford, Conn., 1956), 97–129. Trumbull, who always maintained the appearance of a wealthy man, never invoked either "his" act or a successor insolvency statute. Instead, he proved quite adept at stiffing his creditors, large and small. When he died in 1785, his apparently ample estate was insolvent. See ibid., 131–159.

48. See Oscar Zeichner, *Connecticut's Years of Controversy, 1750–1776* (Chapel Hill, N.C., 1949), 46–47.

49. *CCR*, 12:127–133.

50. Ibid., 12:228. See WSJ to Stephen Forman, [July 9, 1763], Johnson Papers, Letterbook 12; WSJ to James McEvers, Nov. 7 and Dec. 7, 1763, ibid.

51. WSJ to John Hancock, Nov. 18, 1763, Johnson Papers, Letter-book 12; WSJ to John and Jonathan Simpson, Nov. 21, 1763, ibid.; WSJ to James McEvers, Nov. 17, 1763, ibid.; WSJ to John Tweedy, Dec. 8, 1763, ibid.; WSJ to Samuel Deming, Jan. 21, 1764, Letterbook 13.

52. Max Farrand, ed., *The Records of the Federal Convention of 1787*, rev. ed., 4 vols. (New Haven, Conn., 1937), 2:489 (Sept. 3, 1787).

53. *CCR*, 12:357–366.

54. Letter of license (copy), May 23, 1772, John Tabor Kempe Papers, box (Lawsuits) C–F, NYHS. Five years was an unusually long term for a letter of license. However, within nine months DeLyon was in jail in New York at the suit of two of the assignees, although it is not clear if they sued him on a new debt, on a reaffirmation of an old debt, or in violation of the letter. See papers relating to Isaac DeLyon v. Joseph Dean and Isaac DeLyon v. Philip Francis in ibid.

55. James Beekman & Sons, Leonard Kip, Kip & Duryea to Reuben Schuyler and Ahasuerus Teller, Nov. 1, 1787, Beekman Papers, box 15, NYHS. Schuyler and Teller, who had initially asked for thirty months with no conditions, appear to have declined the terms. Schuyler & Teller to Kip & Duryea, Sept. 26, 1787; Dirck TenBroeck to James Beekman & Sons, Nov. 30, 1787, ibid.

56. Petition of Peter R. Livingston, n.d. [1794], Robert R. Livingston Papers, Livingston Family Correspondence, 1743–1886, ser. 1 (reel 6, frames 483–484), NYHS; [ ] to [James Beekman], Mar. 1, 1765, Beekman Papers, box 15; Samuel Hazard to Stephen Haven, Nov. 18, 1751, "To the Creditors of S.H.," Dec. 16, 1755, and Hazard to Dennys DeBerdt, Dec. 17, 1755, Samuel Hazard Letterbook, 1749–1758, PrU.

57. Gerard G. Beekman to Henry Lloyd, Feb. 3, 1755, *Beekman Mercantile Papers*, 1:245. Despite his resolve Beekman agreed to a letter of license for Gamaliel Wallice, a Boston merchant, on Lloyd's assurance that Wallice's estate would fetch at least 12s to the pound. When Wallice failed, his estate sold for rather less, prompting Beekman to observe ruefully that among debtors it "is generally the Case to Rate them More than they Sell to Encourage the Creditors to Sign." Beekman to Lloyd, Jan. 18, 1756, in ibid., 1:271.

58. Remarks on a letter of license, Peter Stephen DuPonceau Papers, Precedent Book, 1785–1798, at 355–356, HSP; Thomas Moland to John Tabor Kempe, May 23, 1765, Kempe Papers, box (Lawsuits) M–O; [ ] to [James Beekman], Mar. 1, 1765, Beekman Papers, box 15.

59. Daniel King to Samuel Abbot, Apr. 11, 21, May 7, 12, 1763, Papers of Samuel Abbot, Domestic (Inland) Letters, box 1.

60. Hazard to Dennys DeBerdt, Dec. 17, 1755, Hazard Letterbook; John Kidd to Thomas Preston, Sept. 21, 1756, John Kidd Letterbook, 1749–1763, HSP; WSJ to Sidney Breese, May 30, 1751, Johnson Papers, Letterbook 5; WSJ to William Smith, Jr., July 8, 1751, Letterbook 6; WSJ to Breese, June 15, 1752, Letterbook 7.

61. WSJ to Benjamin and Edward Davis, Nov. 20, 1762, Johnson Papers, Letterbook 12.

62. Petition of Jacob Frye et al., July 5, 1771, Kempe Papers, box (Lawsuits) C-F; Petition of David McKendless and John Shaw, Jan. 24, 1774, ibid., box (Lawsuits) M-O. Peter Coleman counted eight such special acts, which discharged nearly 260 insolvent debtors between 1772 and 1775. See Coleman, *Debtors and Creditors*, 113-114; *Colonial Laws of New York*, 5:416-417 (Mar. 24, 1772), 418-421 (Mar. 24, 1772), 595-596 (Mar. 8, 1773), 596-600 (Mar. 8, 1773), 701-706 (Mar. 19, 1774), 706-707 (Mar. 19, 1774), 826-831 (Apr. 3, 1775), 832-833 (Apr. 3, 1775). The special acts permitted the debtors named in them to apply for a discharge under the act that had expired in 1770.

63. Only two petitions predate 1765—the notorious one from John and Jabez Cable in April 1762 and a second by Thomas Allen two months later. Apart from these catalysts, one would not expect insolvent debtors to petition for relief until the legislature had created, and then withdrawn, a category of relief for them to request. Allen was a merchant in New London and Newport who suffered large losses in the West Indies during the Seven Years' War. When his creditors lost patience and seized his shop inventory for auction, he assigned some of his real estate to trustees for his New York creditors, shut himself up in his house to avoid process, and appealed to the Connecticut assembly to enact a bankruptcy statute. The assembly took no action on the petition, not even deferring it as it had for the Cables. Three years later, in 1765, Allen petitioned the Rhode Island assembly for an insolvency act, claiming that while his Rhode Island creditors had agreed to give him a discharge, his creditors in Connecticut, New York, and Massachusetts refused to do so. However, Allen withdrew the petition. He then gave up on securing release from his debts and, after a stint in debtors' prison in New York, persuaded his Connecticut creditors to join his petition for insolvency under the 1765 Connecticut act, which stripped him of his remaining property except household items and barred future arrest for the same debts. See Petition of Thomas Allen, June 30, 1762, Connecticut Archives, Insolvent Debtors, 1st ser., vol. 1; and Appraisal, Oct. 24, 1761, "Inventory of Sundry Goods sold att Vendue for account of Mr. Thomas Allen," n.d. [1761-1763], Petition of Thomas Allen to Rhode Island General Assembly, Feb. 20, 1765, Proposals of Thomas Allen to his creditors, Nov. 28, 1765, and Insolvency Papers, Connecticut [1766], all in Allen Family Collection, 1718-1838, box 7, folder 1, AAS.

64. Petition of Philip Daggett, Oct. 1, 1772, Petition of Azariah Smith, Apr. 18, 1774, and Petition of Ebenezer Martin, May 19, 1771, Connecticut Archives, Insolvent Debtors, 1st ser., vol. 1.

65. Petition of Abijah Beach, Apr. 6, 1772, Connecticut Archives, Insolvent

Debtors, 1st ser., vol. 1. For the same recital of losses at sea, bad foreign markets, and other misfortunes common to merchants, see Petition of Ebenezer Keeney and Judson Burton, Sept. 17, 1772, ibid. Losses at sea was the reversal cited most frequently by merchants and traders, more often than delinquent debtors or illness, which is hardly surprising among people dependent on maritime commerce. Risks at sea loomed large, whether they were storms, pirates, privateers, or the sunken rock that John Herttell's sloop managed to hit before it had even cleared New London harbor. See Petition of John Herttell, Sept. 21, 1774, ibid.

66. Petition of Mary Bellamy, Apr. 20, 1772, Connecticut Archives, Insolvent Debtors, 1st ser., I.

67. Petition of Clement Minor [Sr.], May 6, 1765, and Petition of Clement Minor [Jr.], May 5, 1772, Connecticut Archives, Insolvent Debtors, 1st ser., vol. 1.

68. Petition of Nathaniel Eells, Sept. 27, 1774, Connecticut Archives, Insolvent Debtors, 1st ser., vol. 1.

69. Peter Coleman cites Mary Bellamy as a rare recipient of a full bankruptcy discharge, but this is a misreading of a confusingly written assembly resolution. See Coleman, *Debtors and Creditors*, 79. The resolution is in *CCR*, 13:603–604.

70. See Petition of John Herpin, Sept. 16, 1766, Report of committee, Oct. 29, 1767, and General Assembly resolution, May 1772, Connecticut Archives, Insolvent Debtors, 1st ser., vol. 1; *CCR*, 13:594–595. Herpin's timing was unfortunate—he negotiated the composition a few months before the assembly passed the 1763 bankruptcy act but did not give up on his creditors until after the act was repealed.

71. For Abijah Beach, see Petition, Apr. 6, 1772, Report of committee, Oct. 6, 1772, General Assembly resolution, October 1772, and *CCR*, 14:29–31; for Ebenezer Keeney and Judson Burton, see Petition, Sept. 17, 1772, Report of committee, May 4, 1773, General Assembly resolution, May 1773, and *CCR*, 14:106–107. All petitions, reports, and resolutions are in Connecticut Archives, Insolvent Debtors, 1st ser., vol. 1.

72. For Clement Minor, Jr., see Report of committee, Apr. 23, 1773, and *CCR*, 14:109–110; for Mary Bellamy, see Report of committee, n.d. [May 28, 1772], and *CCR*, 13:603–604; for Elisha Royce, see Report of committee, May 24, 1772. All reports and resolutions are in Connecticut Archives, Insolvent Debtors, 1st ser., vol. 1.

73. Joseph Nash to Samuel Abbot, Nov. 11, 1774, Papers of Samuel Abbot, Domestic (Inland) Letters, box 3. Abbot immediately backed off, sending his Providence agent a copy of Nash's letter and adding that "I think it best not to push the matter so far with Mr. Nash as to force him to take the advantage of the Bankrupt act." Abbot to Ephraim Starkweather, Nov. 17, 1774, Papers of Samuel Abbot, Inland Letterbook,

1771–1776. For the Rhode Island regime and figures, see Coleman, *Debtors and Creditors*, 92–101. South Carolina had a statutory bankruptcy system that discharged only the debts owed to creditors who accepted dividends from the bankrupt debtor's estate, which meant that a full discharge required the unanimous participation of all creditors. Thomas Cooper and David J. McCord, eds., *The Statutes at Large of South Carolina*, 10 vols. (Columbia, S.C., 1836–1841), 4:86–94 (Apr. 7, 1759).

3. IMPRISONED DEBTORS IN THE EARLY REPUBLIC

1. John Pintard, Commonplace Book, n.d. [ca. 1806–1809], 26, John Pintard Papers, box 1, NYHS. Pintard recorded the length of his imprisonment on the day of his release. See Pintard, Journal of Studies, 1797–1804 (Aug. 6, 1798), Pintard Papers, box 2. His distinction rests, for historians, on his role as a founder of the New-York Historical Society in 1804.

2. After Rodney's death in 1811, his son, Caesar Augustus Rodney, entered a notation at the beginning of the gap that his father "was cruelly imprisoned in the lowest state of health in the common jail of Dover." Thomas Rodney, Accounts, 1774–1791, at 227 [June 1791], Rodney Family Papers, box 3, LC (C. A. Rodney's notation dated Aug. 10, 1811). Thomas Rodney's later, indirect references to his imprisonment, which he referred to as "the Bastille of Dover," are at Accounts, 1797–1799, at 235 (Aug. 30, 1797), and Journal, 1798–1799 (Dec. 10, 1798), ibid.

3. Most of the literature on imprisonment for debt focuses on the statutory frameworks for imprisonment and release. For example, see Peter J. Coleman, *Debtors and Creditors: Insolvency, Imprisonment for Debt, and Bankruptcy, 1607–1900* (Madison, Wis., 1974); Robert A. Feer, "Imprisonment for Debt in Massachusetts before 1800," *Mississippi Valley Historical Review*, 48 (1961): 252–269; Abraham L. Freedman, "Imprisonment for Debt," *Temple Law Quarterly*, 2 (1928): 330–365; S. Laurence Shaiman, "The History of Imprisonment for Debt and Insolvency Laws in Pennsylvania as They Evolved from the Common Law," *American Journal of Legal History*, 4 (1960): 205–225; and George Philip Bauer, "The Movement against Imprisonment for Debt in the United States" (Ph.D. diss., Harvard University, 1935).

4. Debt servitude was fairly common in Maryland. See Christine Daniels, "'Without Any Limitacon of Time': Debt Servitude in Colonial America," *Labor History*, 36 (1995): 232–250. Elsewhere it may have been less so, as it was simple enough for creditors to bind debtors to them in dependent relations that resembled debt peonage, either by continually rolling over debts in return for interest payments, accompanied by threats of foreclosure or arrest, or by paying off a debtor's obliga-

tions to other creditors in return for the debtor's labor until the amount was satisfied. Christine Leigh Heyrman and Daniel Vickers have examined the latter practice as well as debt clientage in the fishing industry of Essex County, Massachusetts, while Stephen Innes has discussed William Pynchon's use of the former in Springfield, Massachusetts. See Heyrman, *Commerce and Culture: The Maritime Communities of Colonial Massachusetts, 1690–1750* (New York, 1984), 239–241; Vickers, *Farmers and Fishermen: Two Centuries of Work in Essex County, Massachusetts, 1630–1830* (Chapel Hill, N.C., 1994), 103–116, 153–155, 158–167; Innes, *Labor in a New Land: Economy and Society in Seventeenth-Century Springfield* (Princeton, N.J., 1983), 44–71.

5. Samuel Hazard to Dennys DeBerdt, Dec. 17, 1755, Samuel Hazard Letterbook, 1749–1758, PrU. Debtors did sometimes produce cash payments within a few hours of their imprisonment to win release, but that was undoubtedly rare. Two who did were Amasa Parker and John Wheeler, each of whom paid his way out of the Worcester County jail within twenty-four hours of his arrest. See List of prisoners, 1789–1790, Worcester County, Mass., Papers, box 2 (Worcester County Jail Records, 1748–1836), folder 2, AAS. Reasons for release are even harder to come by than lists of imprisoned debtors, but if we take the most detailed list I have seen—one of the several that exist for Worcester County—and make the generous assumption that debtors who were released on the day they were imprisoned or the day after were freed because they paid, the shock of imprisonment abruptly shook money loose from at most seven of the 111 debtors (110 men, one woman) imprisoned in the two years from March 14, 1784, to March 11, 1786. That they were the exception rather than the rule is further confirmed by the fact that the average stay in jail during that period was sixty-eight days—a computation that includes the suddenly solvent seven who left within twenty-four hours. See "A Register of all Prisoners Committed to Gaol in Worcester County Since March 5, 1785," ibid.

6. William Dudley to John Tabor Kempe, Apr. 14, 1766, John Tabor Kempe Papers, box (Lawsuits) C-F, NYHS.

7. This statement applies, of course, only to unsecured and undersecured creditors. For a good brief discussion of the unsatisfactoriness of imprisonment as a creditor's remedy, see Jonathan M. Chu, "Debt Litigation and Shays's Rebellion," in Robert A. Gross, ed., *In Debt to Shays: The Bicentennial of an Agrarian Rebellion* (Charlottesville, Va., 1993), 81–99, esp. 84–86.

8. George Francis Dow, ed., *Records and Files of the Quarterly Courts of Essex County, Massachusetts,* 8 vols. (Salem, Mass., 1911–1921), 7:111. Imprisonment for debt was first authorized by statute in England in the thirteenth century. See William

S. Holdsworth, *A History of English Law,* 16 vols. (London, 1903–1966), 8:230–232; Ralph B. Pugh, *Imprisonment in Medieval England* (Cambridge, England, 1968), 45–46; Jay Cohen, "The History of Imprisonment for Debt and Its Relation to the Development of Discharge in Bankruptcy," *Journal of Legal History,* 3 (1982): 153–171, esp. 154–155.

9. [N.N.], *Some Reflections on the Law of Bankruptcy: Wrote at the Desire of a Friend: Shewing, That such a Law would be beneficial to the Publick, and analogous to Reason and our Holy Religion* (New Haven, Conn., 1755), 9. See also *The Ill Policy and Inhumanity of Imprisoning Insolvent Debtors, Fairly Stated and Discussed* ([Newport, R.I.], 1754). English criticisms include *Imprisonment of Mens Bodys for Debt, as the practice of England now stands* (London, 1641); *The Case of the Poor Prisoners for Debt* (London, 1700); Philanthropos [pseud.], *Proposals for Promoting Industry and Advancing Proper Credit; Advantageous to Creditors in particular and the Nation in general: In a Letter to a Member of Parliament* (London, 1732).

10. Hendrik Oudenarde, *An Expostulatory Letter to the Honourable Daniel Horsmanden, Esq., Concerning the unnecessary and cruel Imprisonment of Henry Oudenarde, Late Merchant in the City of New-York* (New York, 1766); Oudenarde, *Seven Letters to the Honourable Daniel Horsmanden, Esq., Concerning the unnecessary and cruel Imprisonment of Hendrick Oudenarde, Late Merchant in the City of New-York* (New York, 1766); John Wright Stanly, *A State of the Accounts and Disputes betwixt Jonathan Cowpland and John Wright Stanly* (Philadelphia, 1768); Jonathan Cowpland, *A Few Observations, in Answer to Two Pamphlets, published by John Wright Stanly, relative to a Dispute with Jonathan Cowpland* (pamphlet appears not to have survived); Stanly, *John Wright Stanly's Reply to A Few Observations, Lately Published by Jonathan Cowpland* (Philadelphia, 1768); Stanly, *Remarks on Scurrility and Oppression* (Philadelphia, 1769); Gazelena Rousby, *To the Freeholders and Freemen of the City of New-York, January 20, 1769* [New York, 1769]; James Jauncey, *Mr. Jauncey heartily thanks* . . . [New York, 1769]; Rousby, *As Mr. Jauncey* . . . [New York, 1769].

11. *The Ill Policy and Inhumanity of Imprisoning Insolvent Debtors,* 16; Samuel House to John Francis Mercer, Jan. 20 and Feb. 12, 1787, Mercer Family Papers, sec. 33, folder 3, VHS.

12. *The Ill Policy and Inhumanity of Imprisoning Insolvent Debtors,* 3–4.

13. Ibid., 5, 8–9, 17.

14. [N.N.], *Some Reflections on the Law of Bankruptcy,* 3.

15. *The Ill Policy and Inhumanity of Imprisoning Insolvent Debtors,* 34–37; [N.N.], *Some Reflections on the Law of Bankruptcy,* 9–11. See Samuel Moody, *The Debtors*

Monitor, Directory and Comforter: Or, The Way to get and keep Out of Debt, In Three Sermons (Boston, 1715), 9–10.

16. Justinian [pseud.], *A Letter to the Legislative Authority, of Connecticut. Wherein is shewn, that the Law, and Practice of the Colony, in Regard to Debt and Goal, is not according to the Foundation of Civil Law; which is compiled for public Good* ([Hartford, Conn.], 1770), 3–4, 12.

17. For good descriptions of debtors' prisons in England, see Joanna Innes, "The King's Bench Prison in the Later Eighteenth Century: Law, Authority and Order in a London Debtors' Prison," in John Brewer and John Styles, eds., *An Ungovernable People: The English and Their Law in the Seventeenth and Eighteenth Centuries* (New Brunswick, N.J., 1980), 250–298; Paul H. Haagen, "Imprisonment for Debt in England and Wales" (Ph.D. diss., Princeton University, 1986). John F. Watson, the nineteenth-century chronicler of early Philadelphia, described the Stone Prison at Third and High (Market) streets, completed in 1723, as consisting of two two-story stone buildings, one for debtors and one for criminals. Roberts Vaux, however, indicated that there was no separation between debtors and criminals, which was more likely the case. See John F. Watson, *Annals of Philadelphia, and Pennsylvania, in the Olden Time; being a Collection of Memoirs, Anecdotes, and Incidents of the City and Its Inhabitants,* ed. Willis P. Hazard, 3 vols. (Philadelphia, 1905), 1:360–361; Roberts Vaux, *Notices of the Original, and Successive Efforts to Improve the Discipline of the Prison at Philadelphia* (Philadelphia, 1826), 13.

18. Charles Woodmason, *The Carolina Backcountry on the Eve of the Revolution: The Journal and Other Writings of Charles Woodmason, Anglican Itinerant,* ed. Richard J. Hooker (Chapel Hill, N.C., 1953), 236; Philip Klein, *Prison Methods in New York State: A Contribution to the Study of the Theory and Practice of Correctional Institutions in New York State* (New York, 1920), 32–33; Report of John Fessenden et al., "The Committee appointed to view the County Goal," Dec. 8, 1785, Worcester County, Mass., Papers, box 2, folder 4. The attic location in New York's city hall at least allowed access to the roof, although one debtor accidentally fell to his death while "airing himself under the Cupola." See I. N. Phelps Stokes, *The Iconography of Manhattan Island, 1498–1909,* 6 vols. (New York, 1915–1928), 4:701.

19. *Minutes of the Common Council of the City of New York, 1784–1831,* 21 vols. (New York, 1917–1930), 19:185 (July 26, 1830). A sepia wash drawing of the prison is reproduced in Raymond A. Mohl, "The Humane Society and Urban Reform in Early New York, 1787–1831," *New-York Historical Society Quarterly,* 54 (1970): 31. For descriptions and brief histories of the building, see Stokes, *The Iconography of Manhattan*

Island, 1:333, 4:707; Sidney I. Pomerantz, *New York: An American City, 1783–1803, A Study of Urban Life,* 2d ed. (Port Washington, N.Y., 1965), 312; Klein, *Prison Methods in New York State,* 32–33; James Ciment, "In Light of Failure: Bankruptcy, Insolvency and Financial Failure in New York City, 1790–1860" (Ph.D. diss., City University of New York, 1992), 123–124. For the ghost rumors, see *Gazette of the United States* (Philadelphia), Jan. 19, 1798; *Aurora, or General Advertiser* (Philadelphia), Feb. 28, 1798.

20. Watson, *Annals of Philadelphia,* 3:179–180. See Robert J. Turnbull, *A Visit to the Philadelphia Prison; being an Accurate and Particular Account of the Wise and Humane Administration Adopted in Every Part of that Building; containing also An Account of the Gradual Reformation, and Present Improved State, of the Penal Laws of Pennsylvania: with Observations on the Impolicy and Injustice of Capital Punishments* (Philadelphia, 1796), 4–5. For another contemporary description, see Caleb Lownes, *An Account of the Alteration and Present State of the Penal Laws of Pennsylvania, Containing Also an Account of the Goal and Penitentiary House of Philadelphia and the Interior Management Thereof, by Caleb Lownes, of Philadelphia* (Philadelphia, 1793), 80. Negley K. Teeters quotes a later, more detailed description of the Walnut Street complex in *They Were in Prison: A History of the Pennsylvania Prison Society, 1787–1937* (Philadelphia, 1937), 18. He also reproduced a modern drawing of the debtors' apartment, based on a mid-nineteenth-century sketch, in ibid., 32, and in Teeters, *The Cradle of the Penitentiary: The Walnut Street Jail at Philadelphia, 1773–1835* (Philadelphia, 1955), 20.

21. *Forlorn Hope* (New York), Mar. 24, 1800; De Rivafinoli v. Corsetti, 4 Paige Ch. (New York) 264, 270 (1833); [Joseph Dewey Fay], *Essays of Howard: or, Tales of the Prison. Originally Printed in the New-York Columbian, and Supposed to be Written by a Debtor, Who Has Been Confined for Sixteen Years in the New-York Debtor's Jail* (New York, 1811), 65.

22. Holdsworth, *History of English Law,* 8:233; Dive v. Maningham, 1 Plowden 60, 68, 73 Eng. Rep. 96, 108–109 (K.B., 1551).

23. William Moore to John Tabor Kempe, Sept. 23, 1767, Kempe Papers, box (Lawsuits) M-O; Thomas Moland to Kempe, May 23, 1765, ibid.; Petition of Jacob Frye et al., July 5, 1771, box (Lawsuits) C-F, ibid.; John Young to Kempe, Jan. 29, 1770, box (Lawsuits) V-Z, ibid.; Petition of Abel Butterfield, June 1786, Worcester County, Mass., Papers, box 2, folder 4; Andrew G. Fraunces to William Duer, Mar. 7 and May 2, 1796, William Duer Papers, box 3, NYHS; Duer to Fraunces, Sept. 24, 1796, ibid. When Butterfield escaped from the Worcester County jail four months

later, the escape advertisement noted his single arm but said nothing of his nakedness. Escape advertisement, Oct. 8, 1786, Worcester County, Mass., Papers, box 2, folder 4.

24. Hugh McEwan to John Tabor Kempe, Sept. 28, 1767, Kempe Papers, box (Lawsuits) M-O; Protest by prisoners, Dec. 7, 1785, Worcester County, Mass., Papers, box 2, folder 4. The twenty-three debtors were joined in the petition by five other prisoners—three men jailed for failure to pay taxes, one who was listed as being imprisoned for "fornication" but who was probably kept in jail for not paying a fine or child support, and one man whose reason for incarceration I have not been able to determine. The number of debtors imprisoned in the Worcester County jail on a given day can be computed from "A Register of all Prisoners Committed to Gaol in Worcester County Since March 5, 1785," ibid., box 2, folder 2.

25. *A Sketch of the Origin and Progress of the Humane Society of the City of New-York* (New York, 1814), 3, 7. The curious additional charge was in imitation of the Royal Humane Society in London. Good brief accounts of the Humane Society are in David M. Schneider, *The History of Public Welfare in New York State, 1609–1866* (Chicago, 1938), 143–146, and Raymond A. Mohl, *Poverty in New York, 1783–1825* (New York, 1971), 121–136. On the Philadelphia Society, see Teeters, *They Were in Prison;* Harry E. Barnes, *The Evolution of Penology in Pennsylvania: A Study in American Social History* (Indianapolis, 1927), 80–105; Marvin E. Wolfgang, "Consensus and Conflict about Imprisonment: The Philadelphia Society for Alleviating the Miseries of Public Prisons, 1787–1829," in Randolph S. Klein, ed., *Science and Society in Early America: Essays in Honor of Whitfield J. Bell, Jr.* (Philadelphia, 1986), 225–249. A similar relief organization, the Philadelphia Society for Assisting Distressed Prisoners, appears to have existed for nineteen months after the outbreak of the Revolution until the British occupied the city in September 1777. See Philadelphia Society for Alleviating the Miseries of Public Prisons, Minutes, 1787–1793, at 36–37 (Oct. 12, 1789), Association, Club, and Society Records, 1764–1937, HSP. The one reference I have seen to the Newark committee is in John Pintard, Diary, Newark (Oct. 11–12, 1793), Pintard Papers, box 2. The American societies followed their principal English counterpart, popularly known as the Thatched House Society, by a decade. See [James Nield], *An Account of the Rise, Progress and Present State of the Society for the Discharge and Relief of Persons Imprisoned for Small Debts throughout England* (London, 1796).

26. For examples, see Meeting and report of the Acting Committee, Philadelphia Society for Alleviating the Miseries of Public Prisons, Minutes, 1787–1793, at 69–74 (Aug. 6, 1788), Association, Club, and Society Records; Meeting of the Acting Committee, ibid., 76 (Sept. 19, 1788); Representation to the Supreme Executive

Council, Dec. 15, 1788, Philadelphia Society for Alleviating the Miseries of Public Prisons, Minutes, vol. 1, 1787–1809, Pennsylvania Prison Society, Records, HSP; Grand jury presentment (Sept. 19, 1787), in *Pennsylvania Gazette* (Philadelphia), Sept. 26, 1787. The volume labeled "Minutes, 1787–1793" in the Association, Club, and Society Records is a contemporaneous copy of the first portion of the volume labeled "Minutes, I, 1787–1809" in the Pennsylvania Prison Society Records. The Philadelphia Society (hereafter cited as PSAMPP) changed its name to the Pennsylvania Prison Society in 1886.

27. Charles Brockden Brown, *Arthur Mervyn; or, Memoirs of the Year 1793, First and Second Parts*, in Sydney J. Krause et al., eds., *The Novels and Related Works of Charles Brockden Brown, Bicentennial Edition*, (Kent, Ohio, 1980), 3:253–254. Brown's depiction of the Prune Street jail appears in the Second Part, which was originally published in New York in 1800. In taking his characters inside the debtors' prison, Brown used a device common to earlier English novelists such as Henry Fielding and Tobias Smollett, whose picaresque novels were well known in America. Fielding and Smollett had the literary advantage of having experienced imprisonment for debt firsthand. Brown may also have been familiar with William Hogarth's series of eight prints, "A Rake's Progress" (1733–1734), based on his paintings now in Sir John Soane's Museum, London. Hogarth, too, had been imprisoned for debt.

28. Address from "a Prisoner" to the Committee, Jan. 30, 1788, PSAMPP Papers, 1787–1848, folder 2.

29. See *The Columbian* (New York), Jan. 28, 1811; "Summary of the Charges exhibited . . . against Benjamin F. Haskins," July 24, 1795, Duer Papers, box 6; "Proclamation of sentence against Benjamin Haskins," n.d. [July 24, 1795], ibid.

30. See Representation of the prisoners in jail, Aug. 15, 1787, PSAMPP Papers, 1787–1848, folder 2; Representation of prisoners in jail, Nov. 10, 1787, ibid. The keeper of the debtors' prison in Philadelphia, as elsewhere, did not receive a salary but rather subsisted on fees from the debtors. The liquor concession was a major source of his income—a fact the Philadelphia Society acknowledged when it seconded the keeper's petition to be made a salaried officer, arguing that "by annexing a Competent salary to the office of keeper, he is freed from the temptation of vending spirituous liquors to the prisoners." Representation in support of keeper's petition, PSAMPP Minutes, 1787–1793, at 45–47 (Dec. 21, 1790).

31. Representation to the Supreme Executive Council, Dec. 15, 1788, PSAMPP Minutes, vol. 1, 1787–1809; Representation in support of keeper's petition, PSAMPP Minutes, 1787–1793, at 45–47 (Dec. 21, 1790); *A Sketch of the Origin and Progress of the*

Humane Society, 4–5; Benjamin Rush, *An Inquiry into the Effects of Spirituous Liquors on the Human Body, and their Influence upon the Happiness of Society* (Philadelphia, 1787); Grand jury presentment (Sept. 19, 1787), in *Pennsylvania Gazette*, Sept. 26, 1787. For a good, brief discussion of the connection between temperance and republican culture, see Michael Meranze, *Laboratories of Virtue: Punishment, Revolution, and Authority in Philadelphia, 1760–1835* (Chapel Hill, N.C., 1996), 99–102.

32. Meranze, *Laboratories of Virtue*, 143. Negley Teeters lists the names and occupations of the 37 charter members and the 138 others who joined within the first year. Merchants, ministers, doctors, lawyers, and other professionals comprised at least two-thirds of that first year's membership. See Teeters, *They Were in Prison*, 90–99.

33. Meeting of the Acting Committee, PSAMPP Minutes, 1787–1793, at 69 (Aug. 6, 1788); Constitution, ibid., 1–5 (May 8, 1787).

34. John K. Alexander seems to consider the plight of imprisoned debtors as the principal spur to the formation of the Philadelphia Society, but the Society records confirm that debtors were of secondary importance. See Alexander, *Render Them Submissive: Responses to Poverty in Philadelphia, 1760–1800* (Amherst, Mass., 1980), 67–68.

35. Representation to the Supreme Executive Council, Dec. 15, 1788, PSAMPP Minutes, vol. 1, 1787–1809 (passage in brackets torn in original, supplied from transcript in Teeters, *They Were in Prison*, 450). The jailing of acquitted defendants for the costs of their prosecution raises the question of how many people were imprisoned for debt. Regrettably, there is only occasional anecdotal evidence. Jail lists such as have survived for Worcester County, Massachusetts, do not exist for Philadelphia. One Philadelphia newspaper reported that 4,061 debtors and 3,999 criminals had been imprisoned in the city in the ten-year period 1780–1790. *Federal Gazette and Philadelphia Daily Advertiser*, Oct. 8, 1790. Another stated that seventy-five debtors were in prison in December 1785, sixty of whom were "so *miserably poor* that they must *perish* with *hunger* and *cold*, unless fed and cloathed by the charitable inhabitants of the city!" "Justice in Mercy," *Pennsylvania Gazette*, Dec. 7, 1785. Both claimed to derive their figures from the journals or reports of the jailer. By a third account, 297 debtors were jailed for small amounts in 1793. *Pennsylvania Gazette*, Jan. 13, 1794. All the things we would like to know about the debtors—who they were, how long they were confined, how many were in jail at any one time, were they imprisoned on *mesne* process or execution process, how many were held just for costs of prosecution or for jail fees—are undiscoverable. What we do know is that the Philadelphia Society fre-

quently paid jail fees and small debts to secure the release of poor debtors whose characters met its standards, and that it lobbied the legislature to end the practice of charging acquitted criminals for the costs of their prosecution. See Alexander, *Render Them Submissive*, 64–70.

36. James Bland Burges, *Considerations on the Law of Insolvency, with a Proposal for a Reform* (London, 1783), 379; Turnbull, *A Visit to the Philadelphia Prison*, 63–64.

37. After inspecting the debtors' apartment in January 1799, the visiting committee reported that "the improper Intercourse of the Sexes, so long a subject of Complaint was not yet prevented" and that the keeper had informed them "that Idle Loose Women Contrived to be sent there for small or fictitious debts (as he supposed for the purpose of Communication with the Men Prisoners)." Report of visiting committee, Jan. 14, 1799, PSAMPP Minutes, vol. 1, 1787–1809.

38. Report on Society constitution, PSAMPP Minutes, 1787–1793, at 57 (July 9, 1792). The reference to "trifling debts" is at Meeting of the Acting Committee, ibid., 69 (Aug. 6, 1788). In January 1799 the Acting Committee reported that "the prison for Debtors also continues to require particular attention," upon which the Society directed the Committee "to apply to the Sheriff and County Commissioners to aid them in such measures as may, on investigation, be judged most likely to produce the desired reform in that place of confinement." This would seem to indicate a continuing interest in the plight of imprisoned debtors, but I suspect it is misleading. It was only the second mention of debtors in the Society records since mid-1792, and it was the last mention in the volume of Minutes that extends through 1809. Report of Acting Committee, Jan. 14, 1799, PSAMPP Minutes, vol. 1, 1787–1809.

39. Inspectors of the Jail and Penitentiary House, Minutes, 1794–1835 (6 vols.), vol. 1, Feb. 4, 1795, Dec. 19, 1797, Jan. 23 and Feb. 27, 1798, Record Group 38, PCA.

40. See ibid., entries for May 26 and Oct. 27, 1794; Feb. 4, Mar. 11, and Apr. 29, 1795; Dec. 19, 1797; Jan. 23, Feb. 6, Feb. 27, and Apr. 24, 1798. The first volume of minutes begins in May 1794, so it is possible that the Board had worked tirelessly on behalf of debtors for the five unrecorded years before then. Not likely, but possible. There does not appear to have been a set of formal rules and regulations for the debtors' apartment until 1808. See Teeters, *Cradle of the Penitentiary*, 140–141.

41. Thomas Mifflin, "To the Assembly concerning the present State of the Debtors' Apartment in the Philadelphia Prison," Dec. 22, 1791, in George Edward Reed, ed., *Pennsylvania Archives*, 4th ser. (Harrisburg, Pa., 1900), 4:212–214.

42. Prison limits, also known as prison bounds or prison liberties, were a defined area—sometimes as small as the jail yard, but more commonly at least including the

neighboring streets—into which a debtor who provided sureties could be bailed. The bail terms varied. They might allow a debtor to leave the jail during the day, as long he stayed within a prescribed area and returned at night. Or they could allow him to live outside the jail, as long as he stayed within the bounds. Either one permitted the debtor to ply his trade. There is some indication that small-town county seats offered more extensive limits than cities like Boston, New York, or Philadelphia, sometimes including much of the town center. There is no reliable information on how many debtors had the freedom of the limits, although the bonding requirement makes it unlikely that the numbers were significant. More is known about prison bounds in the nineteenth century, when they were greatly expanded. There is also occasional evidence of "mercy" releases to the limits without requiring sureties. In September 1798, Oliver Wolcott, the secretary of the treasury, authorized the release of William Duer and Jose Joaquin da Costa to the New York prison bounds for the duration of the yellow fever epidemic as long as they pledged not to leave the limits and to return to confinement when the contagion had passed. See Oliver Wolcott to William W. Parker, Sept. 19, 1798, Misc. Wolcott, NYHS. A few months later, Duer's creditors allowed him to live within the limits to spare him from dying in jail. See Elbert Roosevelt to James Morris, Jan. 3, 1799, Morris Family Papers, NYPL; J. LeTurc to James Morris, Apr. 15, 1799, Duer Papers, box 4. Peter Stephen DuPonceau negotiated an agreement that permitted Philip Sanchez, who also was dying, to leave the Prune Street jail for daily walks or rides "for his health," since Sanchez's creditors were "anxious that he should not end his days in a common gaol." See Peter Stephen DuPonceau to Edward Tilghman, Feb. 7, 1801, Peter Stephen DuPonceau Papers, Letterbooks, 1797–1801, at 213, HSP; DuPonceau to William Davy, Feb. 18, 1801, ibid., 215–217.

43. Andrew Fraunces to William Duer, May 2, 1796, Duer Papers, box 3; Jonathan Wallace, *Fellow-Citizens* . . . [Carlisle, Pa., 1798]; *Argus, Greenleaf's Daily Advertiser* (New York), Apr. 30 and May 4, 1798. The initial account of the escape is in *Argus*, Apr. 26, 1798. Reward notices and progress reports appeared regularly until May 7. See *Argus*, Apr. 26 and 30, May 1 and 7, 1798. On aid dispensed to debtors by the Humane Society, see Mohl, *Poverty in New York*, 124–126.

44. Thomas C. Amory to Forsyth Smith & Co., Aug. 21, 1798, Thomas C. Amory Letterbook, 1797–1798, HBS. Cancellation of court sessions could, of course, inure to the benefit of debtors. For example, see Peter Stephen DuPonceau to Benjamin Stoddart and J. Mason, Aug. 31, 1797, and William Tilghman and Peter Stephen DuPonceau to Benjamin Stoddart and J. Mason, Dec. 9, 1797, DuPonceau Papers, Letterbooks, 1797–1801, at 15–19.

45. *Forlorn Hope,* Aug. 2, 1800; [Fay], *Essays of Howard,* 28. See William Duer to Hugh Peebles, Sept. 29, 1795, Duer Papers, box 3. A writer to the *Aurora* in 1797—early in a yellow fever season that would finish with half again the mortality of the three preceding years but only a third that of the following year—took a more cynical view of the flight from Philadelphia: "This alarm [i.e., the fever] has no doubt driven many into the country; others have gone because it was fashionable to go; some to avoid the importunity of creditors, and some because there was little to be done in town, owing to the number of inhabitants that had previously removed." *Aurora,* Sept. 2, 1797. An enumeration of deaths from yellow fever recorded in Philadelphia for ten of the thirteen years from 1793 through 1805 is in Teeters, *They Were in Prison,* 345 note 2.

46. *Gazette of the United States,* Sept. 18, 19, 27, and 28, 1798; Robert Morris to John Nicholson, Sept. 29, 1798, Robert Morris Papers, box 3, NYPL; Morris to Nicholson, Oct. 15, 1798, Conarroe Autograph Collection, box 13, at 16–17, HSP; Morris to Nicholson, Oct. 16, 1798, ibid., 18–19. For an example of an imprisoned debtor tracking the epidemic through newspaper accounts, see Morris to Nicholson, Aug. 27, 1798, Morris Papers, box 3. On Elijah Weed's sacrifice in 1793, see J. H. Powell, *Bring Out Your Dead: The Great Plague of Yellow Fever in Philadelphia in 1793* (Philadelphia, 1949), 188–189.

47. Charles Young to Thomas Hawthorn, Sept. 21, 1798, Meredith Family Papers, box 9, folder 6, HSP; *Gazette of the United States,* Sept. 24, 1798. Hawthorn relented and released Young for sixty days upon his giving security to return. Young returned to the New Gaol by early January. See Samuel Young to Thomas Hawthorn, n.d. [October 1798], Meredith Family Papers, box 9, folder 13; Thomas Ogden to William Meredith, Jan. 7, 1799, ibid., box 10, folder 1. During his brief liberty Young traveled to Philadelphia and met with Robert Morris, who was imprisoned for debt there and who brokered an impromptu compromise when one of Young's bailsmen arrived with the sheriff to arrest him. See Robert Morris to John Nicholson, Nov. 25, 1798, Morris Papers, box 3.

48. Charles Young to Thomas Hawthorn, Sept. 21, 1798, Meredith Family Papers, box 9, folder 6; Memorial of Alexander Lamb, Apr. 22, 1799, Common Council Documents, box 17, NYCMA; *Minutes of the Common Council,* 2:536–537 (Apr. 22, 1799). Lamb's generosity is noted in *Forlorn Hope,* Mar. 24, 1800.

49. The city inspectors sent criminal prisoners to the Chester County jail in West Chester and female prisoners and "the Vagrants and disorderly Servants who were likely to crowd the House and endanger the health of the Prisoners" to Robert

Morris's unfinished mansion, "Morris's Folly." See *Gazette of the United States*, Sept. 19, 1798; Inspectors of the Jail and Penitentiary House, Minutes, vol. 1, Nov. 21, 1798. According to his biographer, Morris, whose son William succumbed to yellow fever in the 1798 epidemic, declined an offer to be removed to the countryside. See Ellis P. Oberholtzer, *Robert Morris: Patriot and Financier* (New York, 1903), 352. During the next year's fever season Morris took the precaution of "establish[ing] the means of a temporary removal in case the danger approaches too near." Morris to James Rees, Sept. 7, 1799, Morris Papers, box 3.

50. See *Forlorn Hope*, Mar. 24, 1800; Report of the visiting committee, Apr. 5, 1798, in Teeters, *They Were in Prison*, 66. The rental market was not unregulated. The New York Common Council once investigated the keeper, Arent Van Hook, for "extort[ing] from Debtors . . . unreasonable Compensation for indulgencies in the Use of certain Rooms in the Goal." *Minutes of the Common Council*, 2:314–315 (Dec. 28, 1796).

51. Robert Morris to John Nicholson, Feb. 20, 1798, Private Letterbooks, 1794–1798, 3:255, Papers of Robert Morris, LC; Morris to Theophile Cazenove, Feb. 26, 1798, ibid., 3:259; "Inventory of Articles found in Possession of Robert Morris in his Rooms, Debtors Apartment," Aug. 1, 1801, in BA 1800-PA, reel 7.

52. Robert Morris to John Nicholson, Oct. 4, 1797, Private Letterbooks, 2:606. Allison may have been able to rent a room large enough to accommodate his card-playing acquaintances, but the additional comfort did not save him from succumbing to yellow fever. Morris to Nicholson, Sept. 29, 1798, Morris Papers, box 3.

53. Pintard, Journal of Studies, 1797–1804 (various entries, July 14 to Aug. 3, 1797), Pintard Papers, box 2; Pintard, Reading Diary in Newark Prison, 37 (July 23, 1797), 38 (Aug. 6, 1797), ibid.; Jonathan Mason, Jr. to Harrison Gray Otis, Mar. 26, 1798, Loose Manuscripts, 1793–1799, Harrison Gray Otis Papers, MHS; *Aurora*, July 17, 1797; Julian Ursyn Niemcewicz, *Under Their Vine and Fig Tree: Travels through America in 1797–1799, 1805, with some further account of life in New Jersey* (Metchie J. E. Budka, trans. and ed.), in *Collections of the New Jersey Historical Society* (Elizabeth, N.J., 1965), 14:17; Robert Morris to Standish Forde, July 26, 1798, Reed & Forde Papers, folder "Robert Morris Papers, 1798–1799," HSP; Robert Morris to John Nicholson, Nov. 12, 1798, Conarroe Autograph Collection, box 13; Brockholst Livingston to Andrew G. Fraunces, July 30, 1795, Duer Papers, box 4. William Wood recalled in his memoir that, as a young actor imprisoned for debt in the Prune Street jail in 1798, the keeper's wife let him go to the theater once or twice a week.

William B. Wood, *Personal Recollections of the Stage, Embracing Notices of Actors, Authors, and Auditors, during a Period of Forty Years* (Philadelphia, 1855), 40.

54. "Record of Private Meeting of the Judges of the Supreme Court," 30 (Mar. 11, 1797), Duer Papers, box 6. On the other hand, only four months later an anonymous New York writer reported that "a considerable dissatisfaction prevails in the gaol of this city . . . in consequence of the discrimination in favor of" debtors who occupied rooms by themselves. See *Aurora*, July 17, 1797.

55. "An act for the relief of Debtors, with respect to the imprisonment of their persons," 12th sess., ch. 23, Feb. 13, 1789, *Laws of the State of New-York . . . Twelfth Session* (New York, 1789). The £10 limit was extended to £1,000 two years later by the One-Thousand-Pound Act. "An Act supplementary to the act, entitled, 'An Act for giving Relief in cases of Insolvency,' and the Act, entitled, 'An act for the Relief of Debtors with respect to the imprisonment of their Persons,'" 14th sess., ch. 29, Mar. 10, 1791, *Laws of the State of New-York . . . Fourteenth Session* (New York, 1791). New York enacted the Ten-Pound Act in response to lobbying by the Humane Society, which presented the assembly with evidence that 716 of the 1,162 debtors imprisoned between January 1787 and December 1788 owed amounts small enough—less than 40s—to be recoverable before a justice of the peace, many less than 20s. *A Sketch of the Origin and Progress of the Humane Society*, 5. Thirty-five years earlier, the New York attorney general accused justices of the peace—many of whom he dismissed as "low mean illiterate and ignorant"—of encouraging creditors to bring lawsuits for trifling sums as low as 4d so they could generate court fees. William Kempe to David Jones, n.d. [August or September 1754], Theodore Sedgwick (Sedgwick II) Papers, box 1, folder 9, MHS.

56. See Seth Johnson to Andrew Craigie, Sept. 6 and 16, 1792, Andrew Craigie Papers, box 6, folder 5, AAS; Robert Morris to John Nicholson, Feb. 28, 1798, Private Letterbooks, 3:261–262; Morris to Nicholson, Mar. 3, 1798, ibid., 3:266. John Pintard, on the other hand, a "wealthy debtor" by most measures but a minor speculator alongside Duer or Morris, spent most of his time in prison reading—up to fourteen hours a day of Greek, Latin, English literature and poetry, sermons, and more. When he had to prepare his accounts and inventory to petition for release, it was a "disagreeable tho' necessary" task that interrupted his reading. See Pintard, Reading Diary in Newark Prison, 84 (Mar. 31, 1798) and passim, and Journal of Studies, passim, Pintard Papers, box 2; Pintard, Recollections, 35, Pintard Papers, box 16.

57. For example, Robert Morris's partner, John Nicholson, died in Prune Street. James Wilson, an associate justice of the United States Supreme Court who had once

been imprisoned in Prune Street, died in North Carolina, where he had fled to avoid arrest and return to prison. William Duer died shortly after he had been paroled into the prison limits, where he had been sent so that he would not have to die in jail.

58. Alfred F. Young, *The Democratic Republicans of New York: The Origins, 1763–1797* (Chapel Hill, N.C., 1967), 394. Keteltas spent five weeks in jail in 1796 for contempt of the New York assembly in connection with his advocacy of two Irish ferrymen who had been punished for their insolence to a Federalist alderman. Ibid., 476–495.

59. *Forlorn Hope*, Mar. 24, 1800.

60. John Young, *Narrative of the Life, Last Dying Speech and Confession of John Young, Condemned to be executed on this Day, for the Murder of Robert Barwick, One of the Deputy Sheriffs* (New York, 1797), 6. For discussions of the reform of American criminal punishment after the Revolution, see Adam J. Hirsch, *The Rise of the Penitentiary: Prisons and Punishments in Early America* (New Haven, Conn., 1992), 47–68; Louis P. Masur, *Rites of Execution: Capital Punishment and the Transformation of American Culture, 1776–1865* (New York, 1989), 25–92; Meranze, *Laboratories of Virtue*, 63–72, 80–84; David J. Rothman, *The Discovery of the Asylum: Social Order and Disorder in the New Republic* (Boston, 1971), 30–78.

61. "On the Impolicy of Imprisonment for Debt (No. 5)," *Forlorn Hope*, June 14, 1800; "The Prisoner; a sentimental morsel founded on a fact," ibid., June 21, 1800; "A Comparison between the situation of a Debtor and a Criminal under the law of this state," ibid., Aug. 2, 1800; "The memorial of A.B. and C.D. . . . to . . . their father's creditor," ibid., Aug. 9, 1800. The Beccaria chapter appeared in "On the Impolicy of Imprisonment for Debt (No. 2)," ibid., Apr. 19, 1800.

62. "A Case in Point," *Forlorn Hope*, Mar. 24, 1800; "Inquisitor," ibid., Apr. 7, 1800; "For the Forlorn Hope," ibid., June 21, 1800; Obituary of Dr. Samuel Lereaux, ibid., July 26, 1800; "A Comparison between the situation of a Debtor and a Criminal . . . ," ibid., Aug. 2, 1800. Obituary notices of imprisoned debtors who committed suicide also appeared in general newspapers. See *Aurora*, Aug. 15, 1797. On a lighter note, Keteltas printed a letter to the president and directors of the Manhattan Company in response to their advertisements of life insurance. The writers, "doomed to confinement in a loathesome prison," wanted "to know at what rate you would insure our lives, individually" and whether, conceding "that our dismal situation increases your risk," the company would require higher premiums. "To the President and Directors of the Manhattan Company," *Forlorn Hope*, Apr. 7, 1800.

63. "On Punishment," *Forlorn Hope*, May 10, 1800.

64. The treatment of fraudulent and absconding debtors as criminals is a limited and highly specific exception to this statement.

65. *A Letter on insolvency* (Philadelphia, 1803), 4, 10. See also [Fay], *Essays of Howard*, 18–19.

66. *Prisoner of Hope* (New York), May 3, 10, and 21, 1800. Sing and Keteltas each spilled a significant amount of ink in their feud. For the various attacks and counterattacks, see *Prisoner of Hope*, May 10, 21, June 18, 1800; *Forlorn Hope*, May 17, 24, 31, June 14, Aug. 9, Sept. 13, 1800. Sing stated his intended dedication of the profits in the first issue. In what turned out to be the last number, he announced that he was suspending publication because the paper was losing money. *Prisoner of Hope*, May 3 and Aug. 23, 1800.

67. [Fay], *Essays of Howard*, 27–28.

4. THE IMAGERY OF INSOLVENCY

1. John Pintard, Reading Diary in Newark Prison, 219–223 (July 4, 1798), John Pintard Papers, box 2, NYHS. The New York Common Council reimbursed Pintard £14 15s for his expenses in organizing the 1791 celebrations. See *Minutes of the Common Council of the City of New York, 1784–1831*, 21 vols. (New York, 1917–1930), 1:655 (July 8, 1791).

2. John Pintard to Elisha Boudinot, Jan. 27, 1784, Bayard-Boudinot-Pintard Papers, NYHS. Robertson declined the honor. Pintard to Boudinot, Mar. 8, 1784, ibid. Boudinot, like Pintard of French Huguenot descent, was the younger brother of Elias Boudinot, recently president of the Continental Congress and later United States congressman from New Jersey, whose wife's sister was the wife of Pintard's uncle and guardian, Lewis Pintard.

3. The only biographies of Pintard are an old hagiography by James G. Wilson, *John Pintard, Founder of the New-York Historical Society* (New York, 1902), and an unpublished dissertation by David L. Sterling, "New York Patriarch: A Life of John Pintard, 1759–1844" (Ph.D. diss., New York University, 1958). For brief sketches, see the entry on Pintard in the *Dictionary of American Biography*, 22 vols. (New York, 1928–1958), 14:629–630; the introduction to *Letters from John Pintard to His Daughter, Eliza Noel Pintard Davidson, 1816–1833*, in *Collections of the New-York Historical Society*, 70–73 (4 vols., New York, 1940–1941), 1:ix–xxii; and Walter Barrett, pseud. [Joseph A. Scoville], *The Old Merchants of New York City*, 5 vols. (New York, 1863–1869), 2:217–244.

4. John Pintard to Elisha Boudinot, Sept. 21, Oct. 3, and Nov. 20, 1790, Bayard-Boudinot-Pintard Papers.

5. A good analysis of the ambiguous relationship between profit and virtue among these merchants is Cathy Matson, "Public Vices, Private Benefit: William Duer and His Circle, 1776–1792," in William Pencak and Conrad Edick Wright, eds., *New York and the Rise of American Capitalism: Economic Development and the Social and Political History of an American State, 1780–1870* (New York, 1989), 72–123. See also E. Wayne Carp, *To Starve the Army at Pleasure: Continental Army Administration and American Political Culture, 1775–1783* (Chapel Hill, N.C., 1984); E. James Ferguson, *The Power of the Purse: A History of American Public Finance, 1776–1790* (Chapel Hill, N.C., 1961).

6. The details of the scheme were rather more complex. Duer and his partners, who referred to themselves as "the six percent club," floated rumors about a planned "Million Bank," which in a hot speculative environment quickly attracted promises of subscriptions that would have resulted in a large capitalization. They parlayed the promised subscriptions into a petition to the New York legislature to charter the plan as the "State Bank." The idea was to use rumors of the State Bank's strength to drive down the price of stock in the Bank of New York, which Duer and his partners would then buy up with borrowed funds—an early leveraged buyout. They would then fold the State Bank plan, watch their Bank of New York stock rise, and use the profits to continue their effort to corner the market on government six percents, which stockholders in the Bank of the United States needed in July 1792 to pay an installment due to the Bank for subscriptions. See Matson, "Public Vices, Private Benefit," 104–105. The best discussion of Duer's speculations and eventual collapse is Joseph Stancliffe Davis, "William Duer, Entrepreneur, 1744–99," in his *Essays in the Earlier History of American Corporations,* 2 vols. (Cambridge, Mass., 1917), 1:109–345. See also Robert F. Jones, *"The king of the Alley," William Duer: Politician, Entrepreneur, and Speculator, 1768–1799* (Philadelphia, 1992); Robert F. Jones, "William Duer and the Business of Government in the Era of the American Revolution," *WMQ,* 3d ser., 32 (1975): 393–416; David L. Sterling, "William Duer, John Pintard, and the Panic of 1792," in Joseph R. Frese and Jacob Judd, eds., *Business Enterprise in Early New York* (Tarrytown, N.Y., 1979), 99–132. For a different explanation of what led to the panic, see David J. Cowen, "The First Bank of the United States and the Securities Market Crash of 1792," *Journal of Economic History,* 60 (2000): 1041–1060.

7. James Watson to Jeremiah Wadsworth, Mar. 14, 1792, quoted in Davis, *Essays in the Earlier History of American Corporations,* 1:285.

8. Seth Johnson to Andrew Craigie, Mar. 25, 1792, Andrew Craigie Papers, box 6, folder 4, AAS.

9. John Adams to Oliver Wolcott, Sr., Jan. 30, 1792, quoted in Davis, *Essays in the Earlier History of American Corporations,* 1:288; Seth Johnson to Andrew Craigie, Aug. 20, 1791, Craigie Papers, box 6, folder 3; William Duer to [ ], Oct. 27, 1791, William Duer Papers, box 3, NYHS.

10. The phrase is Thomas Jefferson's, for whom Duer's "kingdom" was populated by "gambling scoundrels." Jefferson to Thomas Mann Randolph, Jr., Mar. 16, 1792, in *TJP,* 23:287.

11. John Pintard to Elisha Boudinot, Apr. 26, 1784, Bayard-Boudinot-Pintard Papers.

12. John Pintard to Elisha Boudinot, Nov. 24, 1796, Bayard-Boudinot-Pintard Papers; Pintard, Diary, Newark, Oct. 1, 1793, Pintard Papers, box 2.

13. Pintard, Diary, Newark, Oct. 2, 1793.

14. Seth Johnson to Andrew Craigie, Mar. 25, 1792, Craigie Papers, box 6, folder 4; Pintard, Reading Diary, 37 (July 23, 1797); Pintard, Journal of Studies, 1797–1804, Aug. 6, 1798, Sept. 17, 1800, Pintard Papers, box 2; "John Pintard," BA1800-NY, reel 6. Pintard's release did not free him from debt. Indeed, had he been four years younger and unmarried, the New Jersey statute would have required him to work off his debts as an indentured servant for up to seven years. See William Patterson, comp., *Laws of the State of New Jersey* (Newark, N.J., 1800), 184–189. It may not be a coincidence that Charles Brockden Brown named a particularly vengeful creditor "Farquhar." See Charles Brockden Brown, *Arthur Mervyn; or, Memoirs of the Year 1793, First and Second Parts,* in Sydney J. Krause et al., eds., *The Novels and Related Works of Charles Brockden Brown, Bicentennial Edition* (Kent, Ohio, 1980), 3:365–366.

15. Pintard, Recollections, 35, Pintard Papers, box 16; Pintard, Diary, Newark, Nov. 13, 1793; Pintard, Journal of Studies, Aug. 22, 1797. On Pintard's prison reading, see Larry E. Sullivan, "Books, Power, and the Development of Libraries in the New Republic: The Prison and Other Journals of John Pintard of New York," *Journal of Library History,* 21 (1986): 407–424. By the day of his release, Pintard had walked 1,096 miles—113,984 lengths of the prison hall.

16. Pintard, Journal of Studies, July 4, 1797; David Cressy, *Bonfires and Bells: National Memory and the Protestant Calendar in Elizabethan and Stuart England* (Berkeley, Calif., 1989), 1; Pintard, Reading Diary, 115 (May 27, 1798). The reference to "red letter days" is at Journal of Studies, Sept. 17, 1800.

17. Pintard, Commonplace Book, n.d. [ca. 1806–1809], 2, Pintard Papers, box 1.

Another imprisoned debtor who professed to find redemptive value in adversity was Thomas Rodney, who wrote from "the Bastille" in Dover, Delaware, that "there is a certain point in the progress of adversity where virtue disarms even enmity itself of its poison sting." [Thomas Rodney] to [ ], n.d. [June–November 1791], Rodney Collection, box 10, folder 8, HSD. See also Thomas Rodney to Caesar Augustus Rodney, June 19, 1791, ibid.

18. Pintard, Diary, Newark, Oct. 4 and 11–12, 1793.

19. Pintard, Journal, Aug. 25 to Sept. 25, 1800, at Aug. 25 and 27, 1800, Pintard Papers, box 12; Rosemarie Zagarri, "The Rights of Man and Woman in Post-Revolutionary America," *WMQ*, 3d ser., 55 (1998): 203–230, esp. 207.

20. Pintard, Diary, Newark, Oct. 3, 10, and 24, 1793; Pintard to Elisha Boudinot, Nov. 24, 1796, Bayard-Boudinot-Pintard Papers; Pintard, Reading Diary, 108 (May 21, 1798), 109 (May 24, 1798), 111 (May 25, 1798), 112 (May 26, 1798); Pintard, Journal of Studies, May 23 and June 19–20, 1798; Pintard, Journal, Aug. 25 to Sept. 25, 1800, at Aug. 27, 1800.

21. For Burr's recommendation, see Aaron Burr to Theodosia Prevost Burr, Feb. 16, 1793, in Matthew L. Davis, ed., *Memoirs of Aaron Burr, with Miscellaneous Selections from His Correspondence* (New York, 1836), 1:363. For Wollstonecraft's reception in America, see R. M. Janes, "On the Reception of Mary Wollstonecraft's *A Vindication of the Rights of Woman*," *Journal of the History of Ideas*, 39 (1978): 293–302; Marelle Thiebaux, "Mary Wollstonecraft in Federalist America, 1791–1802," in Donald H. Reiman et al., eds., *The Evidence of the Imagination: Studies of Interactions between Life and Art in English Romantic Literature* (New York, 1978), 195–245.

22. Elias Boudinot, *An Oration Delivered at Elizabeth-Town, New-Jersey, Agreeably to a Resolution of the State Society of Cincinnati on the Fourth of July MDCCXCIII* (Elizabethtown, N.J., 1793), 24. On Boudinot, see George Adams Boyd, *Elias Boudinot: Patriot and Statesman, 1740–1821* (Princeton, N.J., 1952); Jane J. Boudinot, ed., *The Life, Public Services, Addresses and Letters of Elias Boudinot, LL.D., President of the Continental Congress*, 2 vols. (Boston, 1896). On the female franchise in New Jersey, see Judith Apter Klinghoffer and Lois Elkis, "'The Petticoat Electors': Women's Suffrage in New Jersey, 1776–1807," *Journal of the Early Republic*, 12 (1992): 159–194.

23. William Duer to Walter Livingston, Apr. 14, 1792, Robert R. Livingston Papers, Livingston Family Correspondence, 1743–1886, ser. 1, NYHS; Robert Morris to John Nicholson, Aug. 29, 1796, Private Letterbooks, 1794–1798, 2:86, Papers of Robert Morris, LC; John Hook to Samuel Gist, Mar. 15, 1773, John Hook Letterbooks, 1772–1774, LVa; *A Letter on insolvency* (Philadelphia, 1803), 7.

24. Sandra Sherman, *Finance and Fictionality in the Early Eighteenth Century: Accounting for Defoe* (Cambridge, 1996), 40–54; Daniel Defoe, *The Review of the State of the British Nation*, vol. 3, no. 5 (Jan. 10, 1706); J. G. A. Pocock, *Virtue, Commerce, and History: Essays on Political Thought and History, Chiefly in the Eighteenth Century* (New York, 1985), 99. See also Pocock, *The Machiavellian Moment: Florentine Political Thought and the Atlantic Republican Tradition* (Princeton, N.J., 1975), 452–458; Paula R. Backscheider, "Defoe's Lady Credit," *Huntington Library Quarterly* 44 (1981): 89–100. On the precariousness of manly identity and reputation among merchants, see Toby L. Ditz, "Shipwrecked, or, Masculinity Imperiled: Mercantile Representations of Failure and the Gendered Self in Eighteenth-Century Philadelphia," *Journal of American History*, 81 (1994): 51–80.

25. Pintard, Diary, Newark, Oct. 17 and 25, 1793. For the account of Pintard's hiding, see ibid., Nov. 8–22, 1793; Pintard to Elisha Boudinot, Nov. 20, 1793, Bayard-Boudinot-Pintard Papers. Pintard's first refuge was with the sheriff's brother. After a few days, he slipped home under cover of darkness by way of back lanes and fields. The writ he avoided was returnable to the court that was then in session. The writ lapsed with the rising of the court, which meant that there could be no further action on the matter until the court next sat in six months. Pintard's mortification over the report that he had absconded evidently came from the distress it had caused local tradesmen to whom he owed money. He had already been formally labeled an "absconding debtor" in New York. See Affidavit of George Knox, Apr. 15, 1793, Petitions against Absconding Debtors, New York County Clerk's Office, New York.

26. Robert Morris to John Nicholson, Dec. 12, 1797, Jan. 22, 27, and Feb. 7, 1798, Private Letterbooks, 3:146–147, 227, 236, 243; John Pintard to Elisha Boudinot, Apr. 27, 1797, Bayard-Boudinot-Pintard Papers.

27. Sullivan, "Books, Power, and the Development of Libraries in the New Republic," 411; Sterling, "New York Patriarch," 205.

28. Pintard, Reading Diary, 91–92 (Apr. 19, 1798), 103–104 (Apr. 29, 1798), 109–110 (May 24, 1798).

29. For good discussions of the symbols and imagery of Independence Day celebrations, see Simon P. Newman, *Parades and the Politics of the Street: Festive Culture in the Early American Republic* (Philadelphia, 1997), 83–119; Len Travers, *Celebrating the Fourth: Independence Day and the Rites of Nationalism in the Early Republic* (Amherst, Mass., 1997); David Waldstreicher, *In the Midst of Perpetual Fetes: The Making of American Nationalism, 1776–1820* (Chapel Hill, N.C., 1997); Albrecht Koschnik, "Political Conflict and Public Contest: Rituals of National Celebration in Philadelphia,

1788–1815," *Pennsylvania Magazine of History and Biography,* 118 (1994): 209–248. Pintard's substitution for the liberty cap—"for Liberty alas! has nothing to do within this walls, unless the blessings we enjoy may be deemed a specimen of French Liberty"—was also a Federalist swipe at Republican francophiles. J. David Harden has traced the migration of the liberty cap from the Netherlands to England to colonial America to revolutionary France in "Liberty Caps and Liberty Trees," *Past and Present,* no. 146 (1995): 66–102.

30. Nine months earlier, Harper had moved the appointment of a committee to prepare a bankruptcy bill. He was a major investor in the North American Land Company, all of whose principals—Robert Morris, John Nicholson, and James Greenleaf—were imprisoned for debt. See *Annals of Congress,* 5th Cong., 2d sess., 7:643 (Nov. 27, 1797); Charles Warren, *Bankruptcy in United States History* (Cambridge, Mass., 1935), 12–13.

31. *Forlorn Hope* (New York), Mar. 24, 1800. See also [David Longworth, ed.,] *Longworth's American Almanac, New-York Register and city Directory for the twenty-fourth year of American independence* (New York, 1799), 26–29, in which the editor noted the "pleasure with which [he] has frequently perused the following Toasts" and said of Pintard that his "loss to this city is generally deplored by those who knew his worth intrinsically as a man." For illuminating discussions of toasting rituals and their significance for popular political culture in the period, see Newman, *Parades and the Politics of the Street,* 29–31, 92–94, 137–138; Waldstreicher, *In the Midst of Perpetual Fetes;* Peter Thompson, "'The Friendly Glass': Drink and Gentility in Colonial Philadelphia," *Pennsylvania Magazine of History and Biography,* 113 (1989): 549–573.

32. Pintard, Journal of Studies, 1797–1804, Jan. 11, 1800.

33. Upon his release, Simpson ran an advertisement in the *Newark Gazette* announcing his return to business in Newark. In soliciting customers, he wished "only to partake a share of the crumbs of comfort . . . that he may be hereafter enabled to face the importunity of duns, and avoid the vigilance of shoulder friends ycleped catchpoles." The reference in the last phrase is to the standard image of the constable (catchpole) taking debtors by the shoulder as he arrested them. The ad was reprinted in Philadelphia with the added editorial comment that the author was a "sable son of misery . . . on whose natural vivacity of disposition the horrors of a Goal have not been able to make any impression." *Aurora, or General Advertiser* (Philadelphia), Aug. 4, 1798. The likelihood of any encounter between Pintard and Simpson is entirely speculative. Pintard never mentioned Simpson or any other fellow prisoner in his diaries. Seven years earlier, Thomas Rodney, imprisoned for debt in Dover, Delaware,

asked a friend to procure the release of an imprisoned black debtor named Cuffe. Rodney had not seen Cuffe, but he had heard him praying through the walls and was astonished by "the natural force of [his] genius and inspiration." He thought Cuffe should be "at liberty to teach his fellow blacks." See Rodney to Abraham Pryor, Nov. 6, 1791, Rodney Collection, box 10, folder 8.

34. Pintard, Journal of Studies, Jan. 27, 1800; Pintard, Journal, Aug. 25 to Sept. 25, 1800, at Sept. 2, 1800. For one letter of introduction, see James Wilkinson to William Dunbar, Jan. 30, 1801, Mss 142, The Historic New Orleans Collection, New Orleans.

35. See Woody Holton, *Forced Founders: Indians, Debtors, Slaves, and the Making of the American Revolution in Virginia* (Chapel Hill, N.C., 1999), 3–38.

36. J. B. C. Lucas to Mme [ ], n.d. [ca. 1787], Letterbook, John B. C. Lucas Papers, box 1, MoHS. The letters in this volume, all in French, are to unidentified correspondents in France. The quotation is from an English translation made in 1957 filed with the volume. Lucas later sat in Congress and, after moving farther west to St. Louis, was United States district judge for the northern district of Louisiana.

37. *Virginia Gazette* (Williamsburg), Dec. 25, 1766; James Mercer to John Francis Mercer, May 27, 1783, Mercer Family Papers, sec. 29, VHS; Charles Smith to Jonathan Meredith, Feb. 2, 1798, Meredith Family Papers, box 8, folder 3, HSP. See Charles Royster, *The Fabulous History of the Dismal Swamp Company: A Story of George Washington's Times* (New York, 1999), 370–371, 379–382.

38. Theodore Foster to Dwight Foster, Aug. 7, 1788, Dwight Foster Papers, MHS; Peregrine Foster to Dwight Foster, Apr. 30, 1791, Foster Family Papers, box 2, folder 1, AAS.

39. Peregrine Foster to Dwight Foster, Nov. 16, 1791, Feb. 2, 1792, Foster Family Papers, box 2, folder 1; Dwight Foster to Mrs. Dorothy Foster, Feb. 16, 1792, ibid., box 2, folder 2; Peregrine Foster to Dwight Foster, Oct. 27, 1794, Dec. 18, 1796, Dwight Foster Papers; Dwight Foster to Rufus Putnam, June 16, 1796, ibid.

40. Jonathan Wallace, *Fellow-Citizens* . . . [Carlisle, Pa., 1798].

41. [Benjamin Franklin], *Father Abraham's Speech To a great Number of People, at a Vendue of Merchant-Goods; Introduced to the Publick by Poor Richard* (Boston, [1758]), 14; [N.N.], *Some Reflections on the Law of Bankruptcy: Wrote at the Desire of a Friend: Shewing, That such a Law would be beneficial to the Publick, and analogous to Reason and our Holy Religion* (New Haven, Conn., 1755), 5.

42. "Notes of St. George Tucker on Manuscript Copy of William Wirt's *Life of Patrick Henry* (September 25, 1815)," *WMQ*, 1st ser., 22 (1914): 252.

43. On the centrality of tobacco, see T. H. Breen, *Tobacco Culture: The Mentality of the Great Tidewater Planters on the Eve of Revolution* (Princeton, N.J., 1985); Allan Kulikoff, *Tobacco and Slaves: The Development of Southern Cultures in the Chesapeake, 1680–1800* (Chapel Hill, N.C., 1986); Gloria L. Main, *Tobacco Colony: Life in Early Maryland, 1650–1720* (Princeton, N.J., 1982); Edmund S. Morgan, *American Slavery, American Freedom: The Ordeal of Colonial Virginia* (New York, 1975).

44. On tobacco cultivation, habits of consumption, the tobacco trade, and the vagaries of the international tobacco market, see Breen, *Tobacco Culture;* Jacob M. Price, *France and the Chesapeake: A History of the French Tobacco Monopoly, 1674–1791, and of Its Relationship to the British and American Tobacco Trades,* 2 vols. (Ann Arbor, Mich., 1973); Jacob M. Price, *Capital and Credit in British Overseas Trade: The View from the Chesapeake, 1700–1776* (Cambridge, Mass., 1980).

45. Edmund Wilcox to James Russell, May 6, 1760, Hubard Family Papers, Southern Historical Collection, University of North Carolina, Chapel Hill, quoted in Royster, *The Fabulous History of the Dismal Swamp Company,* 27.

46. The growing indebtedness of Virginia planters before the Revolution has long been known to historians, who have debated not its existence but its causes and consequences. The most notable early interpretations were Charles A. Beard, *Economic Origins of Jeffersonian Democracy* (New York, 1915), and Isaac Samuel Harrell, *Loyalism in Virginia: Chapters in the Economic History of the Revolution* (Durham, N.C., 1926). Modern interpretations date from Emory G. Evans's seminal article, "Planter Indebtedness and the Coming of the Revolution in Virginia," *WMQ,* 3d ser., 19 (1962): 511–533. Recent work by T. H. Breen, Woody Holton, and Charles Royster extend, modify, and add considerable texture to Evans's argument.

47. See Holton, *Forced Founders,* 67.

48. See generally Neil McKendrick, John Brewer, and J. H. Plumb, *The Birth of a Consumer Society: The Commercialization of Eighteenth-Century England* (Bloomington, Ind., 1982); John Brewer and Roy Porter, eds., *Consumption and the World of Goods* (London, 1993); Cary Carson, Ronald Hoffman, and Peter J. Albert, eds., *Of Consuming Interests: The Style of Life in the Eighteenth Century* (Charlottesville, Va., 1994); and, in particular, the following articles by T. H. Breen: "An Empire of Goods, The Anglicization of Colonial America," *Journal of British Studies,* 25 (1986): 467–499; "'Baubles of Britain': The American and Consumer Revolutions of the Eighteenth Century," *Past and Present,* no. 119 (1988): 73–104; "Narrative of Commercial Life: Consumption, Ideology, and Community on the Eve of the American Revolution," *WMQ,* 3d ser., 50 (1993): 471–501; and "The Meaning of Things: Inter-

preting the Consumer Economy in the Eighteenth Century," in Brewer and Porter, eds., *Consumption and the World of Goods*, 249–260.

49. The best brief account of Robinson's embezzlement, which came to light only after he died, is Joseph A. Ernst, "The Robinson Scandal Redivivus: Money, Debts, and Politics in Revolutionary Virginia," *Virginia Magazine of History and Biography*, 77 (1969): 146–173. For the administrator's list of debtors, see David John Mays, *Edmund Pendleton, 1721–1803: A Biography*, 2 vols. (Cambridge, Mass., 1952), vol. 1, app. ii.

50. On credit exchanges as "cultural conversations" and the consequences of that perception, see Breen, *Tobacco Culture*, 94–118.

51. [Peyton Randolph], *A Letter to a Gentleman in London, from Virginia* (Williamsburg, Va., 1759), 11; Robert Beverley to [John Bland], n.d. [1764], Robert Beverley Letterbook, 1761–1793, LC; Thomas Jefferson, "Additional Questions of M. de Meusnier, and Answers," 1786, in *TJP*, 10:27. For a full discussion of Jefferson and debt, see Herbert E. Sloan, *Principle and Interest: Thomas Jefferson and the Problem of Debt* (New York, 1995).

52. For the British side of the distress, see Julian Hoppit, *Risk and Failure in English Business, 1700–1800* (Cambridge, England, 1987), 122–139.

53. For different, yet complementary, analyses of the convergence of debt and revolutionary ideology in Virginia, see Breen, *Tobacco Culture*, 191–203, and Holton, *Forced Founders*, 39–130.

54. Brent Tarter, ed., *The Order Book and Related Papers of the Common Hall of the Borough of Norfolk, Virginia, 1736–1798* (Richmond, Va., 1979), 101; Robert Beverley to [John Bland], n.d. [1764], Robert Beverley Letterbook.

55. "Humphrey Ploughjogger," *Boston Gazette*, Oct. 14, 1765. For other examples, as well as for a stimulating argument about the development of American nationalism, see T. H. Breen, "Ideology and Nationalism on the Eve of the American Revolution: Revisions *Once More* in Need of Revising," *Journal of American History*, 84 (1997): 13–39.

56. "An American," Purdie's *Virginia Gazette* (Williamsburg, Va.), Mar. 29, 1776. For extended discussions of the relationship between slavery and revolutionary ideology, see Breen, *Tobacco Culture;* Holton, *Forced Founders;* Morgan, *American Slavery, American Freedom;* F. Nwabueze Okoye, "Chattel Slavery as the Nightmare of the American Revolutionaries," *WMQ*, 3d ser., 37 (1980): 3–28.

57. James Mercer to John Francis Mercer, Apr. 5, 1783, Mercer Family Papers; Thomas Jefferson to Lucy Ludwell Paradise, Aug. 27, 1786, in *TJP*, 10:304–305.

Good accounts of postwar British efforts to collect pre-war debts are Emory G. Evans, "Private Indebtedness and the Revolution in Virginia, 1776 to 1796," *WMQ*, 3d ser., 28 (1971): 349–374; Charles F. Hobson, "The Recovery of British Debts in the Federal Circuit Court of Virginia, 1790 to 1797," *Virginia Magazine of History and Biography*, 92 (1984): 176–200.

58. "To Mr. William Keteltas," *Prisoner of Hope* (New York), May 21, 1800; "To Mr. William Sing," *Forlorn Hope*, May 24, 1800.

59. "To the Public," *Forlorn Hope*, Mar. 24, 1800.

60. John Nicholson published *The Supporter, or Daily Repast* from the Prune Street jail in Philadelphia from April 1800 until shortly before his death eight months later, but it was a general paper meant to turn a profit to support Nicholson's family and was indistinguishable from newspapers published elsewhere in the city. See Clarence S. Brigham, *A History and Bibliography of American Newspapers, 1690–1820*, 2 vols. (Worcester, Mass., 1947), 2:953; Rosalind Remer, *Printers and Men of Capital: Philadelphia Book Publishers in the New Republic* (Philadelphia, 1996), 32–33. It may have been the newspaper Keteltas referred to when he noted "that proposals are issued from the debtor's apartment in Philadelphia, for the publication of a newspaper," and expressed the hope that "[i]f the talents of the prisoners confined for debt, in the several jails of the United States, are moderately and judiciously exerted for their emancipation, it must ultimately flash conviction on the mind of the most obdurate creditor." "Intelligence," *Forlorn Hope*, Apr. 19, 1800. If it was, Keteltas was doubtless disappointed. Other debtors published broadsides or pamphlets, but these were limited pieces of special pleading that argued nothing beyond the injustice of their own imprisonment.

61. "The Sharks' Petition," *Forlorn Hope*, Mar. 31, 1800.

62. "On Imprisonment for Debt (No. 1)," *Forlorn Hope*, June 28, 1800; "On the impolicy of Imprisonment for Debt (No. 4)," ibid., May 24, 1800; "On Imprisonment for Debt (No. 2)," ibid., July 5, 1800; "The Last Will and Testament of a Debtor," ibid., Mar. 24, 1800; "Communication from a Gentleman of Veracity," ibid., June 7, 1800; "Hotchpotch (No. 2)," ibid., Apr. 7, 1800; "The memorial of A.B. and C.D. . . . to . . . their father's creditor," ibid., Aug. 9, 1800.

63. "For the FORLORN HOPE . . . [from] Z.," *Forlorn Hope*, Mar. 24, 1800; Extracts from Laws of New York, ibid., Mar. 24 and Mar. 31, 1800.

64. "What a Hum!," *Forlorn Hope*, July 26, 1800.

65. "The Last Will and Testament of a Debtor," *Forlorn Hope*, Mar. 24, 1800; "Remarks," ibid., Aug. 30, 1800.

66. "Newark Prison," *Forlorn Hope,* Mar. 24, 1800; "To the Editor . . . [from] P.Q.," ibid., July 5, 1800.

67. See "Record of Private Meeting of the Judges of the Supreme Court," 14 (Dec. 26, 1796), Duer Papers, box 6.

68. [Hugh Williamson], *Letters from Sylvius to the Freemen Inhabitants of the United States. Containing Some Remarks on the Scarcity of Money; Paper Currency; National Dress; Foreign Luxuries; the Federal Debt; and Public Taxes* (New York, 1787), 29; [Joseph Dewey Fay], *Essays of Howard: or, Tales of the Prison. Originally Printed in the New-York Columbian, and Supposed to be Written by a Debtor, Who Has Been Confined for Sixteen Years in the New-York Debtor's Jail* (New York, 1811), 11; *A Letter on insolvency,* 4; *Debtor and Creditor* (Philadelphia, 1810), 26.

69. Parker Chase to William Duer, Jan. 21, 1792, Duer Papers, box 3; "For the Forlorn Hope . . . [from] Inquisitor," *Forlorn Hope,* Apr. 7, 1800; "On Imprisonment for Debt (No. 1)," ibid., June 28, 1800.

5. A SHADOW REPUBLIC

1. The description of Oeller's assembly room is that of an English traveler, Henry Wansey. See David John Jeremy, ed., *Henry Wansey and His American Journal: 1794* (Philadelphia, 1970), 104 (originally published as Henry Wansey, *Journal of an Excursion of the United States of North America, in the Summer of 1794* [Salisbury, Eng., 1796]). That of the New Gaol is from [Joseph Dewey Fay], *Essays of Howard: or, Tales of the Prison. Originally Printed in the New-York Columbian, and Supposed to be Written by a Debtor, Who Has Been Confined for Sixteen Years in the New-York Debtor's Jail* (New York, 1811), 65. The Lyceum advertised its meeting in the *Aurora, or General Advertiser* (Philadelphia), Apr. 14, 1797. The meeting in the New Gaol is recorded in "Record of Private Meeting of the Judges of the Supreme Court," 35 (Apr. 15, 1797), William Duer Papers, box 6, NYHS (hereafter cited as Supreme Court Records).

2. Statement of purposes and rules, n.d., doc. no. 26, Duer Papers, box 6. No copy of the debtors' constitution survives, but its outlines can be inferred from the order it created. The evidence is fragmentary—a sixty-six-page record of court proceedings and several dozen file papers from individual cases and other items of business. The record book covers the fourteen months from October 1796 to December 1797, with a three-month gap near the end. The file papers span a longer period, from March 1795 to January 1798. The most significant document is a statement of purposes and rules of the court. It is a sheet of paper, folded once to create four pages, with writing on three of them. The bottom half of the folded sheet is gone, leaving

only the top half of each of the four pages. Unless otherwise noted, all manuscripts cited in this chapter are in the Duer Papers, box 6.

3. "Supreme Court convened in No. 5," Sept. 15, 1796; Oaths, Oct. 11, 1796, doc. no. 20; Notice, Nov. 18, 1795, doc. no. 50; Notice, Oct. 10, 1796; Supreme Court Records, 31 (Mar. 11, 1797); Election of attorney general, ibid., 20–21 (Jan. 24, 1797).

4. For the clerk's duties, see Supreme Court Records, 31 (Mar. 11, 1797), 58 (Sept. 7, 1797). For those of the wardens, see ibid., 58 (Sept. 7, 1797); "General Meeting at No. 2," ibid., 66 (Dec. 18, 1797). For prosecutions of wardens, see Summons to Joseph Brantingham, Nov. 11, 1796, doc. no. 68; People v. William Duer and Joseph Brantingham, Supreme Court Records, 6–7 (Nov. 11, 1796); People v. Peter Hardenbrook and William Humphreys, ibid., 22–23 (Jan. 24, 1797). For the appointment of stewards, see Supreme Court Records, 28–29 (Feb. 25, 1797). On room governors and spittoons, see "Charge against William I. Nott," Apr. 1, 1797; "The People vs. Wm. I. Nott," Supreme Court Records, 34 (Apr. 3, 1797).

5. Supreme Court Records, 5 (Oct. 29, 1796), 6–7 (Nov. 11, 1796); Summons to Joseph Brantingham, Nov. 11, 1796, doc. no. 68.

6. Supreme Court Records, 7 (Nov. 11, 1796).

7. "The People vs. Wm. I. Nott," Supreme Court Records, 34 (Apr. 3, 1797); Complaint of Edward M. Mills v. William Davis, Apr. 21, 1797, doc. no. 12; Supreme Court Records, 36 (Apr. 21, 1797).

8. See the prosecution of Peter Hardenbrook and William Humphreys, Supreme Court Records, 22–23 (Jan. 24, 1797). The case is also noteworthy for its procedural elements—a "citizen" using formal process to charge breach of duty by public officials, defendants contesting the issue by pleading not guilty, and a finding of fact by the judges using testimony from witnesses.

9. Call for meeting, Mar. 18, 1795, doc. no. 50; Minutes of meeting, Mar. 7, 1796, doc. no. 72. Hazard replied to each request on the bottom half of the document.

10. Minutes, Sept. 15, 1796, doc. no. 37; Letter from "The Lower Hall" to "The Committee of the Middel Hall," Sept. 16, 1796, doc. no. 22.

11. Complaint of James E. Millet v. Hugh Hagarty, May 31, 1796, doc. no. 18; Supreme Court Records, 46–51 (July 22, 26–27, 1797); Report of committee, n.d. (probably July 27, 1797).

12. Complaint of William Duer v. William Mumford, Sept. 10, 1795, doc. no. 70. The complaint antedates the beginning of the surviving record, so the disposition is unknown.

13. Call for meeting, Apr. 22, 1797, doc. no. 27; Record of "a Special Court," Apr.

24, 1797, doc. no. 28. It is not clear if Duer's sacrifice was for the remainder of his confinement. When he gave up his room, his fellow prisoners asked the jailer "to appropriate to him Exclusively" a room on the upper hall. Nine months later, however, Duer was listed as in Room 6, his old room on the middle hall. Since he had remained a judge in the interim, it is unlikely that he had ever moved to the third floor, but whether he shared the room is unknown. See Supreme Court Records, 30 (Mar. 11, 1797), 65 (Dec. 16, 1797).

14. Complaint of Isaac Sherman v. William I. Nott and Jacob Canter, May 16, 1797, doc. no. 41.

15. Supreme Court Records, 11–13 (Dec. 23, 24, and 26, 1796). At the end of the month, the court instructed the sheriff to release Snow "from his Custody" upon Snow paying the fine for his dereliction when warden. See ibid., 23 (Jan. 23, 1797).

16. On the communal nature of church discipline, see Emil Oberholzer, Jr., *Delinquent Saints: Disciplinary Action in the Early Congregational Churches of Massachusetts* (New York, 1956), 43–163, 186–215. For an analysis of church disciplinary procedure, see Bruce H. Mann, *Neighbors and Strangers: Law and Community in Early Connecticut* (Chapel Hill, N.C., 1987), 137–155. On the mock seriousness of club procedures, where the community was no less real, see Andrew Hamilton, *The History of the Ancient and Honorable Tuesday Club*, ed. Robert Micklus, 3 vols. (Chapel Hill, N.C., 1990). In what may be another link to the sociability of clubmen, the court directed the stewards to "Regulate the distribution of the provisions after the Entertainment" in coordination with the jailer. Unfortunately, all we know of "the Entertainment" is that it evidently involved food. See Supreme Court Records, 28 (Feb. 25, 1797).

17. Supreme Court Records, 14–17 (Dec. 26 and 28, 1796).

18. Supreme Court Records, 45 (July 22, 1797); Newel Narine to "Brother Morison," July 19, 1797, doc. no. 59; Complaint of Robert Turner v. Newel Narine, n.d., doc. no. 67; Summons, July 21, 1797, doc. no. 58; "The People vs. N. Narine," n.d. [July 22, 1797], doc. no. 42.

19. Petition of Newel Narine, Sept. 11, 1797, doc. no. 53; Supreme Court Records, 58 (Sept. 11, 1797).

20. Supreme Court Records, 56–59 (Sept. 7, 11, and 12, 1797); Complaint of Thomas King v. James Devan, Sept. 7, 1797, doc. no. 54; Complaint of James Devan v. Thomas King, n.d. [Sept. 11, 1797], doc. no. 51; Writ, King v. Devan, Sept. 11, 1797, doc. no. 52; Thomas King to "the Honourabell the Judges of the Court," Sept. 12, 1797, doc. no. 47. Devan's name is spelled variously Devan, DeVan, Davan, and Duvan in the several documents.

21. See Complaint of Peter Sackett v. David Grigg, Oct. 3, 1797, doc. no. 61; Complaint of William James et al. v. Cornelius Cooper, Oct. 7, 1797, doc. no. 57. Entries in the record book skip from September 12 to December 13, 1797, so there is no record of any action on these complaints. The complainants against Cooper were his roommates in No. 4.

22. See Complaint of Isaac Sherman v. William I. Nott and Jacob Canter, May 16, 1797, doc. no. 41; People v. William I. Nott and Jacob Canter, Supreme Court Records, 41 (May 17, 1797); [Charles Simpson], Supreme Court Records, 19 (Jan. 21, 1797); Complaint of John Van Sice v. Hutchinson, Mar. 16, 1797, doc. no. 15; People v. Hutchinson, Supreme Court Records, 32 (Mar. 17, 1797). There is passing indication that such renovations might have required the approval of the Common Council. The Council once received a letter from several debtors asking permission "to make certain Improvements to their Room" and referred the request to the Committee on Repair to the Gaol for examination. *Minutes of the Common Council of the City of New York, 1784–1831*, 21 vols. (New York, 1917–1930), 2:367–368 (July 12, 1797).

23. Arbitration award in David Beattie [Baty] v. Jacob Canter, Dec. 14, 1796, doc. no. 36. Thirteen months later the court formally adjudicated a similar dispute between a debtor who had purchased the right to occupy an "apartment" from a previous occupant, "as had been customary," and the other residents of the room, who barred his entry. The room had probably been subdivided. The members of the middle hall voted in favor of the purchaser. See Petition of James Smith, Jan. 2, 1798, doc. no. 16; Minutes of General Meeting, Jan. 2, 1798, doc. no. 17; "General Meeting on Occupancy of Room No. 3 by Purchase," Supreme Court Records, 68 (Jan. 3, 1798). For more on this dispute, see the discussion in the text accompanying note 27.

24. For a discussion of this process, see Mann, *Neighbors and Strangers*, 101–136. For more detail, see also Bruce H. Mann, "The Formalization of Informal Law: Arbitration before the American Revolution," *New York University Law Review*, 59 (1984): 443–481.

25. Minutes of General Meeting, Jan. 3, 1798, doc. no. 17; Recommendation of committee, n.d. [February 1797], doc. no. 45.

26. Under the new procedure adopted by the court, applicants needed the sponsorship of two members and the approval first of a committee, which investigated the circumstances of the applicant's imprisonment, and then of the full membership. See Supreme Court Records, 61–66 (Dec. 12–18, 1797), 69 (n.d. [Jan. 11, 1798]); Application of Alexander McDonald, Jan. 10, 1798, doc. no. 29; Application of John Daniels, Jan. 10, 1797 [1798], doc. no. 30.

27. See Petition of James Smith "To the Judges of the Hall," Jan. 2, 1798, doc. no. 16; Minutes of General Meeting, Jan. 3, 1798, doc. no. 17; "General Meeting on Occupancy of Room No. 3 by Purchase," Supreme Court Records, 68 (Jan. 3, 1798); ibid., 69 (Jan. 6, 1798).

28. Complaint of William Arebeck v. Edward Jamison, Aug. 10, 1797, doc. no. 73; Complaint of Margaret Frean v. Charles Ellison, Aug. 15, 1795, doc. no. 33; "Summary of the Charges exhibited . . . against Benjamin F. Haskins," July 24, 1795; "Proclamation of sentence against Benjamin Haskins," n.d. [July 24, 1795]; Minutes of proceedings, July 17, 1795, doc. no. 2. That said, the debtors may have been affirming something else when they expelled Timothy Wales from the hall "as a public Informer and Disturber of the Peace" for having snitched to the jailer that someone had brought in liquor "and by that means endeavouring to prevent the admission of that article to the manifest injury of the Prisoners in General." See Complaint against Timothy Wales, May 18, 1796, doc. no. 18; "People vs. Timothy Wales," May 18, 1796, doc. no. 32.

29. See Robert J. Turnbull, *A Visit to the Philadelphia Prison; being an Accurate and Particular Account of the Wise and Humane Administration Adopted in Every Part of that Building; containing also An Account of the Gradual Reformation, and Present Improved State, of the Penal Laws of Pennsylvania: with Observations on the Impolicy and Injustice of Capital Punishments* (Philadelphia, 1796), 20. Joanna Innes describes a debtors' court in King's Bench prison, but she does not discuss its procedure. See Innes, "The King's Bench Prison in the Later Eighteenth Century: Law, Authority and Order in a London Debtors' Prison," in John Brewer and John Styles, eds., *An Ungovernable People: The English and Their Law in the Seventeenth and Eighteenth Centuries* (New Brunswick, N.J., 1980), 250–298, esp. 276–286. None of the prisoner-of-war accounts suggest any attention to legal procedure. For example, see Charles Herbert, *A Relic of the Revolution* (Boston, 1847), 68, 71, 116, 145–146, 148, on Mill Prison in Plymouth, England; Andrew Sherburne, *Memoirs of Andrew Sherburne: A Pensioner of the Navy of the Revolution* (Utica, N.Y., 1828), 83, also on Mill Prison; "Diary of William Widger of Marblehead, Kept at Mill Prison, England, 1781," *Essex Institute Historical Collections*, 73 (1937): 311–347, 74 (1938): 22–48, 142–158, esp. 144–145; Albert G. Greene, ed., *Recollections of the Jersey Prison-Ship: Taken, and Prepared for Publication, from the Original Manuscript of the Late Captain Thomas Dring, of Providence, R.I., One of the Prisoners* (New York, 1831), 102–111. See also Jesse Lemisch, "Listening to the 'Inarticulate': William Widger's Dream and the Loyalties of American Revolutionary Seamen in British Prisons," *Journal of Social History*, 3 (1969): 20–25. There is some indication

that captured American sailors in the War of 1812 added a constitutional dimension to their self-government in prison. See Robin F. A. Fabel, "Self-Help in Dartmoor: Black and White Prisoners in the War of 1812," *Journal of the Early Republic,* 9 (1989): 177–179. One can only speculate as to why legal authority and formality were so much more rudimentary in the Revolutionary War prisons than in the New York debtors' prison fifteen years later. One explanation may lie in the fact that the sailors' self-government was just that—an organization of sailors. Officers—a more likely source of authority and formality—were kept in separate prisons.

30. *The Debtor and Creditor's Assistant* (London, 1793), 43, quoted in Innes, "The King's Bench Prison in the Later Eighteenth Century," in Brewer and Styles, eds., *An Ungovernable People,* 276.

31. "An act for the relief of Debtors, with respect to the imprisonment of their persons," 12th sess., ch. 23, Feb. 13, 1789, *Laws of the State of New-York . . . Twelfth Session* (New York, 1789), amended by "An Act supplementary to the act, entitled, 'An Act for giving Relief in cases of Insolvency,' and the Act, entitled, 'An act for the Relief of Debtors with respect to the imprisonment of their Persons,'" 14th sess., ch. 29, Mar. 10, 1791, *Laws of the State of New-York . . . Fourteenth Session* (New York, 1791). Isaac Sherman addressed his renegade call for a meeting to "the Debtors confined on sums exceeding Ten pounds," which, since he was summoning the entire membership of the hall, suggests that all the members owed too much money to be eligible for gaol delivery. See Call for meeting, Apr. 22, 1797, doc. no. 27. See also Supreme Court Records, 66 (Dec. 18, 1797).

32. On Bedlow, see Paul A. Gilje, *The Road to Mobocracy: Popular Disorder in New York City, 1763–1834* (Chapel Hill, N.C., 1987), 87–88. Brantingham, Fowler, and Harrison are listed as merchants in various annual New York directories for the 1790s. On Brantingham in particular, see Julius Goebel, Jr., and Joseph H. Smith, eds., *The Law Practice of Alexander Hamilton: Documents and Commentary,* 5 vols. (New York, 1964–1981), 4:179–207; Robert Morris to Thomas Brantingham, Feb. 23, 1795, Papers of Robert Morris, Private Letterbooks, 1794–1798, 1:47–48, LC.

33. On Joseph Brantingham, see Goebel and Smith, eds., *The Law Practice of Alexander Hamilton,* 4:181 note 5. For Langworthy, see ibid., 5:106–107 note 1. For Mumford's bankruptcy, see BA1800-NY, reel 5. For Blanchard, see *Minutes of the Common Council,* 1:59 (July 21, 1784), 517 (Jan. 15, 1790).

34. Charge against James Blanchard, Dec. 13, 1797, doc. no. 74. When Blanchard realized they were serious, he resigned. Supreme Court Records, 62 (Dec. 15, 1797).

35. *Forlorn Hope* (New York), Apr. 7 and Apr. 19, 1800.

6. THE POLITICS OF INSOLVENCY

1. "Bon Mot," *Aurora, or General Advertiser* (Philadelphia), Jan. 25, 1797. On Bache, see Jeffery A. Smith, *Franklin and Bache: Envisioning the Enlightened Republic* (New York, 1990); James Tagg, *Benjamin Franklin Bache and the Philadelphia Aurora* (Philadelphia, 1991).

2. See Peter Thompson, *Rum Punch and Revolution: Taverngoing and Public Life in Eighteenth-Century Philadelphia* (Philadelphia, 1999), 146–154, 172–175, 190–191.

3. "To the People of the United States," *Aurora*, Jan. 17, 1797; "To the Farmers and other industrious citizens of America, particularly those of Connecticut," ibid., Mar. 26, 1798.

4. "Convention of DOGS," *Gazette of the United States* (Philadelphia), Feb. 19, 1798; *Aurora*, Jan. 7, 1797, Mar. 19, 1798. The emblem was first suggested by the editor of the weekly *Farmer's Museum, or Lay Preacher's Gazette* in Walpole, New Hampshire, and quickly reprinted in various other papers, including the *Gazette of the United States*, May 18, 1799.

5. Max Farrand, ed., *The Records of the Federal Convention of 1787*, rev. ed., 4 vols. (New Haven, Conn., 1937), 2:489 (Sept. 3, 1787); William Samuel Johnson to James McEvers, Nov. 17, 1763, William Samuel Johnson Papers, Letterbook 12, CHS.

6. *Considerations on the Subject of Finance, In which the causes of the depreciation of the Bills of Credit emitted by Congress are briefly stated and examined, and a Plan proposed for restoring Money to a certain, known value* (Philadelphia, 1779), 1.

7. E. James Ferguson, *The Power of the Purse: A History of American Public Finance, 1776–1790* (Chapel Hill, N.C., 1961), 29; John Henry, Jr., to the Governor of Maryland [Thomas Johnson, Jr.], Feb. 14, 1778, in Edmund C. Burnett, ed., *Letters of Members of the Continental Congress*, 8 vols. (Washington, D.C., 1921–1936), 3:85. Ferguson's book, on which this section draws, remains the authority on currency finance and the public debt. For a more recent analysis, see Janet A. Riesman, "Money, Credit, and Federalist Political Economy," in Richard Beeman, Stephen Botein, and Edward C. Carter II, eds., *Beyond Confederation: Origins of the Constitution and American National Identity* (Chapel Hill, N.C., 1987), 128–161. See also Cathy Matson, "The Revolution, the Constitution, and the New Nation," in Stanley L. Engerman and Robert E. Gallman, eds., *The Cambridge Economic History of the United States*, vol. 1: *The Colonial Era* (New York, 1996), 363–401. For a catalog of the myriad

national and state debt certificates, see William G. Anderson, *The Price of Liberty: The Public Debt of the American Revolution* (Charlottesville, Va., 1983).

8. For a brief overview, see John J. McCusker and Russell R. Menard, *The Economy of British America, 1607–1789, with Supplementary Bibliography* (Chapel Hill, N.C., 1991), 351–377.

9. Thomas Stoughton to Dominick Lynch, Mar. 11, 1785, Lynch & Stoughton Letterbook, 1783–1787, at 102a–b, NYHS; [Hugh Williamson], *Letters from Sylvius to the Freemen Inhabitants of the United States. Containing Some Remarks on the Scarcity of Money; Paper Currency; National Dress; Foreign Luxuries; the Federal Debt; and Public Taxes* (New York, 1787), 9.

10. Thomas Jefferson to Archibald Stuart, Jan. 25, 1786, Archibald Stuart Papers, 1786–1822, folder 2, VHS. Jefferson remarked on the silver lining of the collapse of credit to others as well. For example, see Jefferson to G. K. van Hogendorp, Oct. 13, 1785, in *TJP*, 8:632.

11. Harrison Gray Otis to Harrison Gray, Nov. 9, 1790, Harrison Gray Otis Letterbook, 1788–1807, at 107–109, Harrison Gray Otis Papers, MHS; George Skillern to Archibald Stuart, Nov. 4, 1785, Stuart Family Papers, sec. 1, folder 11, VHS; Robert Morris to Tench Tilghman & Co., Jan. 3, 1786, Robert Morris Papers, box 2, NYPL; Nicholas Power to James Beekman, Oct. 21, 1782, Beekman Papers, box 15, NYHS; George Read to William Clay, Sept. 10, 1792, Read Mss, HSP.

12. For example, see [William Barton], *Observations on the Nature and Use of Paper-Credit; and the Peculiar Advantages to be Derived from It, in North-America: From Which Are Inferred the Means of Establishing and Supporting It, Including Proposals for Founding a National Bank* (Philadelphia, 1781). Barton later became disillusioned with the bank. See Riesman, "Money, Credit, and Federalist Political Economy," 158–159.

13. See Thomas Paine, *Dissertations on Government, the Affairs of the Bank, and Paper-Money* (Philadelphia, 1786); Mathew Carey, ed., *Debates and Proceedings of the General Assembly of Pennsylvania, on the memorials praying a repeal or suspension of the law annulling the charter of the bank* (Philadelphia, 1786), 66; [Pelatiah Webster], *An Essay on Credit, in which the Doctrine of Banks is Considered, and some Remarks are made on the present State of the Bank of North-America* (Philadelphia, 1786), 3. For a recent analysis of the controversy, see George David Rappaport, *Stability and Social Change in Revolutionary Pennsylvania: Banking, Politics, and Social Structure* (University Park, Pa., 1996), 137–221. On the early banks, see Bray Hammond, *Banks and Politics in America from the Revolution to the Civil War* (Princeton, N.J., 1957), 40–88; Robert A. East, *Business Enterprise in the American Revolutionary Era* (New York,

1938), 285–305. For the best brief discussion of the role of banks and commercial paper in the financial modernization of Philadelphia after the Revolution, see Thomas M. Doerflinger, *A Vigorous Spirit of Enterprise: Merchants and Economic Development in Revolutionary Philadelphia* (Chapel Hill, N.C., 1986), 296–310.

14. William Hart, Jr., *To the Public . . . 14th February, 1780* [Hartford, Conn., 1780].

15. Pelatiah Webster, "Strictures on Tender-Acts," Dec. 13, 1780, in Webster, *Political Essays on the Nature and Operation of Money, Public Finances, and Other Subjects: Published during the American War, and continued up to the present Year, 1791* (Philadelphia, 1791), 132; [Williamson], *Letters from Sylvius,* 9, 34. During the ratification debates Federalists routinely excoriated their opponents as "Debtors in desperate circumstances, who have not resolution to be either honest or industrious . . . *Paper money* and *tender acts* is the only atmosphere in which they can breathe and live." "A Landholder II" [Oliver Ellsworth], *Connecticut Courant* (Hartford), Nov. 12, 1787. On tender laws in particular, Henry Lee's denunciation at the Virginia ratifying convention can stand for all: "Permit me to ask, if there be an evil which can visit mankind, so injurious and oppressive in its consequence and operation, as a tender law? If Pandora's box were on one side of me, and a tender law on the other, I would rather submit to the box than to the tender law. The principle, evil as it is, is not so base and pernicious as the application. It breaks down the moral character of your people— robs the widow of her maintenance, and defrauds the offspring of his food. The widow and orphans are reduced to misery, by receiving in a depreciated value, money which the husband and father had lent out of friendship. This reverses the natural course of things. It robs the industrious of the fruits of their labor, and often enables the idle and rapacious to live in ease and comfort at the expence of the better part of the community." Virginia Convention, June 9, 1788, in *DHRC,* 9:1074.

16. Society of Friends, *To the General Assembly of the State of Rhode-Island, next to be holden at Providence. The Petition and Memorial of the Representatives of the People called Quakers, in New-England, being met together in Capacity of a Meeting for Sufferings* ([Providence, R.I.], 1788). Linking the two issues may also have been an attempt to bridge the divide between Quakers who supported the new Constitution for its prohibition of state tender laws and fellow Friends who opposed it for its protection of the slave trade.

17. [Barton], *Observations on the Nature and Use of Paper-Credit,* 19. For examples of currency arbitrage, see East, *Business Enterprise in the American Revolutionary Era,* 33. See also Matson, "The Revolution, the Constitution, and the New Nation," 367–368.

18. See Ferguson, *The Power of the Purse*, 252–253; Edward C. Papenfuse, *In Pursuit of Profit: The Annapolis Merchants in the Era of the American Revolution, 1763–1805* (Baltimore, 1975), 94; Charles Royster, *A Revolutionary People at War: The Continental Army and American Character, 1775–1783* (Chapel Hill, N.C., 1979), 342.

19. Webster, "A Seventh Essay on Free Trade and Finance; In which the Expediency of Funding the Public Securities, Striking further Sums of Paper Money, and other important Matters, are considered," Jan. 10, 1785, in Webster, *Political Essays*, 273, 278–279, 290; [Andrew Craigie] to [Samuel Rugers], n.d. [March 1787], Andrew Craigie Papers, box 11, folder 2, AAS.

20. See Doerflinger, *A Vigorous Spirit of Enterprise*, 135–136, 242–249; Henry Drinker to Frederick Pigou, Jr., Jan. 29, 1785, Henry Drinker Letterbook, 1762–1786, at 104, HSP; Thomas Stoughton to Dominick Lynch, Dec. 1, 1784, Lynch & Stoughton Letterbook, 1783–1787, at 86b.

21. James T. Mitchell and Henry Flanders, comps., *The Statutes at Large of Pennsylvania from 1682 to 1801*, 16 vols. (Harrisburg, Pa., 1896–1911), 12:70–86. Although not entirely clear on its face, the statute was interpreted to cover debts incurred before it was enacted. Only the petitioning creditor had to claim a debt incurred subsequent to enactment. See Edward Shippen's jury charge in Pleasants v. Meng et al., 1 Dallas 380, 389 (C.P., Phila. County, 1788).

22. *Annals of Congress*, 5th Cong., 3d sess., 9:2654–2655 (Jan. 14, 1799).

23. See Bankruptcy File, 1785–1790, in Records of Pennsylvania's Revolutionary Governments, 1775–1790, Record Group 27, PHMC. My count of petitions does not include the second petition filed against Jeremiah Fisher and Abraham Rogers, both of Philadelphia, five days after the first, which was incomplete, or the second petition against James Newport, also of Philadelphia, which was filed eight days after the presumably defective first one. I have, however, counted the two petitions against Samuel Emery of Philadelphia and the two against Aaron Musgrave, Jr., of Westchester separately and Emery and Musgrave twice as debtors because each petition represents a separate bankruptcy, forty-five months after the first one in Emery's case and eighteen months in Musgrave's. The disparity between the number of petitions and the number of debtors stems from the ten petitions filed against partners, each of whom counts as a separate debtor, given the joint and several liability of partners. Eleven creditors filed two petitions, one filed three, and two—Benjamin James and William Wistar, both of Philadelphia—each filed four.

24. Clement Biddle to Brother and Sister Tiller, Apr. 24, 1789, Biddle to Richard Smith, Apr. 25, 1789, Clement Biddle Letterbook, 1789–1792, HSP. See "At a

Meeting of the Subscribers Creditors of Manuel Noah of the City of Philadelphia Merchant of the City Tavern in Philadelphia," Jan. 11, 1786, Bankruptcy File, 1785–1790. Noah's creditors acted in sufficient concert that they agreed to share equally "in all the Risk and Expences" of the bond required by the statute as security that the petitioning creditor would prove both his debt and that the debtor was bankrupt in the event. Twenty-one of the petitions were filed by creditors with the same surname as their debtors. Some of these may have been vengeful relatives, but it seems unlikely that most were. Other ties are harder to find.

25. "Draft opinion on Case of Jonathan Williams," n.d. [1787 or 1788], Richard Harison Papers, box 3, NYHS. See also "Draft opinion of Case respecting Messrs Isaac Moses, Samuel Myers, and Moses Myers for Mr. Daniel Ludlow," January 1786, ibid. For a summary of the New York statutory vacillations in the 1780s, see Julius Goebel, Jr., and Joseph H. Smith, eds., *The Law Practice of Alexander Hamilton: Documents and Commentary*, 5 vols. (New York, 1964–1981), 2:332–336.

26. The litigation figures are from David P. Szatmary, *Shays' Rebellion: The Making of an Agrarian Insurrection* (Amherst, Mass., 1980), 29. Although Shays's Rebellion was, above all, a conflict over debt and taxes, it was not a straightforward clash between debtors and creditors. For the most nuanced analyses, see John L. Brooke, *The Heart of the Commonwealth: Society and Political Culture in Worcester County, Massachusetts, 1713–1861* (New York, 1989), 189–229; and the essays in Robert A. Gross, ed., *In Debt to Shays: The Bicentennial of an Agrarian Rebellion* (Charlottesville, Va., 1993). For additional brief insights, see Christopher Clark, *The Roots of Rural Capitalism: Western Massachusetts, 1780–1860* (Ithaca, N.Y., 1990), 44–50; Ferguson, *The Power of the Purse*, 245–50. For a superb study of how debtors and creditors became winners and losers not by weakness or oppression but in the step-by-step process of dealing with an unfamiliar and volatile economy, see Jonathan M. Chu, "Debt and Taxes: Public Finance and Private Economic Behavior in Postrevolutionary Massachusetts," in Conrad Edick Wright and Katheryn P. Viens, eds., *Entrepreneurs: The Boston Business Community, 1700–1850* (Boston, 1997), 121–149.

27. Ironically, the vigor with which eastern authorities suppressed the Shaysites strengthened Antifederalism in Massachusetts and threatened the state's ratification of the Constitution. See Richard D. Brown, "Shays's Rebellion and the Ratification of the Federal Constitution in Massachusetts," in Beeman et al., eds., *Beyond Confederation*, 113–127. Other acts of resistance or defiance by debtors were more fleeting but nonetheless unsettling for the specter of class violence they raised. Backcountry planters in South Carolina forcibly closed the local court of common pleas in April

1785. Two hundred armed men surrounded the New Hampshire legislature for a day in September 1786 demanding paper money and other debt relief before they were routed by the militia. Debtors torched jails and courthouses in Virginia in the spring and summer of 1787. See Robert A. Becker, ed., "John F. Grimké's Eyewitness Account of the Camden Court Riot, April 27–28, 1785," *South Carolina Historical Magazine*, 88 (1983): 209–213; Alan Taylor, "Regulators and White Indians: The Agrarian Resistance in Post-Revolutionary New England," in Gross, ed., *In Debt to Shays*, 145–160; *DHRC*, 8:xxviii.

28. See Stephen E. Patterson, "The Federalist Reaction to Shays's Rebellion," in Gross, ed., *In Debt to Shays*, 106–109; Szatmary, *Shays' Rebellion*, 100–104.

29. See *An Address from the General Court, to the People of the Commonwealth of Massachusetts* (Boston, 1786), 33–35.

30. Farrand, ed., *Records*, 2:447–448 (Aug. 31, 1787), 488–489 (Sept. 3, 1789). For a summary of South Carolina's ever-changing bankruptcy system, see Peter J. Coleman, *Debtors and Creditors in America: Insolvency, Imprisonment for Debt, and Bankruptcy, 1607–1900* (Madison, Wis., 1974), 181–187. The only extended study of the bankruptcy clause is Kurt H. Nadelmann, "On the Origin of the Bankruptcy Clause," *American Journal of Legal History*, 1 (1957): 215–228.

31. See the petitions in Connecticut Archives, Insolvent Debtors, 1st ser. (1 vol.) and 2d ser. (13 vols.), CSL.

32. James et al. v. Allen, 1 Dallas 188, 191 (C.P., Phila. County, 1786). Most of the lawyers' arguments are in the published case report. A slightly fuller version of the arguments, which I have used here, is in "James & Carsen v. Andrew Allan," Peter Stephen DuPonceau, Precedent Book, 1785–1798, at 149–157, Peter Stephen DuPonceau Papers, HSP.

33. See Millar v. Hall, 1 Dallas 229, 231 (Sup. Ct. Pa., 1788).

34. Proceedings and Debates of the Convention, Dec. 7, 1787, in *DHRC*, 2:519; *The Federalist* (no. 42), ed. Jacob E. Cooke (Middletown, Conn., 1961), 287. Madison discussed the full faith and credit clause in the very next paragraph, thus maintaining the juxtaposition of the clauses in the convention despite their separation in the document he was defending.

35. For example, a delegate to the Connecticut ratifying convention explained that "[t]he general laws of bankruptcy appear to be necessary both for creditors and debtors, and it appears reasonable, when conformed to in one state, they should be effectual to secure the debtor throughout the union." Samuel Holden Parson to William Cushing, Jan. 11, 1788, in *DHRC*, 3:572.

36. [Oliver Ellsworth], "A Landholder II," *Connecticut Courant*, Nov. 12, 1787; "A Dialogue between Mr. Z and Mr. &," *Massachusetts Centinel* (Boston), Nov. 7, 1787. Even foreign observers recited the damning litany. The French minister in New York reported to Paris that "one can count . . . among the Antifederalists the Bankrupts, the men of bad faith, [and] the needy." Comte de Moustier to Comte de Montmorin, Mar. 16, 1788, in *DHRC*, 16:403.

37. *An Additional Number of Letters from the Federal Farmer to the Republican Leading to a Fair Examination of the System of Government Proposed by the Late Convention; To Several Essential and Necessary Alterations in It; And Calculated to Illustrate and Support the Principles and Positions Laid Down in the Preceding Letters* (New York, 1788), in Herbert J. Storing, ed., *The Complete Anti-Federalist*, 7 vols. (Chicago, 1981), 2:344. The "Federal Farmer" had revised his opinion—three months earlier he had written that he did not know enough to say how federal bankruptcy laws would affect the states, but "[i]f uniform bankrupt laws can be made without producing real and substantial inconveniences, I wish them to be made by Congress." *Observations Leading to a Fair Examination of the System of Government Proposed by the Late Convention; and to Several Essential and Necessary Alterations in It. In a Number of Letters from the Federal Farmer to the Republican* (New York, 1787), in Storing, ed., ibid., 2:243. For a good example of Antifederalist reservations about the power of the federal judiciary, see Luther Martin, *The Genuine Information Delivered to the Legislature of the State of Maryland Relative to the Proceedings of the General Convention Lately Held at Philadelphia* (Philadelphia, 1788), in Storing, ed., ibid., 2:69–71. The contract clause raised similar issues. See Steven R. Boyd, "The Contract Clause and the Evolution of American Federalism, 1789–1815," *WMQ*, 3d ser., 44 (1987): 529–548.

38. *Freeman's Journal* (Philadelphia), Feb. 20, 1788, in Storing, ed., *Complete Anti-Federalist*, 3:180; [Aristocrotis], *The Government of Nature Delineated or An Exact Picture of the New Federal Constitution* (Carlisle, Pa., 1788), in ibid., 3:196–197.

39. See "Cassius" II, *Massachusetts Gazette* (Boston), Nov. 23, 1787; [George Bryan], Response to questions concerning the Constitutional Convention and ratification, n.d. [1789], George Bryan Papers, box 2, folder 4, HSP; Arthur Bryan to George Bryan, Apr. 9, 1788, ibid., box 3, folder 2. On George Bryan's failure after nineteen years as a merchant in Philadelphia, see Joseph S. Foster, *In Pursuit of Equal Liberty: George Bryan and the Revolution in Pennsylvania* (University Park, Pa., 1994), 10–12.

40. *Annals of Congress*, 1st Cong., 1st sess., 1:417 (June 1, 1789); 1st Cong., 2d sess., 1:1105–1106 (Feb. 1, 1790). On Smith, see George C. Rogers, Jr., *Evolution of a Federalist: William Loughton Smith of Charleston (1758–1812)* (Columbia, S.C., 1962).

41. Robert A. Rutland, ed., *The Papers of George Mason*, 3 vols. (Chapel Hill, N.C., 1970), 3:989–990. See Joseph J. Persky, *The Burden of Dependency: Colonial Themes in Southern Economic Thought* (Baltimore, 1992), 28–33.

42. Harrison Gray Otis to Sally Otis, July 5, 1792, Harrison Gray Otis Papers, Loose Manuscripts, 1691–1792, MHS; Seth Johnson to Andrew Craigie, Aug. 11, 14, and 29, 1791, Craigie Papers, box 6, folder 3; Thomas Jefferson to Thomas Mann Randolph, Jr., Mar. 16, 1792, in *TJP*, 23:287; Alexander Macomb to William Constable, June 6, 1792, Constable-Pierrepont Collection, NYPL; *Annals of Congress*, 2d Cong., 1st sess., 3:166 (Nov. 9, 1791).

43. Benjamin Rush, *The Autobiography of Benjamin Rush: His "Travels through Life" together with His Commonplace Book for 1789–1813*, ed. George W. Corner (Princeton, N.J., 1948), 218 (Apr. 18, 1792), 219 (Apr. 25, 1792); Henrietta Maria Colden to John Laurance, Apr. 11, 1792, John Laurance Papers, NYHS.

44. See Harry Remsen to Thomas Jefferson, Apr. 23, 1792, in *TJP*, 23:447–448; Seth Johnson to Andrew Craigie, Mar. 25, 1792, Craigie Papers, box 6, folder 4; Rush, *Autobiography*, 217 (Mar. 30, 1792); Thomas Jones, *History of New York during the Revolutionary War*, ed. Edward Floyd de Lancey, 2 vols. (New York, 1879), 2:589.

45. Seth Johnson to Andrew Craigie, Mar. 25, 1792, Craigie Papers, box 6, folder 4; Jones, *History of New York*, 2:589; Philip H. Livingston to Walter Livingston, Apr. 20, 1792, Robert R. Livingston Papers, Livingston Family Correspondence, 1743–1886, ser. 1, NYHS. The threat of violence was real enough that when a false report reached Philadelphia that the militia had fired on and killed several of the rioters in New York, Thomas Jefferson thought the rumor credible because "[n]othing was wanting to fill up the criminality of this paper system, but to shed the blood of those whom it had cheated of their substance." Jefferson to Harry Remsen, Apr. 14, 1792, in *TJP*, 23:426.

46. Henrietta Maria Colden to John Laurance, Apr. 11, 1792, Laurance Papers; Jefferson to Thomas Mann Randolph, Jr., Apr. 19, 1792, in *TJP*, 23:436; Rush, *Autobiography*, 219 (Apr. 18, 1792); Richard Platt to Winthrop Sargent, Mar. 25, 1792, Winthrop Sargent Papers, MHS; Thomas Randall to Henry Knox, Mar. 18, 1792, Henry Knox Papers, MHS; Seth Johnson to Andrew Craigie, Apr. 18, 1792, Craigie Papers, box 6, folder 4.

47. Samuel Blodget, Jr., to Thomas Jefferson, Apr. 20, 1792, in *TJP*, 23:437; John Pintard to John Templeman, July 9, 1792, John Pintard Papers, box 11, folder 2, NYHS.

48. Philip Key to Matthew Blair, Mar. 28, 1792, Misc. Key, NYHS; Seth Johnson to Andrew Craigie, Apr. 11, 1792, Craigie Papers, box 6, folder 4; *Boston Gazette*, Apr. 23, 1792. The abandoned copper mines in Simsbury, Connecticut, were used as a prison from 1773 to 1827. See Richard H. Phelps, *Newgate of Connecticut: A History of the Prison, Its Insurrections, Massacres, &c., Imprisonment of the Tories, in the Revolution* (Hartford, Conn., 1844).

49. William Duer to Walter Livingston, Apr. 14, 1792, Robert R. Livingston Papers, Livingston Family Correspondence; Seth Johnson to Andrew Craigie, Apr. 18, 1792, Craigie Papers, box 6, folder 4; Alexander Macomb to William Constable, Mar. 28 and June 6, 1792, Constable-Pierrepont Collection; Walter Livingston to Philip H. Livingston, Apr. 17, 1792, Robert R. Livingston Papers, ser. 6, vols. 1761–1885; Livingston to Duer, May 2, 1792, ibid.; Livingston to William S. Smith, Feb. 13, 1793, ibid.

50. *Annals of Congress*, 2d Cong., 2d sess., 3:708 (Nov. 21, 1792), 618 (Dec. 3, 1792), 741 (Dec. 10, 1792). See Rogers, *Evolution of a Federalist*, 252. When the bill died is unclear. The last reference to it is in a letter to Theodore Sedgwick from a constituent in Northampton, Massachusetts, inquiring "What has become of the Bankrupt Bill? I feel very anxious, on account of a number of valuable friends, to have that pass." Samuel Henshaw to Sedgwick, Jan. 23, 1793, Theodore Sedgwick (Sedgwick I) Papers, box 2, folder 7, no. 102, MHS. No reply survives.

51. "Extempore thoughts and doubts on very superficially running over the bankruptcy bill," [ca. Dec. 10, 1792], in *TJP*, 24:722–723. Jefferson sent the "loose thoughts" to James Madison. See Jefferson to Madison, [ca. Dec. 10, 1792], in ibid., 24:717.

52. See Thomas Jefferson to David Humphreys, Apr. 9, 1792, in ibid., 23:387.

53. For a detailed analysis of Otis's argument, see M. H. Smith, *The Writs of Assistance Case* (Berkeley, Calif., 1978).

54. Thomas Jefferson to Thomas Mann Randolph, Jr., Dec. 21, 1792, in *TJP*, 24:775; Jefferson to John Francis Mercer, Dec. 19, 1792, in ibid., 24:757.

55. See *Annals of Congress*, 3d Cong., 1st sess., 4:142 (Dec. 13, 1793), 256 (Jan. 22, 1794); ibid., 3d Cong., 2d sess., 4:970 (Dec. 9, 1794); ibid., 4th Cong., 1st sess., 5:149 (Dec. 16, 1795), 240 (Jan. 13, 1796); ibid., 4th Cong., 2d sess., 6:1739–1740 (Dec. 29, 1796).

56. John Pintard, Diary, Newark, Oct. 2, 1793, Pintard Papers, box 2; [James Sullivan], *The Path to Riches: An Inquiry into the Origin and Use of Money, and into the Principles of Stocks and Banks* (Boston, 1792), 10; Hugh Henry Brackenridge, *Modern*

Chivalry: containing the Adventures of a Captain, and Teague O'Regan, his Servant (Philadelphia, 1815 [originally published in installments, 1792–1815]); Philip Freneau, "The Projectors," in *Poems Written between the Years 1768 and 1794* (Monmouth, N.J., 1795); Freneau, "Plan for a Nobility in the United States," *National Gazette* (Philadelphia), May 7, 1792; *Columbian Herald* (Charleston, S.C.), July 25, 1793; "A Sufferer by Swindlers," *Columbian Gazetteer* (New York), Feb. 8, 1794. For a good account of newspaper attacks on speculation and speculators in the 1790s, see Donald H. Stewart, *The Opposition Press of the Federalist Period* (Albany, N.Y., 1969), 33–70.

57. Doerflinger, *A Vigorous Spirit of Enterprise*, 316. Doerflinger also offers the best brief overview of the forces that drove land speculation, in ibid., 314–329.

58. See Robert Morris to James Greenleaf, Dec. 23, 1794, Papers of Robert Morris, Private Letterbooks, 1794–1798 (3 vols.), 1:4, LC; Morris to Greenleaf, Jan. 6, 1795, ibid., 1:13; Morris to John Swanwick, Jan. 12, 1795, ibid., 1:19; Morris to Greenleaf, Feb. 23, 1795, ibid., 1:46–47.

59. This is a drastic simplification of extraordinarily complex investments, the details of which are, fortunately, not relevant here. The clearest account of the Federal City speculation is in Robert D. Arbuckle, *Pennsylvania Speculator and Patriot: The Entrepreneurial John Nicholson, 1757–1800* (University Park, Pa., 1975), 114–138, and of the North American Land Company in ibid., 165–184, and in Shaw Livermore, *Early American Land Companies: Their Influence on Corporate Development* (Cambridge, Mass., 1939), 162–171. Charles Royster lucidly treats both in *The Fabulous History of the Dismal Swamp Company: A Story of George Washington's Times* (New York, 1999), 356–360, 372–377, 382–390. For a recent analysis of the founding of Washington, see C. M. Harris, "Washington's Gamble, L'Enfant's Dream: Politics, Design, and the Founding of the National Capital," *WMQ*, 3d ser., 56 (1999): 526–564. See also Bob Arnebeck, *Through a Fiery Trial: Building Washington, 1790–1800* (Lanham, Md., 1991); Stanley Elkins and Eric McKitrick, *The Age of Federalism* (New York, 1993), 169–181. An older, uncritical treatment is Allen C. Clark, *Greenleaf and Law in the Federal City* (Washington, D.C., 1901). Greenleaf's persuasiveness was such that even William Duer invested—and lost—as much as $80,000 with him in a failed attempt to speculate his way out of debtors' prison and back to solvency. See Duer to Henry Knox, Feb. 17, 1797, Knox Papers.

60. Robert Morris to James Chalmers, Mar. 17, 1795, Private Letterbooks, 1:92–94; Morris to Willem and Jan Willink, Mar. 16, 1795, ibid., 1:82–90; Morris to James Pasley, Mar. 18, 1795, ibid., 1:99–102; Morris to Christian Gottlieb Frege, May 13, 1795, ibid., 1:256–258.

61. Freeman's auction house in Philadelphia advertised that "Notes, Bills, Drafts and Bonds of Messrs MORRIS & NICHOLSON, or either of them will be taken in payment at their current value." *Aurora*, Apr. 26, 1797.

62. See the hundreds of protest notes in Sequestered John Nicholson Papers, MG96, Legal Papers, boxes 4–5, PHMC.

63. A. C. Duplaine to J. B. C. Lucas, Feb. 18, 1794, John B. C. Lucas Papers, box 1, MoHS ("Il semble que les hommes et les élémens se soient conjures contre notre malheureuse ville . . . [L]es banqueroutes se multiplient.").

64. See Rush, *Autobiography*, 236–237 (December 1796); Robert Morris to John Nicholson, Dec. 8, 1796, Private Letterbooks, 2:184–186; Morris to James Carey, Dec. 16, 1796, ibid., 2:199–200; Morris to William Cranch, Dec. 23, 1796, ibid., 2:208. For the rumor of Morris's imprisonment, see Seth Johnson to Andrew Craigie, Dec. 15, 1796, Craigie Papers, box 7, folder 3. For an excellent brief account of one man's reckless obsession with land speculation, see Jacob E. Cooke, *Tench Coxe and the Early Republic* (Chapel Hill, N.C., 1978), 311–333.

65. Theodore Sedgwick to Ephraim Williams, Dec. 24 1796, Theodore Sedgwick (Sedgwick III) Papers, box 2, folder 6, MHS; Sedgwick to Henry Van Schaack, Dec. 29, 1796, ibid.; *Annals of Congress*, 4th Cong., 2d sess., 6:1739–1740 (Dec. 29, 1796); Robert Morris to John Nicholson, Jan. 28, 1797, Private Letterbooks, 2:249.

66. Thomas Jefferson to James Madison, Jan. 3, 1798, in Paul Leicester Ford, ed., *The Writings of Thomas Jefferson*, 10 vols. (New York, 1892–1899), 7:188; Robert Morris to John Nicholson, Jan. 31, 1798, Private Letterbooks, 3:233–234; William B. Wood, *Personal Recollections of the Stage, Embracing Notices of Actors, Authors, and Auditors, during a Period of Forty Years* (Philadelphia, 1855), 39–40; Theodore Sedgwick to Rufus King, Apr. 9, May 1, and July 1, 1798, Copies of Letters from Theodore Sedgwick to Rufus King, 1787–1802, Theodore Sedgwick (Sedgwick II) Papers, box 9, vol. 10, MHS. For Wilson's end, see Charles Page Smith, *James Wilson: Founding Father, 1742–1798* (Chapel Hill, N.C., 1956), 376–388. For Nicholson's descent into Prune Street, see Arbuckle, *Pennsylvania Speculator and Patriot*, 185–201.

67. *Aurora*, Jan. 7, Mar. 17, May 1, and Aug. 17, 1797. For Washington's land speculations, see Royster, *Fabulous History of the Dismal Swamp Company*.

68. *Annals of Congress*, 5th Cong., 2d sess., 7:643–644 (Nov. 27, 1797), 692 (Dec. 8, 1797), 786–788 (Jan. 1, 1798).

69. John Pintard, Reading Diary in Newark Prison, 221 (July 4, 1798), Pintard Papers, box 2; *Annals of Congress*, 5th Cong., 2d sess., 7:796–797 (Jan. 3, 1798).

70. *Gazette of the United States*, Feb. 8, 1798; "To the Commercial World, the

Framers of our Laws, and the Creditors of Insolvent Debtors," ibid., Jan. 18, 1798; Pintard, Reading Diary, 221 (July 4, 1798), Pintard Papers, box 2.

71. Arthur Bryan to George Bryan, Apr. 9, 1788, Bryan Papers, box 3, folder 2; Drew R. McCoy, *The Elusive Republic: Political Economy in Jeffersonian America* (Chapel Hill, N.C., 1980), 178.

72. For the early discussions, see *Annals of Congress*, 5th Cong., 3d sess., 9:2426 (Dec. 11, 1798), 2441–2442 (Dec. 14, 1798), 2465–2469 (Dec. 20, 1798), 2489–2490 (Dec. 26, 1798), 2552–2553 (Jan. 1, 1799), 2556 (Jan. 2, 1799), 2577–2582 (Jan. 8, 1799), 2582–2583 (Jan. 9, 1799). The procedural delays led John W. Fenno to complain, as usual, of a Jacobin plot to subvert the civil order. There could be, he wrote, "but one reason for the opposition to the Bankrupt Law, which is, to make as many desperate men as possible, throughout the United States; who, seeing no end to their calamities, may effect a subversion of all order both civil and religious;—then *Huzza for Liberty and Equality, à la François, à la Guillotine.*" "A Card," *Gazette of the United States*, Dec. 22, 1798.

73. Kenneth R. Bowling and Helen E. Veit, eds., *The Diary of William Maclay and Other Notes on Senate Debates* (Baltimore, 1988), 225 (Mar. 22, 1790); John Pintard to Elisha Boudinot, Apr. 6, 1797, Bayard-Boudinot-Pintard Papers, NYHS; *Aurora*, Apr. 16, 1797; "The Economist," *Gazette of the United States*, Feb. 16, 1798.

74. *Annals of Congress*, 5th Cong., 3d sess., 9:2656–2658 (Jan. 15, 1799).

75. Ibid., 9:2649–2651, 2654 (Jan. 14, 1799). Ironically, Gallatin here echoed a common refrain of land speculators, who often complained that they were sitting on more than enough wealth to pay their debts, if only they could reach it. Gallatin also ignored the extent to which bank credit rested on mortgages of land as well as pledges of stock.

76. *Annals of Congress*, 5th Cong., 3d sess., 9:2666–2667 (Jan. 15, 1799). It is not clear whether anyone was listening to Gordon's jab. Two days later the *Aurora* noted the apparent inattentiveness of the members: "While Mr. Gordon was *hammering away* on Tuesday last at the Bankrupt Bill, and *see-sawing* from foot to foot, with his hand alternately in his *fob* and under his nose, . . . the members were marching about the house as if it had been adjourned." *Aurora*, Jan. 17, 1799.

77. *Annals of Congress*, 5th Cong., 3d sess., 9:2669–2670 (Jan. 15, 1799).

78. Ibid., 9:2658–2659, 2669 (Jan. 15, 1799).

79. Ibid., 9:2660, 2675 (Jan. 15, 1799).

80. For the failures of Otis's father and uncle, see Samuel Eliot Morison, *The Life and Letters of Harrison Gray Otis, Federalist, 1765–1848*, 2 vols. (Boston, 1913), 1:27–28.

On Otis and Pintard, see Harrison Gray Otis to John Pintard, Mar. 21, 1792, and Otis to Nathaniel Prince and John Atkinson, Mar. 21, 1792, Otis Letterbook, 1788–1807, at 125–126. On friends in financial distress, see Otis to Sally Otis, Dec. 3, 18, 26, 30, 1797, Jan. 3, 7, Feb. 14, Mar. 14, 23, 1798, Harrison Gray Otis Papers, Loose Manuscripts, 1793–1799. The description of Morris's arrest is in Otis to Sally Otis, Feb. 16, 1798, ibid.

81. *Annals of Congress*, 5th Cong., 3d sess., 9:2650–2651, 2654 (Jan. 14, 1799), 2667–2668 (Jan. 15, 1799). On Gallatin's land speculations, see Raymond Walters, Jr., *Albert Gallatin: Jeffersonian Financier and Diplomat* (New York, 1957), 16–21, 47–48, 174, 220–221. When Robert Morris went to jail in 1798, he still owed Gallatin $3,000 for land he had bought from him four years earlier. See ibid., 63, 136.

82. *Annals of Congress*, 5th Cong., 3d sess., 9:2663, 2669 (Jan. 15, 1799).

83. See *Annals of Congress*, 5th Cong., 3d sess., 9:2668 (Jan. 15, 1799); Dwight Foster, Journal, Jan. 15, 1799, Foster Family Papers, AAS. For McClenachan's indiscretions, see Robert Morris to John Nicholson, Dec. 11, 1796, Private Letterbooks, 2:188; *The Minerva, & Mercantile Evening Advertiser* (New York), Jan. 2, 1797 (publishing a caution from a committee of McClenachan's creditors); *Gazette of the United States*, Mar. 20, 1799. On Livingston, see *Aurora*, Feb. 2, 1797; Peter Stephen DuPonceau to Richard Riker, Feb. 27, 1800, Letterbooks, 1797–1801, at 144, DuPonceau Papers. DuPonceau, a rising young French émigré lawyer in Philadelphia, once remarked somewhat acidly of Livingston, who had failed to repay a loan, that "were I in his place I would undoubtedly sell my last pair of breeches to pay such a debt . . . , but tho' he calls himself a *Democrat*, I suppose he would not like to be a *Sans culotte*." DuPonceau to Richard Riker, Aug. 10, 1799, ibid., 93. The vote is at *Annals of Congress*, 9:2676–2677 (Jan. 15, 1799). Harper lamented the loss to his constituents but assured them that the bill was "now in such a state as to be brought forward at next session with good prospects of success." Robert Goodloe Harper, Circular Letter, Mar. 20, 1799, in Noble E. Cunningham, Jr., ed., *Circular Letters of Congressmen to Their Constituents, 1789–1829*, 3 vols. (Chapel Hill, N.C., 1978), 1:167. For another account of Bayard's role, see Morton Borden, *The Federalism of James A. Bayard* (New York, 1955), 62–72.

84. *Annals of Congress*, 6th Cong., 1st sess., 10:247 (Jan. 6, 1800); Pintard, Journal of Studies, 1797–1804, Jan. 10–11, 1800, Pintard Papers, box 2; Theodore Sedgwick to Henry Van Schaack, Jan. 15, 1800, Sedgwick III Papers, box 3, folder 1; John Dawson to James Madison, Mar. 30, 1800, Madison Papers, LC. Bayard, Harper, Chauncey Goodrich, Samuel Sewall, and John Marshall constituted the two committees. See Herbert A. Johnson, Charles T. Cullen, Charles F. Hobson et al., eds., *The*

Papers of John Marshall, 10 vols. (Chapel Hill, N.C., 1974–), 4:34. The judiciary bill, which reorganized and expanded the federal judiciary, was deferred to the next session, where it became the famous Judiciary Act of 1801. See Kathryn Turner, "Federalist Policy and the Judiciary Act of 1801," *WMQ*, 3d ser., 22 (1965): 3–32.

85. Theodore Sedgwick to Rufus King, Mar. 20, Nov. 15, 1799, Feb. 11, 1800, Copies of Letters from Theodore Sedgwick to Rufus King, Sedgwick II Papers, box 9, vol. 10; Sedgwick to Henry Van Schaack, Feb. 9, 1800, Sedgwick III Papers, box 3, folder 1. The printed version of Sedgwick's letters to King has "acceptable" for "accessible." See Charles R. King, ed., *The Life and Correspondence of Rufus King, Comprising His Letters, Private and Official, His Public Documents and His Speeches*, 6 vols. (New York, 1894–1900), 3:147.

86. James A. Bayard to Richard Bassett, Feb. 1, 1800, Bayard Family Papers, LC. The printed version has "negotiate" for "ingratiate." See Elizabeth Donnan, ed., *Papers of James A. Bayard, 1796–1815*, in *Annual Report of the American Historical Association for the Year 1913*, 2 vols. (Washington, D.C., 1915), 2:95.

87. Theodore Sedgwick to Rufus King, Feb. 6, 1800, Copies of Letters from Theodore Sedgwick to Rufus King, Sedgwick II Papers, box 9, vol. 10. Sedgwick proudly adopted the label "ultra federalist," which originated among his friends. See Sedgwick to Henry Van Schaack, Jan. 15, 1800, Sedgwick III Papers, box 3, folder 1. On Sedgwick generally, see Richard E. Welch, Jr., *Theodore Sedgwick, Federalist: A Political Portrait* (Middletown, Conn., 1965).

88. "A True Friend," *Virginia Independent Chronicle* (Richmond), Nov. 14, 1787, in *DHRC*, 8:160–61; *Annals of Congress*, 5th Cong., 3d sess., 9:2660–2661, 2676 (Jan. 15, 1799).

89. Theodore Sedgwick to Rufus King, Feb. 6 and May 11, 1800, Copies of Letters from Theodore Sedgwick to Rufus King, Sedgwick II Papers, box 9, vol. 10.

90. *Annals of Congress*, 6th Cong., 1st sess., 10:110–111 (Mar. 17, 1800), 126 (Mar. 28, 1800), 534 (Feb. 21, 1800); *Gazette of the United States*, Feb. 25, 1800; Pintard, Journal of Studies, Jan. 22, Feb. 3, 14, 26, 1800, Pintard Papers, box 2. Two Republicans, Edward Livingston of New York and Samuel Smith of Maryland, voted for the bill. Pintard had long known that a bankruptcy law would be "too irritable a measure for the Southern States." Pintard to Elisha Boudinot, Apr. 6, 1797, Bayard-Boudinot-Pintard Papers.

91. Pintard, Journal of Studies, Apr. 1, 1800, Pintard Papers, box 2; *Forlorn Hope* (New York), Mar. 24, Apr. 7, and Apr. 26, 1800. The text took up three-and-a-half pages of the four-page newspaper.

92. *Aurora*, Mar. 18 and Mar. 29, 1800; Anthony New, Circular Letter, Apr. 8, 1800, in Cunningham, ed., *Circular Letters*, 1:196; Thomas T. Davis, Circular Letter, Mar. 29, 1800, in ibid., 1:184; John Fowler, Circular Letter, May 15, 1800, in ibid., 1:209.

93. Theodore Sedgwick to Rufus King, May 11, 1800, Copies of Letters from Theodore Sedgwick to Rufus King, Sedgwick II Papers, box 9, vol. 10; Caleb Strong to Benjamin Goodhue, Mar. 4, 1800, Foster Family Papers, box 34, folder 1; Strong to Sedgwick, Mar. 8, 1800, Sedgwick I Papers, box 4, folder 6.

7. THE FACES OF BANKRUPTCY

1. See "Thomas Dawes, Jr.," BA1800-MA, Bankruptcy Case Files, box 13. The two bankruptcy volumes in Dawes's library presumably were Thomas Davies, *The Law relating to Bankrupts* (London, 1744), and Thomas Goodinge, *The Law against Bankrupts, or, A Treatise wherein the Statutes against Bankrupts Are Explained*, 3d rev. ed. (London, 1719). Dawes left the state supreme court in 1803 and served as a Boston Municipal Court judge for twenty years thereafter. One suspects that his voluntary demotion to the less prestigious court was attractive for the opportunity to collect fees. Fifteen years before his discharge, Dawes had touted the advantages of uniform national legislation in a Fourth of July oration delivered while the Constitutional Convention sat in Philadelphia—it "will render property secure, and convince us that the payment of debts is our truest policy and highest honour." He may have been referring to public debts, but the irony, even if only small, remains. Thomas Dawes, Jr., *An Oration, Delivered July 4, 1787, at the Request of the Inhabitants of the Town of Boston, in Celebration of the Anniversary of American Independence* (Boston, 1787), 18.

2. "An Act to establish an uniform system of Bankruptcy throughout the United States," 2 Stat. ch. 19, §§1–2, in *The Public Statutes at Large of the United States of America, from the Organization of the Government in 1789, to March 3, 1845* (Boston, 1845), 2:19–36.

3. See Thomas Cooper, *The Bankrupt Law of America, compared with the Bankrupt Law of England* (Philadelphia, 1801), 1–36. For a brief description of English bankruptcy law in the eighteenth century, see Julian Hoppit, *Risk and Failure in English Business, 1700–1800* (Cambridge, England, 1987), 35–37.

4. See M. S. Servian, "Eighteenth-Century Bankruptcy Law: From Crime to Process" (Ph.D. diss., University of Kent at Canterbury, 1985), 151–178.

5. Robert Fields, *A Practical Treatise upon the Bankrupt Law of the United States* (Boston, 1800), 2; Cooper, *The Bankrupt Law of America*, viii.

6. Opinions, Questions, and Answers on the Bankruptcy Act, May 27 and 31, 1800, in Mary-Jo Kline, ed., *The Papers of Aaron Burr, 1736–1836* (microfilm ed., 1977), ser. 1, reel 4, frames 656–683.

7. For example, only twelve different men were appointed to fill 708 of the 802 available positions on the 271 commissions issued in Massachusetts for which we have the names of the commissioners (three commissioners per commission, except for eleven commissions to which only two commissioners were appointed). Thirty other men served as commissioners a total of 94 times—all for bankrupt debtors who lived far from Boston. Thomas Dawes, Jr., sat on 120 commissions, William Tudor and Nathan Goodale on 98, Joseph Blake on 83, Thomas Edwards on 81, George Richards Minot on 60. The same three-man panel tended to comprise successively appointed commissions—which meant that they were conducting many commissions simultaneously—until one died or, perhaps, lost interest, to be succeeded by someone who continued serving on successive commissions with his predecessor's former colleagues. Bankruptcy proceedings in Boston, the commercial hub of the state which produced nearly 60 percent of the bankrupt debtors, were thus supervised by an essentially permanent panel of increasingly experienced commissioners. The same pattern prevailed in New York, where sixteen men—each of whom almost always sat with the same two co-commissioners—filled 245 of the 264 positions available on the 88 commissions for which we have the commissioners' names, and in Pennsylvania, where eleven prominent Philadelphians filled all 528 seats on the 176 commissions for which we have the names. Congress unintentionally ratified this pattern in April 1802, when, as a consequence of repealing the Judiciary Act of 1801, it ordered district judges to direct bankruptcy commissions to commissioners appointed by the president. John Quincy Adams, who had just started receiving commissions under the old system, was not appointed under the new one—an oversight or insult that became a bone of contention between his mother and Thomas Jefferson. See Morris Weisman, "Of Jefferson and Adams and a Commissioner in Bankruptcy," *Commercial Law Journal*, 48 (1943): 248–251. Figures compiled from BA1800-MA; BA1800-NY; BA1800-PA. Unless otherwise noted, these and BA1800-CT are the sources for all numbers in the text and notes.

8. Of the 241 discharges recorded in Massachusetts, 158 (66 percent) were issued less than five months after the date of the commission—that is, before the earliest first dividend date permitted by the statute. In Pennsylvania and Connecticut, 72 percent were (130 of 180 and 47 of 65, respectively), and in New York, 81 percent (71

of 88). Technically, it was the commissioners who ordered the dividend, but they did so on the basis of the accounts submitted by the assignees.

9. Charles Warren alone recognized the voluntary potential of the Act, even as he largely dismissed the Act itself as derivative. However, he assumed without looking at the records that collusive or cooperative filings were perforce fraudulent or unscrupulous. See Warren, *Bankruptcy in United States History* (Cambridge, Mass., 1935), 19–20.

10. Thomas Clark to Nathan Frazier, Nov. 30, 1801, in "Thomas Clark," BA1800-MA, Bankruptcy Case Files, box 11; Memorandum, May 1801, in "John J. White," BA1800-CT, Bankruptcy Case Files, box 11.

11. See "Thomas Dawes, Jr.," BA1800-MA, Bankruptcy Case Files, box 13; "Records of meetings of the Suffolk County (Mass.) Bar, 1770–1805," in *Proceedings of the Massachusetts Historical Society* (Boston, 1882), 19:153–154; Mary Walton Ferris, comp., *Dawes-Gates Ancestral Lines: A Memorial Volume Containing the American Ancestry of Rufus R. Dawes* (Milwaukee, Wis., 1943), 3.

12. See "William Allis," BA1800-MA, Bankruptcy Case Files, box 1.

13. See "Louis Devotion," ibid., box 14; "Joshua Snow," ibid., box 37.

14. See "Ebenezer Holbrook," ibid., box 20.

15. See "Benjamin Beale, Jr.," ibid., box 5; "Shearjashub Bourne, Jr.," ibid., box 7; "William Lang, Jr.," ibid., box 25; "John Read, Jr.," ibid., box 34. Beale *fils* was no stranger to the drill—five weeks earlier he had taken out a commission of bankruptcy against two other merchants, one of whom may have been a relative. See "Asahel Bigelow and Robert Beale," ibid., box 6.

16. See Opinions, Questions, and Answers on the Bankruptcy Act, in Kline, ed., *Papers of Aaron Burr*, ser. 1, reel 4, frames 656–662; "Memorandum for Mr. [Nicholas] Low respecting Mr. [Jacob] Halletts bankruptcy," [Oct. 18, 1800], Robert Troup Papers, box 2, folder 1, NYPL; "Mr. Troup's account with Mr. Low," Dec. 30, 1801, ibid.; "Draft opinion on Case of Mr. [Jacob] Cuyler," May 11, 1802, Richard Harison Papers, box 4, NYHS. Two days after receiving Troup's advice, Low petitioned for a commission of bankruptcy against Hallett. See Certificates of discharge, October 28, 1800–March 29, 1809, at 134–135, BA1800-NY, reel 11. The second commission empaneled in New York was appointed for William McCready on June 30, 1800. See "William McCready," ibid., reel 5. A commission issued against Cuyler six months after Harison's advice. His discharge proceeded smoothly. See "Jacob Cuyler," ibid., reel 2.

17. *Forlorn Hope* (New York), Apr. 7, 1800.

18. See John Pintard, Journal of Studies, 1797–1804, Jan. 30, June 30, and Aug. 6, 1798, John Pintard Papers, box 2, NYHS; Reading Diary in Newark Prison, 84, 90, 108, 116 (Mar. 31, Apr. 14, May 21, 30, 1798), ibid.; Pintard to Elisha Boudinot, May 7, 1798, Bayard-Boudinot-Pintard Papers, NYHS.

19. Except where otherwise noted, this and the following paragraphs rest on "John Pintard," BA1800-NY, reel 6, and on Pintard's entries in his Journal of Studies (1797–1804), his Diary (July 19–Aug. 25, 1800), and his Journal (Aug. 25–Sept. 25, 1800) for the months April through September. The diary and journals are in the Pintard Papers—the first two in box 2, the third in box 12. The treatise was William Cooke, *The Bankrupt Laws*, in two volumes. Pintard did not record which edition he read, but the most recent was the fourth (London, 1799).

20. Livingston was also one of Pintard's creditors—$4,666 on a note Isaac Whippo had given Willian Duer in February 1792, endorsed by both Duer and Pintard. Livingston had given up on the debt years earlier with no apparent rancor, but he proved it in the bankruptcy proceedings against Pintard anyway so he could vote for Pintard's discharge.

21. See "John Blagge," BA1800-NY, reel 1. A new commission to the same three commissioners eventually issued against Blagge, who received a discharge in January 1801. However, the interruption gave one creditor the opportunity to imprison him, where he remained until released by the commissioners. One of the commissioners, Caleb S. Riggs, was the attorney for another of Blagge's creditors, in which capacity he informed the commissioners—himself included—that his client would not consent to a discharge. Riggs did not recuse himself nor did he join his co-commissioners in declaring Blagge a bankrupt or in signing the certificate of conformity for Blagge's discharge.

22. The debtor was released after a week when his wife came forward and swore that she had buried the silver, which she considered hers, without her husband's knowledge. See "William McCready," BA1800-NY, reel 5.

23. The three were Richard Platt, who was petitioned into bankruptcy twelve days after Pintard received his discharge, and Benjamin Seixas and John Halsey, against whom commissions issued one and two years later, respectively.

24. See "Joseph Callender," BA1800-MA, Bankruptcy Case Files, box 8; "Thomas Dennie," ibid., box 14; "Gurdon Jason Miller," BA1800-CT, Bankruptcy Case Files, box 7.

25. See [William Meredith] to [Alexander J. Dallas], May 4, 1802, and reply, May 5, 1802, in William Meredith, Court Notes, 1800–1815, Meredith Family Papers,

HSP; "Joseph Bacon," BA1800-MA, Bankruptcy Case Files, box 3; "William Ladd," ibid., box 25; "Zadock Pomeroy," ibid., box 32. Ironically, Bacon had petitioned another, much smaller trader into bankruptcy just three days before he closed his own business. See "John Benson," ibid., box 6. For examples of arbitrated claims, see "John Chapman," BA1800-NY, reel 2; "Daniel R. Durning," ibid., reel 3; "Joseph Lyon," ibid., reel 5; "Nathaniel Olcott," ibid., reel 6.

26. See "Thomas Walter," BA1800-MA, Bankruptcy Case Files, box 42. The median time from commission to discharge in Massachusetts was 109 days, with one-third of the discharges (81 of 241) taking 90 days or less. Proceedings in Pennsylvania moved at a similar pace, with a median time from commission to discharge of 108 days and 31 percent of the discharges (55 of 180) taking 90 days or less. By comparison, New York was a model of efficiency—the median was a scant 71 days, with 72 percent of the discharges (63 of 88) taking 90 days or less. Connecticut lay in between—a median of 98 days, with 43 percent of the discharges (28 of 65) taking 90 days or less.

27. See "Benjamin Alley," ibid., box 1; Abner Alley and James Alley v. Benjamin Alley, September 1801, Records of the United States District Court for Massachusetts, Case Papers, box 13, Record Group 21, National Archives—Northeast Region (Boston), Waltham, Mass. Two months later, one of the jurors, Henry Chapman, was among the creditors who accused Thomas Walter of making a fraudulent conveyance. A second juror, John Soley, was himself petitioned into bankruptcy six months afterward and endured a protracted process that took two years to negotiate a discharge.

28. The numbers for Massachusetts were 241 discharges in 290 commissions, with 174 of the 241 (72 percent) producing discharges within six months, and 27 of 241 (11 percent) taking a year or more. Pennsylvania was less stringent—one in nine commissions (22 of 202) failed to produce a discharge, while 83 percent of the ones that did (150 of 180) did so within six months, and only eight (4 percent) took a year or more. New York and Connecticut were more severe. Fully one-third of the commissions in New York (43 of 131) did not result in a discharge, although 82 percent of those that did (72 of 88) did so within six months, and only five (6 percent) took a year or more. In Connecticut nearly one-fourth of the commissions (23 of 100) failed to produce a discharge; 77 percent of the ones that did for which dates are known (50 of 65—there were 77 discharges in all, but 12 were in proceedings on undated commissions) did so within six months, but 14 percent (9 of 65) took a year or more. These figures should be treated as approximations and are offered only as broad descriptions. The bankruptcy records for the various states, though voluminous, are not

necessarily complete. The absence of a discharge in a file or a discharge volume may not mean that there was none. However, enough proceedings clearly concluded without releasing the debtor to be able to say that, although a bankrupt debtor was likely to win a discharge, it was by no means certain that he would. It is also clear that creditors often withheld their consent for months and sometimes years.

29. Wolcott reprimanded the commissioners for defects as large as omitting supporting documentation and as small as using numbers rather than words to state the amount of the claims, reminding them that it was "important that the proceedings under all Commissions of Bankruptcy, should as soon as practicable be governed by established forms." He granted the discharge when the commissioners resubmitted a corrected file. See Oliver Wolcott to Joseph Darling, Naphtali Daggett, and Elihu Monson, Aug. 21, 1801, in "Ezra Kimberly," BA1800-CT, Bankruptcy Case Files, box 6.

30. For example, see "Joseph Donaldson, Jr.," BA1800-PA, reel 18; "John Hopkins," ibid.; "John Hyde," ibid., reel 21; "Lot Merkel," ibid., reel 20; "Thomas Mifflin," ibid., reel 15; Stephen Sayre," ibid., reel 22; "William Sterrett," ibid., reel 18; "Abijah Peck," BA1800-CT, Bankruptcy Case Files, box 8; "Edmund Bartlett, Jr.," BA1800-MA, Bankruptcy Case Files, box 4; "Elihu Bates and Isaac Walker," ibid. The commissioners also examined each debt submitted by creditors and rejected or reduced those not proved to their satisfaction.

31. See "Peter Blight," BA1800-PA, reels 4–5. Blight's creditors eventually received twenty-five cents on the dollar in six dividends spread across thirty-three years, the last one in 1839. Four of the dividends were paid long after Blight himself was dead.

32. See "Robert Crommelin and John Betts," BA1800-NY, reel 2.

33. See "John Palmer," BA1800-PA, reel 16. For an example of arbitration between assignees, see "Nathan Adams," BA1800-MA, Bankruptcy Case Files, box 1. The one instance of the assignees of one bankrupt petitioning another debtor into bankruptcy is "Peter H. Colt," BA1800-CT, Bankruptcy Case Files, box 3.

34. See "Jabez Perkins," BA1800-CT, Bankruptcy Case Files, box 8; "Jacob Huistis," BA1800-NY, reel 3; "An abstract of the property of C. Sands," n.d., ibid., reel 8; "Assignee's exhibit of the Estate and Effects of Thomas Clark," July 5, 1802, in "Thomas Clark," BA1800-MA, Bankruptcy Case Files, box 11; "Joshua Blanchard," ibid., box 7.

35. Pintard, Diary (July 19–Aug. 25, 1800), July 20, 1800, Pintard Papers, box 2. See "Richard Yates," BA1800-NY, reel 11; "Carlisle Pollock," ibid., reel 6; "George Pollock," ibid.

36. See "John Field, Jr.," BA1800-PA, reel 14; "John Field, Sr.," ibid., reel 23; "John Miller, Jr.," ibid., reel 21; "John Miller, Sr.," ibid., reel 23; "Thomas Murgatroyd & Sons [Samuel and Daniel Murgatroyd]," ibid., reel 12; "Richard Tittermary & Son [Robert Tittermary]," ibid., reel 14; "Nicholas Coverly, Sr.," BA1800-MA, Bankruptcy Case Files, box 12; "Nicholas Coverly, Jr.," ibid.; "George Keith, Sr.," ibid., box 24; "George Keith, Jr.," ibid.

37. See "Jonas Prentice, Jr.," BA1800-NY, reel 7; "Jonas Prentice, Sr.," BA1800-CT, Bankruptcy Case Files, box 8.

38. See "Susannah Kneeland," BA1800-MA, Bankruptcy Case Files, box 25; "William Kneeland," ibid.

39. See "Nathaniel G. Ingraham," BA1800-NY, reel 4; "Nathaniel Olcott," ibid., reel 6.

40. See *Annals of Congress*, 7th Cong., 2d sess., 12:378–379 (Jan. 13, 1803), 547–550 (Feb. 18, 1803). On Bayard's switch, see Morton Borden, *The Federalism of James A. Bayard* (New York, 1955), 73–105; Richard E. Welch, Jr., *Theodore Sedgwick, Federalist: A Political Portrait* (Middletown, Conn., 1965), 228–230.

41. *Annals of Congress*, 7th Cong., 2d sess., 12:377–378, 379 (Jan. 13, 1803), 531, 532 (Feb. 16, 1803), 546, 549 (Feb. 18, 1803). The Virginia bankruptcy records, which presumably were destroyed during the Civil War, were fragmentary as early as 1822, when the clerk of the federal district court in Richmond reported that he could find only incomplete files on forty-five commissions. See Report of Richard Jeffries, Jan. 18, 1822, in Walter Lowrie and Walter S. Franklin, comps., *American State Papers: Documents, Legislative and Executive, of the Congress of the United States*, Class 10, Miscellaneous, 2 vols. (Washington, D.C., 1834), 2:914–915, doc. no. 514.

42. See *Annals of Congress*, 7th Cong., 2d sess., 12:546–547, 551–552, 557–562 (Feb. 18, 1803).

43. See *Annals of Congress*, 8th Cong., 1st sess., 13:616–622 (Nov. 23, 1803). For the Senate debate, see Everett Somerville Brown, ed., *William Plumer's Memorandum of Proceedings in the United States Senate, 1803–1807* (New York, 1923), 74, 83–86. For the Senate vote, see *Annals of Congress*, 8th Cong., 1st sess., 13:215 (Dec. 13, 1803). For Mitchill's comment, see ibid., 7th Cong., 2d sess., 12:531 (Feb. 16, 1803).

44. Manasseh Cutler to Joseph Dana, Nov. 30, 1803, in William Parker Cutler and Julia Perkins Cutler, eds., *The Life, Journals and Correspondence of Rev. Manasseh Cutler, LL.D.*, 2 vols. (Cincinnati, 1888), 2:143; see also Cutler to Fitch Poole, Dec. 30, 1803, in ibid., 2:151–152.

45. *Annals of Congress*, 7th Cong., 2d sess., 12:548 (Feb. 18, 1803). The claim

that small or nonexistent dividends had been a major objection to the Act first appeared in print in 1808. See *Debtor and Creditor* (Philadelphia, 1810), 2, 28–31.

46. Robert Morris to William Lewis, May 24, 1800, Letter Press Copies, 1798–1800, Sequestered John Nicholson Papers, MG-96, General Correspondence, box 1, folder 3, PHMC; Peter Stephen DuPonceau to Peter Mitchell, Sept. 12, 1801, Peter Stephen DuPonceau Papers, Letterbooks, 1797–1801, at 261, HSP; Robert Morris to Thomas Morris, Mar. 23 and Dec. 5, 1801, Morris Collection, box 6, Huntington Library, San Marino, Calif.; "Robert Morris," BA1800-PA, reel 7. Morris's son Thomas, who served only one term, joined James A. Bayard and forty-eight others in February 1803 to postpone the issue of repealing the Act. *Annals of Congress,* 7th Cong., 2d sess., 12:564 (Feb. 18, 1803).

CONCLUSION

1. See Edward J. Balleisen, *Navigating Failure: Bankruptcy and Commercial Society in Antebellum America* (Chapel Hill, N.C., 2001); Charles Warren, *Bankruptcy in United States History* (Cambridge, Mass., 1935); David Frum, "Bankruptcy Reform Is a Moral Issue," *Wall Street Journal,* Feb. 11, 2000, at A14. The overwhelming majority of American consumer bankruptcy filings at the close of the twentieth century were precipitated by one or more of three events—job loss, uninsured medical expenses, and, for women, divorce. See Teresa A. Sullivan, Elizabeth Warren, and Jay Lawrence Westbrook, *As We Forgive Our Debtors: Bankruptcy and Consumer Credit in America* (New York, 1989); Sullivan, Warren, and Westbrook, *The Fragile Middle Class: Americans in Debt* (New Haven, Conn., 2000).

2. Robert Morris to Thomas Morris, Feb. 24, 1798, Morris Collection, box 6, Huntington Library, San Marino, Calif.; Last Will and Testament of Robert Morris (copy), June 13, 1804, in "Robert Morris," BA1800-PA, reel 7; John Pintard, Reading Diary in Newark Prison, 138 (June 10, 1798), John Pintard Papers, box 2, NYHS; John Pintard to Walter Livingston, Sept. 1, 1792, Robert R. Livingston Papers, Livingston Family Correspondence, 1743–1886, ser. 1, NYHS.

3. For a richly textured analysis of bankruptcy in the first half of the nineteenth century, see Balleisen, *Navigating Failure.*

4. See *Annals of Congress,* 5th Cong., 2d sess., 7:796 (Jan. 3, 1798); ibid., 5th Cong., 3d sess., 9:2582–2583 (Jan. 9, 1799); ibid., 6th Cong., 1st sess., 10:111 (Mar. 17, 1800). The estimate of how many commercial debtors would have been barred from bankruptcy by Harper's amendment is based on the debts proved against bankrupt debtors' estates in Massachusetts.

5. Theodore Sedgwick, Jr., to Theodore Sedgwick, Mar. 28 and Apr. 22, 1800, Theodore Sedgwick (Sedgwick III) Papers, box 3, folder 2, MHS; Donald M. Roper, "The Elite of the New York Bar as Seen from the Bench: James Kent's Necrologies," *New-York Historical Society Quarterly*, 56 (1972); 199–237, esp. 232; Gordon S. Wood, *The Radicalism of the American Revolution* (New York, 1991), 266. For a superb study of the business and financial strategies of artisanal entrepreneurs, see Donna J. Rilling, *Making Houses, Crafting Capitalism: Builders in Philadelphia, 1790–1850* (Philadelphia, 2001). For one of printers, see Rosalind Remer, *Printers and Men of Capital: Philadelphia Book Publishers in the New Republic* (Philadelphia, 1996).

6. See Robert Emory, *History of the Discipline of the Methodist Episcopal Church* (New York, 1844), 142–144. On the spread of southern evangelicalism, see Christine Leigh Heyrman, *Southern Cross: The Beginnings of the Bible Belt* (New York, 1997).

7. John Pintard to John Templeman, July 9, 1792, Pintard Papers, box 11, folder 2; *Forlorn Hope* (New York), Apr. 7, 1800; *Annals of Congress*, 7th Cong., 2d sess., 12:378 (Jan. 13, 1803); *A Letter on insolvency* (Philadelphia, 1803), 5.

8. William Duer to Henry Knox, May 5, 1792, Henry Knox Papers, MHS; James Greenleaf, "To the Gentlemen Creditors of James Greenleaf," Dec. 16, 1796, in "James Greenleaf," BA1800-PA, reel 16; James Greenleaf to John Coffin Jones, Patrick Jeffrey, and Joseph Russell, Jan. 14, 1797, John Coffin Jones Papers, case 3, HBS; Peter Stephen DuPonceau to James Greenleaf, Dec. 6, 1803, Peter Stephen DuPonceau Papers, Letterbooks, 1803–1809, at 5, HSP; Robert Morris to Samuel Clarkson, Nov. 28, 1796, Papers of Robert Morris, Private Letterbooks, 1794–1798 (3 vols.), 2:152, LC; Morris to John Nicholson, Nov. 1, 1797, ibid., III, 3:48; Peter Stephen DuPonceau to Daniel Thuun, Nov. 11 and 12, 1799, DuPonceau Papers, Letterbooks, 1797–1801, at 106–109.

9. See Bertram Wyatt-Brown, *Southern Honor: Ethics and Behavior in the Old South* (New York, 1982), 41, 72–73, 345–346; Kenneth S. Greenberg, *Honor and Slavery: Lies, Duels, Noses, Masks, Dressing as a Woman, Gifts, Strangers, Humanitarianism, Death, Slave Rebellions, the Proslavery Argument, Baseball, Hunting, and Gambling in the Old South* (Princeton, N.J., 1996), 70–86; T. H. Breen, "Horses and Gentlemen: The Cultural Significance of Gambling among the Gentry of Virginia," *WMQ*, 3d ser., 34 (1977): 239–257. For an intriguing argument on the role of entrepreneurship—specifically, the lack thereof—in the South's economic stagnation after the Revolution, see Thomas M. Doerflinger, *A Vigorous Spirit of Enterprise: Merchants and Economic Development in Revolutionary Philadelphia* (Chapel Hill, N.C., 1986), 344–364.

10. See Joanne B. Freeman, *Affairs of Honor: National Politics in the New Republic* (New Haven, Conn., 2001).

11. Robert Morris to Alexander Hamilton, Jan. 17, 1798, Private Letterbooks, 3:220; Morris to Thomas Morris, Feb. 24, 1798, Morris Collection, box 6. For an exploration of some of these themes in early modern England, see Alexandra Shepard, "Manhood, Credit and Patriarchy in Early Modern England *c.* 1580–1640," *Past and Present,* no. 167 (2000): 75–106.

12. William Maclay recorded Morris's announced disregard of money with more than a little skepticism. See Kenneth R. Bowling and Helen E. Veit, eds., *The Diary of William Maclay and Other Notes on Senate Debates* (Baltimore, 1988), 134 (Aug. 25, 1789).

INDEX